1964

LINEAR ALGEBRA

This book is in the

ADDISON-WESLEY
SERIES IN MATHEMATICS

Consulting Editor
LYNN H. LOOMIS

LINEAR ALGEBRA

PAUL C. SHIELDS

Wayne State University

ADDISON-WESLEY PUBLISHING COMPANY, INC.

READING, MASS. · PALO ALTO · LONDON

To Debbie

Preface

The recent past has seen a considerable upgrading of the usual under-graduate mathematics curriculum. This has taken place for both mathematics majors and for nonmajors. A consequence of this trend is that many schools now offer a course in linear algebra for undergraduates. Such a course is usually offered independently of the calculus, advanced calculus, differential equations sequence. Linear algebra can be used, however, to unify and clarify much of the subject matter of advanced calculus and differential equations, and is also useful early in the physics and engineering sequences. Accordingly, the feeling is current that linear algebra can and should be given immediately after the student has had introductory calculus. This textbook has been explicitly designed for such a course in the undergraduate mathematics curriculum.

Those topics which are of use in the calculus sequence have been selected for treatment in the text proper. Thus the study of linear independence, linear transformations, inner products, and the spectral theorem for real symmetric operators are emphasized. On the other hand, such favorite topics as linear programming, convex geometry, elementary matrices, canonical forms, quadratic forms, and group theory have been included only in the exercises.

Two approaches are possible for the study of linear algebra. The study of matrices is the simpler one. Computational tools are easily obtained. Such an approach, however, makes the geometric ideas of the subject more difficult to understand, tends to obscure the formal algebraic ideas, and makes generalization somewhat difficult. I have chosen the alternative approach, which is to study linear transformations, treating matrices as important devices for computation. This approach requires that the student learn many new concepts. In spite of the simplicity of the concepts, this is not an easy task. Nevertheless, I feel that the end result is worth the effort: in addition to acquiring the tools of "modern" linear algebra, the student becomes familiar with and begins to use the abstract ideas which are so characteristic of mathematics today.

Several techniques have been employed to assist the student in learning the concepts of linear algebra. The most basic of these techniques is a strong emphasis on low-dimensional examples. As a general rule, all material is introduced after a careful consideration of one or more examples.   This not only helps the student learn the material, but also stresses the fact that much of linear algebra has arisen from generalizing critical low-dimensional examples.   In addition, I have used a minimum of notation, generally omitting notational devices which serve only as shorthand. I have usually omitted proofs which require complicated notation to keep track of the generality. Instead, several examples have been given to clarify the results. Proofs of familiar material, such as the division algorithm for polynomials, have also been omitted. Except for occasional exercises and Sections 4, 5, and 6 of Chapter 4, all results are given only for real numbers.

To further assist the student, Chapters 1 and 2 have the same format: elementary material, followed by concepts and generality, followed by elementary material. Thus Chapter 1 begins with systems of equations, proceeds to the concepts of vector space, subspace, independence, and linear transformation, then terminates with a long section on matrix computation. Chapter 2 begins with the familiar dot product, generalizes this, and terminates with a discussion of the familiar determinant and cross product. This sequence should make it possible for the concepts to become clear while the student is working on more elementary material.

The material of Chapter 3 is the most difficult and most important part of this book. The first section takes a careful look at a few key examples, stressing the ease of computation with diagonalizable operators. (The exercises of this section give a complete discussion of the two-dimensional case.)   The problem then shifts to determining when an operator is diagonalizable, and the study of polynomials is begun. The relevant facts about polynomials are then given in Sections 2 and 3. General criteria for diagonalizability, and the spectral theorem for real symmetric matrices, are given in Section 4. The results are cast in the terminology of projections, the form most easily generalized to infinite dimensions.

Chapter 4 contains additional material to be used if time permits. This chapter divides into four independent units: Section 1 on commuting operators; Section 2 on positive definite operators; Section 3 on orthogonal operators; and Sections 4 through 6 on the complex case. Sections 4 through 6 of this chapter can also be taken up immediately following Theorem 21 (in Section 4 of Chapter 3).

The exercises are roughly of three types. Many are computational, to assist the student in developing this often neglected skill. These also provide drill, a necessity for many nonmathematics majors. Other exercises test the student's grasp of the concepts by asking for proofs of text results or related results. A third class of exercises contains material which is not included in the text proper. A very large number of exercises of each of these types has been provided. This makes possible a considerable variation in the amount of time spent on each section, according to the needs of the class, and also provides the student with an adequate supply of review exercises. Answers to odd parts of all computational exercises have been provided.

In addition to the regular exercises, seven "Special Exercises" have been provided. These are designed to encourage sustained thought by the student on a single series of ideas. These may be assigned to the entire class or to selected students, allowing one or more weeks for the completion of each problem.

Only the most important results are designated by the name "Theorem." Three of the fundamental tools of the subject are given the name "Lemma." All other results, including examples, are numbered consecutively in each section. I have separated some of the material into paragraphs called "Remarks." This was done somewhat arbitrarily, chiefly in order to maintain a reasonable flow of discussion in the main text. These remarks contain comment on computation, relations with other ideas, and extensions of the text material, and should be studied carefully by the student. At the end of each chapter a short section entitled "Notes" has been provided. These notes are designed to encourage further reading by the student in various areas related to linear algebra. They are in no way exhaustive, but contain those references which my students have found of interest.

Enough material has been provided to make this book usable for a two-quarter sophomore course or a one-semester upper-class course. A one-semester sophomore course should be able to complete Chapters 1, 2, and 3, and parts of Chapter 4 (omitting Chapter 2, Section 7, if desirable). A one-quarter sophomore course should be able to complete Chapters 1 and 2 and possibly give a sketchy treatment of Chapter 3. The material from Chapters 1 and 2 can also be used to supplement a calculus course.

Acknowledgements

Seldom is a textbook the direct result of the efforts of just one person, and this one is no exception. I am grateful to Professors Arthur Mattuck and Kenneth Hoffman, who were particularly helpful in my early teaching of linear algebra. I am very indebted to Professor Lynn H. Loomis and Mr. Robert Riley, who read the manuscript and whose valuable suggestions have been incorporated into many parts of this book. To my wife Dorothy I owe considerable thanks for typing the manuscript, assisting with the proofreading, drawing preliminary sketches for the figures, and suffering through many hours of enforced discussion. Thanks are also due to Miss Mabel Black who helped with the proofreading.

August 1963   P.C.S.
Ann Arbor, Michigan

Contents

CHAPTER 1

Basic Concepts

Section 1. SYSTEMS OF LINEAR EQUATIONS

We shall begin our study of linear algebra by taking a careful look at a method, which should be familiar to the reader, for solving systems of linear equations. Our purpose is to obtain a precise formulation of the method so that we can easily answer questions about the existence and nature of solutions.

Suppose we are given the system

(1)
$$2x + 3y = 1$$
$$x - y = 2.$$

A solution to this system is a pair of numbers x and y such that each equation of (1) is valid. For example, $x = \frac{7}{5}$, $y = -\frac{3}{5}$ is a solution, while $x = 3$, $y = 1$ is not a solution. In the usual rectangular coordinate system for the plane, each equation of (1) is the equation of a straight line. These lines meet in the point $x = \frac{7}{5}$, $y = -\frac{3}{5}$, so we see that this is the only solution to (1). (See Fig. 1)

The equations of (1) are called *linear* equations. An example of a system of *nonlinear* equations would be

$$2x^2 + 3y = 1$$
$$x - xy = 2.$$

The first equation of this system gives a parabola, the second a hyperbola. These equations involve powers and products of the variables. In this book we shall concentrate on linear systems such as (1).

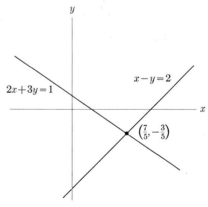

FIGURE 1

1

The most general linear system of two equations in three unknowns is of the form

(2)
$$ax + by + cz = d$$
$$ex + fy + gz = h.$$

In this we are given a, b, c, d, e, f, g, h and seek a solution x, y, and z. To describe the most general system of m equations in n unknowns we shall use a more convenient notation. We shall represent the unknowns by $x_1, x_2, \ldots, x_n$ and the constants on the right-hand side by $y_1, y_2, \ldots, y_m$. We will use a double subscript to denote the coefficients in each equation, the first subscript to denote the equation, the second subscript the unknown. With these conventions we can rewrite (2) as

$$A_{11}x_1 + A_{12}x_2 + A_{13}x_3 = y_1$$
$$A_{21}x_1 + A_{22}x_2 + A_{23}x_3 = y_2.$$

Using the above conventions the most general linear system of m equations in n unknowns is of the form

(3)
$$A_{11}x_1 + A_{12}x_2 + \cdots + A_{1n}x_n = y_1$$
$$A_{21}x_1 + A_{22}x_2 + \cdots + A_{2n}x_n = y_2$$
$$\vdots$$
$$A_{m1}x_1 + A_{m2}x_2 + \cdots + A_{mn}x_n = y_m.$$

Usually we are given the numbers $A_{11}, A_{12}, \ldots, A_{1n}, A_{21}, A_{22}, \ldots, A_{2n}, \ldots, A_{m1}, A_{m2}, \ldots, A_{mn}$, which are called the *coefficients* of the system (3), and the numbers $y_1, y_2, \ldots, y_m$, which are called the *constants* of the system (3). We want to find numbers $x_1, x_2, \ldots, x_n$, such that each equation of (3) is valid. Such a set of numbers, namely a set $\{x_1, x_2, \ldots, x_n\}$, such that each equation of (3) is valid, is called a *solution* to (3). We seek a method for finding solutions to (3).

How did we solve (1)? One easy method is as follows. We multiply the second equation of (1) by 3 and add the result to the first equation. This gives

(4) $5x = 7, \quad x - y = 2.$

Now we divide the first equation by -5 and add the result to the second equation:

(5) $5x = 7, \quad -y = \frac{3}{5}.$

Dividing the first equation by 5 and the second by -1 gives our solution

(6) $x = \frac{7}{5}, \quad y = -\frac{3}{5}.$

From Fig. 1 we see that this is the only solution to (1).

The method is: Multiply an equation by a number and add the result to another equation, or merely multiply an equation by a number. Repeat this process, eliminating as many unknowns as possible until a solution is obtained. If no solution exists, the method is still useful since it will then give us an equation which can never be valid. An example of this phenomenon would be the following:

(7)
$$2x + 3y = 1$$
$$4x + 6y = 3.$$

The two lines determined by this system are parallel; hence they have no intersection. (See Fig. 2.) If we multiply the first equation by -2 and add the result to the second equation, we obtain

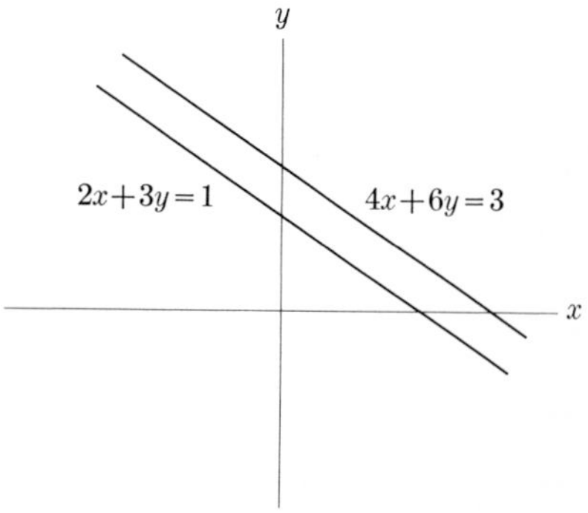

(8)
$$2x + 3y = 1$$
$$0 = 1.$$

FIGURE 2

The second equation of (8) can never hold. Thus the geometric fact of nonintersection corresponds to our obtaining mathematical nonsense with our method. This leads us to ask two questions about a system such as (3). First: Does a solution exist? Second: If a solution exists, how many solutions can we find? Our method will answer both of these questions.

Let us treat the case where we know in advance that at least one solution exists. In system (3), this is the case when $y_1 = y_2 = \cdots = y_m = 0$. For if this is true, then $x_1 = 0, x_2 = 0, \ldots, x_n = 0$ is always a solution to (3). A system (3) in which $y_1 = y_2 = \cdots = y_m = 0$ is called a *homogeneous system;* the solution

$$x_1 = 0, \qquad x_2 = 0, \ldots, \qquad x_n = 0$$

is called the *trivial solution*. In this section we shall use our method on homogeneous systems. For such systems the only questions of interest are those of the existence and nature of *nontrivial* solutions. Therefore, in general, we seek to find $\{x_1, x_2, \ldots, x_n\}$, *not all zero*, such that

(9)
$$A_{11}x_1 + A_{12}x_2 + \cdots + A_{1n}x_n = 0$$
$$A_{21}x_1 + A_{22}x_2 + \cdots + A_{2n}x_n = 0$$
$$\vdots$$
$$A_{m1}x_1 + A_{m2}x_2 + \cdots + A_{mn}x_n = 0.$$

We consider the system

(10)
$$3x + 2y - z = 0$$
$$x - 3y + z = 0$$
$$8x - 2y = 0.$$

Multiply the second equation by -3; add the result to the first equation:

(11)
$$11y - 4z = 0$$
$$x - 3y + z = 0$$
$$8x - 2y = 0.$$

Multiply the second equation by -8; add the result to the third equation:

(12)
$$11y - 4z = 0$$
$$x - 3y + z = 0$$
$$22y - 8z = 0.$$

Divide the first equation by 11 and the third equation by 22. Then the first and third equations are identical. We can eliminate the first equation by multiplying the third equation by -1 and adding the result to the first equation:

(13)
$$0 = 0$$
$$x - 3y + z = 0$$
$$y - \tfrac{4}{11}z = 0.$$

The first equation is now superfluous. We shall keep it only to indicate that we began with three equations. Multiply the third equation by 3; add the result to the second equation:

(14)
$$0 = 0$$
$$x - \tfrac{1}{11}z = 0$$
$$y - \tfrac{4}{11}z = 0.$$

This is as far as we need to go. We can now assign an arbitrary value to z, compute x and y from (14), and thereby obtain a solution to (10). For example, we can let $z = 1$ and compute $x = \tfrac{1}{11}$, $y = \tfrac{4}{11}$, or we can let $z = 11$ and compute $x = 1$, $y = 4$. Each set, $\{x = \tfrac{1}{11}, y = \tfrac{4}{11}, z = 1\}$ or $\{x = 1, y = 4, z = 11\}$ is a solution to (10). Any choice of z, except $z = 0$, gives a nontrivial solution to (10). Geometrically, each equation of (10) represents a plane. These planes intersect in the line given by (14). In parametric form this is the line $x = t/11$, $y = 4t/11$, $z = t$.

We can simplify our procedure by noting that we operated only on the coefficients of the equations of (10), successively changing them to the coefficients of (11), (12), (13), and finally (14). All we need is a means of keeping track of which coefficients go with which variables in which equations. This is usually done as follows.

Definition. A *matrix* is a rectangular array of real numbers. In general,

(15)
$$\begin{bmatrix} A_{11} & A_{12} & \ldots & A_{1n} \\ A_{21} & A_{22} & \ldots & A_{2n} \\ \vdots & & & \\ A_{m1} & A_{m2} & \ldots & A_{mn} \end{bmatrix}$$

is a matrix, where A_{ij} is a real number for each i and j, $1 \leq i \leq$ $1 \leq j \leq n$.

Remark. The first subscript of A_{ij} refers to the *row* in which entry A_{ij} appears, while the second subscript refers to the *column* which A_{ij} appears. If the matrix has m rows and n columns, we say that it is $m \times n$, and call this the *size* of the matrix. If the size the matrix is known, we will usually replace the symbols of (15) by shorter symbol (A_{ij}). In many cases we will not even refer to the size of the matrix and will replace it with a single capital letter such (Usually we will denote matrices with capital letters from the first of the alphabet.)

If $A = (A_{ij})$ is a matrix of size $m \times n$ and if the entries are the same as the coefficients of a system such as (3), then we say is the *matrix of coefficients* of (3). Hence if A is the matrix of coeff of the system (3), then the entry in the ith row and jth column of A sponds to the coefficient of the jth variable in the ith equation of (

For example, the matrix of coefficients of (10) is the matrix

$$\begin{bmatrix} 3 & 2 & -1 \\ 1 & -3 & 1 \\ 8 & -2 & 0 \end{bmatrix} .$$

This matrix is 3×3. The matrix of coefficients of (7) is

$$\begin{bmatrix} 2 & 3 \\ 4 & 6 \end{bmatrix} ,$$

which is 2×2.

Clearly the matrix of coefficients of a system is a convenient way to keep track of which coefficients belong to which equations. Instead of writing down the variables and the equations, we merely write down the matrix. In the homogeneous case the matrix completely describes the system. (In Section 2 we shall give another matrix which conveniently describes a nonhomogeneous system.)

The matrix of coefficients of (11) is

$$\begin{bmatrix} 0 & 11 & -4 \\ 1 & -3 & 1 \\ 8 & -2 & 0 \end{bmatrix}.$$

We obtained the system (11) by multiplying the second equation of (10) by -3 and adding to the first equation of (10). In terms of the matrix of coefficients we can obtain

$$A = \begin{bmatrix} 0 & 11 & -4 \\ 1 & -3 & 1 \\ 8 & -2 & 0 \end{bmatrix} \quad \text{from } B = \begin{bmatrix} 3 & 2 & -1 \\ 1 & -3 & 1 \\ 8 & -2 & 0 \end{bmatrix}$$

by multiplying each entry of the second row of B by -3 and adding to the corresponding entry of row one of A. Similarly the matrix of coefficients for (12) is obtained by multiplying each entry of the second row of A by -8 and adding to the corresponding entry of the third row of A.

This is our basic operation. In matrix terms we replace each entry of row i_0 by adding to it a fixed multiple of the corresponding entry of another row, say i_1. In moving from (12) to (13) we used a second type of operation; we replaced each entry of a given row by a fixed nonzero multiple of that entry. (The restriction "nonzero" is needed, for if we replaced each entry of a row by 0, we might change the solutions.) The reference to "entries" in these operations is somewhat cumbersome. For this reason we adopt the following shorthand convention. A *row operation* is an operation performed on each entry of a row. With this convention, our two operations can be stated, respectively: Add to row i_0 a multiple of row i_1, $i_1 \neq i_0$. Multiply row i by $a \neq 0$.

A third operation is of little computational value, but is a technical device useful for stating results. This is: Interchange two rows of a matrix. This operation will enable us to place the rows of the matrix in convenient order.

Let us summarize our method. We replace (10) by the matrix

(16)
$$\begin{bmatrix} 3 & 2 & -1 \\ 1 & -3 & 1 \\ 8 & -2 & 0 \end{bmatrix}.$$

We multiply the second row of this by -3 and add the result to the first row:

$$(17) \qquad \begin{bmatrix} 0 & 11 & -4 \\ 1 & -3 & 1 \\ 8 & -2 & 0 \end{bmatrix}, \qquad \text{i.e., the matrix of coefficients of (11)}.$$

Multiplying the second row of this by -8 and adding the result to the third row gives

$$(18) \qquad \begin{bmatrix} 0 & 11 & -4 \\ 1 & -3 & 1 \\ 0 & 22 & -8 \end{bmatrix}, \qquad \text{i.e., the matrix of (12)}.$$

We multiply row one by $\frac{1}{11}$ and row 3 by $\frac{1}{22}$, obtaining

$$(19) \qquad \begin{bmatrix} 0 & 1 & -\frac{4}{11} \\ 1 & -3 & 1 \\ 0 & 1 & -\frac{4}{11} \end{bmatrix}.$$

Multiplying row three by -1, and adding the result to row one gives

$$(20) \qquad \begin{bmatrix} 0 & 0 & 0 \\ 1 & -3 & 1 \\ 0 & 1 & -\frac{4}{11} \end{bmatrix}, \qquad \text{i.e., the matrix of (13)}.$$

We then multiply row three by 3, and add the result to row two, to get

$$(21) \qquad \begin{bmatrix} 0 & 0 & 0 \\ 1 & 0 & -\frac{1}{11} \\ 0 & 1 & -\frac{4}{11} \end{bmatrix}, \qquad \text{i.e., the matrix of (14)}.$$

We are finished. Matrix (21) is the matrix of (14), and we can easily read off our solutions from (21). The row of zeros in (21) merely indicates that one equation of (10) has been entirely eliminated. It will be convenient to place this row at the bottom. This is easily done by interchanging rows one and three of (21), then interchanging rows one and two of this new matrix. This gives the convenient form

$$(22) \qquad \begin{bmatrix} 1 & 0 & -\frac{1}{11} \\ 0 & 1 & -\frac{4}{11} \\ 0 & 0 & 0 \end{bmatrix}.$$

In computation we seldom perform such an interchange. However, the form of (22) will be easier to use in stating general results.

Our method should be clear. Form the matrix of coefficients, then eliminate certain coefficients by multiplying one row by a number and adding the result to another row. Make leading coefficients 1 by multiplying a row by a nonzero number. Interchange rows to obtain a form like (22) and read off the solutions. In order to clarify the nature of this final form, let us look at two more examples.

To solve

(23)
$$x + 3y \qquad = 0$$
$$2x + 6y + 4z = 0,$$

form the matrix

(24)
$$\begin{bmatrix} 1 & 3 & 0 \\ 2 & 6 & 4 \end{bmatrix}.$$

Multiply row one by -2; add the result to row two:

(25)
$$\begin{bmatrix} 1 & 3 & 0 \\ 0 & 0 & 4 \end{bmatrix}.$$

Multiply row two by $\frac{1}{4}$:

(26)
$$\begin{bmatrix} 1 & 3 & 0 \\ 0 & 0 & 1 \end{bmatrix}.$$

This is the matrix of coefficients for

(27)
$$x + 3y = 0, \qquad z = 0.$$

We can assign y any value, then compute x and z (z must be zero) from (27). This gives a solution to (23).

Another example:

(28)
$$3x + 2y - z = 0$$
$$x - y + 2z = 0$$
$$x + y - 6z = 0.$$

The matrix of coefficients is

(29)
$$\begin{bmatrix} 3 & 2 & -1 \\ 1 & -1 & 2 \\ 1 & 1 & -6 \end{bmatrix}.$$

Multiply row two by -3; add the result to row one. Then multiply row two by -1 and add the result to row three:

(30)
$$\begin{bmatrix} 0 & 5 & -7 \\ 1 & -1 & 2 \\ 0 & 2 & -8 \end{bmatrix}.$$

Multiply row three by $\frac{1}{2}$; then multiply the resulting row three by -5 and add to row one. Then multiply by 1 and add to row two:

(31)
$$\begin{bmatrix} 0 & 0 & 13 \\ 1 & 0 & -2 \\ 0 & 1 & -4 \end{bmatrix}.$$

Multiply row one by $\frac{1}{13}$; then multiply the resulting row one by 2 and add to row two. Then multiply the resulting row one by 4 and add to row three:

(32)
$$\begin{bmatrix} 0 & 0 & 1 \\ 1 & 0 & 0 \\ 0 & 1 & 0 \end{bmatrix}.$$

Interchange rows one and two, then rows two and three:

(33)
$$\begin{bmatrix} 1 & 0 & 0 \\ 0 & 1 & 0 \\ 0 & 0 & 1 \end{bmatrix}.$$

This is the matrix of coefficients for

(34) $x = 0, \qquad y = 0, \qquad z = 0.$

We conclude from (34) that (28) has only trivial solutions.

What do the matrices (22), (26), and (33) have in common? The most obvious fact is that the first nonzero entry in each row is a 1 and that all other entries in the column in which this 1 appears are zeros. Thus in (22) the leading coefficient of row one is a 1, and we have "eliminated" the corresponding unknown from the second and third equations. The leading coefficient of row two is a 1, and we have "eliminated" the corresponding unknown from the first and third equations. In (26) the coefficient of x is 1 in equation one, and we eliminated x from equation two. In the process of eliminating x, we also eliminated y, so that the first nonzero entry of row two appears in column three.

We note also that the first nonzero entry in row one is to the left of the first nonzero entry in row two in (22), (26), and (33). In (22) the row of zeros is at the bottom, and in (33) the first nonzero entry in row two is to the left of the first nonzero entry in row three. We repeat, this fact is accomplished by interchanging rows and will be of some theoretical use. For solving systems of equations, the facts given in the previous paragraph are the essential ones.

The general form we desire is called the *row reduced echelon* form, or more simply, the *echelon* form. A matrix R is *echelon* if:

(35)

(a) All the zero rows of R are at the bottom of R (i.e., every row, all of whose entries consist entirely of zeros, is below every row which contains any nonzero entry).

(b) The first nonzero entry in each row is a 1 (i.e., the leading coefficient of each equation is a 1).

(c) If the first nonzero entry in row i appears in column k_i, then all other entries in column k_i are zeros (i.e., if x_{k_i} is the first variable in equation i, then x_{k_i} has been eliminated from all the other equations).

(d) If r is the number of nonzero rows, then $k_1 < k_2 < \cdots < k_r$ (i.e., the first nonzero entry in row i is to the left of the first nonzero entry in row $i + 1$).

Parts (b) and (c) of the above definition are essential; parts (a) and (d) will make later results easier to establish. Our first theorem should be clear. Because its proof involves only bookkeeping-type devices to keep track of the generality, we shall omit the proof.

Theorem 1.   In order to solve the homogeneous system

(9)
$$
\begin{aligned}
A_{11}x_1 + A_{12}x_2 + \cdots + A_{1n}x_n &= 0 \\
A_{21}x_1 + A_{22}x_2 + \cdots + A_{2n}x_n &= 0 \\
&\;\;\vdots \\
A_{m1}x_1 + A_{m2}x_2 + \cdots + A_{mn}x_n &= 0,
\end{aligned}
$$

form the matrix of coefficients $A = (A_{ij})$. Operate on A with row operations to obtain a row reduced echelon matrix R. Then the solutions to (9) are the same as the solutions to

(36)
$$
\begin{aligned}
R_{11}x_1 + R_{12}x_2 + \cdots + R_{1n}x_n &= 0 \\
R_{21}x_1 + R_{22}x_2 + \cdots + R_{2n}x_n &= 0 \\
&\;\;\vdots \\
R_{m1}x_1 + R_{m2}x_2 + \cdots + R_{mn}x_n &= 0.
\end{aligned}
$$

The peculiar nature of a row reduced echelon matrix, such as R of (36), gives us our solutions explicitly. From the above description of R we know that if r is the number of nonzero rows, and the first nonzero entry of row i appears in column k_i, then all other entries in column k_i are zeros and $k_1 < k_2 < \cdots < k_r$. Since each k_i is a column subscript, we have $1 \leq k_1 < k_2 < \cdots < k_r \leq n$. Suppose that $r \geq n$. How many ways can we write r whole numbers $\{k_1, k_2, \ldots, k_r\}$ such that

$1 \leq k_1 < k_2 < \cdots < k_r \leq n$? If $r > n$, this cannot be done, and if $r = n$, this can be done in exactly one way, namely $k_i = i$. (Thus, for example, if $n = 3$ and $r = 4$, we cannot choose k_1, k_2, k_3, k_4 from among $\{1, 2, 3\}$ such that $1 \leq k_1 < k_2 < k_3 < k_4 \leq 3$. If $r = 3$, then the only way we can choose k_1, k_2, k_3 from among $\{1, 2, 3\}$ such that $1 \leq k_1 < k_2 < k_3 = 3$ is $k_1 = 1$, $k_2 = 2$, $k_3 = 3$.) Thus if $r = n$, then $k_i = i$, i.e., the first nonzero entry in the ith equation of (36) is the coefficient of x_i and this is a 1. All other entries in this column are zeros; i.e., we have eliminated x_i from all the other equations. Then (36) becomes

$$\begin{aligned} x_1 &= 0 \\ x_2 &= 0 \\ &\vdots \\ x_n &= 0. \end{aligned}$$

(37)

This is the situation in (33) where $n = 3$ and $r = 3$. In this case we have a unique solution, namely the trivial solution.

If $r < n$, it would appear that there are many choices for each k_i, depending on the sequence of operations used to obtain R. Actually it can be shown that our method always yields the same echelon matrix R for a given matrix A. This result will be left as a special exercise. Let k_i be the column subscript of the column in which the first nonzero entry in row i appears. Then the coefficient of x_{k_i} in the ith equation is a 1 and x_{k_i} has been eliminated from all the other equations. To obtain a description of (36) let us change notation. Let $u_1, u_2, \ldots, u_{n-r}$ denote the variables not included among $x_{k_1}, x_{k_2}, \ldots, x_{k_r}$. Let c_{ij} denote the coefficient of u_j in the ith equation of (36). Then we have

$$\begin{aligned} x_{k_1} + c_{11}u_1 + c_{12}u_2 + \cdots + c_{1(n-r)}u_{n-r} &= 0 \\ x_{k_2} + c_{21}u_1 + c_{22}u_2 + \cdots + c_{2(n-r)}u_{n-r} &= 0 \\ &\vdots \\ x_{k_r} + c_{r1}u_1 + c_{r2}u_2 + \cdots + c_{r(n-r)}u_{n-r} &= 0. \end{aligned}$$

(38)

Thus the solutions to (38) are the same as the solutions to (36), since (38) is the same as (36) with a change of notation. But the solutions to (36) are the solutions to (9), so that (38) gives the solutions to (9). To solve (38) we can assign any values we want to $u_1, u_2, \ldots, u_{n-r}$ and compute $x_{k_1}, x_{k_2}, \ldots, x_{k_r}$ from (38). This will give a solution to (9). In some sense (to be made precise in Section 3) we have $(n - r)$ "choices" in (38).

In order to clarify (38) let us look at (22) and (26). In (22) we have $n = 3$, $r = 2$, $k_1 = 1$, $k_2 = 2$. The remaining variable is z, so $u_1 = z$, $c_{11} = -\frac{1}{11}$, and $c_{21} = -\frac{4}{11}$. In (26) we have $n = 3$, $r = 2$, $k_1 = 1$,

$k_2 = 3$. The remaining variable is y, so we have $u_1 = y$, $c_{11} = 3$, and $c_{21} = 0$. Let us gather this information into a theorem.

Theorem 2. Having found the row reduced echelon matrix R as in Theorem 1, then (9) has only the trivial solution if and only if $n = r$, and (9) has a nontrivial solution if and only if $n > r$. Here r is the number of nonzero rows of R. If $n > r$, then we obtain all solutions to (9) by assigning $u_1, u_2, \ldots, u_{n-r}$ arbitrary values and computing $x_{k_1}, x_{k_2}, \ldots, x_{k_r}$ by using (38).

We have one situation when we know in advance that $n > r$.

Corollary. If we have more unknowns than equations in (9), then we always have a nontrivial solution to (9).

Proof. The matrix of coefficients is $m \times n$, where m is the number of equations, and n is the number of unknowns. By assumption $m < n$. Operate on this matrix as in Theorem 1 to obtain an $m \times n$ echelon matrix R. Let r be the number of nonzero rows of R. Then $r \leq m$, since m is the number of rows of R. Thus $r < n$ and Theorem 2 assures us that (9) has a nontrivial solution.

———

Remarks. This corollary is a basic result. We can find a nontrivial solution to (9) whenever we have more unknowns than equations. If we have at least as many equations as unknowns, we can find a nontrivial solution provided that enough equations are superfluous and can be eliminated. This is what Theorem 2 tells us. The process of finding an echelon matrix is in fact the process of removing all superfluous equations, i.e., those which give no new information. Thus we eliminate those equations which are "dependent" on the remaining equations. The equations remaining after determination of R are "independent." Our system (9) has a nontrivial solution if and only if the maximum number of "independent" equations is less than the number of unknowns. If $n = r$, we have no freedom to choose; the only solution must be (37). If $n > r$, then we have $n - r$ "choices" or $n - r$ "degrees of freedom." In some sense, the solutions to (9) have "dimension" $n - r$. These concepts of "dimension," "choice," "degrees of freedom," "independence," and "dependence" will be made precise in Section 3.

The process of finding a row reduced echelon matrix R described in Theorem 1 is called the process of *elimination*, or *row reduction*. We say that we have *row reduced A* to the matrix R, or if we need not stress "row," we merely say that we have *reduced A* to echelon form. We could describe a method of column reduction; however, since this is not so useful in solving equations, we shall omit such a discussion.

The method of row reduction can be applied to more general number systems than the real numbers. All that is necessary is that we be able to add, subtract, multiply, and divide. Systems which satisfy the same addition, subtraction, multiplication, and division rules as the real numbers are called *fields*. In Chapter 4 we shall be interested in the fact that the complex numbers are a field, and hence that our results hold for systems of complex equations. The complex numbers are those numbers of the form $a + ib$, where a and b are real and $i^2 = -1$. Addition and multiplication are defined by $(a + ib) + (c + id) = (a + c) + i(b + d)$ and $(a + ib)(c + id) = (ac - bd) + i(ad + bc)$. Subtraction and division can be defined easily in terms of these two operations.

EXERCISES

1. Write the matrix of coefficients of each of the following systems of equations.

(a) $2x + y = 0$

(b)
$$7x_3 + x_4 = 0$$
$$2x_1 + x_2 - x_4 = 0$$
$$x_2 - x_3 + 3x_4 = 0$$

(c) $x_1 + 2x_2 = 0$
$3x_1 + 4x_2 = 0$

(d) $ax_1 + a^2x_2 = 0$
$bx_1 + b^2x_2 = 0$

where $a \neq b$, $a \neq 0$, $b \neq 0$.

(e)
$$6x_2 + x_3 = 0$$
$$9x_1 + 12x_2 - 8x_3 = 0$$
$$12x_1 + 62x_2 - 3x_3 = 0$$
$$-3x_1 + 8x_2 - 2x_3 = 0$$

(f) $x_1 - x_2 + x_3 - x_4 + x_5 = 0$
$x_1 - x_3 + x_4 - x_5 = 0$
$x_1 - x_4 + x_5 = 0$
$x_1 - x_5 = 0$

(g) $x_2 + 2x_3 - x_4 = 0$
$x_1 - 3x_2 = 0$
$x_2 - x_1 = 0$

(h) $x_1 + 2x_2 = 0$
$x_1 + 3x_2 = 0$
$x_1 - x_2 = 0$
$3x_2 = 0$

(i) $x_1 + x_2 + x_3 = 0$
$ax_1 + ax_2 + ax_3 = 0$
$a^2x_1 + a^2x_2 + a^2x_3 = 0$

(j) $a^2x_1 + ax_2 + 3x_3 = 0$
$x_1 = 0$
$ax_1 + 2x_2 = 0$

2. For each of the matrices of Exercise 1, reduce to echelon form and solve the system of equations.

3. Solve each of the following systems of equations.

(a) $x_1 + x_2 + 2x_3 = 0$
$-2x_1 - x_3 = 0$
$x_1 + 3x_2 + 5x_3 = 0$

(b) $3x_1 + x_2 + 4x_3 = 0$
$x_1 + x_4 = 0$
$x_2 + x_4 = 0$

(cont.)

(c) $x_1 + 2x_2 + 3x_3 + 4x_4 = 0$ (d) $7x_1 - x_2 - x_3 = 0$
        $5x_1 + 6x_2 + 7x_3 + 8x_4 = 0$ $6x_1 - 3x_2 + x_3 = 0$
        $9x_1 + 10x_2 + 11x_3 + 12x_4 = 0$ $13x_1 - 4x_2 = 0$
        $13x_1 + 14x_2 + 15x_3 + 16x_4 = 0$

4. Which of the following systems of equations possess nontrivial solutions?

(a) $3x_1 + 2x_2 = 0$ (b) $8x + 9y + 10z = 0$

$$x - y + z = 0$$
$$x + \sqrt{2}y + z = 0$$

(c) $6x + \sqrt{5}y - \sqrt{2}z + w = 0$ (d) $7x_1 - x_2 - x_3 = 0$
    $x - \sqrt{3}y + \sqrt{6}z = 0$ $6x_1 - 3x_2 + x_3 = 0$
    $x + y - 7z - w = 0$ $13x_1 - 4x_2 = 0$

(e) $x + y + z = 0$ (f) $x - y + z = 0$
     $x + y + 3z = 0$ $3x - \sqrt{2}z = 0$
     $x + y + 2z = 0$
     $x - y - z = 0$

(g) $x - y - z - w = 0$
       $x + 3y - z + w = 0$
       $3x - 7y - z - 6w = 0$
       $2x + 2y - 2z = 0$
       $6x - 2y - 4z - 5w = 0$

5. A homogeneous linear equation in three unknowns represents a plane passing through the origin. Using this interpretation, describe geometrically the possible solutions to a system of m equations in three unknowns. Also use this to interpret the corollary to Theorem 2.

6. Solve each of the following complex systems of equations by forming the matrix of coefficients and reducing it to echelon form.

(a) $x_1 + ix_2 + 3x_3 = 0$
    $x_1 - x_2 + (1 + i)x_3 = 0$

(b) $x_1 + 2x_2 + 4x_3 - x_4 = 0$
    $ix_1 + (2 + 3i)x_2 - x_3 + ix_4 = 0$
       $-x_1 + 7x_2 + 2ix_3 - 7x_4 = 0$
    $-ix_1 + (3 - i)x_2 + x_3 - ix_4 = 0$

7. Let A be the matrix of coefficients of a homogeneous system. Suppose that $A_{ij} = 0$ if $i < j$, and that A is $n \times n$. Show that the system of equations has a nontrivial solution if and only if $A_{ii} = 0$ for at least one i.

8. Show that the system

$$ax + by = 0$$
$$cx + dy = 0$$

has a nontrivial solution if and only if $ad = bc$.

9. Show that the system

$$A_{11}x + A_{12}y + A_{13}z = 0$$
$$A_{21}x + A_{22}y + A_{23}z = 0$$
$$A_{31}x + A_{32}y + A_{33}z = 0$$

has a nontrivial solution if and only if $A_{11}A_{22}A_{33} + A_{12}A_{23}A_{31} + A_{13}A_{32}A_{21} - A_{13}A_{22}A_{31} - A_{12}A_{21}A_{33} - A_{11}A_{23}A_{32} = 0$.

10. Let A and B be $m \times n$ matrices. We say that B is *row equivalent* to A if we can obtain B from A by a finite sequence of row operations of the type used in Theorem 1. Show that if B is row equivalent to A, then A is row equivalent to B. [*Hint:* Show that each operation on page 6 has an inverse operation of the same type. For example, show that if B is obtained from A by multiplying row i of A by a and adding to row j of A, then A is obtained from B by multiplying row i of B by $-a$ and adding to row j of B.]

11. Let A and B each be the matrix of coefficients of homogeneous systems of equations. Suppose that A and B are $m \times n$ and row equivalent. Show that the systems have the same solutions. [*Hint:* Show that both A and B can be reduced to the same echelon matrix and apply Theorem 2.]

12. Show that any 2×2 matrix is row equivalent to *exactly* one of the following matrices:

$$\begin{bmatrix} 1 & 0 \\ 0 & 1 \end{bmatrix}, \quad \begin{bmatrix} 0 & 1 \\ 0 & 0 \end{bmatrix}, \quad \begin{bmatrix} 0 & 0 \\ 0 & 0 \end{bmatrix}, \quad \begin{bmatrix} 1 & a \\ 0 & 0 \end{bmatrix}, \quad a \text{ arbitrary.}$$

[*Hint:* These are the possible 2×2 echelon matrices. Use Theorem 1 to deduce that any 2×2 matrix is row equivalent to at least one of the above. By using Exercise 11, show that none of the above are row equivalent.]

13. Find the maximum number of multiplications needed to solve a homogeneous system of three equations in three unknowns by the method given in Theorem 1. Do the same for a system of four equations in four unknowns.

14. Many problems in linear algebra can be solved with computers. In this exercise and exercises in later sections we will discuss the writing of flow diagrams for some of those problems. We shall restrict our attention to a simple type of flow diagram, using a circle to indicate "Start" or "End," a rectangular box to indicate operations, and an ellipse to indicate alternatives. The flow will be indicated by arrows. For example, Fig. 3 is a part of a flow diagram for solving the system

$$a_1x + b_1y = 0, \qquad a_2x + b_2y = 0.$$

Box E changes notation, while box D carries out the "elimination," then changes notation. The "Yes" arrow from C is not completed.   (*cont.*)

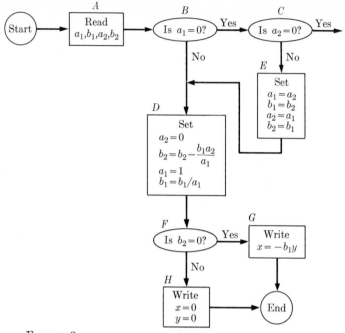

FIGURE 3

(a) Complete the flow diagram.

(b) Write a flow diagram for solving a homogeneous system of three equations in three unknowns.

SPECIAL EXERCISE

Prove Theorem 1. [*Hint*: The only real problem here is notational. If you are systematic, then this is easy. By using row operations, first obtain a 1 in the first row, first column, and zeros in the rest of the first column. Then proceed to column two. If all entries of the first column are zero, proceed directly to column two. What should you do now?]

Section 2. NONHOMOGENEOUS SYSTEMS

In order to solve a nonhomogeneous system, such as [see (1), Section 1]

(1)
$$2x + 3y = 1$$
$$x - y = 2,$$

note that we must keep track of both the coefficients and the constant terms. The following matrix will do this for us.

Given the system of equations

(2)
$$A_{11}x_1 + A_{12}x_2 + \cdots + A_{1n}x_n = y_1$$
$$A_{21}x_1 + A_{22}x_2 + \cdots + A_{2n}x_n = y_2$$
$$\vdots$$
$$A_{m1}x_1 + A_{m2}x_2 + \cdots + A_{mn}x_n = y_m;$$

form the $m \times (n + 1)$ matrix A' defined by

(3)
$$A' = \begin{bmatrix} A_{11} & A_{12} & \cdots & A_{1n} & y_1 \\ A_{21} & A_{22} & \cdots & A_{2n} & y_2 \\ \vdots & & & & \\ A_{m1} & A_{m2} & \cdots & A_{mn} & y_m \end{bmatrix}.$$

This matrix is called the *augmented matrix* of the system (2). The entry in the jth column and ith row of A' is the coefficient of the jth unknown in the ith equation if $j \leq n$, and is the constant term in the ith equation if $j = n + 1$. Thus the first n columns of A' consist of the coefficient matrix of (2), and the last column of A' consists of the constant terms. An operation performed on the rows of A' will clearly correspond to an operation on the equations of (2). Using the operations given in Section 1, we can reduce A' to a form from which we can read off the solutions to (2). Let us look at some examples in order to see what this form looks like.

The augmented matrix for (1) is

(4)
$$\begin{bmatrix} 2 & 3 & 1 \\ 1 & -1 & 2 \end{bmatrix}.$$

We apply the following operations. Multiply row two by 3, add the result to row one, and then multiply row one by $\frac{1}{5}$. Multiplying the resulting row one by -1, adding the result to row two, and then multiplying row two by -1 gives

(5)
$$\begin{bmatrix} 1 & 0 & \frac{7}{5} \\ 0 & 1 & -\frac{3}{5} \end{bmatrix},$$

which is the augmented matrix for the system

(6)
$$x = \tfrac{7}{5}, \qquad y = -\tfrac{3}{5},$$

which is our solution.

For the system [see (7), Section 1]

(7)
$$2x + 3y = 1$$
$$4x + 6y = 3,$$

the augmented matrix is

(8)
$$\begin{bmatrix} 2 & 3 & 1 \\ 4 & 6 & 3 \end{bmatrix}.$$

Multiply row one by -2, and add the result to row two:

(9)
$$\begin{bmatrix} 2 & 3 & 1 \\ 0 & 0 & 1 \end{bmatrix}.$$

This is the augmented matrix for the system

(10)
$$2x + 3y = 1, \qquad 0 = 1.$$

This system has no solution because no choice of x and y will make the second equation valid. In general, we never have to go further than (9) if our system has no solutions. If, while reducing A', we reach a row in which the first n entries are zero, while the $(n + 1)$st entry is *not* zero, then we know that our system has no solution. Such a row would correspond to an equation which *cannot* hold for any choice of the variables.

We have examined two cases. In (4) we had a *unique* solution as shown by (5); in (7) we had *no* solution as shown by (10). Let us look at a case where we have more than one solution.

The augmented matrix for the system

(11)
$$\begin{aligned}
3x - y + 7z &= 0 \\
2x - y + 4z &= \tfrac{1}{2} \\
x - y + z &= 1 \\
6x - 4y + 10z &= 3
\end{aligned}$$

is

(12)
$$\begin{bmatrix} 3 & -1 & 7 & 0 \\ 2 & -1 & 4 & \tfrac{1}{2} \\ 1 & -1 & 1 & 1 \\ 6 & -4 & 10 & 3 \end{bmatrix}.$$

Perform the following operations on (12). Multiply row three by -3, add to row one, then multiply by -2, add to row two, multiply by -6, and add to row four. This gives

(13)
$$\begin{bmatrix} 0 & 2 & 4 & -3 \\ 0 & 1 & 2 & -\tfrac{3}{2} \\ 1 & -1 & 1 & 1 \\ 0 & 2 & 4 & -3 \end{bmatrix}.$$

Note rows one, two, and four. Multiply row two by -2, add to rows one and four, then multiply by 1, add to row three. Interchanging row one and row three gives

(14)
$$\begin{bmatrix} 1 & 0 & 3 & -\frac{1}{2} \\ 0 & 1 & 2 & -\frac{3}{2} \\ 0 & 0 & 0 & 0 \\ 0 & 0 & 0 & 0 \end{bmatrix},$$

which is the augmented matrix for the system

(15)
$$\begin{aligned} x + 3z &= -\tfrac{1}{2} \\ y + 2z &= -\tfrac{3}{2} \\ 0 &= 0 \\ 0 &= 0. \end{aligned}$$

Assign z any value, compute x and y from (15), and we have a solution to (11). Thus we have many solutions, one for each value of z. Geometrically, the four planes given by (11) intersect in the line given by (15).

Our method should be clear. We apply row operations to A', attempting to put the coefficient matrix (the first n columns of A') in echelon form. Two cases result. We get a row in which the first n entries are zero, while the $(n + 1)$st entry is *not* zero (i.e., an equation which can never hold), or we do not get such a row. In the first case there is no solution. In the second case we finally obtain a matrix R' such that the first n columns are in row reduced echelon form *and* in which any row which has its first n entries zero also has its $(n + 1)$st entry zero. In this case, *no* row can have the property that its first nonzero entry appears in the last column. This matrix R' is thus an $m \times (n + 1)$ echelon matrix. Let us describe R': R' has r rows with nonzero entries; these are the first r rows of R'. The first nonzero entry of row i, $i = 1, 2, \ldots, r$, is a 1. Suppose that this appears in column k_i. Then we know that all other entries in column k_i are zero, and that

$$1 \le k_1 < k_2 < \cdots < k_r \le n.$$

(The first nonzero entries go downward and to the right, and no such entry can appear in column $n + 1$.) All entries in the last column are zero below the rth row. We also know that $n \ge r$ [see (35), Section 1].

We proceed as before. If $n = r$, then

$$k_1 = 1, \qquad k_2 = 2, \ldots, \qquad k_n = n.$$

Our system has been reduced to

(16)

$$x_1 = R'_{1(n+1)}$$
$$x_2 = R'_{2(n+1)}$$
$$\vdots$$
$$x_n = R'_{n(n+1)}$$
$$0 = 0$$
$$\vdots$$
$$0 = 0.$$

Here $R'_{i(n+1)}$ is the entry in the ith row and $(n + 1)$st column of R'. The number of trivial equations $(0 = 0)$ is $m - n$. Our system (2) has the unique solution given by (16). If $n > r$, let $u_1, u_2, \ldots, u_{n-r}$ denote those variables not included among $x_{k_1}, x_{k_2}, \ldots, x_{k_r}$. R' is the augmented matrix of a system of equations. Let c_{ij} be the coefficient of u_j in the ith equation of this system where $1 \leq i \leq r$. Let $z_1, z_2, \ldots, z_r$ be the first r entries in the last column of R'. (The remaining entries of that column are zeros.) With this change of notation, our system becomes

(17)

$$x_{k_1} + c_{11}u_1 + c_{12}u_2 + \cdots + c_{1(n-r)}u_{n-r} = z_1$$
$$x_{k_2} + c_{21}u_1 + c_{22}u_2 + \cdots + c_{2(n-r)}u_{n-r} = z_2$$
$$\vdots$$
$$x_{k_r} + c_{r1}u_1 + c_{r2}u_2 + \cdots + c_{r(n-r)}u_{n-r} = z_r$$
$$0 = 0$$
$$\vdots$$
$$0 = 0.$$

Let us translate our examples into these forms. In (1), we obtained (5), which gives

$$n = r = 2, \qquad k_1 = 1, \qquad k_2 = 2,$$
$$R'_{13} = \tfrac{7}{5}, \qquad R'_{23} = -\tfrac{3}{5},$$
$$x_{k_1} = x, \qquad x_{k_2} = y.$$

In (7) we obtained (10), found that we had no solutions, and proceeded no further. In (11) we found (14), which gives $n = 3$, $r = 2$, $k_1 = 1$, $k_2 = 2$, $x_{k_1} = x$, $x_{k_2} = y$, $u_1 = z$, $c_{11} = 3$, $c_{21} = 2$, $z_1 = -\tfrac{1}{2}$, $z_2 = -\tfrac{3}{2}$. In (5), $n = r$, and we had a unique solution. In (11) we had $n > r$, so that we have many solutions.

We now gather these results into a theorem, the proof of which again involves only devices to keep track of the generality.

Theorem 3.   In order to solve

$$
\begin{aligned}
A_{11}x_1 + A_{12}x_2 + \cdots + A_{1n}x_n &= y_1 \\
A_{21}x_1 + A_{22}x_2 + \cdots + A_{2n}x_n &= y_2 \\
&\vdots \\
A_{m1}x_1 + A_{m2}x_2 + \cdots + A_{mn}x_n &= y_m,
\end{aligned}
$$

(2)

form the augmented matrix

(3)
$$
A' = \begin{bmatrix}
A_{11} & A_{12} & \cdots & A_{1n} & y_1 \\
A_{21} & A_{22} & \cdots & A_{2n} & y_2 \\
\vdots & & & & \\
A_{m1} & A_{m2} & \cdots & A_{mn} & y_m
\end{bmatrix}.
$$

Apply row operations to A' to reduce it to echelon form. Either we obtain a row whose first nonzero entry appears in column $n + 1$, in which case we have no solution, or we obtain a row reduced echelon matrix R', in which *no* first nonzero entry appears in column $n + 1$. In this latter case we have solutions. Let r be the number of nonzero rows of this R'. If $n = r$, we have the unique solution given by (16). If $n > r$, then (17) results and we can assign $u_1, u_2, \ldots, u_{n-r}$ arbitrary values and compute $x_{k_1}, x_{k_2}, \ldots, x_{k_r}$ using (17) to obtain a solution.

A special case of this theorem is of some interest. This is the case when $m = n$; that is, we have the same number of equations as unknowns.

Theorem 4.   Suppose that $m = n$ in (2). Form A' as in (3). Let A be the coefficient matrix of (2); i.e., A consists of the first n columns of A'. Then (2) has a unique solution if and only if A can be reduced to the $n \times n$ matrix

$$
I = \begin{bmatrix}
1 & 0 & \cdots & 0 \\
0 & 1 & \cdots & 0 \\
0 & 0 & 1 \cdots & 0 \\
\vdots & & & \\
0 & 0 & \cdots & 1
\end{bmatrix}.
$$

Proof.   Suppose that (2) has a unique solution. Then (16) results. Thus the first n columns of R' form the matrix I; i.e., the first n columns of A' have been reduced to I. Thus A has been reduced to I.

Conversely, if we can reduce A to I, apply these same operations to A'. This gives us the $n \times (n + 1)$ matrix

$$R' = \begin{bmatrix} 1 & 0 & \ldots & 0 & z_1 \\ 0 & 1 & \ldots & 0 & z_2 \\ \vdots & & & & \\ 0 & 0 & \ldots & 1 & z_n \end{bmatrix}.$$

We conclude that we have solutions (since no first nonzero entry appears in column $n + 1$), and that $n = r$. From Theorem 3 we conclude that (2) has a unique solution.

Remark. We have in no way shown that R' is unique. (See Special Exercise, Section 3.)   That is, if we apply row operations in another order, do we get a different matrix R'? The answer is *no!* We always get the same matrix. Even without this result we can give some answers as to the nature of R'. The existence or nonexistence, and uniqueness or nonuniqueness of solutions to (2) is clearly independent of the method used in reducing A'. We conclude that no matter what R' looks like, at least we know that we will have *no* solution if and only if we obtain a row whose first nonzero entry is in column $n + 1$. We have a unique solution if and only if no row has its first nonzero entry in column $n + 1$, and $n = r$. In this case R' must be the augmented matrix of (16); i.e., R' is uniquely determined. If we have solutions and if $n > r$, then all we know thus far is that we have more than one solution. In the next section we will show that r is uniquely determined by (2) with $n - r$ corresponding to the number of "independent" solutions to (2).

We have now shown how to solve the system (2). However, in some cases our system (2) will have no solution. Can we determine the values of $y_1, y_2, \ldots, y_m$ such that (2) has at least one solution? Let us look at two examples, one in which we obtain conditions on $y_1, y_2, \ldots, y_m$ which guarantee the existence of solutions, the other being a case which we can solve no matter what values $y_1, y_2, \ldots, y_m$ have.

Consider the system

$$(18) \qquad \begin{aligned} x + y + 2z &= a_1 \\ -2x - z &= a_2 \\ x + 3y + 5z &= a_3. \end{aligned}$$

The augmented matrix is

$$(19) \qquad \begin{bmatrix} 1 & 1 & 2 & a_1 \\ -2 & 0 & -1 & a_2 \\ 1 & 3 & 5 & a_3 \end{bmatrix}.$$

Multiply row one by 2, and add the result to row two; then multiply by -1, and add the result to row three. Next multiply row two by -1, adding to row three. This gives

(20)
$$\begin{bmatrix} 1 & 1 & 2 & a_1 \\ 0 & 2 & 3 & a_2 + 2a_1 \\ 0 & 0 & 0 & a_3 - a_2 - 3a_1 \end{bmatrix}.$$

According to Theorem 3 we have no solution if $a_3 - a_2 - 3a_1 \neq 0$. Thus a necessary condition for a solution to exist is

(21)
$$a_3 - a_2 - 3a_1 = 0.$$

If (21) is satisfied, we have

(22)
$$\begin{bmatrix} 1 & 1 & 2 & a_1 \\ 0 & 2 & 3 & a_2 + 2a_1 \\ 0 & 0 & 0 & 0 \end{bmatrix},$$

which can be solved, yielding (after discarding the superfluous equation)

(23)
$$x - \frac{1}{2}z = -\frac{a_2}{2}$$
$$y + \frac{3}{2}z = a_1 + \frac{a_2}{2}.$$

Thus (21) is a necessary and sufficient condition for the existence of a solution to (18).

Consider the system

(24)
$$x + 3y - z = a_1$$
$$x - 2y + z = a_2$$
$$2x - y + z = a_3.$$

Reduction of the augmented matrix gives

(25)
$$\begin{bmatrix} 1 & 0 & 0 & a_1 + 2a_2 - a_3 \\ 0 & 1 & 0 & -a_1 - 3a_2 + 2a_3 \\ 0 & 0 & 1 & -3a_1 - 7a_2 + 5a_3 \end{bmatrix}.$$

In this case we always have a solution, for no choice of a_1, a_2, and a_3 will give us a row whose first nonzero entry appears in column four. Also $n = r = 3$, so that *any* choice of a_1, a_2, and a_3 gives a unique solution.

Let us interpret these results geometrically. Changing the values of a_1, a_2, and a_3 in (18) results in changing each equation of (18) (which represents a plane) into the equation of a parallel plane. The planes given by the first two equations intersect in the line given by (23) for any choice of a_1 and a_2. This line will be parallel to the plane of the third equation of (18) unless (21) is satisfied. If (21) is satisfied, then the plane of the third equation of (18) contains the line of (21).

In equations (24), the three planes intersect in a point for any choice of a_1, a_2, and a_3; i.e., no matter how we move the planes, so long as we do it in a parallel fashion, they will continue to meet in a single point.

The generalization of these results is left to the reader.

EXERCISES

1. By forming the augmented matrix and row reducing, determine all solutions, if they exist, for each of the following systems.

(a) $\quad 3x + 4y = 4$
$\quad\quad 9x + 12y = 6$

(b) $\quad x - y = 4$
$\quad\quad x + y = 7$

(c) $\quad 3x - 6y + 7z = 0$
$\quad\quad 2x - y + z = 1$
$\quad\quad 7x + y - 6z = 2$
$\quad\quad 2x + 2y - 4z = 1$

(d) $\quad 6x_1 + 2x_2 - x_3 + x_4 - 3x_5 = 1$
$\quad\quad 2x_1 - 3x_2 + x_3 - 2x_4 - x_5 = 3$
$\quad\quad 5x_1 - \frac{2}{3}x_2 + x_3 - 3x_4 + x_5 = 0$
$\quad\quad -3x_1 + x_2 - x_3 - x_4 = 0$

(e) $\quad x - y + z + w = 0$
$\quad\quad x + 2y - z - w = 1$
$\quad\quad x - y + z/2 - w/2 = 0$
$\quad\quad -3y + z - w = -1$

(f) $\quad x_1 + x_2 + x_3 + x_4 + x_5 = 0$
$\quad\quad 4x_2 + x_3 + 4x_4 + 3x_5 = 0$
$\quad\quad x_1 + 2x_2 + 3x_3 + 4x_4 + 5x_5 = 1$
$\quad\quad x_2 - x_3 - x_4 - x_5 = 0$
$\quad\quad x_1 - x_2 + x_3 - x_4 + x_5 = 1$
$\quad\quad x_4 - x_5 = -\frac{1}{2}$

(g) $\quad x - y = 1$
$\quad\quad x - z = 2$
$\quad\quad x - w = 3$
$\quad\quad y + z + w = 0$

(h) $x_1 + 2x_2 + 2x_3 + 2x_4 + 2x_5 + x_6 + 5x_7 = 0$
$\quad\quad\quad\quad x_1 + x_2 + x_7 = 1$
$\quad\quad\quad\quad x_2 + x_3 + x_7 = 1$
$\quad\quad\quad\quad x_3 + x_4 + x_7 = 1$
$\quad\quad\quad\quad x_4 + x_5 + x_7 = 1$
$\quad\quad\quad\quad x_5 + x_6 + x_7 = 1$

(i) $x - y = 2$
$\quad 2x - 2y = 4$

(j) $x - y + z + w = 1$
$\quad 3x - 4y + 2z - w = 0$
$\quad\quad\; 8x - 10y + 6z = 1$

2. Determine, using Theorem 4, whether each of the following systems has unique solutions.

(a) $x - z = 1$
$\quad y - z = 2$
$\quad y + z = 0$

(b) $x_1 + x_2 + x_3 + x_5 + x_6 = 0$
$\quad 3x_1 - 7x_5 = 1$
$\quad x_2 + x_4 = 0$
$\quad x_3 - x_6 = 0$
$\quad x_1 + x_5 = 6$
$\quad x_6 = 2$

(c) $2x - 3y - 4z - w = 0$
$\quad z + w = 0$
$\quad x - y - z = 0$
$\quad y + z = 1$

(d) $x + y + 2z + w = 0$
$\quad z + w = 0$
$\quad x - y - z = 0$
$\quad y + z = 0$

3. Determine the values of the numbers $y_1, y_2, \ldots, y_n$ for which the following systems have solutions.

(a) $3x - 6y + 7z = y_1$
$\quad 2x - y + z = y_2$
$\quad 7x + y - 6z = y_3$
$\quad 2x + 2y - 4z = y_4$

(b) $3x_1 - 2x_2 = y_1$
$\quad x_1 - 3x_2 = y_2$

(c) $x_1 + x_2 + x_3 + x_4 = 0$
$\quad x_1 + x_2 = y_1$
$\quad x_2 + x_3 = y_2$
$\quad x_3 + x_4 = y_3$

(d) $x_1 - x_2 - x_3 = y_1$
$\quad x_2 + x_3 = y_2$
$\quad x_1 - x_3 = y_3$

4. Solve the following systems.

(a) $ix + (3i + 1)y = 1$
$\quad x - iy = 2$

(b) $(2 - i)x + iy - z = 0$
$\quad 2ix - y = 0$
$\quad x - iz = 1$

(c) $(i + 1)x - 3iy + (1 + i/2)z = -3i/4$
$\quad x + y + iz = i$
$\quad x - 3y - iz = 0$

5. Show that if a system has m equations in n unknowns and $m < n$, then the system either has no solution or has more than one solution. Interpret this geometrically when $n = 3$. (Compare this with the corollary to Theorem 2.)

6. Let A be the matrix of coefficients of a linear system. Suppose $A_{ij} = 0$ if $i < j$ and that A is $n \times n$. Show that the system has a solution if y_i (the constant term in the ith equation) is zero whenever $A_{ii} = 0$. Show that the system has a unique solution if and only if $A_{ii} \neq 0$ for each i. (See Exercise 7, Section 1.)

7. (a) Show that

$$ax + by = y_1, \quad cx + dy = y_2$$

has a unique solution if and only if $ad \neq bc$. (See Exercise 8, Section 1.)

(b) Can you give an extension of Exercise 9, Section 1, to the nonhomogeneous case?

8. Solve each of the systems

$$
\begin{array}{ll}
x + 2y = 1 & x + 2y = 1 \\
x + 2.01y = -1, & x + 1.99y = -1.
\end{array}
$$

Compare your solutions. Note that a small change in the coefficient of y in the second equation leads to a great change in the solutions. This is not true of the systems

$$
\begin{array}{ll}
x + 2y = 1 & x + 2y = 1 \\
x - 2.01y = -1, & x - 1.99y = -1,
\end{array}
$$

where the solutions are nearly the same. Can you give a geometric explanation for this phenomenon? (Graphing each system will be helpful.)

9. In computing with a desk calculator one can use the spaces of the echelon form which are filled with ones and zeros to store information. One method for doing this is as follows. Let A' be as in (3), with $m = n$, and let B be computed as follows.

1. The first column of B is the same as the first column of A'.
2. $B_{1j} = A_{ij}/A_{11}$, $2 \leq j \leq n$, $B_{1(n+1)} = y_1/A_{11}$, i.e., divide the remaining entries of row one by A_{11}.
3. $B_{i2} = A_{i2} - B_{i1}B_{12}$, $\quad i \geq 2$.
4. $B_{2j} = \dfrac{A_{2j} - B_{21}B_{12}}{B_{22}}$, $\quad j \geq 2$, $\quad B_{2(n+1)} = \dfrac{y_2 - B_{21}B_{12}}{B_{22}}$.
5. Having computed the entries in the ith row and ith column of B, we compute the entries of the $(i+1)$st row and $(i+1)$st column by

$$B_{(i+1)j} = A_{(i+1)j} - B_{(i+1)1}B_{1j} + B_{(i+1)2}B_{2j} + \cdots + B_{(i+1)(j-1)}B_{(j-1)j}$$

if $i > j$ and

$$B_{(i+1)j} = \frac{A_{(i+1)j} - B_{(i+1)1}B_{1j} + B_{(i+1)2}B_{2j} + \cdots + B_{(i+1)i}B_{ij}}{B_{(i+1)(i+1)}}$$

if $i < j - 1$.

Show in the case when $n = 3$ that if $A_{11} \neq 0$ and $B_{ii} \neq 0$, $i \geq 2$, then the solutions to (2) are given by

$$x_3 = B_{34}, \quad x_2 = B_{24} - B_{23}x_3, \quad \text{and} \quad x_1 = B_{14} - B_{12}x_2 - B_{13}x_3.$$

10. (a) Write a flow diagram to solve a system of two equations in two unknowns.

(b) Write a flow diagram to determine whether a system of four equations in four unknowns has a solution.

Section 3. VECTOR SPACES, SUBSPACES, AND DIMENSION

In the previous sections we studied a method for solving systems of linear equations. Among the questions which will be treated in this section are those concerning the nature of such solutions. Let us consider an example:

(1)
$$-2x + y + 3z = 0$$
$$2x - y - 3z = 0$$
$$-6x + 3y + 9z = 0.$$

The coefficient matrix for this system is

(2)
$$\begin{bmatrix} -2 & 1 & 3 \\ 2 & -1 & -3 \\ -6 & 3 & 9 \end{bmatrix}.$$

Reduction of (2) gives

(3)
$$\begin{bmatrix} 1 & -\frac{1}{2} & -\frac{3}{2} \\ 0 & 0 & 0 \\ 0 & 0 & 0 \end{bmatrix}.$$

Thus a triple (x, y, z) is a solution to (1) if and only if

(4)
$$x - \tfrac{1}{2}y - \tfrac{3}{2}z = 0.$$

We note that (4) has two arbitrary "choices" (i.e., we can choose x and y, then compute z, or choose x and z, then compute y, or most easily, choose y and z, then compute x). We started with three unknowns and can now choose two arbitrarily, compute the third from (4), and thereby obtain a solution to (1). This concept of "choice," a central concept in linear algebra, will be developed in this chapter. In order to clarify our work, let us look at our example (1), with its solution (4), in a more geometric fashion.

One convenient way to represent triples of numbers (x, y, z) is as points in three-dimensional space. Usually this is done as follows. Pick a point; label it O. Pass three mutually perpendicular straight lines through O. Call one of these lines the x-axis, another the y-axis, another the z-axis. On each of these axes pick a unit of measure. On each axis pick one side of O to be called the "positive" side, the other side of O being called the "negative" side. The triple (x_0, y_0, z_0) is then represented by the point P_0 whose projection on the x-axis is x_0 units from O (on the positive side of O if $x_0 > 0$, on the negative side of O if $x_0 < 0$), whose projection on the y-axis is y_0 (again directed, i.e., on the positive side if $y_0 > 0$ and on the negative side if $y_0 < 0$) and whose projection

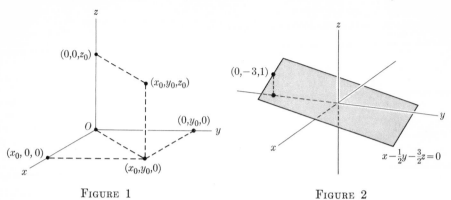

FIGURE 1   FIGURE 2

on the z-axis is z_0 (also directed). The point $(0, 0, 0)$ is represented by O and called the origin. (See Fig. 1.)

With this representation, the solutions to each equation of (1) form a plane passing through O; i.e., each equation is the equation of a plane passing through O. [In our example, each equation is the equation of the same plane, as is the equation (4).] The solutions to (1) form a plane passing through O. (See Fig. 2.)

The following system gives a somewhat less trivial example:

$$\begin{aligned} 2x + 5y + \ z &= 0 \\ x - 2y + \ z &= 0 \\ 3x + 3y + 2z &= 0. \end{aligned}$$
(5)

Row reduction gives the system

$$\begin{aligned} x + \tfrac{7}{9}z &= 0 \\ y - \tfrac{1}{9}z &= 0. \end{aligned}$$
(6)

This pair of equations determines a line. (See Fig. 3.)

Row reduction of the system

$$\begin{aligned} x - y + z &= 0 \\ 2x - y + z &= 0 \\ x + y + z &= 0 \end{aligned}$$
(7)

gives the solution

$$x = y = z = 0.$$
(8)

These are the equations of O. (See Fig. 4.)

In equations (1) we have *two* "choices" and the solutions form a plane, which is a *two*-dimensional object. In (5) we have *one* "choice,"

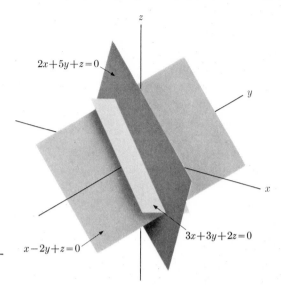

$2x+5y+z=0$

$3x+3y+2z=0$

$x-2y+z=0$

FIG. 3.   Three planes intersecting in a line.

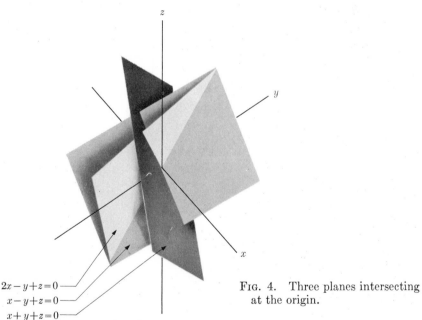

$2x-y+z=0$
$x-y+z=0$
$x+y+z=0$

FIG. 4.   Three planes intersecting
at the origin.

namely z in (6) and the solutions of (6) form a line, which is a *one*-dimensional object. In (7) we have no "choice"; our solution is a single point, which is a zero-dimensional space. In this fashion we can describe our solutions in geometric terms, the number of "choices" corresponding to the dimension of the space of solutions.

This geometric description is very powerful. As we shall see, much of the terminology of linear algebra arises from such geometric considerations. Unfortunately, such a description is limited. For example, what do we do with ten equations in twelve unknowns? We can still use geometric terminology, but our visual perception fails us. We clearly need something more. The concept which has arisen to assist us is that of vector space, a concept which arose to handle certain physical phenomena. Let us consider an example.

Many physical quantities, such as velocity and force, have the property of possessing both magnitude and direction. Such quantities can be represented by an arrow, the length of the arrow representing the magnitude, while the direction in which the arrow points represents the direction in which the quantity acts. Thus we can represent a force acting on a particle at P by an arrow which issues from P, whose length is the magnitude of the force, and whose direction is the direction in which the force acts. If an arrow begins at P and ends at Q, we usually denote this arrow by the symbol $\overrightarrow{PQ}$; P is called the *initial point* and Q the *terminal point* of $\overrightarrow{PQ}$. (See Fig. 5.)

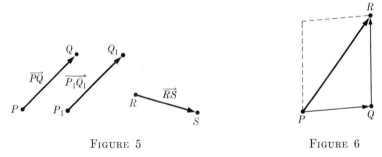

FIGURE 5   FIGURE 6

A quantity, such as force, which can be thus represented by an arrow is usually called a *vector*. Of course the same force can act on a particle at a different point P_1 and can therefore also be represented by an arrow $\overrightarrow{P_1Q_1}$ which points in the same direction and has the same length as $\overrightarrow{PQ}$. In other words, the same vector can be represented by different arrows. In fact, two arrows represent the same vector if and only if they have the same length and point in the same direction. (See Fig. 5 where $\overrightarrow{PQ}$ and $\overrightarrow{P_1Q_1}$ represent the same vector, while $\overrightarrow{RS}$ represents a different vector.)

Suppose that two forces act on a particle at P. The result of both forces acting at the same time is a single force. In order to represent this resultant force we can proceed as follows. Let $\overrightarrow{PQ}$ represent the first force and let $\overrightarrow{QR}$ represent the second force. Then the resultant force is represented by the arrow $\overrightarrow{PR}$. (See Fig. 6.) The arrow $\overrightarrow{PR}$ is called the *vector sum* of the arrows $\overrightarrow{PQ}$ and $\overrightarrow{QR}$.

We can also define a "multiple" of an arrow. If F is a force acting on a particle at P and a is a real number, then aF is defined to be the force whose magnitude is $|a|$ times the magnitude of F and whose direction is the same as F if $a > 0$, and opposite to F if $a < 0$. If $\overrightarrow{PQ}$ represents F and $\overrightarrow{PR}$ represents aF, then the length of $\overrightarrow{PR}$ is $|a|$ times the length of $\overrightarrow{PQ}$, and $\overrightarrow{PR}$ points in the same direction as $\overrightarrow{PQ}$ if $a > 0$, and in the opposite direction if $a < 0$. We usually denote $\overrightarrow{PR}$ by $a\overrightarrow{PQ}$; $\overrightarrow{PR}$ is called the *scalar multiple* of $\overrightarrow{PQ}$ by the scalar (i.e., the real number) a. (In Fig. 7, $2\overrightarrow{PQ}$ is represented by $\overrightarrow{PR}$, and $-\frac{3}{2}\overrightarrow{PQ}$ is represented by $\overrightarrow{PS}$. Also $\overrightarrow{PQ}$ represents $\frac{1}{2}\overrightarrow{PR}$ and $\overrightarrow{PR}$ represents $-\frac{4}{3}\overrightarrow{PS}$.)

FIGURE 7

For convenience we shall generally denote vectors as well as arrows by lower-case boldface letters, with or without subscripts. The zero vector is a vector with no magnitude and any arbitrary direction and will be denoted by $\mathbf{o}$. We shall denote the vector sum of $\mathbf{v}_1$ and $\mathbf{v}_2$ by $\mathbf{v}_1 + \mathbf{v}_2$. If a is a real number, then we denote the scalar multiple a of $\mathbf{v}$ by $a\mathbf{v}$.

These definitions of vector sum and scalar multiple satisfy the usual rules for addition of real numbers and multiplication of real numbers by scalars (i.e., real numbers). To make this precise, we state the following rules:

(a) $\mathbf{v}_1 + \mathbf{v}_2 = \mathbf{v}_2 + \mathbf{v}_1$.

(b) $(\mathbf{v}_0 + \mathbf{v}_1) + \mathbf{v}_2 = \mathbf{v}_0 + (\mathbf{v}_1 + \mathbf{v}_2)$.

(c) There is a vector, denoted by $\mathbf{o}$, such that $\mathbf{v} + \mathbf{o} = \mathbf{v}$.

(d) Given any vector $\mathbf{v}$, there is a vector, namely $(-1)\mathbf{v}$, such that

(9) $\mathbf{v} + (-1)\mathbf{v} = \mathbf{o}$.

(e) $a(b\mathbf{v}) = (ab)\mathbf{v}$.

(f) $(a + b)\mathbf{v} = a\mathbf{v} + b\mathbf{v}$.

(g) $a(\mathbf{v}_1 + \mathbf{v}_2) = a\mathbf{v}_1 + a\mathbf{v}_2$.

(h) $1\mathbf{v} = \mathbf{v}$.

The demonstration that these hold will be left to the exercises. This is the algebraic structure we were looking for. As we shall see, the structure given by (9) enables us to easily discuss questions about ten equations in twelve unknowns. Also we can do more than just discuss questions about solving equations. All we need are the rules (9). Any object with an addition and multiplication by scalars (i.e., real numbers) which satisfies (9) is called a vector space, or linear space. More precisely we have the following definition.

Definition. A collection of objects V, whose members are usually called *vectors*, is called a *vector space* if an addition $X + Y$ and scalar multiplication aX are defined for members of V which satisfy the following laws.

(10)

(a) $X + Y$ is in V if X and Y are in V.

(b) i. $X + Y = Y + X$.

    ii. $X + (Y + Z) = (X + Y) + Z$.

    iii. There is a member of V, usually denoted by O, such that $X + O = X$ for all X in V.

    iv. For each X in V, there is a member of V, usually denoted by $-X$ such that $X + (-X) = O$.

(c) aX is in V if X is in V and a is a real number.

(d) i. $a(bX) = (ab)X$.

    ii. $(a + b)X = aX + bX$.

    iii. $a(X + Y) = aX + aY$.

    iv. $1X = X$.

We stress that a vector space is defined in terms of the algebraic rules given above. Although we use the words "vector" and "space" this does not mean that a vector space can be thought of geometrically or physically. Thus a vector space V is an algebraic object whose only connection with the space of arrows given previously is that the addition and scalar multiplication satisfy the same laws (10). As we shall see below and in the exercises, many mathematical structures possess a vector space structure; i.e., an addition and scalar multiplication can be defined which satisfy the given laws (10).

Let us begin by describing a class of vector spaces which are of considerable computational importance. Let n be an integer (i.e., a whole number), $n \geq 1$. An (ordered) *n-tuple* is a set of the form $(x_1, x_2, x_3, \ldots, x_n)$. For example (x, y) would be a pair or 2-tuple, and $(1, 2, 4, 1, 0)$ would be a 5-tuple. Let R^n be the collection of all ordered n-tuples. We can describe an addition and a scalar multiplication in R^n as follows:

(11)
$$(x_1, x_2, \ldots, x_n) + (y_1, y_2, \ldots, y_n) = (x_1 + y_1, x_2 + y_2, \ldots, x_n + y_n)$$
$$a(x_1, x_2, \ldots, x_n) = (ax_1, ax_2, \ldots, ax_n).$$

Clearly these operations satisfy the rules (10) and hence R^n is a vector space, called *n-dimensional Cartesian space*. In the vector, i.e., n-tuple, $(x_1, x_2, \ldots, x_n)$, x_i is called the ith coordinate. In most of this book when we use the term "vector space" we can if we wish, substitute "R^n." In fact for much of our work R^3 or even R^2 will suffice. In many cases the vector space of arrows described above will be adequate for our purposes. However, most of what we do is a consequence of the rules (10), so that we shall use the general term "vector space" in stating our results. We shall denote a vector space by V, vectors by X, Y, X^1, X^2, ..., Y^1, Y^2, Y^3, Z, Z^1, Z^2, etc., and real numbers by a, b, c, etc. If $V = R^n$ we may denote vectors in V by n-tuples $(x_1, x_2, \ldots, x_n)$ or $(y_1, y_2, \ldots, y_n)$ or by X, Y, etc. We may adopt somewhat different notation as various special cases arise. We shall usually denote our vector space of arrows by $\mathbf{V}$ and its members by $\mathbf{v}_0$, $\mathbf{v}_1$, etc.

The vector space R^3 can be represented geometrically as in Fig. 1. A similar representation for R^2 can be constructed as well as for R^1. We shall usually identify R^1 with the real numbers. The space R^3 can also be represented as the space $\mathbf{V}$. Thus if (x, y, z) is a point in R^3, we can represent this point by the arrow which begins at $(0, 0, 0)$ and terminates at (x, y, z). This representation preserves our definitions of addition in both R^3 and $\mathbf{V}$. For if (x_0, y_0, z_0) corresponds to $\mathbf{v}_0$ and (x_1, y_1, z_1) corresponds to $\mathbf{v}_1$, then $(x_0 + x_1, y_0 + y_1, z_0 + z_1)$ corresponds to $\mathbf{v}_0 + \mathbf{v}_1$ and (ax_0, ay_0, az_0) corresponds to $a\mathbf{v}_0$. The proof of this is left to the exercises. The discussion of the general problem of identifying vector spaces will be left to Section 5.

What are some of the properties of these objects called vector spaces? In our examples (1) through (8) we pointed out that the solutions to systems of equations in three unknowns could be represented as planes, lines, or points. Thus our solutions could be represented as certain subsets of R^3. Can those subsets, i.e., planes, lines, and points, be described algebraically? Clearly there are subsets which are not planes, lines, or points. How can we rule out these? Algebraically, the subsets that we want are easy to define.

Definition. A *subspace* M of a vector space V is a subset of V with the following properties.

    (a) 0 is in M.

(12)   (b) If X and Y are in M, then $X + Y$ is in M.

    (c) If X is in M and a is a real number, then aX is in M.

A subspace of V is a subset M in which we can perform the same operations as we could perform in V and *never* get a vector which is *not* in M. Thus property (b), above, says that we can add in M and property (c) says that we can multiply by real numbers and remain in M. From property (c) we have $-X = (-1)X$ is in M if X is in M. Therefore we can also subtract in M. Thus M is itself a vector space. In fact a subspace of V is just a subset which is also a vector space with the operations as given in V. Let us examine our examples.

If (x_0, y_0, z_0) is a solution to (1) and (x_1, y_1, z_1) is a solution to (1), then

$$
\begin{array}{ll}
& -2x_0 + y_0 + 3z_0 = 0 \qquad\qquad -2x_1 + y_1 + 3z_1 = 0 \\
(13) \quad & 2x_0 - y_0 - 3z_0 = 0 \quad \text{and} \quad 2x_1 - y_1 - 3z_1 = 0 \\
& -6x_0 + 3y_0 + 9z_0 = 0, \qquad\qquad -6x_1 + 3y_1 + 9z_1 = 0.
\end{array}
$$

We form the sum $(x_0, y_0, z_0) + (x_1, y_1, z_1) = (x_0 + x_1, y_0 + y_1, z_0 + z_1)$. This is also a solution to (1):

$$
\begin{aligned}
-2(x_0 + x_1) &+ (y_0 + y_1) + 3(z_0 + z_1) \\
&= (-2x_0 + y_0 + 3z_0) + (-2x_1 + y_1 + 3z_1) = 0 \\
(14) \quad 2(x_0 + x_1) &- (y_0 + y_1) - 3(z_0 + z_1) \\
&= (2x_0 - y_0 - 3z_0) + (2x_1 - y_1 - 3z_1) = 0 \\
-6(x_0 + x_1) &+ 3(y_0 + y_1) + 9(z_0 + z_1) \\
&= (-6x_0 + 3y_0 + 9z_0) + (-6x_1 + 3y_1 + 9z_1) = 0.
\end{aligned}
$$

This shows that if (13) is true, then (14) is true. Similarly, form $a(x_0, y_0, z_0) = (ax_0, ay_0, az_0)$. Then if (x_0, y_0, z_0) is a solution to (1), so is (ax_0, ay_0, az_0). Clearly $(0, 0, 0)$ is a solution to (1). These three statements: $(0, 0, 0)$ is a solution to (1); if (x_0, y_0, z_0) and (x_1, y_1, z_1) are solutions to (1), so is $(x_0 + x_1, y_0 + y_1, z_0 + z_1)$; and if (x_0, y_0, z_0) is a solution to (1), so is (ax_0, ay_0, az_0), merely tell us that the collection of all solutions to (1) is a subspace of R^3.

In a similar elementary fashion, the collection of all solutions to (5) is a subspace of R^3, and the collection of all solutions to (7) is a subspace of R^3. The following result should be clear.

The collection of all n-tuples $(x_1, x_2, \ldots, x_n)$ such that

$$
\begin{aligned}
A_{11}x_1 + A_{12}x_2 + \cdots + A_{1n}x_n &= 0 \\
A_{21}x_1 + A_{22}x_2 + \cdots + A_{2n}x_n &= 0 \\
&\vdots \\
A_{m1}x_1 + A_{m2}x_2 + \cdots + A_{mn}x_n &= 0
\end{aligned}
$$

(15)

is a subspace of R^n. This subspace is called the *null space* of the matrix $A = (A_{ij})$.

Thus the null space of (2) is the collection of all solutions to (1). This is also the null space of (3). The null space of

$$
\begin{bmatrix} 2 & 5 & 1 \\ 1 & -2 & 1 \\ 3 & 3 & 2 \end{bmatrix}
$$

is the collection of solutions to (5), which is also the null space of

$$\begin{bmatrix} 1 & 0 & \frac{7}{9} \\ 0 & 1 & -\frac{1}{9} \\ 0 & 0 & 0 \end{bmatrix},$$

as well as the null space of

$$\begin{bmatrix} 1 & 0 & \frac{7}{9} \\ 0 & 1 & -\frac{1}{9} \end{bmatrix}.$$

The null space of

$$\begin{bmatrix} 1 & -1 & 1 \\ 2 & -1 & 1 \\ 1 & 1 & 1 \end{bmatrix}$$

is the set of solutions to (7), i.e., the single vector $(0, 0, 0)$.

This last example is of some interest. If V is a vector space, we can immediately describe two subspaces of V. If M contains only the zero vector, then M certainly satisfies (12), so that M is a subspace of V. We call M the *zero* subspace of V or, for rather obvious reasons, the *trivial* subspace of V. The space V itself satisfies the conditions of (12), so that V is a subspace of itself. If M is a subspace of V and $M \neq V$, then we usually call M a *proper* subspace.

———

Remarks. It will be left as an exercise to show that a line or a plane through $(0, 0, 0)$ is a subspace of R^3 and that these are the only non-trivial, proper subspaces of R^3. Therefore a circle is not a subspace of R^3. What about lines not passing through $(0, 0, 0)$? These also are *not* subspaces, yet they clearly have many of the same properties, geometrically if not algebraically. A line or plane not through the origin is simply a translation of a line or plane through the origin, i.e., is a translation of a subspace. We shall make this precise below. The exercises will contain many examples of subsets of vector spaces which are subspaces, and some examples which are not.

———

What about the concepts of "dimension" and "choice"? These concepts have rather simple algebraic definitions. Let us again look at (1). We noted that (x_0, y_0, z_0) is a solution to (1) if and only if $x_0 - \frac{1}{2}y_0 - \frac{3}{2}z_0 = 0$, i.e., if (4) is valid. We shall pick two particular solutions to (1), as follows. Let $y_0 = 1, z_0 = 0$; compute x_0 from (4) to obtain the vector $X = (\frac{1}{2}, 1, 0)$. Let $y_0 = 0, z_0 = 1$; compute x_0 from (4) to obtain the vector $Y = (\frac{3}{2}, 0, 1)$.

Then we have the following:

(16) X and Y are in the null space of (2); i.e., both X and Y are solutions to (1).

(17)   If a and b are real numbers, then $Z = aX + bY$ is in the null space of (2).

This follows from the fact that (16) holds and that the null space of (2) is a subspace of R^3. Now let $Z = (x_1, y_1, z_1)$ be any vector in the null space of (2). Then (4) tells us that $x_1 = \frac{1}{2}y_1 + \frac{3}{2}z_1$. Let $W = y_1X + z_1Y$. Then

$$W = y_1(\tfrac{1}{2}, 1, 0) + z_1(\tfrac{3}{2}, 0, 1) = (\tfrac{1}{2}y_1 + \tfrac{3}{2}z_1, y_1, z_1) = Z.$$

This establishes the following:

(18)   If $Z = (x_1, y_1, z_1)$ is in the null space of (2), then $Z = y_1X + z_1Y$.

Statement (18) tells us that any solution to (1) "depends" upon the particular solutions X and Y. Statements (17) and (18) tell us that X and Y completely "describe" the null space of (2). Do we need to use both X and Y, or is one of them enough? Rephrasing this question, does X "depend" on Y, or does Y "depend" on X? Suppose $X = aY$ for some a. Then we would have $(\frac{1}{2}, 1, 0) = a(\frac{3}{2}, 0, 1) = (\frac{3}{2}a, 0, a)$. This cannot be true for any a. Similarly $Y = aX$ cannot be true for any a. The easiest way to state this is as follows:

(19)   If $aX + bY = 0$, then $a = b = 0$.

We have shown that we can pick two vectors, namely X and Y, in the null space of (2) such that any vector in the null space of (2) "depends" upon X and Y [as expressed in (18)], while X and Y are "independent" [as expressed in (19)]. Is our choice of X and Y just magic? Could we describe the null space with only one vector? Is it possible that some other choice might require three vectors? Let Z be in the null space of (2) and suppose that X and Y "depend" on Z, i.e., $X = aZ$ and $Y = bZ$. Choose c_1 and c_2, *not* both zero, such that $ac_1 + bc_2 = 0$. This can be done because of the corollary to Theorem 2. Then

$$c_1X + c_2Y = c_1aZ + c_2bZ = (c_1a + c_2b)Z = 0.$$

This contradicts (19). Thus the null space of (2) *cannot* be described with one vector.

Now let $U = (u_1, u_2, u_3)$, $V = (v_1, v_2, v_3)$, and $W = (w_1, w_2, w_3)$ be any three vectors in the null space of (2). Then by (17) we have $U = u_2X + u_3Y$, $V = v_2X + v_3Y$, and $W = w_2X + w_3Y$. Choose c_1,

c_2, and c_3, *not* all zero, such that:

$$(20) \qquad \begin{aligned} u_2c_1 + v_2c_2 + w_2c_3 &= 0 \\ u_3c_1 + v_3c_2 + w_3c_3 &= 0. \end{aligned}$$

Statement (20) is again an application of the corollary to Theorem 2, for (20) is a set of two equations in three unknowns [c_1, c_2, and c_3] and hence has a nontrivial solution. With this choice of c_1, c_2, and c_3 we have

$$\begin{aligned} c_1 U + c_2 V + c_3 W &= c_1(u_2X + u_3Y) + c_2(v_2X + v_3Y) + c_3(w_2X + w_3Y) \\ &= (u_2c_1 + v_2c_2 + w_2c_3)X + (u_3c_1 + v_3c_2 + w_3c_3)Y \\ &= 0X + 0Y = 0. \end{aligned}$$

This establishes the following:

(21)   If U, V, and W are in the null space of (2), then we can find c_1, c_2, and c_3 not all zero, such that $c_1 U + c_2 V + c_3 W = 0$.

This shows that any three vectors in the null space of (2) must be "dependent." We now have a good candidate for the concept of dimension. The solutions to (1) form a plane, which is a two-dimensional space. This space cannot be described by one vector, can be described by two "independent" vectors, and lastly has the property that three vectors in the space must have a "dependency" relation; i.e., three vectors are too many. The dimension of a subspace should be the number of "independent" vectors which "describe" the subspace. We shall generalize these ideas and make them precise.

Definition.   A collection of vectors $\{X^1, X^2, \ldots, X^k\}$ is said to be:

(22)
(a) *Dependent*, if we can find numbers c_1, c_2, $\ldots$, c_k *not* all zero, such that $c_1X^1 + c_2X^2 + \cdots + c_kX^k = 0$.

(b) *Independent*, if it is not dependent; i.e., if $c_1X^1 + c_2X^2 + \cdots + c_kX^k = 0$ implies that $c_1 = c_2 = \cdots = c_k = 0$.

We often wish to form sums of the form $c_1X^1 + c_2X^2 + \cdots + c_kX^k$. Such sums are given a name.

(23)   A sum of the form $c_1X^1 + c_2X^2 + \cdots + c_kX^k$ is called a *linear combination* of the set $\{X^1, X^2, \ldots, X^k\}$.

In terms of our example we have that any vector in the null space of (2) is a linear combination of X and Y [this is (18)], that any linear combination of X and Y is in the null space of (2) [this is (17)], and that X and Y are independent [this is (19)]. From (21) we see that any three vectors in the null space of (2) must be dependent.

Other simple properties of dependence and independence are easily obtained. For example, the set $\{0\}$ is dependent, for $1 \cdot 0 = 0$ and $1 \neq 0$. Also, if $X \neq 0$, then $\{X\}$ is independent since $aX = 0$ and $a \neq 0$ tell us that $X = 0$. Note that any subset of an independent set must be independent, while any set containing a dependent set must also be dependent. However, we can give independent subsets of dependent sets. For example, the set $\{(1, 0)\}$ in R^2 is independent, while the set $\{(1, 0), (2, 0)\}$ is dependent since $1 \cdot (2, 0) - 2(1, 0) = 0$.

These definitions are given for finite sets of vectors. They can be extended to infinite sets as follows. We say that a set of vectors D is *independent* if every finite subset of D is independent, and *dependent* if some finite subset of D is dependent.

Let us look at the situation of two vectors in R^3. Let $X^1 = (x_1, y_1, z_1)$ and $X^2 = (x_2, y_2, z_2)$. Suppose $\{X^1, X^2\}$ is dependent. Then $aX^1 + bX^2 = 0$ and $a \neq 0$ or $b \neq 0$. Suppose $a \neq 0$. Then $X^1 = (-b/a)X^2$; i.e., $x_1 = (-b/a)x_2$, $y_1 = (-b/a)y_2$, and $z_1 = (-b/a)z_2$. Thus X^1 lies on the line through $(0, 0, 0)$ and (x_2, y_2, z_2). (The equations of this line, in parametric form, are $x = x_2t$, $y = y_2t$, and $z = z_2t$.) If X^1 lies on this line, then $x_1 = x_2t_0$, $y_1 = y_2t_0$, and $z_1 = z_2t_0$ for some t_0. Thus $X^1 = t_0X^2$; i.e., $X^1 - t_0X^2 = 0$. We conclude that $\{X^1, X^2\}$ is a dependent set. From these results we conclude that $\{X^1, X^2\}$ is a dependent set if and only if X^1 and X^2 are collinear with $(0, 0, 0)$. This tells us that $\{X^1, X^2\}$ is an independent set if and only if X^1 and X^2 are *not* collinear with $(0, 0, 0)$.

Let X^1 and X^2 be two vectors. Let X be a linear combination of X^1 and X^2; i.e., $X = aX^1 + bX^2$, where a and b are real numbers. We look at two examples. Let $X^1 = (1, 1, 0)$ and $X^2 = (0, 1, 1)$. Then, since $(1, 1, 0)$ and $(0, 1, 1)$ are not collinear with $(0, 0, 0)$, the set $\{X^1, X^2\}$ is independent. The equation of the plane passing through X^1, X^2, and $(0, 0, 0)$ is $x - y + z = 0$. Since $X = aX^1 + bX^2 = a(1, 1, 0) + b(0, 1, 1) = (a, a + b, b)$, we see that X lies on this plane. Conversely, if $X = (x_0, y_0, z_0)$ lies on this plane, then $x_0 - y_0 + z_0 = 0$ so that $y_0 = x_0 + z_0$. This tells us that $X = x_0X^1 + z_0X^2$. We have shown that a vector X, i.e., a point, is a linear combination of X^1 and X^2 if and only if X lies on the plane through X^1, X^2, and $(0, 0, 0)$.

Suppose that $X^1 = cX^2$; i.e., suppose that X^1, X^2, and $(0, 0, 0)$ are collinear. Then $X = aX^1 + bX^2 = (ac + b)X^2$. Thus X, X^2, and $(0, 0, 0)$ are collinear. If X, X^2, and $(0, 0, 0)$ are collinear, then as we have shown above $X = t_0X^2 = 0 \cdot X^1 + t_0X^2$. We conclude that X is a linear combination of X^1 and X^2 (where $X^2 \neq 0$ and $\{X^1, X^2\}$ is a dependent set) if and only if X lies on the line through $(0, 0, 0)$ and X^2.

From these remarks it should be clear that the collection of all linear combinations of a given set of vectors is of interest. This has a name.

Let V be a vector space and let D be a nonempty subset of V. Let M be the collection of all vectors in V which can be expressed as a linear combination of a finite subset of D. Then M is a subspace, which is called the *subspace spanned by* D. We also say that D *spans* M.

Let us show that M is a subspace. Let X_0 be a vector in D. Then $0 \cdot X_0 = 0$ and $0 \cdot X_0$ is a linear combination of a finite subset of D. Thus 0 is in M. Let X and Y be in M. Then we can find $X^1, X^2, \ldots, X^k$ all in D and $Y^1, Y^2, \ldots, Y^l$, also all in D, such that $X = c_1 X^1 + c_2 X^2 + \cdots + c_k X^k$, and $Y = d_1 Y^1 + d_2 Y^2 + \cdots + d_l Y^l$. Then $aX = (c_1 a)X^1 + (c_2 a)X^2 + \cdots + (c_k a)X^k$, and $X + Y = c_1 X^1 + c_2 X^2 + \cdots + c_k X^k + d_1 Y^1 + d_2 Y^2 + \cdots + d_l Y^l$ so that aX and $X + Y$ are both linear combinations of some finite subset of D. Thus aX and $X + Y$ are in M. We conclude from (12) that M is a subspace.

We restate our results in terms of this concept. Statement (17) says that any linear combination of X and Y must be in the null space of (2). Statement (18) says that any vector in the null space of (2) is a linear combination of X and Y. Thus (17) and (18) together say that $\{X, Y\}$ spans the null space of (2). We have also shown that $\{X, Y\}$ is an independent set in (19). The condition of spanning ensures that the set $\{X, Y\}$ contains enough vectors to describe the null space of (2), while the condition of independence ensures us that we do not have more vectors than we need. These are the algebraic conditions we were looking for. The set $\{X, Y\}$ is called a *basis* for the null space of (2). In general we have the following definition.

> **Definition.**   Let M be a subspace of V. Then a subset D of M which is independent and which spans M is called a *basis* for M. If D is a finite set, then we say that M is *finite dimensional*,
> (24)   and the number of vectors in D is called the *dimension* of M. This number is denoted by "dim M." If M is the zero subspace, we say that dim $M = 0$.

Remarks.   The set $\{(1, 0), (0, 1)\}$ is a basis for R^2. This follows from the fact that $(x, y) = x(1, 0) + y(0, 1)$, so that $\{(1, 0), (0, 1)\}$ spans R^2. If $x(1, 0) + y(0, 1) = 0$, then $(x, y) = 0$, so that $x = y = 0$; i.e., $\{(1, 0), (0, 1)\}$ is independent. We conclude that dim $R^2 = 2$, as it should be. Similarly, dim $R^n = n$.

We have not as yet shown that our definition of dimension is unambiguous. We must show that any two bases for M contain the same number of vectors. This, along with a method for constructing a basis, will be shown below.

If M is *not* finite dimensional, then we say that M is *infinite dimensional*. Much of modern mathematics and physics, e.g., Fourier series, differential equations, and quantum theory, takes place in infinite dimensional spaces. In spite of this we shall confine most of our study in this book to finite dimensional spaces, as a knowledge of such spaces is helpful in understanding the infinite dimensional theories.

Let us look at the concept of basis in another way. Let $\{X^1, X^2, \ldots, X^k\}$ be a basis for M. Then we have two facts: $\{X^1, X^2, \ldots, X^k\}$ spans M, and $\{X^1, X^2, \ldots, X^k\}$ is independent. The first fact tells us that if X is in M, then $X = a_1 X^1 + a_2 X^2 + \cdots + a_k X^k$; i.e., we can find an expression for X in terms of $\{X^1, X^2, \ldots, X^k\}$. The second fact, i.e., independence, tells us that we can find only one such expression. For suppose that $X = b_1 X^1 + b_2 X^2 + \cdots + b_k X^k$. Subtraction gives $0 = (a_1 - b_1)X^1 + (a_2 - b_2)X^2 + \cdots + (a_k - b_k)X^k$. Independence of $\{X^1, X^2, \ldots, X^k\}$ tells us that $a_1 = b_1$, $a_2 = b_2$, $\ldots$, $a_k = b_k$. Thus the statement that $\{X^1, X^2, \ldots, X^k\}$ is a basis for M is the same as the statement that each X in M has a *unique* expression in the form $X = a_1 X^1 + a_2 X^2 + \cdots + a_k X^k$. This fact will be used in Section 4 and systematically exploited in Section 6.

We need two lemmas to assist us in establishing our results. The first lemma uses Theorem 2 heavily and guarantees that independent sets cannot be too large.

Lemma 1. Let V be a vector space which is spanned by a finite set of vectors, say $\{Y^1, Y^2, \ldots, Y^n\}$. Let $D = \{X^1, X^2, \ldots, X^k\}$ be an independent set in V. Then $k \leq n$.

Proof. This lemma is a generalization of (21). In proving (21) we used the fact that (20) possessed a nontrivial solution. This is exactly what we shall do here. Since $\{Y^1, Y^2, \ldots, Y^n\}$ spans V, each vector in D is a linear combination of $\{Y^1, Y^2, \ldots, Y^n\}$; i.e.,

$$
\begin{aligned}
X^1 &= c_{11}Y^1 + c_{21}Y^2 + \cdots + c_{n1}Y^n \\
X^2 &= c_{12}Y^2 + c_{22}Y^2 + \cdots + c_{n2}Y^n \\
&\vdots \\
X^k &= c_{1k}Y^1 + c_{2k}Y^2 + \cdots + c_{nk}Y^n.
\end{aligned}
$$

(25)

Suppose that $k > n$. Then by the corollary to Theorem 2, the system

$$
\begin{aligned}
c_{11}d_1 + c_{12}d_2 + \cdots + d_{1k}d_k &= 0 \\
c_{21}d_1 + c_{22}d_2 + \cdots + c_{2k}d_k &= 0 \\
&\vdots \\
c_{n1}d_1 + c_{n2}d_2 + \cdots + c_{nk}d_k &= 0
\end{aligned}
$$

(26)

has at least one nontrivial solution. Let $(d_1, d_2, \ldots, d_k)$ be such a nontrivial solution. Then $d_1 X^1 + d_2 X^2 + \cdots + d_k X^k = d_1(c_{11} Y^1 + c_{21} Y^2 + \cdots + c_{n1} Y^n) + d_2(c_{12} Y^1 + c_{22} Y^2 + \cdots + c_{n2} Y^n) + \cdots + d_k(c_{1k} Y^1 + c_{2k} Y^2 + \cdots + c_{nk} Y^n) = (c_{11} d_1 + c_{12} d_2 + \cdots + c_{1k} d_k) Y^1 + (c_{21} d_1 + c_{22} d_2 + \cdots + c_{2k} d_k) Y^2 + \cdots + (c_{n1} d_1 + c_{n2} d_2 + \cdots + c_{nk} d_k) Y^n = 0 \cdot Y^1 + 0 \cdot Y^2 + \cdots + 0 \cdot Y^n = 0$. Thus if $k > n$, we can choose d_1, $d_2, \ldots, d_k$, *not* all zero, such that $d_1 X^1 + d_2 X^2 + \cdots + d_k X^k = 0$; i.e., $\{X^1, X^2, \ldots, X^k\}$ is a dependent set. We conclude that $k \leq n$. Q.E.D.

The next lemma gives us a method for "enlarging" independent sets.

Lemma 2. Let $\{X^1, X^2, \ldots, X^r\}$ be an independent set in V. Let M be the subspace spanned by $\{X^1, X^2, \ldots, X^r\}$. Let X be a vector which is in V but *not* in M. Then $\{X^1, X^2, \ldots, X^r, X\}$ is an independent set.

Proof. Let $c_1 X^1 + c_2 X^2 + \cdots + c_r X^r + cX = 0$. We will show that $c_1 = c_2 = \cdots = c_r = c = 0$. If $c \neq 0$, solve for X. This gives

$$X = -\frac{c_1}{c} X^1 - \frac{c_2}{c} X^2 - \cdots - \frac{c_r}{c} X^r.$$

The right-hand side of this expression is a linear combination of $\{X^1, X^2, \ldots, X^r\}$ and hence is in M. The left-hand side is not in M. This is a contradiction. We conclude that $c = 0$. This gives $c_1 X^1 + c_2 X^2 + \cdots + c_r X^r = 0$. Since $\{X^1, X^2, \ldots, X^r\}$ is an independent set, we must have $c_1 = c_2 = \cdots = c_r = 0$. We have shown that $c_1 = c_2 = \cdots = c_r = c = 0$; i.e., $\{X^1, X^2, \ldots, X^r, X\}$ is an independent set. Q.E.D.

These two lemmas give us a method for constructing a basis for a subspace of a vector space V, whenever we know in advance that V is spanned by a finite set of vectors. Let $\{Y^1, Y^2, \ldots, Y^n\}$ span V and let M be a nonzero subspace of V. Let X be an nonzero vector in M. If $\{X\}$ spans M, then $\{X\}$ is a basis. If not, let $X^1 = X$ and let X^2 be a vector in M not in the subspace spanned by $\{X^1\}$. Then by Lemma 2, $\{X^1, X^2\}$ is an independent set in M. If $\{X^1, X^2\}$ spans M, then it is a basis for M. If not, we can find X^3 in M such that X^3 is not in the subspace spanned by $\{X^1, X^2\}$. We proceed in this fashion, knowing that we must eventually get a basis for M. How do we know this? Lemma 1 ensures us that we can never have more than n independent vectors, while Lemma 2 ensures that if $\{X^1, X^2, \ldots, X^r\}$ is an independent set in M which does not span M, we can increase the number of vectors in the set without destroying independence. We conclude that we must in this fashion eventually obtain a basis for M.

Theorem 5.   Let V be a vector space which is spanned by a finite set of vectors. Let M be a nonzero subspace of V. Then M has a basis consisting of a finite number of vectors; i.e., M is finite dimensional. Furthermore, any two bases for M contain the *same* number of vectors.

Proof. We have established all except the last statement of this theorem. This statement is a consequence of Lemma 1. Let D_1 and D_2 both be bases for M. Then Lemma 1 says that the number of vectors in D_1 is not greater than the number of vectors in a set which spans V; hence D_1 is a finite set. Similarly D_2 is a finite set. Since D_1 spans M and D_2 is independent, the number of vectors in D_2 is not greater than the number in D_1. Since D_2 spans M and D_1 is independent, the number of vectors in D_1 is not greater than the number in D_2. We conclude that D_1 and D_2 contain the same number of vectors. This completes the proof of Theorem 5.   Q.E.D.

Remarks. Since R^n is finite dimensional, we conclude the rather obvious fact that any subspace of R^n is also finite dimensional. Thus we can completely describe a subspace of R^n (or any finite dimensional space) by giving a basis for the subspace. This can be done in many ways. Theorem 5 ensures that no matter how we find a basis, the number of vectors in that basis is the same as the number in any other basis.

Some easy consequences of Theorem 5 are the following.

(27)   Let V be a finite dimensional space. Let U be a subspace of V. Then $\dim U \leq \dim V$. If U is a proper subspace of V, then $\dim U < \dim V$.

(28)   If D contains n vectors and spans V, then $\dim V \leq n$. If $\dim V = n$, then D is an independent set.

(29)   If D is an independent set in V containing n vectors, then $\dim V \geq n$. If $\dim V = n$, then D spans V.

The proofs of (27), (28), and (29) are left to the exercises. Statements (28) and (29) are very useful in applications. For if $\dim V = n$ and D is a set containing n vectors, then in order to determine whether D is a basis it is enough to show that D spans V, (28), or that D is independent, (29).

Let us examine our examples again. In (1), the space of solutions has dimension 2, while (3) tells us that all the equations of (1) "depend" on (4). Similarly the space of solutions to (5) has dimension 1; i.e., it is the subspace spanned by the vector $(-\frac{2}{9}, \frac{1}{9}, 1)$ which is obtained from (6) by letting $z = 1$. The three equations of (5) "depend" on the two "independent" equations of (6). In (7) the space of solutions has dimension 0, while the three equations are "independent." These relationships (i.e., the "dependence" or "independence" of equations, and the relations which hold among the number of variables, the number of "independent" equations and the dimension of the solutions) can be easily established with the concepts we now have available.

Clearly the rows of the matrix (2) can be thought of as vectors in R^3: the first row as the vector $(-2, 1, 3)$, the second row as the vector $(2, -1, -3)$, the third row as $(-6, 3, 9)$. Let M be the subspace spanned by these three rows. We assert that $\{(1, -\frac{1}{2}, -\frac{3}{2})\}$ is a basis for this subspace. We see that $(1, -\frac{1}{2}, -\frac{3}{2}) = -\frac{1}{2}(-2, 1, 3)$, so that $(1, -\frac{1}{2}, -\frac{3}{2})$ belongs to M. We also have $(-2, 1, 3) = -2(1, -\frac{1}{2}, -\frac{3}{2})$; $(2, -1, -3) = 2(1, -\frac{1}{2}, -\frac{3}{2})$; and $(-6, 3, 9) = -6(1, -\frac{1}{2}, -\frac{3}{2})$. Thus any vector which is a linear combination of $(-2, 1, 3)$, $(2, -1, -3)$, and $(-6, 3, 9)$ is also a linear combination of $(1, -\frac{1}{2}, -\frac{3}{2})$. Therefore

(30) The nonzero row of (4), i.e., $\{(1, -\frac{1}{2}, -\frac{3}{2})\}$, is a basis for M.

(31) Also $\dim R^3 = 3 = \dim M +$ the dimension of the null space of (2).

Now let M_1 be the subspace of R^3 spanned by the rows of

$$(32) \quad \begin{bmatrix} 2 & 5 & 1 \\ 1 & -2 & 1 \\ 3 & 3 & 2 \end{bmatrix},$$

which is the coefficient matrix of (5). We can row reduce (32) to

$$(33) \quad \begin{bmatrix} 1 & 0 & \frac{7}{9} \\ 0 & 1 & -\frac{1}{9} \\ 0 & 0 & 0 \end{bmatrix},$$

which is the coefficient matrix of (6). Let N be the subspace of R^3 spanned by the rows of (33). We assert that $M_1 = N$ and that $\{(1, 0, \frac{7}{9}), (0, 1, -\frac{1}{9})\}$ is a basis for M_1. The matrix of (33) is obtained from (32) by applying a sequence of row operations to (32). Each such row operation is actually a process of replacing a row of (32) by a linear combination of the rows of (32). Thus each row of (33) is a linear combination of the rows of (32). We conclude that N is contained in M_1. Now we note that each row of (33) is a linear combination of the rows of (32). We can show this directly or we can note that (32) can be obtained from (33) by applying a sequence of row operations to (33). Let us see how this is done. To obtain (33) from (32), apply the following operations to (32). Multiply row two by

-2, and add the result to row one; then multiply by -3, and add the result to row three. Multiply row one by $\frac{1}{9}$. Multiply row one by 2, and add the result to row two; then multiply by -9, and add the result to row three. Interchange rows one and two. To obtain (32) from (33) we need only reverse these operations and cancel out their effect. Thus we apply the following operations to (33). Interchange rows one and two. Multiply row one by 9, and add the result to row three; then multiply by -2, and add the result to row two. Multiply row one by 9. Multiply row two by 3, and add the result to row three; then multiply by 2, and add the result to row one. This gives (32). (The reader should check this.) Thus each row of (32) is a linear combination of the rows of (33) and M_1 is contained in N. Therefore $M_1 = N$. The nonzero rows of (33) are clearly independent, so we have the following statements.

(34)   The nonzero rows of the echelon form (33) are a basis for M_1.

Again we have

(35) $\dim R^3 = 3 = \dim M_1 +$ the dimension of the null space of (32).

We shall now give the general results.

Definition. The *row space* of an $m \times n$ matrix A is the subspace of R^n spanned by the rows of A. The dimension of this space is called the *rank* of A and is denoted by "rank (A)." The dimension of the null space of A is called the *nullity* of A and is denoted by "nullity (A)."

We generalize our results as follows. Let A be an $m \times n$ matrix and let B be obtained from A by applying a row operation to A. Thus B is obtained from A by replacing a row of A by a linear combination of some of the rows of A. We conclude that the row space of B is contained in the row space of A. But, note that A can be obtained from B by applying a row operation to B (e.g., if B is obtained from A by multiplying row i_0 of A by a and adding to row i_1 of A, with $i_0 \neq i_1$, then A is obtained from B by multiplying row i_0 of B by $-a$ and adding to row i_1 of B). We conclude that the row space of A is contained in the row space of B. Therefore A and B have the same row space. In particular, this generalization of the method used to equate the row spaces of (32) and (33) gives the following.

(36)   Let A be an $m \times n$ matrix and suppose that A is reduced to the row reduced echelon matrix R. Then A and R have the same row space.

The following important theorem is a consequence of this.

Theorem 6. If A is an $m \times n$ matrix, then rank (A) + nullity (A) = n.

Proof. We shall only sketch a proof, by indicating a basis for the row space of A and one for the null space of A. First, row reduce A to a row reduced echelon matrix R. Then from (36) we know that A and R have the same row space, and from Theorem 1, that they have the same null space. In terms of R we can describe a basis for each of these spaces. Let R be described as in (35) of Section 1; i.e., let r be the number of nonzero rows of R, and let k_i be the column subscript of the first nonzero entry in row i of R, $1 \le i \le r$.

(37)   The nonzero rows of R form a basis for the row space of R.

Thus rank (A) = rank (R) = r. If $r = n$, then nullity (A) = 0 by Theorem 2, so that n = rank (A) + nullity (A). If $r < n$, let u_1, u_2, ..., u_{n-r} be the variables not included among $\{x_{k_1}, x_{k_2}, \ldots, x_{k_r}\}$ as in Theorem 2. Let X^s be the vector obtained by assigning u_s the value 1 and u_t the value zero for $t \ne s$. The other coordinates of X^s are computed using (38) of Section 1.

(38) $\{X^1, X^2, \ldots, X^{n-r}\}$ is a basis for the null space of A.

Thus nullity $A = n - r = n -$ rank (A).   Q.E.D.

Remarks. The proof of this theorem should be intuitively clear even though the generality involved may cause difficulties. If A is $m \times n$, then we can obtain a basis for the row space of A by removing those rows of A which are superfluous, i.e., by reducing A to echelon form. But this process also enables us to determine the number of "independent" choices for the null space of A; i.e., this was the point of our work in Section 1. Each X^i in (38) clearly corresponds to the "free" variable u_i. All (38) tells us is that X is in the null space of A if and only if its coordinates are uniquely determined by assigning values to u_1, u_2, ..., u_{n-r}. A complete proof of (37) and (38) will be left to the exercises.

Let us interpret these results in R^3. Let M be a line or a plane through $(0, 0, 0)$. How can we describe M? We have essentially two ways to do this. We can either give a set of vectors which span M, or we can give a set of equations for which M is the null space. If we remove all superfluous equations, then we obtain a minimal description of M. Similarly if we require that the spanning set be independent, we also obtain a "minimal" description of M. Theorem 6 tells us that the dimension of M plus the minimal number of equations needed to describe M is always three, the dimension of R^3. Thus if M is a line, we can describe M with a basis consisting of *one* vector or as the intersection of *two* planes. If M is a plane, then a basis for M consists of *two* vectors.

Theorem 6, along with (37) and (38), has many applications. Let us note some of these. Suppose that M is the subspace of R^n spanned by $\{X^1, X^2, \ldots, X^k\}$. What is the dimension of M? From Lemma 1 we know that dim $M \leq k$. We apply Theorem 6. Let A be the $k \times n$ matrix whose ith row consists of the coordinates of X^i, $i = 1, 2, \ldots, k$. Then M is the row space of A. Thus rank $(A) =$ dim M.

How can we find a basis for M? This is answered using (37). We reduce A to an echelon matrix R. Then the rows of R are a basis for the row space of A which is M.

This same technique can be used to answer two other questions. Let X be in R^n and let $\{X^1, X^2, \ldots, X^k\}$ be a set of vectors in R^n. Is $\{X^1, X^2, \ldots, X^k\}$ independent? Is X a linear combination of $\{X^1, X^2, \ldots, X^k\}$? To answer the first question let M be the subspace spanned by $\{X^1, X^2, \ldots, X^k\}$. Then dim $M = k$ if and only if $\{X^1, X^2, \ldots, X^k\}$ is an independent set. [Use (28) with $V = M$ and $D = \{X^1, X^2, \ldots, X^k\}$]. Let A be the matrix constructed above. Then dim $M =$ rank (A). Thus to determine if $\{X^1, X^2, \ldots, X^k\}$ is an independent set, we form the matrix whose rows are the n-tuples $X^1, X^2, \ldots, X^k$. We reduce this matrix to an echelon form R. Then the set is independent if and only if rank $(R) = k$.

To answer the second question, let M be the subspace spanned by $\{X^1, X^2, \ldots, X^k\}$ and M_1 the subspace spanned by $\{X^1, X^2, \ldots, X^k, X\}$. Then M is a subspace of M_1, so dim $M \leq$ dim M_1 [by (27)]. To say that X is a linear combination of $\{X^1, X^2, \ldots, X^k\}$ is the same as saying that X is in M. But if X is in M, then any vector in M_1 is also in M, so that X is a linear combination of $\{X^1, X^2, \ldots, X^k\}$ if and only if $M = M_1$. Again using (27), this is the same as saying that dim $M =$ dim M_1. We can now use the above method. Let A be the $k \times n$ matrix whose ith row is X^i. Let B be the $(k + 1) \times n$ matrix whose ith row is X^i if $i = 1, 2, \ldots, k$, and whose $(k + 1)$st row is X. Then X is a linear combination of $\{X^1, X^2, \ldots, X^k\}$ if and only if rank $(A) =$ rank (B), since dim $M =$ rank (A) and dim $M_1 =$ rank (B). Thus we can answer the second question by reducing A and B.

Of course if we wish to find real numbers $a_1, a_2, \ldots, a_k$ such that $X = a_1 X^1 + a_2 X^2 + \cdots + a_k X^k$, we must do more than the above. An example will be helpful. Let $X^1 = (3, 1, 2)$, $X^2 = (1, -6, 0)$, and $X = (1, \frac{20}{3}, \frac{4}{3})$. Then we wish to determine a and b, if we can, such that $X = aX^1 + bX^2$. This gives the system of equations

$$3a + b = 1, \qquad a - 6b = \tfrac{20}{3}, \qquad 2a = \tfrac{4}{3},$$

which is easily solved, yielding $a = \frac{2}{3}$, $b = -1$.

Let A be an $m \times n$ matrix. Then in an obvious fashion we can identify a column of A with a vector in R^m. The *column space* of A is then the subspace of R^m spanned by the columns of A and the *column rank* of A is the dimension of this space. We shall show in the next section the rather amazing fact that rank (A) = column rank of A. This result is even more useful than Theorem 6.

In this section we have studied the space of solutions to a homogeneous system of equations. What about a nonhomogeneous system? We shall describe this case with an example, then give the general results. We consider the system

$$
\begin{aligned}
2x + y - 3z &= 1 \\
3x + 2y - 2z &= 2 \\
x + y + z &= 1.
\end{aligned}
$$
(39)

Reduction of the augmented matrix of (39) gives

$$
(40) \qquad
\begin{bmatrix}
1 & 0 & -4 & 0 \\
0 & 1 & 5 & 1 \\
0 & 0 & 0 & 0
\end{bmatrix}.
$$

From Theorem 3 we have solutions to (39), in fact, more than one solution. Thus $(4, -4, 1)$ and $(0, 1, 0)$ are solutions to (39), while the sum $(4, -4, 1) + (0, 1, 0) = (4, -3, 1)$ is *not* a solution. The solutions do *not* form a subspace. The solutions *do* form a line, but this line does not pass through $(0, 0, 0)$. Note, however, that the difference $(4, -4, 1) - (0, 1, 0) = (4, -5, 1)$ *is* a solution to the homogeneous system

$$
\begin{aligned}
2x + y - 3z &= 0 \\
3x + 2y - 2z &= 0 \\
x + y + z &= 0.
\end{aligned}
$$
(41)

Conversely $(8, -10, 2)$ is a solution to (41). Add this to $(4, -4, 1)$ and also to $(0, 1, 0)$. This gives $(12, -14, 3)$ and $(8, -9, 2)$, respectively, both of which are solutions to (39). In general, the difference of two solutions to (39) is a solution to (41), while the sum of a solution to (39) and a solution to (41) gives a solution to (39). The general result is the following. Any two solutions to the system

$$
\begin{aligned}
A_{11}x_1 + A_{12}x_2 + \cdots + A_{1n}x_n &= y_1 \\
A_{21}x_1 + A_{22}x_2 + \cdots + A_{2n}x_n &= y_2 \\
&\vdots \\
A_{m1}x_1 + A_{m2}x_2 + \cdots + A_{mn}x_n &= y_m
\end{aligned}
$$
(42)

differ by a vector which is a solution to the homogeneous system

$$(43) \quad \begin{aligned} A_{11}x_1 + A_{12}x_2 + \cdots + A_{1n}x_n &= 0 \\ A_{21}x_1 + A_{22}x_2 + \cdots + A_{2n}x_n &= 0 \\ &\vdots \\ A_{m1}x_1 + A_{m2}x_2 + \cdots + A_{mn}x_n &= 0. \end{aligned}$$

Also the sum of a solution to (42) and a solution to (43) gives a solution to (42). This provides us with a method for solving (42) which is not quite as quick as the method given in Section 2, but which does generalize to other problems. To solve (42), first find one solution to (42) and all solutions to (43). Then any other solution to (42) is obtained by adding our particular solution to (42) to one of the solutions to (43). (This is one of the basic methods for finding the general solution to a nonhomogeneous linear differential equation, where we can find the general solution by adding a particular solution to the general solution of the homogeneous equation.)

In general, if U is a subspace of V and if X is a vector in V, then the collection of all vectors $X + Y$, where Y is in U is called the *parallel translation* of U by the vector X. [Thus a line or plane not through $(0, 0, 0)$ is a parallel translation of a line or plane passing through $(0, 0, 0)$.] A subset K of V which is a parallel translation of a subspace U by a vector X is usually called an *affine* subspace. In this terminology our results can be phrased as follows. The solutions to (42) form an affine subspace which is the parallel translation of the solutions to (43) by a vector which is a solution to (42).

EXERCISES

1. Let **V** be the space of arrows. Establish each of the following. (A careful picture is helpful.)
   (a) $(\mathbf{v}_0 + \mathbf{v}_1) + \mathbf{v}_2 = \mathbf{v}_0 + (\mathbf{v}_1 + \mathbf{v}_2)$.
   (b) The vector $\overrightarrow{PQ}$ is parallel to $\mathbf{v}_1 - \mathbf{v}_2$ and has the same length as $\mathbf{v}_1 - \mathbf{v}_2$. (See Fig. 8.)
   (c) Let O be the point $(0, 0, 0)$, P the point (x, y, z), and Q the point (x_1, y_1, z_1). Show that the terminal point of $\overrightarrow{OP} + \overrightarrow{OQ}$ is $(x + x_1, y + y_1, z + z_1)$.
   (d) Let O be the point $(0, 0, 0)$, and P the point (x, y, z). Show that the terminal point of aOP is (ax, ay, az).

2. Show that each of the following is a vector space. These spaces will be referred to in many later sections.
   (a) Let V be the set of polynomials of degree $\leq n$. If $f = a_0 + a_1t + a_2t^2 + \cdots + a_nt^n$ and $g = b_0 + b_1t + b_2t^2 + \cdots + b_nt^n$, then $f + g$ is defined to be $(a_0 + b_0) + (a_1 + b_1)t + \cdots + (a_n + b_n)t^n$; af is defined to be $(aa_0) + (aa_1)t + \cdots + (aa_n)t^n$.

(b) Let V be the collection of 2×2 matrices. If

$$A_0 = \begin{bmatrix} a_0 & b_0 \\ c_0 & d_0 \end{bmatrix} \quad \text{and} \quad A_1 = \begin{bmatrix} a_1 & b_1 \\ c_1 & d_1 \end{bmatrix},$$

then $A_0 + A_1$ and aA_0 are respectively defined to be

$$\begin{bmatrix} a_0 + a_1 & b_0 + b_1 \\ c_0 + c_1 & d_0 + d_1 \end{bmatrix} \quad \text{and} \quad \begin{bmatrix} aa_0 & ab_0 \\ ac_0 & ad_0 \end{bmatrix}.$$

(c) Let V be the set of expressions $ax + by + cz$, where a, b, and c are real. Addition is defined by $(ax + by + cz) + (a_1x + b_1y + c_1z) = (a + a_1)x + (b + b_1)y + (c + c_1)z$. Multiplication by numbers is defined by $d(ax + by + cz) = (da)x + (db)y + (dc)z$.

(d) Let V be the set of expressions $ax^2 + by^2 + cz^2 + dx + ey + fz$. Addition and multiplication by numbers are defined by

$$(ax^2 + by^2 + cz^2 + dx + ey + fz) + (a_1x^2 + b_1y^2 + c_1z^2 + d_1x + e_1y + f_1z) = (a + a_1)x^2 + (b + b_1)y^2 + (c + c_1)z^2 + (d + d_1)x + (e + e_1)y + (f + f_1)z;$$

and

$$g(ax^2 + by^2 + cz^2 + dx + ey + fz)$$
$$= (ga)x^2 + (gb)y^2 + (gc)z^2 + (gd)x + (ge)y + (gf)z.$$

(e) Let V be the collection of all lines in space which are parallel to a given line l_0. We assume that l_0 passes through the point $(0, 0, 0)$, which we denote by O. If l_1 and l_2 are parallel to l_0, let P_1 and P_2 be the points on l_1 and l_2, respectively, which are closest to O. Let $P = P_1 + P_2$. (Here the addition of points is defined as in R^3.) Let l be the line passing through P which is parallel to l_0. We call l the sum of l_1 and l_2 and write $l = l_1 + l_2$. al_1 is obtained by multiplying each point of l_1 by a.

3. Show that each of the following is *not* a vector space; i.e., at least one of the rules (10) is violated.

(a) V is the set of pairs of real numbers (x, y) such that $x \geq y$. We define addition and multiplication by $(x, y) + (x_1, y_1) = (x + x_1, y + y_1)$ and $a(x, y) = (|a|x, |a|y)$.

(b) V is the set of pairs of real numbers (x, y). We define addition as in R^2 and multiplication by numbers by $a(x, y) = (ax, y)$.

(c) V is the set of polynomials of degree ≤ 1. If $f = a_0 + a_1 t$ and $g = b_0 + b_1 t$, then we define $f + g = (a_0 + b_0) + (a_0 b_1 + a_1 b_0)t$, and $af = (aa_0) + (aa_1)t$.

4. Show that each of the following subsets M is a subspace of the indicated space V.

(a) $V = R^2$, M is the collection of all pairs (x, y) such that $x = y$.

(b) $V = R^2$, M is the collection of all pairs (x, y) such that $x = 0$.

(cont.)

(c) $V = R^3$, M is the collection of all triples (x, y, z) such that $x = z$.

(d) $V = R^3$, M is the collection of all triples (x, y, z) such that $x - 2y + 3z = 0$.

(e) $V = R^3$, M is the collection of all triples (x, y, z) such that $x = y$ and $z = 0$.

(f) $V = R^4$, M is the collection of all 4-tuples (x, y, z, w) such that $x - y = z + w$.

(g) V is the space of Exercise 2(a), with $n = 2$, M is the set of all polynomials $f = a_0 + a_1 t + a_2 t^2$ such that $a_0 = 0$.

(h) V is the space of Exercise 2(d) and M is the space of Exercise 2(c).

(i) V is the space of Exercise 2(b) and M is the collection of matrices of the form

$$\begin{bmatrix} a & b \\ b & c \end{bmatrix}.$$

5. Show that each of the following subsets M of R^3 is *not* a subspace by stating at least one of the properties (12) which is violated.

   (a) M is the collection of all (x, y, z) such that $x^2 + y^2 + z^2 \leq 1$.
   (b) M is the collection of all (x, y, z) such that $x - y + z = 1$.
   (c) M is the collection of all (x, y, z) such that $x \geq y \geq z$.
   (d) M is the collection of all (x, y, z) such that either $x = 0$ or $y = 0$ or both.

6. (a) Is R^2 a subspace of R^3?
   (b) Let U be a subspace of R^2. What are the possible values of dim U?
   (c) Let U be a subspace of R^3. What are the possible values of dim U?
   (d) Show that if U is a proper, nontrivial subspace of R^2, then U is a line through $(0, 0)$.
   (e) Show that U is a proper, nontrivial subspace of R^3 if and only if U is a line or a plane through $(0, 0, 0)$. [*Hint:* Use part (c).]

7. Which of the following subsets of R^2 are independent and which are dependent? [*Hint.* In some cases, Lemma 1 suffices. For others, use the method given in the remarks after Theorem 6.]

   (a) $\{(1, 2), (0, 3)\}$ (b) $\{(1, 1), (-1, -1)\}$
   (c) $\{(2, 1), (1, 2), (3, -1)\}$ (d) $\{(0, 0), (1, 0)\}$
   (e) $\{(3, 1)\}$ (f) $\{(a, b), (c, d)\}$, where $ad \neq bc$.

8. Which of the following subsets of R^3 are independent? [*Hint:* See the hint for Exercise 7.]

   (a) $\{(1, 0, 0), (0, 1, 1), (0, 0, 1), (1, 2, 3)\}$
   (b) $\{(2, 1, 0), (-1, 0, 1)\}$
   (c) $\{(1, 1, 1), (2, 3, 4), (4, 9, 16)\}$
   (d) $\{(1/\sqrt{2}, 0, -1), (\sqrt{3}, 2, 0), (0, -1, 2)\}$
   (e) $\{(1, 2, 1), (-3, 8, 1), (3, -1, -1)\}$

9. Which of the following subsets D of the indicated space V are dependent?

(a) $V = R^4$, $D = \{(1, \sqrt{2}, 0, 1)(2, 1, 0, 0)\}$.

(b) V is the space of Exercise 2(c) with $D = \{x + y, x - y, z\}$.

(c) V is the space of Exercise 3(b) with

$$D = \left\{ \begin{bmatrix} 0 & 1 \\ 1 & 0 \end{bmatrix}, \begin{bmatrix} 0 & -1 \\ 1 & 0 \end{bmatrix}, \begin{bmatrix} 1 & 0 \\ 0 & 1 \end{bmatrix}, \begin{bmatrix} 1 & 0 \\ 0 & -1 \end{bmatrix}, \begin{bmatrix} 1 & 1 \\ 1 & 1 \end{bmatrix} \right\}.$$

(d) V is the space of Exercise 3(a) with $n = 2$ and $D = \{t - 1, t^2 + 1, 3t^2 + 2t + 1\}$.

10. Determine whether $(4, 2, 1, 0)$ is a linear combination of each of the following sets of vectors. If so, find one such combination. (See Remarks after Theorem 6.)

(a) $\{(1, 2, -1, 0), (1, 3, 1, 2), (6, 1, 0, 1)\}$

(b) $\{(3, 1, 0, 1), (1, 2, 3, 1), (0, 3, 6, 6)\}$

(c) $\{(6, -1, 2, 1), (1, 7, -3, -2), (3, 1, 0, 0), (3, 3, -2, -1)\}$

11. Find a basis for the indicated space V which contains a basis for the indicated space M. (See Remarks after Theorem 6, and Lemma 2.)

(a) $V = R^3$, M is the subspace spanned by $\{(1, 2, 1), (0, -1, 0), (2, 0, 2)\}$.

(b) $V = R^3$, M is the subspace spanned by $\{(-1, 1, 1), (1, -1, -1)\}$.

(c) $V = R^4$, M is the subspace spanned by $\{(6, -1, 2, 1), (1, 7, -3, -2), (3, 1, 0, 0), (3, 3, -2, -1)\}$.

(d) $V = R^4$, M is the subspace spanned by $\{(0, 1, -1, 2), (3, 7, 2, 17), (1, 3, 0, 7), (-5, 3, -26, 1)\}$.

(e) V is the space of Exercise 3(a) with $n = 2$, and M is the subspace spanned by $\{t - 1, t^2 + 1, 3t^2 + 2t + 1\}$.

12. For each of the subspaces M of Exercise 11(a)–(d), find a matrix for which M is the null space.

13. For each of the following matrices find the rank, the nullity, a basis for the row space, and a basis for the null space.

(a) $\begin{bmatrix} 2 & 1 \\ 1 & 2 \end{bmatrix}$

(b) $\begin{bmatrix} 2 & -1 & 0 & 1 & 1 \\ 2 & 1 & 0 & 1 & 2 \\ -7 & 0 & 0 & -2 & 0 \\ 3 & -1 & 0 & 1 & 0 \end{bmatrix}$

(c) $\begin{bmatrix} 3 & 6 & 1 & 2 \\ 1 & 0 & \frac{1}{6} & 1 \\ 1 & -7 & 0 & 1 \\ 2 & 1 & 0 & 3 \\ 3 & -6 & 0 & 4 \end{bmatrix}$

(d) $\begin{bmatrix} -2 & -1 & 2 & -5 & 2 & -1 & 2 \\ 3 & 1 & -1 & 6 & 2 & 1 & 0 \\ 4 & 1 & -1 & 7 & 6 & 1 & 2 \end{bmatrix}$

14. Find a basis for each of the spaces of Exercise 2.

15. The following are examples of infinite dimensional vector spaces. They are important in many mathematical investigations. Show that each is a vector space.

   (a) The set of all continuous real (or complex) valued functions $f(t)$ defined for $\alpha \leq t \leq \beta$. Here $f + g$ is the function defined by $\{f + g\}(t) = f(t) + g(t)$ and af is the function defined by $\{af\}(t) = af(t)$.

   (b) The set of all polynomials. Addition and scalar multiplication are as defined in Exercise 2(a). [The space of Exercise 2(a) is a subspace of this space. If we consider a polynomial f as a function defined for $\alpha \leq t \leq \beta$, then this is a subspace of the space of part (a).]

16. Let M and N be subspaces of the vector space V. Let $M \cap N$ be the collection of all vectors belonging to *both* M and N. Let $M \cup N$ be the collection of all vectors belonging to *either* M or N or both.

   (a) Show that $M \cap N$ is a subspace of V.

   (b) Find two subspaces M and N of R^2 such that $M \cup N$ is *not* a subspace of R^2.

   (c) Let M and N be two subspaces of R^3 such that $M \neq N$. Suppose that M and N are planes. Show that $M \cap N$ is a line.

17. (a) Prove (27).   (b) Prove (28).   (c) Prove (29).
    (d) Prove (37).   (e) Prove (38).

18. Show that if A is 2×2, then the row rank and the column rank of A are the same.

19. Show that if A and B are 2×2 row reduced echelon matrices with the same row space, then $A = B$. (See Exercise 12, Section 1.)

20. Many geometric concepts can be formulated in algebraic terms. This allows us to treat these concepts in an arbitrary vector space, often with fruitful results. We shall give some of these here, as well as giving examples of these for the reader to work out. (Often a diagram will be helpful.)

   (a) If X and Y are vectors in V, then the *line (segment) between X and Y* consists of all vectors of the form $aX + (1 - a)Y$, where $0 \leq a \leq 1$.

   (b) If X, Y, and Z are vectors in V, then the *triangle determined by X, Y, and Z* consists of all vectors of the form $aX + bY + cZ$, where $a \geq 0, b \geq 0, c \geq 0$, and $a + b + c = 1$.

   (c) A collection of vectors M contained in V is called a *convex set* if the line between X and Y is contained in M for each X and Y in M.

   (d) A collection of vectors M contained in V is called a (*positive*) *cone* if $aX + bY$ is in M for all X and Y in M and all $a \geq 0, b \geq 0$.

   (e) Draw a graph of the line segment between $(1, 2)$ and $(3, 1)$ in R^2.

   (f) Draw a graph of the triangle determined by $(1, 6)$, $(3, -1)$, and $(0, 2)$ in R^2.

   (g) Show that the collection of all (x, y, z) such that $x^2 + y^2 + z^2 \leq 1$ is a convex set in R^3.

(h) Show that the collection of all (x, y, z) such that $x \geq y \geq z$ is a positive cone in R^3.

(j) Show that the collection of all (x, y) such that $|x| \geq 1$ is *not* a convex set in R^2.

(k) Show that the collection of all (x, y) such that $x \geq 0$, $y \geq 0$, and $xy \geq 1$ is a convex set but is *not* a cone in R^2.

(l) Show that a cone is a convex set.

(m) Show that a triangle is a convex set.

(n) Show that an affine subspace is a convex set.

(o) Show that if M is a convex set and if X, Y, and Z are in M, then the triangle determined by X, Y, and Z is contained in M.

21. Write a flow diagram for each of the following.

(a) Finding the rank of a 3×3 matrix.

(b) Testing the independence of three vectors in R^4.

(c) Testing whether X is a linear combination of Y and Z, where X, Y, and Z are in R^3.

SPECIAL EXERCISE

Show that the echelon form is uniquely determined by the matrix of coefficients. [*Hint*: The above statement needs to be made precise before a proof can be given. It asks you to show that if we obtain an echelon matrix R by reducing A in one fashion and an echelon matrix R' by reducing A in another fashion, then $R = R'$. We know that R and A (also R' and A) have the same row space (Lemma 3). With this the problem is a generalization of Exercise 20. Give a careful description of both R and R' as was given before Theorem 1. Show that the condition that each row of R must be a linear combination of the rows of R' implies that each row of R must be a row of R'. Sketching the 3×3 proof might be helpful.]

Section 4. LINEAR TRANSFORMATIONS

In this section we shall study linear transformations, the fundamental concept in linear algebra. Most of the remainder of this book, especially Chapters 3 and 4, will be concerned with the study of particular types of such transformations. Let us begin by looking at some examples. Consider the system of equations

$$\begin{aligned} 2x + y &= a \\ x - y &= b. \end{aligned}$$

(1)

Heretofore, a and b were given real numbers and we asked for solutions to (1). In this section we shall look at another aspect of (1). For each pair of real numbers (x, y), (1) defines a new pair (a, b). Thus if

$(x, y) = (0, 1)$, then (1) gives $(a, b) = (1, -1)$. In other words, (1) is a *rule* which assigns to each pair (x, y) the pair (a, b) which is computed using (1). Such a rule, or computation scheme, which is defined for pairs (x, y), resulting in pairs (a, b), is called a *transformation (mapping, function)* of R^2 into R^2. We say that the pair (x, y) is *transformed (mapped)* by (1) into the pair (a, b). Thus $(0, 1)$ is transformed, via (1), into $(1, -1)$. Likewise, $(3, 2)$ is mapped, via (1), into $(8, 1)$.

Since we will study computation schemes which are similar to (1), it will be convenient to use a single letter to denote the transformation given by the rules (1). We shall generally use the letter T (or other letters immediately preceding T in the alphabet, such as P, Q, R, and S). To stress that we are interested in the transformation defined by (1), we will generally rewrite it in the form

$$(2) \qquad T(x, y) = (2x + y, x - y).$$

The equation (2) tells us that the pair (x, y) is transformed by T into the pair $(2x + y, x - y)$. In these terms we would then have $T(0, 1) = (1, -1)$ and $T(3, 2) = (8, 1)$.

Consider the transformation given by

$$(3) \qquad S(x, y) = (x^2, y^2).$$

The rule given by (3) differs in an essential way from the rule given by (2), in that the equations defining S are nonlinear, while those defining T are linear. This can be easily stated in terms of the fact that R^2 is a vector space, for T preserves our algebraic structure, while S does not. Consider the vector $c(3, 2) + d(0, 1) = (3c, 2c + d)$. We have

$$(4) \quad \begin{aligned} T(3c, 2c + d) &= \big(2(3c) + (2c + d), (3c) - (2c + d)\big) \\ &= (8c + d, c - d), \end{aligned}$$

$$(5) \quad S(3c, 2c + d) = \big((3c)^2, (2c + d)^2\big) = (9c^2, 4c^2 + 4cd + d^2).$$

Thus

$$(6) \quad T(3c, 2c + d) = c(8, 1) + d(1, -1) = cT(3, 2) + dT(1, -1),$$

$$(7) \quad \begin{aligned} S(3c, 2c + d) &= c^2(9, 4) + (4cd + d^2)(0, 1) \\ &= c^2 S(3, 2) + (4cd + d^2)S(0, 1). \end{aligned}$$

Statement (6) tells us that T transforms a linear combination of $\{(3, 2), (0, 1)\}$ into the same linear combination of $\{T(3, 2), T(0, 1)\}$. Statement (7) tells us that S does not have this property.

Transformations which have the property of preserving linear combinations are called *linear transformations;* all other transformations are said to be nonlinear. We shall confine our study in this book to linear transformations.

An interesting example of a linear transformation can be defined on **V**, the vector space of arrows. Let $\mathbf{v}_0$ be a nonzero vector in **V**. Let **v** be any vector in **V**. Then we define $P(\mathbf{v})$ to be the *projection* of **v** onto $\mathbf{v}_0$. This is defined as follows. Drop a perpendicular from the terminal point of **v** to the line along $\mathbf{v}_0$. Label its intersection with this line by Q. (See Fig. 1.) Then

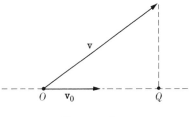

(8) $P(\mathbf{v}) = \overrightarrow{OQ}.$

This transformation also preserves linear combinations, for we have

FIGURE 1

(9) $P(a\mathbf{v}_1 + b\mathbf{v}_2) = aP(\mathbf{v}_1) + bP(\mathbf{v}_2)$ for all $\mathbf{v}_1$ and $\mathbf{v}_2$ in **V** and all real numbers a and b.

To establish (9) directly is somewhat difficult. Let us establish two simpler properties from which (9) will follow. These are

(10) $P(a\mathbf{v}) = aP(\mathbf{v})$ for all **v** in **V** and all numbers a;

(11) $P(\mathbf{v}_1 + \mathbf{v}_2) = P(\mathbf{v}_1) + P(\mathbf{v}_2)$ for all $\mathbf{v}_1$ and $\mathbf{v}_2$ in **V**.

Equations (10) and (11) now follow from simple trigonometric considerations and will be left to the reader. Figures 2 and 3 should be helpful.

We can use (10) and (11) to deduce (9) as follows. Use of (11) gives $P(a\mathbf{v}_1 + b\mathbf{v}_2) = P(a\mathbf{v}_1) + P(b\mathbf{v}_2)$. Use of (10) gives $P(a\mathbf{v}_1) = aP(\mathbf{v}_1)$ and $P(b\mathbf{v}_2) = bP(\mathbf{v}_2)$. These two combine to give (9).

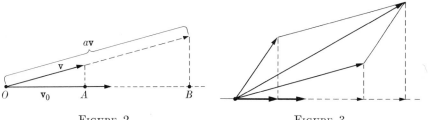

FIGURE 2   FIGURE 3

As we shall see in Section 6, the transformation P can be given an algebraic description similar to (2). We now give the general definition of linear transformation.

Definition.   Let V and W be vector spaces. A *linear transformation* T from V into W is a rule which assigns to each vector X in V, a *unique* vector, denoted by TX, which belongs to W. Furthermore, if X and Y are in V and a and b are real numbers, then

(12) $$T(aX + bY) = aTX + bTY.$$

Remarks. Note that the definition of transformation involves the use of the word "rule" which is an undefined term. Rather than digress enough to remove this undefined word, we shall assume that what we mean by "rule" is clear. (If it is not, it should become so as we accumulate a stock of examples.) The word "transformation" has many synonyms, including "function," "mapping," "single-valued relation," and "correspondence." The analogous notion of function is used in elementary calculus, where we can use the notion of "graph" in order to clarify its meaning. In linear algebra, graphs are essentially useless. For example, a graph of (2) would involve a four-dimensional figure, which is difficult to envision.

As we shall see in Section 6, a linear transformation always has a rule similar to (2). However, except in computation, it is easier to think of linear transformations as rules which satisfy (12).

The relation (12) could be restated as

(13)   (a) $T(aX) = aTX$ for all X in V and all real numbers a;
         (b) $T(X + Y) = TX + TY$ for all X and Y in V.

We used just this fact in deducing (9) from (10) and (11). The proof of the equivalence of (12) and (13) will be left as an exercise, as it duplicates our deduction of (9) from (10) and (11). Since (12) is shorter than (13), we shall generally use (12).

We shall also adopt the convention of omitting parentheses whenever no confusion will result. Hence we shall write TX, rather than $T(X)$, whenever it is clear that T is a transformation and X is a vector in V.

Many transformations are not linear, i.e., do not satisfy (12), but still have properties analogous to linear transformations. The following is an example:

(14) $$S(x, y) = (2x + 1, y - 2).$$

Thus S is a transformation of R^2 into R^2. The equations defining S are linear, yet S does not possess property (12); e.g., $S\big(2(3, 2) + (0, 1)\big) \neq 2S(3, 2) + S(0, 1)$. However, if we rewrite S as $S(x, y) = (2x, y) + (1, -2)$, then S is the "sum" of two transformations. The first transforms (x, y)

into $(2x, y)$, while the second transforms every vector into the vector $(1, -2)$. Thus S is an example of an *affine* transformation. An *affine transformation* S of a vector space V into a vector space W is a transformation of V into W of the form

$$(15) \qquad\qquad SX = TX + Y^0,$$

where T is a linear transformation of V into W, and Y^0 is a fixed vector in W. The exercises will extend some of our results to affine transformations.

The property (12) immediately extends to more than two vectors.

(16) If T is a linear transformation of V into W, then $T(a_1X^1 + a_2X^2 + \cdots + a_kX^k) = a_1TX^1 + a_2TX^2 + \cdots + a_kTX^k$, for any X^1, X^2, $\ldots$, X^k in V and any real numbers $a_1, a_2, \ldots, a_k$.

To prove (16) for three vectors, for example, we have $T(a_1X^1 + a_2X^2 + a_3X^3) = T((a_1X^1 + a_2X^2) + a_3X^3) = T(a_1X^1 + a_2X^2) + a_3TX^3 = a_1TX^1 + a_2TX^2 + a_3TX^3$.

If T is a transformation of V into W, then we usually call V the *domain* of T, or the space on which T is defined. The collection of all vectors in W of the form TX for X in V, is called the *range*, or *image*, of T. This is the set of all Y in W for which the equation $TX = Y$ has at least one solution X in V. If $W = V$, then we usually say that T is an *operator* on V. Our examples will clarify these concepts. The transformation defined by (2) has R^2 as its domain *and* R^2 as its range, since any vector (a, b) in R^2 has the form $(2x + y, x - y)$, where

$$x = \frac{a + b}{3} \qquad \text{and} \qquad y = \frac{a - 2b}{3} \, ;$$

i.e., the equations (1) have a solution for *any* pair (a, b). The transformation defined in (8) has **V** as its domain. Its range consists of all arrows whose terminal points lie on the line through $\mathbf{v}_0$.

The transformations of (2) and of (8) are linear operators. The following is a linear transformation which is not a linear operator:

$$(17) \qquad\qquad T(x, y, z) = (2x + y - z, x + y - z).$$

The domain of (17) is R^3, while its range is R^2, which is *not* contained in R^3.

Two linear transformations are particularly simple. We can transform each vector in V into the zero vector in W. We usually denote this transformation by 0 and call it the *zero transformation* of V into W. Formally, 0 is defined by

(18) $0X = 0$ for all X in V.

Usually it is less confusing to use the same symbol for this transformation as we do for the zero vector in W (as well as in V). Clearly the transformation defined by (18) satisfies (12).

A simple linear operator on V is the one defined by the following rule:

(19) $I_V X = X$ for all X in V;

I_V leaves each vector in V fixed and, for obvious reasons, is called the *identity* operator on V. Clearly the operator defined by (19) satisfies (12). When the space V is understood, we replace I_V by the single symbol I.

The transformation (2) has a close connection with the matrix of coefficients of (1). Let us generalize this. Let T be a linear transformation from R^n into R^m. Let $X^1 = (1, 0, \ldots, 0)$, $X^2 = (0, 1, 0, \ldots, 0)$, $\ldots$, $X^n = (0, 0, \ldots, 0, 1)$. Then $\{X^1, X^2, \ldots, X^n\}$ is a basis for V. Since TX^j is a vector in R^m, for $j = 1, 2, \ldots, n$, we can write

(20) $TX^j = (A_{1j}, A_{2j}, \ldots, A_{mj})$.

The numbers A_{ij} form a matrix, which is called the *matrix* of T; i.e., A is the matrix of T, where

(21)
$$A = \begin{bmatrix} A_{11} & A_{12} & \ldots & A_{1n} \\ A_{21} & A_{22} & \ldots & A_{2n} \\ \vdots & & & \\ A_{m1} & A_{m2} & \ldots & A_{mn} \end{bmatrix}.$$

The jth column of A consists of the coordinates of TX^j for $j = 1, 2, \ldots, m$.

In our example (2), we have $T(1, 0) = (2, 1)$ and $T(0, 1) = (1, -1)$. Thus the matrix of T is

$$\begin{bmatrix} 2 & 1 \\ 1 & -1 \end{bmatrix}$$

which is the matrix of coefficients of (1).

In our example (17), we have $T(1, 0, 0) = (2, 1)$, $T(0, 1, 0) = (1, 1)$, and $T(0, 0, 1) = (-1, -1)$ so that the matrix of T is

$$\begin{bmatrix} 2 & 1 & -1 \\ 1 & 1 & -1 \end{bmatrix}.$$

Any linear transformation from R^n into R^m can be expressed in a form like (2) or (17). To see this, let $\{X^1, X^2, \ldots, X^n\}$ be the basis for R^n constructed to define (20). Let $X = (x_1, x_2, \ldots, x_n)$. Then $X = x_1 X^1 + x_2 X^2 + \cdots + x_n X^n$, and $TX = x_1 TX^1 + x_2 TX^2 + \cdots + x_n TX^n$ using (16). Thus $TX = x_1(A_{11}, A_{21}, \ldots, A_{m1}) + x_2(A_{12}, A_{22}, \ldots, A_{m2}) + \cdots + x_n(A_{1n}, A_{2n}, \ldots, A_{mn})$. Rewriting gives

$$(22) \quad \begin{aligned} T(x_1, x_2, \ldots, x_n) = (&A_{11}x_1 + A_{12}x_2 + \cdots + A_{1n}x_n, \\ &A_{21}x_1 + A_{22}x_2 + \cdots + A_{2n}x_n, \ldots, \\ &A_{m1}x_1 + A_{m2}x_2 + \cdots + A_{mn}x_n). \end{aligned}$$

Remarks. Using (21) or (22) we could treat the theory of linear transformations from R^n into R^m in terms of coordinates or in matrix terms. Historically, this is the manner in which the study of linear transformations arose. Computationally, (21) or (22) is much more useful than (12). However, the use of (21) or (22) is generally very cumbersome, with excess notation often obscuring the simplicity of the results. In addition to this, many linear transformations arise geometrically. Often the expression of such transformations in terms of (21) or (22) is a waste of time. For these reasons we shall stress the property (12) and treat (21) and (22) as helpful computational devices.

Another question arises. Why not define the matrix of T as the matrix whose jth row is (20)? There is no binding reason why we could not do this and many texts in linear algebra do so. We use our definition (21) because this will simplify later results.

How can we compute the range of T if T is as given in (22)? Let $(y_1, y_2, \ldots, y_m)$ be a vector in R^m. Then $(y_1, y_2, \ldots, y_m)$ is in the range of T if and only if $T(x_1, x_2, \ldots, x_n) = (y_1, y_2, \ldots, y_m)$ has a solution $(x_1, x_2, \ldots, x_n)$ in R^n. Rewriting, using (22), we have the following result.

$(y_1, y_2, \ldots, y_m)$ is in the range of T if and only if the following system has at least one solution:

$$(23) \quad \begin{aligned} y_1 &= A_{11}x_1 + A_{12}x_2 + \cdots + A_{1n}x_n \\ y_2 &= A_{21}x_1 + A_{22}x_2 + \cdots + A_{2n}x_n \\ &\vdots \\ y_m &= A_{m1}x_1 + A_{m2}x_2 + \cdots + A_{mn}x_n. \end{aligned}$$

Techniques for treating (23) were given in Section 2, (18) ff.

We shall give a few general results about linear transformations. The first of these is the following.

Theorem 7. Let T be a linear transformation from V into W. Then the following are true.

(a) $T0 = 0$.

(b) If U is a subspace of V, then the image of U, i.e., the set of all TX with X in U, is a subspace of W.

Proof. We have $T0_V = T(0 \cdot 0_V) = 0 \cdot T(0_V) = 0_W$, where 0 is the number, 0_V is the zero of V and 0_W is the zero of W. Now let U be a subspace of V and let U_0 be the image of U. Then 0 is in U_0, since 0 is in U and $T0 = 0$. If Y^1 and Y^2 are in U_0, then we can find vectors X^1 and X^2 in U such that $TX^1 = Y^1$ and $TX^2 = Y^2$. Since U is a subspace, $X^1 + X^2$ is in U. But $T(X^1 + X^2) = TX^1 + TX^2 = Y^1 + Y^2$. Thus $Y^1 + Y^2$ is in U_0 since we found a vector, namely $X^1 + X^2$, in U which is transformed into $Y^1 + Y^2$. Let Y be in U_0 and choose X in U such that $TX = Y$. Then $aY = a(TX) = T(aX)$ so that aY is also in U_0. Hence U_0 is a subspace of W. Q.E.D.

Let T be a linear operator on R^2. Theorem 7 tells us that T transforms lines through the origin onto subspaces of R^2, i.e., onto the point $(0, 0)$, a line through $(0, 0)$, or R^2 itself. We shall show below that T cannot increase dimension. From this we conclude that T maps lines through the origin onto the origin or a line through the origin.

One particular case of Theorem 7 is of interest. If $U = V$, then U is certainly a subspace of V. In this case the image of U is the *range* of T, so that we conclude that the range of T is a subspace of W.

Suppose T, V, W, and U are as in Theorem 7. Let U_0 be the image of U. Let $\{X^1, X^2, \ldots, X^k\}$ span U. Let Y be in U_0 and let X be in U such that $TX = Y$. Since $\{X^1, X^2, \ldots, X^k\}$ spans U, we can find numbers $c_1, c_2, \ldots, c_k$ such that $X = c_1 X^1 + c_2 X^2 + \cdots + c_k X^k$. Then $Y = TX = c_1 TX^1 + c_2 TX^2 + \cdots + c_k TX^k$; i.e., Y is a linear combination of $\{TX^1, TX^2, \ldots, TX^k\}$. This tells us that T maps spanning sets into spanning sets, or more precisely

(24)   if $\{X^1, X^2, \ldots, X^k\}$ spans U, then $\{TX^1, TX^2, \ldots, TX^k\}$ spans the image of U.

As a consequence of this we have the following.

(25)   The dimension of U is greater than or equal to the dimension of the image of U; i.e., T does not increase dimension.

To see this, let $\{X^1, X^2, \ldots, X^k\}$ be a basis for U. Then from (24) we have that $\{TX^1, TX^2, \ldots, TX^k\}$ spans the image of U. By (28) of Section 3 we have that the dimension of the image of $U \leq k = \dim U$.

The dimension of the range of T is an important number. We shall show below that this number is the same as the rank of the matrix of T

in the case where $V = R^n$ and $W = R^m$. Meanwhile no harm comes from calling this number the *rank* of T. We denote this by rank (T). Thus rank (T) is the dimension of the range of T.

Another important subspace connected with T is given by the following.

(26)   The collection of vectors X in V such that $TX = 0$ is a subspace of V. This subspace is called the *null space* of T, its dimension being called the *nullity* of T, usually written as nullity (T).

Let M be the null space of T. Since $T0 = 0$, we see that 0 is in M. Let X^1 and X^2 be in M. Then $TX^1 = TX^2 = 0$. Thus $0 = TX^1 + TX^2 = T(X^1 + X^2)$, so that $X^1 + X^2$ is in M. If $TX = 0$, then

$$0 = aTX = T(aX),$$

so that if X is in M, so is aX. This establishes (26).

Let us clarify these results with our examples. Let T be the transformation defined by (2). Then $T(3, 2) = (8, 1)$. Also $T(3c, 2c) = (8c, c)$; i.e., T transforms the subspace spanned by $\{(3, 2)\}$ into the subspace spanned by $\{T(3, 2)\}$. The null space of T consists of $(0, 0)$ only, as the equation $T(x, y) = (0, 0)$ necessitates that $(x, y) = (0, 0)$. The rank of T is 2 since the range of T is R^2.

In the example (8), any plane through $\mathbf{o}$, perpendicular to $\mathbf{v}_0$ is transformed by P into $\mathbf{o}$. Any other plane through $\mathbf{o}$ has the line through $\mathbf{v}_0$ as its image. Any vector which is transformed by P into $\mathbf{o}$ must lie in the plane through $\mathbf{o}$ perpendicular to $\mathbf{v}_0$. Thus nullity $(P) = 2$. Furthermore rank $(P) = 1$, since the range of P consists of all multiples of $\mathbf{v}_0$.

In our example (18), we have nullity $(0) = \dim V$ and rank $(0) = 0$. In (19) we have nullity $(I_V) = 0$ and rank $(I_V) = \dim V$. In (17) we have rank $(T) = 2$, since the equations

$$a = 2x + y - z$$
$$b = x + y - z$$

have a solution for any choice of (a, b). The null space of this transformation is the same as the null space of the matrix

$$\begin{bmatrix} 2 & 1 & -1 \\ 1 & 1 & -1 \end{bmatrix},$$

which has dimension 1.

In general, if T is a linear transformation from R^n into R^m, then the null space of T is the same as the null space of the matrix (21). This fact follows easily from (22), for to say that $T(x_1, x_2, \ldots, x_n) = (0, 0, \ldots, 0)$ is the same as saying that

$$(27) \quad \begin{aligned} A_{11}x_1 + A_{12}x_2 + \cdots + A_{1n}x_n &= 0 \\ A_{21}x_1 + A_{22}x_2 + \cdots + A_{2n}x_n &= 0 \\ &\vdots \\ A_{m1}x_1 + A_{m2}x_2 + \cdots + A_{mn}x_n &= 0, \end{aligned}$$

so that $(x_1, x_2, \ldots, x_n)$ is in the null space of T if and only if it is a solution to (27).

The general relation between rank (T) and nullity (T) is given in the following theorem.

Theorem 8. If V is finite dimensional and T is a linear transformation from V into W, then rank (T) + nullity (T) = dim V.

Proof. Let $\{X^1, X^2, \ldots, X^k\}$ be a basis for the null space of T. Using Lemma 2 we can find vectors $\{X^{k+1}, X^{k+2}, \ldots, X^n\}$ such that $\{X^1, X^2, \ldots, X^n\}$ is a basis for V. (We may have $k = 0$, in which case just choose a basis for V.) Then by (24) $\{TX^1, TX^2, \ldots, TX^n\}$ spans the range of T. However, $\{X^1, X^2, \ldots, X^k\}$ is contained in the null space of T. Thus $TX^1 = TX^2 = \cdots = TX^k = 0$. We conclude that $\{TX^{k+1}, TX^{k+2}, \ldots, TX^n\}$ spans the range of T. We shall show that $\{TX^{k+1}, TX^{k+2}, \ldots, TX^n\}$ is an independent set and hence is a basis for the range of T. Let $c_{k+1}, c_{k+2}, \ldots, c_n$ be numbers such that $c_{k+1}TX^{k+1} + c_{k+2}TX^{k+2} + \cdots + c_nTX^n = 0$. Then $0 = T(c_{k+1}X^{k+1} + c_{k+2}X^{k+2} + \cdots + c_nX^n)$; i.e., the vector $X = c_{k+1}X^{k+1} + c_{k+2}X^{k+2} + \cdots + c_nX^n$ belongs to the null space of T, which is spanned by $\{X^1, X^2, \ldots, X^k\}$. Thus we can find numbers $c_1, c_2, \ldots, c_k$ such that $X = c_1X^1 + c_2X^2 + \cdots + c_kX^k$. Rewriting this gives $0 = X - X = -c_1X^1 - c_2X^2 - \cdots - c_kX^k + c_{k+1}X^{k+1} + c_{k+2}X^{k+2} + \cdots + c_nX^n$. The independence of $\{X^1, X^2, \ldots, X^n\}$ gives $-c_1 = -c_2 = \cdots = -c_k = c_{k+1} = c_{k+2} = \cdots = c_n = 0$. We have shown that if $c_{k+1}TX^{k+1} + c_{k+2}TX^{k+2} + \cdots + c_nTX^n = 0$, then $c_{k+1} = c_{k+2} = \cdots = c_n = 0$. We conclude that $\{TX^{k+1}, TX^{k+2}, \ldots, TX^n\}$ is a basis for the range of T. We have nullity $(T) = k$, dim $V = n$, and rank $(T) = n - k$ which is our desired result. Q.E.D.

Remarks. This is such a basic theorem that the reader should study it very carefully. Note that we chose a basis for the null space of T, expanded to a basis for V, and showed that the images of the additional vectors formed a basis for the range of T. We used the fact that $\{X^1, X^2, \ldots, X^k\}$ was contained in the null space, that $\{X^1, X^2, \ldots, X^n\}$

spanned V, that $\{X^1, X^2, \ldots, X^k\}$ spanned the null space, and finally that $\{X^1, X^2, \ldots, X^n\}$ was independent. This technique of carefully choosing bases will be used to obtain results later and also will be useful in some of the exercises.

If $V = R^n$ and $W = R^m$, then we can use Theorems 6 and 8 to show that rank $(T) =$ rank (A) if A is the matrix of T. This follows from the fact that nullity $(T) =$ nullity $(A) = n -$ rank $(A) = n -$ rank (T). A more careful examination of A and T reveals more than this. The columns of A are the vectors $TX^1, TX^2, \ldots, TX^n$, where $X^1 = (1, 0, \ldots, 0)$, $X^2 = (0, 1, 0, \ldots, 0), \ldots, X^n = (0, 0, \ldots, 0, 1)$. Since $\{X^1, X^2, \ldots, X^n\}$ spans R^n, we know from (24) that $\{TX^1, TX^2, \ldots, TX^n\}$ spans the range of T. But the set of linear combinations of the columns of A is the column space of A. We conclude:

(28)   rank $(A) =$ the dimension of the column space of A.

The dimension of the row space of A is often called the *row* rank, and the dimension of the column space of A is often called the *column* rank; (28) tells us that these two numbers are equal.

Statement (28) gives us a convenient means for computing the rank of a linear transformation T from R^n into R^m. We merely find the matrix of T and compute its row rank using row reduction. But we may want to find a basis for the range of T. How do we do this? We could just form the matrix of T and column reduce until we reach a column reduced echelon form. (The definitions of column reduction and column reduced echelon form are analogous to those used in row reduction.) We shall give another method. How do we find a basis for the null space of T? We have done this before in the proof of Theorem 6. We form the matrix of T, row reduce this matrix, and compute $\{X^1, X^2, \ldots, X^{n-r}\}$ as in (38) of Section 3. Let us use the proof of Theorem 8 to construct a basis for the range of T. Let $x_{k_1}, x_{k_2}, \ldots, x_{k_r}$ be the remaining variables after row reduction. (See the proof of Theorem 6.) Let Z^j, $j = 1, 2, \ldots, r$, be the vector whose k_jth component is 1 and whose other components are zero. Then

(29) $\{X^1, X^2, \ldots, X^{n-r}, Z^1, Z^2, \ldots, Z^r\}$ is a basis for R^n.

This is easy to show. According to the proof of Theorem 8, $\{TZ^1, TZ^2, \ldots, TZ^r\}$ is a basis for the range of T. The advantage of this method is that we can obtain several items of information by row reducing the matrix of T. We can find a basis for the row space of this matrix, a basis for the null space of T, and a basis for the range of T.

The next result shows us that a linear transformation is completely determined by its effect on a basis. This should not be surprising. The result (22) shows that a linear transformation from R^n into R^m is completely determined by its effect on a basis, i.e., by (21). To establish our result, we need a definition of equality for linear transformations. Two linear transformations are said to be *equal* if they have the same domain and have the same effect. Thus $T = S$ if and only if T and S both have the same space, say V, as domain, and $TX = SX$ for all X in V. We express our result as a theorem.

> **Theorem 9.** Let $\{X^1, X^2, \ldots, X^n\}$ be a basis for V. Let $\{Y^1, Y^2, \ldots, Y^n\}$ be any set contained in W. Then there is precisely *one* linear transformation T from V into W such that $TX^i = Y^i$, $i = 1, 2, \ldots, n$.

Proof. We define T as follows. If X is in V, then $X = c_1 X^1 + c_2 X^2 + \cdots + c_n X^n$. Since $\{X^1, X^2, \ldots, X^n\}$ is a basis for V, this expression for X is unique. [See the remarks after (24) in Section 3.] We define TX to be $c_1 Y^1 + c_2 Y^2 + \cdots + c_n Y^n$. Then T is a transformation from V into W, as we have assigned to each vector X in V a unique vector TX in W. That T satisfies (12) is easy. Since $X^i = 0 \cdot X^1 + 0 \cdot X^2 + \cdots + 0 \cdot X^{i-1} + 1 \cdot X^i + 0 \cdot X^{i+1} + \cdots + 0 \cdot X^n$, we have $TX^i = Y^i$ for $1 \leq i \leq n$. This shows the existence of T.

Now suppose that S is a linear transformation from V into W such that $SX^i = Y^i$, $i = 1, 2, \ldots, n$. If $X = c_1 X^1 + c_2 X^2 + \cdots + c_n X^n$, then $TX = c_1 Y^1 + c_2 Y^2 + \cdots + c_n Y^n = c_1 SX^1 + c_2 SX^2 + \cdots + c_n SX^n = S(c_1 X^1 + c_2 X^2 + \cdots + c_n X^n) = SX$. Therefore $S = T$. Q.E.D.

Remarks. The heart of the proof of Theorem 9 resides in the fact that X can be uniquely expressed in terms of the basis $\{X^1, X^2, \ldots, X^n\}$. This theorem is really just a restatement of this fact. This will be exploited further in Section 6.

Theorem 9 tells us that it is enough to give the effect of T on a basis. Because of this we will say that T is *defined* by the equations $TX^i = Y^i$, $i = 1, 2, \ldots, n$, where $\{X^1, X^2, \ldots, X^n\}$ is a basis for V, meaning that T is so defined on other vectors in V that T is that unique linear transformation from V into W such that $TX^i = Y^i$, $i = 1, 2, \ldots, n$.

Thus the linear operator of (2) is defined by the two equations

$$T(1, 0) = (2, 1), \qquad T(0, 1) = (1, -1).$$

Since $\{(3, 2), (0, 1)\}$ is also a basis for R^2, T is also defined by $T(3, 2) = (8, 1)$ and $T(0, 1) = (1, -1)$. The linear transformation of (17) is defined by the three equations

$$T(1, 0, 0) = (2, 1), \quad T(0, 1, 0) = (1, 1) \quad \text{and} \quad T(0, 0, 1) = (-1, -1).$$

Let us look at (8). Let $\mathbf{v}_1$ and $\mathbf{v}_2$ be chosen such that $\{\mathbf{v}_0, \mathbf{v}_1, \mathbf{v}_2\}$ consists of mutually perpendicular vectors. Then P is defined by the equations

$$P(\mathbf{v}_0) = \mathbf{v}_0, \qquad P(\mathbf{v}_1) = P(\mathbf{v}_2) = \mathbf{0}.$$

We now have several ways to describe a linear transformation. We can use (21) or (22) if the spaces involved are Cartesian spaces. We can use Theorem 9 and prescribe the effect on a basis. Often we can also give geometric descriptions. We shall look at some of these below.

Our final task in this section is to introduce some of the elementary operations that can be performed on linear transformations. As we shall see, under the right conditions we can "add," "multiply," "scalar multiply," and in some cases even "divide" linear transformations. The most important of these operations is multiplication, the others being more elementary and somewhat formal devices for handling linear transformations.

Let S and T be linear transformations from V into W. Apply S to a vector X and also apply T to a vector X. We obtain SX and TX, both vectors in W. Add these two vectors: $SX + TX$. This is also a vector in W, uniquely determined by X, S, and T. Thus we have a new transformation from V into W, namely the one which sends X into $SX + TX$. We denote this rule by the symbol "$S + T$" and call this the *sum* of S and T. The rule for $S + T$ is then

(30) $$(S + T)X = SX + TX \text{ for all } X \text{ in } V.$$

The transformation $S + T$ is linear, for

$$
\begin{aligned}
(S + T)(aX + bY) &= S(aX + bY) + T(aX + bY) \\
&= aSX + bSY + aTX + bTY \\
&= a(SX + TX) + b(SY + TY) \\
&= a(S + T)X + b(S + T)Y.
\end{aligned}
$$

In a similar manner we can define a scalar multiple of a linear transformation. Let T be a linear transformation from V into W and let a be a real number. Let X be in V. Then TX is in W. So is aTX. The vector aTX is uniquely determined by X, T, and a. We denote this new rule by the symbol "aT" and call this the *scalar multiple of T by a*. Formally, aT is the linear transformation from T into W defined by the rule

(31) $$(aT)X = aTX \text{ for all } X \text{ in } V.$$

The linearity of aT is easy to prove.

We consider an example. Suppose that T is the linear transformation of R^2 into R^2 given by (2). Let S be the linear transformation of R^2 into R^2 defined by

$$(32) \qquad S(x, y) = (3x + 2y, -6x + y).$$

Then $S + T$ is given by

$$(33) \qquad (S + T)(x, y) = (5x + 3y, -5x),$$

and aS and aT are given by

$$(34) \qquad \begin{aligned} (aS)(x, y) &= (3ax + 2ay, -6ax + ay), \\ (aT)(x, y) &= (2ax + ay, ax - ay). \end{aligned}$$

The matrix of S is

$$\begin{bmatrix} 3 & 2 \\ -6 & 1 \end{bmatrix}.$$

The matrix of T is

$$\begin{bmatrix} 2 & 1 \\ 1 & -1 \end{bmatrix}.$$

The matrix of $S + T$ is

$$\begin{bmatrix} 5 & 3 \\ -5 & 0 \end{bmatrix}.$$

This is obtained from the matrices of S and T by a form of addition. The general definitions are the following. If $A = (A_{ij})$ and $B = (B_{ij})$ are $m \times n$ matrices, then $A + B$ is defined to be the $m \times n$ matrix $(A_{ij} + B_{ij})$; i.e.,

$$(35) \quad A + B = \begin{bmatrix} A_{11} + B_{11} & A_{12} + B_{12} & \ldots & A_{1n} + B_{1n} \\ A_{21} + B_{21} & A_{22} + B_{22} & \ldots & A_{2n} + B_{2n} \\ \vdots & & & \\ A_{m1} + B_{m1} & A_{m2} + B_{m2} & \ldots & A_{mn} + B_{mn} \end{bmatrix}.$$

Also, aA is defined to be the $m \times n$ matrix (aA_{ij}); i.e.,

$$(36) \qquad aA = \begin{bmatrix} aA_{11} & aA_{12} & \ldots & aA_{1n} \\ aA_{21} & aA_{22} & \ldots & aA_{2n} \\ \vdots & & & \\ aA_{m1} & aA_{m2} & \ldots & aA_{mn} \end{bmatrix}.$$

These are defined in such a fashion that if S and T are linear transformations of R^n into R^m, and if A is the matrix of S and B of T, then $A + B$ is the matrix of $S + T$ and aA is the matrix of aS.

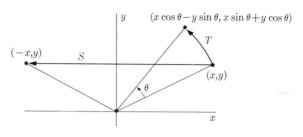

FIGURE 4

We now wish to discuss a multiplication for linear transformations. For example, let T be a rotation of R^2 about $(0, 0)$ through the angle θ, and let S be a reflection of R^2 in the y-axis. Then we can define two new transformations of R^2 into R^2 as follows. Apply T, thus rotating through the angle θ. Then apply S, reflecting in the y-axis. We could also perform the operations in the reverse order. Let us see what these new "composite" transformations look like.

We have (see Fig. 4)

(37) $T(x, y) = (x \cos \theta - y \sin \theta, x \sin \theta + y \cos \theta)$,

(38) $S(x, y) = (-x, y)$.

We first operate with T, then with S. The pair (x, y) is sent by T into $(x \cos \theta - y \sin \theta, x \sin \theta + y \cos \theta)$. This point is then sent by S into $(-x \cos \theta + y \sin \theta, x \sin \theta + y \cos \theta)$. We have defined a transformation which sends (x, y) into $(-x \cos \theta + y \sin \theta, x \sin \theta + y \cos \theta)$. Denoting this by P, we have

(39) $P(x, y) = (-x \cos \theta + y \sin \theta, x \sin \theta + y \cos \theta)$.

Now we operate with S, then with T. The pair (x, y) is sent by S into $(-x, y)$. This point is sent by T into $(-x \cos \theta - y \sin \theta, -x \sin \theta + y \cos \theta)$. We have defined a transformation which sends (x, y) into $(-x \cos \theta - y \sin \theta, -x \sin \theta + y \cos \theta)$. Denoting this by Q, we have

(40) $Q(x, y) = (-x \cos \theta - y \sin \theta, -x \sin \theta + y \cos \theta)$.

Figures 5 and 6 show the relation between S, T, P, and Q. P and Q have some relation to S and T. To denote this we write "$P = ST$" and "$Q = TS$." The expression $P = ST$ says that P is the result of operating by T, then by S; $Q = TS$ says that Q is the result of operating by S, then by T. We have that $Q \neq P$ (unless θ is an integral multiple of π).

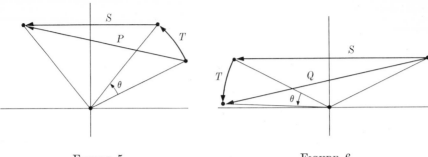

FIGURE 5   FIGURE 6

These concepts are special cases of the following considerations. Let T be a linear transformation from V into W and S a linear transformation from W into U. Then ST is the linear transformation from V into U defined by

(41) $(ST)X = S(TX)$ for all X in V.

The rule (41) can be defined and is a rule which assigns to each X in V a unique vector in U. This is done by first applying T to X, obtaining the vector TX in W, then applying S to TX, giving a vector in U. The transformation ST of V into U is called the *product* of S and T. The order of the factors is important even in the case when $V = W = U = R^2$, as shown in (39) and (40).

ST is a linear transformation of V into U. To see this, compute: $(ST)(aX + bY)$ is by (41) equal to $S(T(aX + bY))$. But $T(aX + bY) = aTX + bTY$ by (12). Thus $S(T(aX + bY)) = S(aTX + bTY)$. Again (12) gives $S(aTX + bTY) = aS(TX) + bS(TY)$. Rule (41) gives $aS(TX) + bS(TY) = a(ST)X + b(ST)Y$. Combining these gives

$$(ST)(aX + bY) = a(ST)X + b(ST)Y;$$

i.e., ST satisfies (12).

Let T be the operator defined by (2) and S the operator defined by (32). Then ST and TS are the linear operators on R^2 defined by

(42)
$$\begin{aligned}
(ST)(x, y) &= S(T(x, y)) = S(2x + y, x - y) \\
&= (3(2x + y) + 2(x - y), -6(2x + y) + (x - y)) \\
&= (8x + y, -11x - 7y),
\end{aligned}$$

(43)
$$\begin{aligned}
(TS)(x, y) &= T(S(x, y)) = T(3x + 2y, -6x + y) \\
&= (2(3x + 2y) + (-6x + y), (3x + 2y) - (-6x + y)) \\
&= (5y, 9x + y).
\end{aligned}$$

This is another example of the fact that in general $ST \neq TS$.

However, some other rules are true. If T is a linear transformation from V_1 into V_2, and if S is a linear transformation of V_2 into V_3, and if R is a linear transformation of V_3 into V_4, then

$$(44) \qquad\qquad (RS)T = R(ST).$$

If S and T are linear transformations of V_1 into V_2 and R is a linear transformation of V_2 into V_3, then

$$(45) \qquad\qquad R(S + T) = RS + RT.$$

If T is a linear transformation of V_1 into V_2, and if S is a linear transformation of V_2 into V_3, and a is a real number, then

$$(46) \qquad\qquad a(ST) = (aS)T = S(aT).$$

Let us establish (44), which is called the *associative law for transformation multiplication*. Since S transforms V_2 into V_3 and R transforms V_3 into V_4, RS transforms V_2 into V_4 and $(RS)T$ transforms V_1 into V_4. Since ST transforms V_1 into V_3, $R(ST)$ transforms V_1 into V_4. We conclude that the domain of $(RS)T$ is the same as the domain of $R(ST)$. Let X be in V_1. Then $((RS)T)X = (RS)(TX) = R(S(TX)) = R((ST)X) = (R(ST))X$; i.e., $R(ST) = (RS)T$. (This is just an exercise in the placing of parentheses.) Statements (45) and (46) are even easier and will be left to the exercises.

The most important case of the product is the case when $V = W = U$ in (41). For if S and T are linear operators on V, then ST and TS are always defined. In general $ST \neq TS$ and other strange things can happen. Some of these will be given in the exercises.

If T is a linear operator on V, then we can form TT, $(TT)T$, $T(TT)$, etc., and all of these will be linear operators on V. We usually use the notation: $T^2 = TT$, $T^3 = (TT)T$, etc. Since $(TT)T = T(TT)$, no ambiguity will result from this notation.

As examples of this we have

$$(47) \quad T^2(x, y) = T(2x + y, x - y) = (2(2x + y) + (x - y), (2x + y) - (x - y)) = (5x + y, x) \text{ if } T \text{ is as defined in (2)}.$$

$$(48) \quad \text{If } T \text{ is as in (37), then } T^2 \text{ is a rotation through the angle } 2\theta, T^3 \text{ is a rotation through the angle } 3\theta, \text{ etc.}$$

$$(49) \quad \text{If } S \text{ is as in (38), then } S^2 = I_{R^2}.$$

Statements (48) and (49) are geometrically clear and are easily established by using (37) and (38).

Just as addition of linear transformations gives rise to matrix addition [see (35)], so multiplication of linear transformations gives rise to matrix multiplication. We shall discuss only the 2×2 case here, leaving the general case to Section 6.

Let S and T be linear operators on R^2. Let

$$A = \begin{bmatrix} A_{11} & A_{12} \\ A_{21} & A_{22} \end{bmatrix}$$

be the matrix of S and

$$B = \begin{bmatrix} B_{11} & B_{12} \\ B_{21} & B_{22} \end{bmatrix}$$

the matrix of T. Then

(50) $\qquad S(x, y) = (A_{11}x + A_{12}y, A_{21}x + A_{22}y),$

(51) $\qquad T(x, y) = (B_{11}x + B_{12}y, B_{21}x + B_{22}y),$

and

$$\begin{aligned}
(ST)(x, y) = S(T(x, y)) &= S(B_{11}x + B_{12}y, B_{21}x + B_{22}y) \\
&= (A_{11}(B_{11}x + B_{12}y) + A_{12}(B_{21}x + B_{22}y), \\
&\qquad A_{21}(B_{11}x + B_{12}y) + A_{22}(B_{21}x + B_{22}y)) \\
&= ((A_{11}B_{11} + A_{12}B_{21})x + (A_{11}B_{12} + A_{12}B_{22})y, \\
&\qquad (A_{21}B_{11} + A_{22}B_{21})x + (A_{21}B_{12} + A_{22}B_{22})y).
\end{aligned}$$

(52)

The matrix of ST is

(53)
$$\begin{bmatrix} A_{11}B_{11} + A_{12}B_{21} & A_{11}B_{12} + A_{12}B_{22} \\ A_{21}B_{11} + A_{22}B_{21} & A_{21}B_{12} + A_{22}B_{22} \end{bmatrix}.$$

This is called the *product* of A and B and written as AB (again the order of A and B is important). The entry in the ith row and jth column of AB is obtained by multiplying the entries in the ith row of A with the corresponding entries in the jth column of B and adding these up. The following examples illustrate this:

(54)
$$\begin{bmatrix} 2 & 1 \\ 1 & -1 \end{bmatrix}\begin{bmatrix} 3 & 2 \\ -6 & 1 \end{bmatrix} = \begin{bmatrix} 2 \cdot 3 + 1 \cdot (-6) & 2 \cdot 2 + 1 \cdot 1 \\ 1 \cdot 3 + (-1) \cdot (-6) & 1 \cdot 2 + (-1) \cdot 1 \end{bmatrix}$$

$$= \begin{bmatrix} 0 & 5 \\ 9 & 1 \end{bmatrix},$$

(55)
$$\begin{bmatrix} 3 & 2 \\ -6 & 1 \end{bmatrix}\begin{bmatrix} 2 & 1 \\ 1 & -1 \end{bmatrix} = \begin{bmatrix} 3 \cdot 2 + 2 \cdot 1 & 3 \cdot 1 + 2 \cdot (-1) \\ (-6) \cdot 2 + 1 \cdot 1 & (-6) \cdot 1 + 1 \cdot (-1) \end{bmatrix}$$

$$= \begin{bmatrix} 8 & 1 \\ -11 & -7 \end{bmatrix},$$

$$(56) \quad \begin{bmatrix} \cos\theta & -\sin\theta \\ \sin\theta & \cos\theta \end{bmatrix}^2 = \begin{bmatrix} \cos^2\theta - \sin^2\theta & -2\cos\theta\sin\theta \\ 2\cos\theta\sin\theta & -\sin^2\theta + \cos^2\theta \end{bmatrix}$$

$$= \begin{bmatrix} \cos 2\theta & -\sin 2\theta \\ \sin 2\theta & \cos 2\theta \end{bmatrix},$$

$$(57) \quad \begin{bmatrix} -1 & 0 \\ 0 & 1 \end{bmatrix}^2 = \begin{bmatrix} 1 & 0 \\ 0 & 1 \end{bmatrix}.$$

These are the matrix analogues of (43), (42), (48), and (49), respectively. It is important that the reader be able to quickly compute 2×2 matrix products.

Remarks. The collection of all linear transformations from V into W, equipped with the addition and scalar multiplication given by (30) and (31) is actually a vector space; i.e., the addition and scalar multiplication satisfy the rules (10) of Section 3. In a similar fashion the collection of $m \times n$ matrices forms a vector space with the addition and scalar multiplication given by (35) and (36). In case $V = W$ or $m = n$, these spaces have a multiplication defined. Such vector spaces are examples of *algebras*. Most of the advanced theory of linear algebra is concerned with these algebras. Except for occasional exercises and remarks, we shall not treat these spaces in this book.

Note that we have not shown that the matrix of a linear transformation T of R^n into R^m uniquely determines T. This follows from Theorem 9 and the definition of the matrix of T given in (20) and (21). We have also not shown that a matrix always gives rise to a linear transformation. This is easy for if A is an $m \times n$ matrix, then (22) defines a linear transformation from R^n into R^m whose matrix is A.

EXERCISES

1. Which of the following define linear transformations from R^3 into R^2?

(a) $T(x, y, z) = (x - y, x - z)$
(b) $T(x, y, z) = (|x|, y - z)$
(c) $T(x, y, z) = (x + 1, y + z)$
(d) $T(x, y, z) = (0, z)$
(e) $T(x, y, z) = (x + y/z, z)$
(f) $T(x, y, z) = (3x - y, y - z, 3x - 2y + z)$
(g) $T(x, y, z) = (3x - 2y + z, x - 3y - 2z)$

2. By expressing in terms of coordinates, as in (2), show that each of the following transformations of R^3 is linear.

   (a) A rotation, through the angle $\pi/3$, about the line through $(0, 0, 0)$ and $(1, 0, 0)$, leaving $(0, 0, 0)$ fixed.

   (b) A reflection in the plane determined by $(2, 0, 3)$, $(1, 0, 2)$, and $(0, 0, 0)$.

   (c) A projection onto the plane of (b).

   (d) A change of scale; i.e., (x, y, z) is changed into (ax, by, cz), where $a > 0, b > 0$, and $c > 0$.

3. Show that each of the following defines a linear operator on R^3.

   (a) $T(x, y, z) = (x - y, z + y, x)$

   (b) $T(x, y, z) = (x, y, 0)$

   (c) $T(x, y, z) = (x + y, -x - y, z)$

   (d) $T(x, y, z) = (y, -x, -z)$

4. (a) Find the matrix of each of the operators of Exercise 2.

   (b) Find the matrix of each of the operators of Exercise 3.

5. Each of the following matrices is the matrix of a linear transformation from R^n into R^m. For each matrix determine n and m and write the transformation in terms of coordinates as in (22).

   (a) $\begin{bmatrix} 3 & 1 & 2 \\ 0 & 1 & 1 \\ -1 & 1 & 1 \end{bmatrix}$ (b) $\begin{bmatrix} 3 & 1 & 0 & 2 & 1 \\ 1 & 0 & 6 & 1 & 1 \\ 0 & -1 & 1 & 1 & 1 \end{bmatrix}$

   (c) $\begin{bmatrix} 2 & 1 & 1 \\ 1 & 1 & 1 \end{bmatrix}$ (d) $\begin{bmatrix} 6 & -1 \\ 1 & 2 \\ 1 & 3 \end{bmatrix}$

6. Let V be the space of polynomials of degree $\leq n$. Show that differentiation is a linear operator on V. Find the rank and nullity of this operator.

7. Describe geometrically the range and null space of each of the operators of Exercise 3.

8. Determine the rank and nullity of each of the linear transformations whose matrices are the following.

   (a) $\begin{bmatrix} 2 & -1 & 0 \\ 1 & 1 & 3 \end{bmatrix}$.   (b) $\begin{bmatrix} 3 & 1 & 1 \\ 2 & 1 & 0 \\ 0 & 1 & -2 \\ 2 & 1 & 0 \end{bmatrix}$ (c) $\begin{bmatrix} 3 & 2 & 1 \\ -1 & 1 & 0 \\ 0 & 5 & 1 \end{bmatrix}$

9. Find a basis for the null space and a basis for the range of each of the linear transformations of Exercise 8.

10. Let T be the linear operator on R^2 defined by each of the following. Express T in terms of coordinates as in (22) and compute $T(1, 0)$.

    (a) $T(3, 1) = (1, 2)$, $T(-1, 0) = (1, 1)$

    (b) $T(1, 1) = (2, 1)$, $T(-1, 1) = (6, 3)$

11. Let dim $V > $ dim W. Let T be a linear transformation from V into W and let S be a linear transformation from W into V.

(a) Show that there is a vector $X \neq 0$ in V such that $TX = 0$.

(b) Show that there is a vector X in V such that $SY = X$ has *no* solution Y in W.

12. Let S be the linear operator on R^3 defined by $S(x, y, z) := (3x - y, 0, z)$. Express ST, TS, $S + T$, and $3S^2 - 2T^3$ in terms of coordinates for each of the operators T of Exercise 3.

13. Compute each of the following products.

(a) $\begin{bmatrix} 2 & 1 \\ 1 & 1 \end{bmatrix} \begin{bmatrix} -1 & 1 \\ 1 & 1 \end{bmatrix}$

(b) $\begin{bmatrix} 3 & 1 \\ -1 & 1 \end{bmatrix} \begin{bmatrix} 1 & 2 \\ -1 & 1 \end{bmatrix}$

(c) $\begin{bmatrix} 2 & 1 \\ 0 & 1 \end{bmatrix} \begin{bmatrix} 3 & -1 \\ 0 & 1 \end{bmatrix}$

(d) $\begin{bmatrix} 3 & 1 \\ 0 & 1 \end{bmatrix} \left[\begin{pmatrix} 2 & 1 \\ -1 & 0 \end{pmatrix} + \begin{pmatrix} -1 & 0 \\ 1 & 1 \end{pmatrix} \right]$

(e) $\begin{bmatrix} 3 & 1 \\ 6 & 1 \end{bmatrix} \begin{bmatrix} -1 & 1 \\ 2 & 1 \end{bmatrix} \begin{bmatrix} 3 & 2 \\ 1 & 1 \end{bmatrix}$

(f) $\begin{bmatrix} 0 & 1 \\ 0 & 1 \end{bmatrix} \begin{bmatrix} 0 & -1 \\ 0 & 1 \end{bmatrix} \begin{bmatrix} 0 & 0 \\ 1 & 0 \end{bmatrix}$

14. Find linear operators on R^3 with the following properties.

(a) $T \neq 0$, $T^2 \neq 0$, $T^3 = 0$ (b) $T \neq 0, S \neq 0, ST \neq 0, TS = 0$

(c) $T^n \neq 0$ for any $n > 1$ (d) $S + T = S - T$

(e) $S^2 = T^2$ and $S \neq T$ (f) $(S - 2I)^2 = 0$, yet $S \neq 2I$

(g) $ST^2 = T^2S$, yet $ST \neq TS$ (h) $T^2 = I$ and $T \neq I$

15. (a) Establish (10) and (11).

(b) Establish (37).

(c) If P and Q are as given in (39) and (40), show that $P = Q$ if and only if $\theta = n\pi$ for some integer n.

(d) Establish (48) by expressing T^2 and T^3 in terms of coordinates and using trigonometric identities.

16. Show that $Tf(t) = \int_0^t f(u)\, du$ defines a linear operator on each of the following spaces.

(a) The space of continuous real valued functions defined for $0 \leq u \leq 1$.

(b) The space of polynomials.

17. (a) Show that differentiation defines a linear operator on the space of polynomials.

(b) Show that differentiation does *not* define a linear operator on the space of Exercise 16(a). (Many of the deepest problems of analysis come from this fact.)

18. (a) Prove that (13) is equivalent to (12).

(b) Show that aT is linear, where aT is given by (31).

(c) Prove (45) and (46).

19. Let T be a linear operator on R^2. Establish each of the following.

(a) If $T \neq 0$ and $T^2 = 0$, then there is a basis $\{X^1, X^2\}$ for R^2 such that $TX^1 = X^2$ and $TX^2 = 0$.   (*cont.*)

(b) If $T \neq 0$, $T \neq I$, and $T^2 = T$, then there is a basis $\{X^1, X^2\}$ for R^2 such that $TX^1 = X^1$ and $TX^2 = 0$.

(c) If rank $(T) = 1$, then there is a basis $\{X^1, X^2\}$ for R^2 such that $TX^1 = 0$ and $TX^2 \neq 0$.

20. (a) Show that if the range of T is the same as the null space of T, then dim V is even. (V is finite dimensional and T is a linear operator on V.)

(b) Let T be a linear transformation from V into W and let S be a linear transformation from W into V. Suppose that dim $V >$ dim W. Show that rank $(ST) <$ dim V.

21. Let V be finite dimensional and let S and T be linear operators on V.

(a) Show that rank $(ST) \leq$ the minimum of rank (S) and rank (T).

(b) If dim $V =$ rank (S), then rank $(ST) =$ rank (T).

(c) What is rank (ST) when rank $(T) =$ dim V?

22. Establish (29). [*Hint*: Give a proof of (29) when n is small.]

23. Let T be a linear operator on V.

(a) Show that T maps the line between X and Y onto the line between TX and TY.

(b) Show that T maps the triangle determined by X, Y, and Z onto the triangle determined by TX, TY, and TZ.

(c) Show that T maps convex sets onto convex sets; i.e., if M is convex, then the image of M is convex.

(d) Show that T maps positive cones into positive cones.

24. Let T be an affine transformation of V.

(a) What is the image of the line between X and Y?

(b) What is the image of the triangle determined by X, Y, and Z?

(c) Show that T maps convex sets onto convex sets.

(d) Give an example in R^2 to show that T may not map positive cones onto positive cones.

25. Let $\{X^1, X^2, X^3\}$ be a basis for R^3. Let f_1 be the linear transformation from R^3 into R defined by $f_1 X^1 = 1, f_1 X^2 = f_1 X^3 = 0$. Similarly, let f_2 and f_3 be defined by $f_2 X^2 = f_3 X^3 = 1, f_2 X^1 = f_2 X^3 = f_3 X^1 = f_3 X^2 = 0$. (These are given by Theorem 9.) Let f be any linear transformation from R^3 into R. Use Theorem 9 to show that $f = (fX^1)f_1 + (fX^2)f_2 + (fX^3)f_3$.

26. (a) Write a flow diagram to find the range of T, where T is a linear operator on R^3 expressed as in (22).

(b) Write a flow diagram to find TX, where T is a linear operator on R^3 and X is in R^3.

(c) Suppose S and T are linear operators on R^3 and that we are given flow diagrams for computation of TX and SX. Use these diagrams to write a flow diagram for $(ST)X$ and $(S + T)X$.

SPECIAL EXERCISE

Let $L(V, W)$ be the vector space of all linear transformations from V into W. [See the Remarks after (57).] Show that if V and W are finite dimensional, then $\dim L(V, W) = \dim V \dim W$. [*Hint*: Let $\{X^1, X^2, \ldots, X^n\}$ be a basis for V and $\{Y^1, Y^2, \ldots, Y^m\}$ a basis for W. Use Theorem 9 to construct the transformations $E_{i,j}$ defined by $E_{i,j}(X^k) = 0$ if $k \neq i$ and $E_{i,j}(X^i) = Y^j$. Use Theorem 9 to show that $\{E_{1,1}, E_{1,2}, \ldots, E_{1,m}, E_{2,1}, E_{2,2}, \ldots, E_{2,m}, \ldots, E_{n,1}, E_{n,2}, \ldots, E_{n,m}\}$ is a basis for $L(V, W)$.]

Section 5. INVERTIBLE LINEAR OPERATORS

In most of the remainder of this book we shall be interested in studying the properties of special kinds of linear transformations. In this section we will study those transformations with nullity zero. We will obtain a characterization of such transformations in terms of transformation multiplication. As we shall see, those transformations with nullity zero are precisely those with which we can "divide."

We begin with an example. Let T be a counterclockwise rotation about the origin in R^2 through the angle θ. Then

$$(1) \qquad T(x, y) \neq (0, 0) \text{ if } (x, y) \neq (0, 0); \text{ i.e., nullity } (T) = 0.$$

Thus rank $(T) = 2$ so that $\{T(1, 0), T(0, 1)\}$ is an independent set in R^2. This can also be verified directly from

$$(2) \qquad T(1, 0) = (\cos \theta, \sin \theta), \qquad T(0, 1) = (-\sin \theta, \cos \theta).$$

[See Fig. 1, where we have shown (2) for $0 < \theta < \pi/2$.]

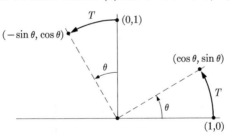

FIGURE 1

The most important property of T for our purposes is that we can "undo" its effect. Let T_1 be a counterclockwise rotation about $(0, 0)$ through the angle $-\theta$; i.e., T_1 is a clockwise rotation through the angle θ. Then

$$(3) \qquad T_1T = TT_1 = I, \text{ the identity on } R^2.$$

Statements (1), (2), and (3) are all important. As we shall see, each expresses the same concept in a different manner. Let us look at some other properties of T. The following is geometrically clear:

(4) T preserves dimension; i.e., if M is a subspace of R^2 and N is the image of M under T, then dim M = dim N.

In our case, (4) says that lines are mapped onto lines.

Now let S be any other linear operator on R^2 and suppose that $TS = 0$. Multiply on the left by T_1. This gives $0 = T_1 0 = T_1(TS) = (T_1 T)S = IS = S$. Thus

(5)   If $TS = 0$, then $S = 0$.

Similarly we can multiply on the right by T_1 in the equation $ST = 0$, to conclude that $S = 0$, so that

(6)   If $ST = 0$, then $S = 0$.

We shall see below that (4), (5), and (6) also express the same property as (1), (2), or (3). We shall take (3) as our property to generalize. We do this because this is the easiest property to use, and because it will give us further insight into operator multiplication.

Let T be a linear operator on V. T is said to be *invertible*, or *nonsingular*, if there is a linear operator T_1 on V such that

(7) $TT_1 = T_1 T = I$, the identity on V.

T_1 is uniquely determined by (7). For if $T_2 T = I$, then $T_1 = IT_1 = (T_2 T)T_1 = T_2(TT_1) = T_2 I = T_2$, just an exercise in placing parentheses! We call T_1 the *inverse* of T and denote T_1 by T^{-1} (read "T-inverse"). Note that if T is invertible, then T^{-1} is also invertible as it also satisfies (7).

When V is finite dimensional we have several ways to describe invertible operators.

The following generalizes (2) and uses Theorem 9 heavily.

(8) Let $\{X^1, X^2, \ldots, X^n\}$ be a basis for V. Let T be a linear operator on V. Then T is invertible if and only if $\{TX^1, TX^2, \ldots, TX^n\}$ is a basis for V.

Suppose that T is invertible and let T^{-1} be the inverse of T. Suppose that $a_1 TX^1 + a_2 TX^2 + \cdots + a_n TX^n = 0$. Apply T^{-1}. Then $0 = T^{-1}(a_1 TX^1 + a_2 TX^2 + \cdots + a_n TX^n) = a_1(T^{-1}T)X^1 + a_2(T^{-1}T)X^2 + \cdots + a_n(T^{-1}T)X^n = a_1 X^1 + a_2 X^2 + \cdots + a_n X^n$. We conclude that $a_1 = a_2 = \cdots = a_n = 0$, so that $\{TX^1, TX^2, \ldots, TX^n\}$ is independent and hence a basis for V (since dim $V = n$).

Conversely, suppose that $\{TX^1, TX^2, \ldots, TX^n\}$ is a basis for V. Apply Theorem 9 (with $\{X^1, X^2, \ldots, X^n\}$ in the statement of that theorem replaced by $\{TX^1, TX^2, \ldots, TX^n\}$ and $\{Y^1, Y^2, \ldots, Y^n\}$ replaced by $\{X^1, X^2, \ldots, X^n\}$.) Let T_1 be the linear operator on V such that $T_1(TX^i) = X^i, i = 1, 2, \ldots, n$. Then $T_1T = I$, since by Theorem 9, I is the only linear operator on V which sends X^i into X^i for $i = 1$, $2, \ldots, n$; I is also the only operator on V which sends TX^i into TX^i for $i = 1, 2, \ldots, n$. But $(TT_1)(TX^i) = T(T_1(TX^i)) = TX^i$, for $i = 1, 2$, $\ldots, n$. Thus $TT_1 = T_1T = I$. This establishes (8).

From (8) we conclude, using Theorem 8, the following.

(9) Let V be finite dimensional and let T be a linear operator on V. Then T is invertible if and only if rank $(T) = \dim V$, or equivalently, if and only if nullity $(T) = 0$.

Statements (8) and (9) generalize statements (1) and (2). Statement (4) also generalizes. In fact the proof of (8) also gives the following.

(10) Let V be finite dimensional. Let T be a linear operator on V. Then T is invertible if and only if $\{TX^1, TX^2, \ldots, TX^k\}$ is independent whenever $\{X^1, X^2, \ldots, X^k\}$ is independent.

We can also derive (10) from (9) directly. For suppose that nullity $(T) = 0$ and $a_1TX^1 + a_2TX^2 + \cdots + a_kTX^k = 0$. Then $T(a_1X^1 + a_2X^2 + \cdots + a_kX^k) = 0$. Thus $a_1X^1 + a_2X^2 + \cdots + a_kX^k = 0$, so that if $\{X^1, X^2, \ldots, X^k\}$ is independent, then $a_1 = a_2 = \cdots = a_k = 0$; that is, $\{TX^1, TX^2, \ldots, TX^k\}$ is independent. Conversely, suppose that nullity $(T) \neq 0$. Let $X \neq 0$ be such that $TX = 0$. Then $\{X\}$ is an independent set and $\{TX\}$ is not. Thus (10) is the same as (9).

What about (5) and (6)? The proofs we gave of (5) and (6) used only (3). Thus the same proofs using (7) give the following.

(11) Let T be an invertible linear operator on V. Let S be a linear operator on V such that $TS = 0$ or $ST = 0$. In either case $S = 0$.

Statement (11) has a converse which we will leave to the exercises. (See Exercise 9.)

When V is finite dimensional, (7) can be weakened to the following.

(12) If there is a linear operator T_1 on V such that $T_1T = I$, then T is invertible and $T_1 = T^{-1}$.

Statement (12) is generally easier to verify than is (7). If $T_1T = I$, let X be in V such that $TX = 0$. Apply T_1. Then $0 = T_1(TX) = (T_1T)X = IX = X = 0$. Thus nullity $(T) = 0$, so that (9) tells us that T is invertible. That $T_1 = T^{-1}$ follows from the proof of the uniqueness of the inverse given in (7) ff.

We turn now to the problem of finding the inverse for a product of linear operators on V. We consider an example. Let T be as in (1). Let S be a reflection in the x-axis. Let P be a change of scale; i.e.,

(13) $S(x, y) = (x, -y),$

(14) $P(x, y) = (ax, by), \quad a > 0, \quad b > 0.$

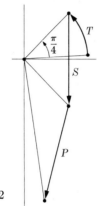
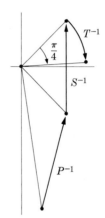

FIGURE 2   FIGURE 3

Then PST consists of a rotation, followed by a reflection, followed by a change of scale. (See Fig. 2, where T is a rotation through $\pi/4$ and $a = \frac{1}{2}, b = 3$.) Then to "undo" the effect of PST we can change scale back again, then reflect, then rotate in the opposite direction. (See Fig. 3.) Thus we have

(15) $P^{-1}(x, y) = \left(\dfrac{1}{a}x, \dfrac{1}{b}y\right),$

(16) $S^{-1} = S,$

(17) T^{-1} is a clockwise rotation through $\pi/4$,

(18) $(PST)^{-1} = T^{-1}S^{-1}P^{-1}.$

Statement (18) is a special case of the following.

(19)   Let V be finite dimensional and let S and T be linear operators on V. Then ST is invertible if and only if S and T are invertible and $(ST)^{-1} = T^{-1}S^{-1}.$

Suppose that S and T are invertible. Then

$$(T^{-1}S^{-1})(ST) = T^{-1}(S^{-1}S)T = T^{-1}IT = T^{-1}T = I.$$

From (12) we conclude that ST is invertible and $(ST)^{-1} = T^{-1}S^{-1}$. Now suppose that ST is invertible. Let $Q = (ST)^{-1}$. Then $I = Q(ST) =$

$(QS)T$. From (12) we conclude that T is invertible and $QS = T^{-1}$. Since T^{-1} is invertible and $S = (ST)T^{-1}$, we conclude that S is invertible. This proves (19). [The assumption that V is finite dimensional in (19) is necessary, as will be shown in the exercises.] Statement (19) clearly extends to a product of more than two operators, so that (18) is a special case of (19).

In the next section we will show how to compute T^{-1} by using the matrix of T. In this section we shall give the 2×2 case.

Let T be a linear operator on R^2 and let

$$A = \begin{bmatrix} a & b \\ c & d \end{bmatrix}$$

be the matrix of T. Then T is invertible if and only if rank $(T) = 2$ [by (9)]. Thus T is invertible if and only if rank $(A) = 2$. But rank $(A) = 2$ if and only if the rows of A are independent, i.e., if and only if $ad - bc \neq 0$. Thus

(20) T is invertible if and only if $ad - bc \neq 0$. Furthermore, the matrix of T^{-1} is

$$\frac{1}{ad - bc} \begin{bmatrix} d & -b \\ -c & a \end{bmatrix}.$$

The last statement of (20) gives us a quick way to compute T^{-1}. It follows from the identity

(21)
$$\frac{1}{ad - bc} \begin{bmatrix} d & -b \\ -c & a \end{bmatrix} \begin{bmatrix} a & b \\ c & d \end{bmatrix} = \begin{bmatrix} 1 & 0 \\ 0 & 1 \end{bmatrix}.$$

We summarize our results for convenient future reference.

Theorem 10. Let V be finite dimensional and let T be a linear operator on V. Then the following are equivalent.

(7)   There is a linear operator T_1 on V such that $TT_1 = T_1T = I$.

(12)   There is a linear operator T_1 on V such that $T_1T = I$.

(9)   Rank $(T) = \dim V$, or nullity $(T) = 0$.

(8) $\{TX^1, TX^2, \ldots, TX^n\}$ is a basis for V whenever $\{X^1, X^2, \ldots, X^n\}$ is a basis for V.

(10) $\{TX^1, TX^2, \ldots, TX^k\}$ is independent whenever $\{X^1, X^2, \ldots, X^k\}$ is independent.

Remarks. The word "invertible" has synonyms. If T is an invertible linear operator on V, we sometimes say that T is *regular* or that T is an *automorphism.*

Our results extend to the study of linear transformations. Let T be a linear transformation from V into W. We say that T is *invertible*, or that T is an *isomorphism of V onto W* if the range of T is all of W and if nullity $(T) = 0$. If V and W are finite dimensional, then it is necessary that $\dim V = \dim W$. Theorem 10 extends to this case.

Theorem 11. Let V and W be finite dimensional vector spaces such that $\dim V = \dim W$. Let T be a linear transformation from V into W. Then the following are equivalent.

(22) T is an isomorphism of V onto W.

(23) There is a linear transformation T_1 from W into V such that $T_1T = I_V$ and $TT_1 = I_W$.

(24) There is a linear transformation T_1 from W into V such that $T_1T = I_V$.

(25) Rank $(T) = \dim$ V, or nullity $(T) = 0$.

(26) $\{TX^1, TX^2, \ldots, TX^n\}$ is a basis for W whenever $\{X^1, X^2, \ldots, X^n\}$ is a basis for V.

(27) $\{TX^1, TX^2, \ldots, TX^k\}$ is independent in W whenever $\{X^1, X^2, \ldots, X^k\}$ is independent in V.

Since the proof of Theorem 11 is almost identical with the proof of Theorem 10, we shall omit it. The transformation T_1 given by (23) is uniquely determined by the condition $T_1T = I_V$ and is called the *inverse* of T; T_1 is an isomorphism of W onto V.

Theorem 10 will be used often in the remainder of this book. Theorem 11 will be used in the next section in our discussion of coordinates.

EXERCISES

1. By expressing both T and T_1 in terms of coordinates establish (3).

2. Which of the following linear operators on R^3 is invertible? If the operator is invertible, construct T^{-1}.

   (a) $T(x, y, z) = (x + y + z, y + z, z)$
   (b) $T(x, y, z) = (x + y - z, x - y + z, x + y + z)$
   (c) $T(x, y, z) = (2x + y + z, 3x + y - z, x + y + 3z)$

3. Which of the following linear operators on R^3 is invertible? If the operator is invertible, describe T^{-1} geometrically.

   (a) T projects onto the plane of the x- and y-axes.
   (b) T reflects in the plane determined by $(3, 1, 2)$, $(2, 1, 0)$, and $(0, 0, 0)$.
   (c) T is a rotation through $\pi/2$ about the line through $(0, 0, 0)$ and $(1, 1, 1)$ which leaves $(0, 0, 0)$ fixed.

(d) T sends the x-axis into the y-axis, the y-axis into the z-axis, and leaves the z-axis fixed.

4. Let V be the space of polynomials of degree ≤ 3. Which of the following linear operators on V is invertible?

   (a) $T(a_0 + a_1t + a_2t^2 + a_3t^3) = t(d/dt)(a_0 + a_1t + a_2t^2 + a_3t^3)$

   (b) $T(a_0 + a_1t + a_2t^2 + a_3t^3) = 1/t \cdot \int_0^t (a_0 + a_1u + a_2u^2 + a_3u^3)\, du$

5. In each of the following, A is the matrix of a linear operator T on R^2. Determine whether T is invertible. If T is invertible find the matrix of T^{-1}.

   (a) $A = \begin{bmatrix} 3 & 2 \\ 1 & 0 \end{bmatrix}$

   (b) $A = \begin{bmatrix} 3 & -1 \\ 0 & 1 \end{bmatrix}\begin{bmatrix} 2 & 0 \\ 1 & 2 \end{bmatrix}\begin{bmatrix} 1 & 2 \\ 0 & 0 \end{bmatrix}$

   (c) $A = \begin{bmatrix} 6 & -1 \\ -1 & \frac{1}{6} \end{bmatrix}$

   (d) $A = \begin{bmatrix} 2 & 1 \\ 1 & 1 \end{bmatrix}\begin{bmatrix} 3 & 2 \\ -1 & 0 \end{bmatrix}$

   (e) $A = \begin{bmatrix} 1 & 2 \\ 0 & 1 \end{bmatrix}\begin{bmatrix} 1 & 0 \\ 0 & 3 \end{bmatrix}\begin{bmatrix} 0 & 1 \\ 1 & 0 \end{bmatrix}$

   (f) $A = \begin{bmatrix} a-1 & -2 \\ 1 & a+1 \end{bmatrix}$, where a is a real number.

   (g) $A = \begin{bmatrix} a-1 & 2 \\ 1 & a+1 \end{bmatrix}$, where a is a real number.

6. One might expect that every invertible linear operator on R^2 is a product of rotations, reflections, and changes of scale. Show that the linear operator whose matrix is

$$\begin{bmatrix} 1 & 1 \\ 0 & 1 \end{bmatrix}$$

cannot be expressed as a product of rotations, reflections, and changes of scale. [*Hint:* Rotations, reflections, and changes of scale *do not* change angles between lines.]

7. Let V be the space of polynomials. Let D and T be defined by $(Df)(t) = (d/dt)(f(t))$ and $(Tf)(t) = \int_0^t f(u)\, du$, where $f = a_0 + a_1t + a_2t^2 + \cdots a_nt^n$.

   (a) Show that $DT = I$.   **(b)** Show that $TD \neq I$.

   This shows that (12) may not be valid when V is not finite dimensional.

8. **(a)** Suppose that V is not finite dimensional. Let S and T be invertible operators on V. Show that ST is invertible and $(ST)^{-1} = T^{-1}S^{-1}$. [*Hint:* Show that $(T^{-1}S^{-1})(ST) = (ST)(T^{-1}S^{-1}) = I$.]

   (b) Let V be the space of polynomials. Find operators S and T which are *not* invertible yet ST is invertible. [*Hint:* Show that the operators of Exercise 7 are *not* invertible; then use part (a) of that exercise.]

9. Let V be finite dimensional and let T be a linear operator on V which is *not* invertible. Show how to find linear operators S_1 and S_2 on V such that $S_1 \neq 0$, $S_2 \neq 0$, and $S_1 T = T S_2 = 0$. [*Hint:* Choose S_2 so that the range of S_2 is contained in the null space of T. Choose S_1 so that the range of T is contained in the null space of S_1. This can be done using the bases given in Theorem 8, then using Theorem 9 to describe S_1 and S_2.]

10. Let S be a linear transformation from V into W and let T be a linear transformation from W into V. Suppose that dim $W >$ dim V. Show that ST is *not* an invertible operator on W. [*Hint:* Show that nullity $(ST) \neq 0$ by showing that nullity $T \neq 0$.]

11. Show that if $n \neq m$, then there is *no* isomorphism of R^n onto R^m. [*Hint:* Let T be a linear transformation from R^n into R^m. If $n > m$, can nullity (T) be zero? If $n < m$, can rank $(T) = m$?]

12. Which of the following linear transformations from R^n into R^m are isomorphisms of R^n onto R^m?

    (a) $T(x, y, z, w) = (x - y, z + w, x - y + z, 0, w)$
    (b) $T(x, y, z, w) = (x - y, z + w, x - y + z)$
    (c) $T(x, y, z) = (x - 3y + 2z, 5x - y + 4z, 2x + y + z)$
    (d) $T(x, y, z, w) = (x, x + y, x + y + z, x + y + z + w)$

13. (a) Find an isomorphism of the space of polynomials of degree ≤ 2 onto R^3.

    (b) Find an isomorphism of the space of expressions of the form $ax + by + cz$ onto the space of polynomials of degree ≤ 2. (See Exercise 2(c) of Section 3 for a definition of this space.)

14. Show that if dim $V =$ dim W, then there is at least one isomorphism of V onto W. [*Hint:* Choose a basis for V and a basis for W. Use Theorem 9 and (26).]

15. Let V be finite dimensional and let T be a linear operator on V. Let T_1 be another linear operator such that $T T_1 = I$. Show that T is invertible, and $T^{-1} = T_1$. [*Hint:* Apply (19).]

Section 6.   MATRIX MULTIPLICATION

This section is primarily computational, and very few new results will be established. We shall look carefully at transformation multiplication and derive rules for computation. We will confine our attention initially to Cartesian spaces, and then show how we can "choose coordinates" in spaces which are not Cartesian spaces and thereby obtain means of computation in such spaces.

In Section 4 we showed that a linear transformation from R^n into R^m can be described by an $m \times n$ matrix. We then defined the sum of transformations and the sum of matrices in such a way that these two concepts corresponded; i.e., $A + B$ is the matrix of $S + T$, whenever A is the matrix of S and B is the matrix of T. We also defined aA in such a way that aA is the matrix of aT whenever A is the matrix of T and a is a real number.

In this section we shall define a product AB of two matrices such that AB is the matrix of ST, whenever ST is defined, A is the matrix of S, and B is the matrix of T. The matrix product gives us a means of computation for transformation products.

Let T be a linear transformation from R^n into R^m and let $B = (B_{ij})$ be the matrix of T. Let S be a linear transformation from R^m into R^k and let $A = (A_{ij})$ be the matrix of S. Then B is $m \times n$ and A is $k \times m$. Furthermore [see (22) of Section 4]

$$
(1) \quad
\begin{aligned}
T(x_1, x_2, \ldots, x_n) = (&B_{11}x_1 + B_{12}x_2 + \cdots + B_{1n}x_n, \\
&B_{21}x_1 + B_{22}x_2 + \cdots + B_{2n}x_n, \ldots, \\
&B_{m1}x_1 + B_{m2}x_2 + \cdots + B_{mn}x_n),
\end{aligned}
$$

$$
(2) \quad
\begin{aligned}
S(y_1, y_2, \ldots, y_m) = (&A_{11}y_1 + A_{12}y_2 + \cdots + A_{1m}y_m, \\
&A_{21}y_1 + A_{22}y_2 + \cdots + A_{2m}y_m, \ldots, \\
&A_{k1}y_1 + A_{k2}y_2 + \cdots + A_{km}y_m).
\end{aligned}
$$

ST is a linear transformation from R^n into R^k. Let $C = (C_{ij})$ be the matrix of ST. Then C is $k \times n$ and

$$
(3) \quad
\begin{aligned}
(ST)(x_1, x_2, \ldots, x_n) = (&C_{11}x_1 + C_{12}x_2 + \cdots + C_{1n}x_n, \\
&C_{21}x_1 + C_{22}x_2 + \cdots + C_{2n}x_n, \ldots, \\
&C_{k1}x_1 + C_{k2}x_2 + \cdots + C_{kn}x_n).
\end{aligned}
$$

We can also arrive at (3) by using (1) and (2). We have $ST(x_1, x_2, \ldots, x_n) = S(T(x_1, x_2, \ldots, x_n)) = S(B_{11}x_1 + B_{12}x_2 + \cdots + B_{1n}x_n, B_{21}x_1 + B_{22}x_2 + \cdots + B_{2n}x_n, \ldots, B_{m1}x_1 + B_{m2}x_2 + \cdots + B_{mn}x_n) = (A_{11}(B_{11}x_1 + B_{12}x_2 + \cdots + B_{1n}x_n) + A_{12}(B_{21}x_1 + B_{22}x_2 + \cdots + B_{2n}x_n) + \cdots + A_{1m}(B_{m1}x_1 + B_{m2}x_2 + \cdots + B_{mn}x_n), A_{21}(B_{11}x_1 + B_{12}x_2 + \cdots + B_{1n}x_n) + A_{22}(B_{21}x_1 + B_{22}x_2 + \cdots + B_{2n}x_n) + \cdots + A_{2m}(B_{m1}x_1 + B_{m2}x_2 + \cdots + B_{mn}x_n), \ldots, A_{k1}(B_{11}x_1 + B_{12}x_2 + \cdots + B_{1n}x_n) + A_{k2}(B_{21}x_1 + B_{22}x_2 + \cdots + B_{2n}x_n) + \cdots + A_{km}(B_{m1}x_1 + B_{m2}x_2 + \cdots + B_{mn}x_n)) = ((A_{11}B_{11} + A_{12}B_{21} + \cdots + A_{1m}B_{m1})x_1 + (A_{11}B_{12} + A_{12}B_{22} + \cdots + A_{1m}B_{m2})x_2 + \cdots + (A_{11}B_{1n} + A_{12}B_{2n} + \cdots + A_{1m}B_{mn})x_n, (A_{21}B_{11} + A_{22}B_{21} + \cdots + A_{2m}B_{m1})x_1 + (A_{21}B_{12} + A_{22}B_{22} + \cdots + A_{2m}B_{m2})x_2 + \cdots + (A_{21}B_{1n} + A_{22}B_{2n} + \cdots + A_{2m}B_{mn})x_n, \ldots, (A_{k1}B_{11} + A_{k2}B_{21} + \cdots + A_{km}B_{m1})x_1 + (A_{k1}B_{12} + A_{k2}B_{22} + \cdots + A_{km}B_{m2})x_2 + \cdots + (A_{k1}B_{1n} + A_{k2}B_{2n} + \cdots + A_{km}B_{mn})x_n)$. Thus

$$
(4) \quad
\begin{aligned}
C_{ij} &= A_{i1}B_{1j} + A_{i2}B_{2j} + \cdots + A_{im}B_{mj}, \\
&i = 1, 2, \ldots, k, \quad j = 1, 2, \ldots n.
\end{aligned}
$$

The matrix C is called the *product* of A and B and we write $C = AB$. (Just as in transformation multiplication the order of factors is important.) The entry in the ith row and jth column of AB is obtained, according to (4), by adding together the products of the entries in the ith row of A with the corresponding entries of the jth column of B. A simple way to become familiar with (4) is to work out some examples, carefully substituting in (4). The definition (4) should become so familiar that the reader can use it automatically.

$$(5) \quad \begin{bmatrix} 2 & 1 & 0 \\ 1 & 0 & 1 \\ 0 & 1 & 3 \end{bmatrix} \begin{bmatrix} 2 & 0 \\ 1 & 1 \\ 3 & 1 \end{bmatrix} = \begin{bmatrix} 2 \cdot 2 + 1 \cdot 1 + 0 \cdot 3 & 2 \cdot 0 + 1 \cdot 1 + 0 \cdot 1 \\ 1 \cdot 2 + 0 \cdot 1 + 1 \cdot 3 & 1 \cdot 0 + 0 \cdot 1 + 1 \cdot 1 \\ 0 \cdot 2 + 1 \cdot 1 + 3 \cdot 3 & 0 \cdot 0 + 1 \cdot 1 + 3 \cdot 1 \end{bmatrix}$$

$$= \begin{bmatrix} 5 & 1 \\ 5 & 1 \\ 10 & 4 \end{bmatrix}.$$

$$(6) \quad \begin{bmatrix} 3 & 1 & 2 & 1 \\ 1 & 0 & 1 & 2 \\ 0 & 1 & -1 & 0 \end{bmatrix} \begin{bmatrix} 1 & 2 \\ 0 & 1 \\ 1 & 1 \end{bmatrix}.$$

This is not defined since the number of columns of the first matrix is not the same as the number of rows of the second matrix.

$$(7) \quad \begin{bmatrix} a & 1 & 0 \\ 1 & -1 & 1 \end{bmatrix} \begin{bmatrix} 2 & 0 \\ 1 & 0 \\ 1 & 0 \end{bmatrix}$$

$$= \begin{bmatrix} a \cdot 2 + & 1 \cdot 1 + 0 \cdot 1 & a \cdot 0 + & 1 \cdot 0 + 0 \cdot 0 \\ 1 \cdot 2 + (-1) \cdot 1 + 1 \cdot 1 & 1 \cdot 0 + (-1) \cdot 0 + 1 \cdot 0 \end{bmatrix}$$

$$= \begin{bmatrix} 2a + 1 & 0 \\ 2 & 0 \end{bmatrix}.$$

$$(8) \quad \begin{bmatrix} 1 & 2 \\ 0 & 0 \end{bmatrix} \begin{bmatrix} 1 & 1 & 2 \\ 0 & 1 & 1 \end{bmatrix}$$

$$= \begin{bmatrix} 1 \cdot 1 + 2 \cdot 0 & 1 \cdot 1 + 2 \cdot 1 & 1 \cdot 2 + 2 \cdot 1 \\ 0 \cdot 1 + 0 \cdot 0 & 0 \cdot 1 + 0 \cdot 1 & 0 \cdot 2 + 0 \cdot 1 \end{bmatrix}$$

$$= \begin{bmatrix} 1 & 3 & 4 \\ 0 & 0 & 0 \end{bmatrix}.$$

$$(9) \quad \begin{bmatrix} 1 & 0 & 0 \\ 0 & 1 & 0 \\ 0 & 0 & 1 \end{bmatrix} \begin{bmatrix} 3 & 1 & 1 & 0 \\ 1 & 0 & 1 & 1 \\ a & 1 & -1 & 4 \end{bmatrix}$$

$$= \begin{bmatrix} 1 \cdot 3 + 0 \cdot 1 + 0 \cdot a & 1 \cdot 1 + 0 \cdot 0 + 0 \cdot 1 \\ 0 \cdot 3 + 1 \cdot 1 + 0 \cdot a & 0 \cdot 1 + 1 \cdot 0 + 0 \cdot 1 \\ 0 \cdot 3 + 0 \cdot 1 + 1 \cdot a & 0 \cdot 1 + 0 \cdot 0 + 1 \cdot 1 \end{bmatrix}$$

$$\begin{bmatrix} 1 \cdot 1 + 0 \cdot 1 + 0 \cdot (-1) & 1 \cdot 0 + 0 \cdot 1 + 0 \cdot 4 \\ 0 \cdot 1 + 1 \cdot 1 + 0 \cdot (-1) & 0 \cdot 0 + 1 \cdot 1 + 0 \cdot 4 \\ 0 \cdot 1 + 0 \cdot 1 + 1 \cdot (-1) & 0 \cdot 0 + 0 \cdot 1 + 1 \cdot 4 \end{bmatrix}$$

$$= \begin{bmatrix} 3 & 1 & 1 & 0 \\ 1 & 0 & 1 & 1 \\ a & 1 & -1 & 4 \end{bmatrix}.$$

We can draw some conclusions from our definition (4) which often speed up computation. If one row of A consists of zeros, then the corresponding row of AB consists of zeros, as in (8). If one column of B consists of zeros, then the corresponding column of AB consists of zeros, as in (7). The following is an obvious consequence of this.

(10)   If B is the $k \times m$ zero matrix or if A is the $m \times n$ zero matrix, then BA is the $k \times n$ zero matrix.

If we denote the zero matrix by 0, then we have $0A = B0 = 0$. No confusion should result from the fact that each use of 0 may represent a zero matrix of different size. Of course, in order to write $0A$ or $B0$, we need to know that these products are defined; i.e., $0A$ makes sense if the number of columns of 0 is the same as the number of rows of A. The matrix

$$\begin{bmatrix} 1 & 0 & 0 \\ 0 & 1 & 0 \\ 0 & 0 & 1 \end{bmatrix}$$

is called the 3×3 identity matrix. On the diagonal the entries are ones; off the diagonal the entries are zeros. Let us make this precise.

(11)   If A is $m \times n$, then the *diagonal* of A consists of the entries A_{ii}. The number of diagonal entries is either m or n, whichever is smaller.

(12)   The $n \times n$ *identity* matrix, denoted by I_n, is the $n \times n$ matrix whose diagonal entries are ones and whose nondiagonal entries are zeros.

The following notation is common. We write $I_n = (\delta_{ij})$, where $\delta_{ij} = 1$, if $i = j$, and $\delta_{ij} = 0$, if $i \neq j$. The symbol "δ_{ij}" is quite common and is called the *Kronecker delta*. If the size of I_n is clear, we shall drop the n. We have the general case of (9).

(13)   If A is $m \times n$, then $I_m A = A I_n = A$.

We can deduce further rules. Let us look at some more examples.

(14) $\begin{bmatrix} 2 & 0 & 0 \\ 0 & 1 & 0 \\ 0 & 0 & 3 \end{bmatrix} \begin{bmatrix} \frac{3}{2} & 1 & -1 & 0 \\ 1 & 0 & 1 & 1 \\ 0 & 1 & 1 & 1 \end{bmatrix}$

$$= \begin{bmatrix} 2 \cdot \frac{3}{2} & 2 \cdot 1 & 2 \cdot (-1) & 2 \cdot 0 \\ 1 \cdot 1 & 1 \cdot 0 & 1 \cdot 1 & 1 \cdot 1 \\ 3 \cdot 0 & 3 \cdot 1 & 3 \cdot 1 & 3 \cdot 1 \end{bmatrix} = \begin{bmatrix} 3 & 2 & -2 & 0 \\ 1 & 0 & 1 & 1 \\ 0 & 3 & 3 & 3 \end{bmatrix}.$$

(15) $\begin{bmatrix} 1 & 0 & 1 \\ -1 & 1 & 1 \end{bmatrix} \begin{bmatrix} 1 & 0 & 0 \\ 0 & -1 & 0 \\ 0 & 0 & x \end{bmatrix}$

$$= \begin{bmatrix} 1 \cdot 1 & 0 \cdot (-1) & 1 \cdot x \\ (-1) \cdot 1 & 1 \cdot (-1) & 1 \cdot x \end{bmatrix} = \begin{bmatrix} 1 & 0 & x \\ -1 & -1 & x \end{bmatrix}.$$

(16) $\begin{bmatrix} 2 & 1 & 1 \\ 0 & 1 & -1 \\ 0 & 0 & 1 \end{bmatrix} \begin{bmatrix} 1 & -2 & 1 \\ 0 & 1 & 1 \\ 0 & 0 & -1 \end{bmatrix} = \begin{bmatrix} 2 & -3 & 2 \\ 0 & 1 & 2 \\ 0 & 0 & -1 \end{bmatrix}.$

An $n \times n$ matrix A is said to be *diagonal* if $A_{ij} = 0$ for $i \neq j$. The general form of (13) and (14) is as follows.

(17) If A is a diagonal $n \times n$ matrix and B is $n \times k$, then AB is obtained from B by multiplying row i of B by A_{ii}, $i = 1, 2, \ldots, n$.

An $n \times n$ matrix A is said to be *upper triangular* if $A_{ij} = 0$ for $i > j$. The general form of (16) is as follows.

(18) If A and B are upper triangular $n \times n$ matrices, then AB is an upper triangular $n \times n$ matrix.

Statements (10), (13), (17), and (18) are easily proved by using the definitions. The proofs involve only some bookkeeping to keep track of the generality. The reader should be able to state and prove many other multiplication theorems for special kinds of matrices. The exercises will contain more results of this type. These results will help the reader become familiar with matrix multiplication and will serve as checks on results.

We will now show how we can describe a linear transformation from R^n into R^m via left multiplication by the matrix of the transformation.

If $(x_1, x_2, \ldots, x_n)$ is a vector in R^n, then we can consider this vector as the $n \times 1$ column matrix

$$\begin{bmatrix} x_1 \\ x_2 \\ \vdots \\ x_n \end{bmatrix}$$

or as the $1 \times n$ row matrix $[x_1\ x_2\ \ldots\ x_n]$. Let T be a linear transformation of R^n into R^m, and let A be the matrix of T. We have

$$T(x_1, x_2, \ldots, x_n) = (y_1, y_2, \ldots, y_m) \text{ if and only if}$$

(19)
$$A \begin{bmatrix} x_1 \\ x_2 \\ \vdots \\ x_n \end{bmatrix} = \begin{bmatrix} y_1 \\ y_2 \\ \vdots \\ y_m \end{bmatrix},$$

i.e., the action of T is performed by left multiplication by A. We also have

$$T(x_1, x_2, \ldots, x_n) = (y_1, y_2, \ldots, y_m) \text{ if and only if}$$

(20)
$$[x_1\ x_2\ \ldots\ x_n] \begin{bmatrix} A_{11} & A_{21} & \cdots & A_{m1} \\ A_{12} & A_{22} & \cdots & A_{m2} \\ \vdots & & & \\ A_{1n} & A_{2n} & \cdots & A_{mn} \end{bmatrix} = [y_1\ y_2\ \ldots\ y_m].$$

The matrix in (20) is obtained from A by interchanging the rows and columns of A. Statements (19) and (20) can be established easily using (4) and (1). Let us exhibit these with an example. Let T be the linear transformation from R^2 into R^3 defined by $T(1, 0) = (1, 1, 0)$ and $T(0, 1) = (0, 1, 1)$. Then the matrix of T is

$$\begin{bmatrix} 1 & 0 \\ 1 & 1 \\ 0 & 1 \end{bmatrix}.$$

We have $T(x, y) = T(x(1, 0) + y(0, 1)) = xT(1, 0) + yT(0, 1) = (x, x + y, y)$. This is the same as

$$\begin{bmatrix} 1 & 0 \\ 1 & 1 \\ 0 & 1 \end{bmatrix} \begin{bmatrix} x \\ y \end{bmatrix} = \begin{bmatrix} x \\ x + y \\ y \end{bmatrix},$$

which is (19), or

$$[x\ \ y] \begin{bmatrix} 1 & 1 & 0 \\ 0 & 1 & 1 \end{bmatrix} = [x\ \ x + y\ \ y],$$

which is (20).

Remarks. For linear transformations defined on Cartesian spaces we can use either (19) or (20) to reduce computational questions to matrix equations. We shall generally use (19), for two reasons. We have been writing the letter denoting the transformation to the left of the variable; i.e., we write TX rather than XT. We use (19) so that we can write the matrix A on the left also. The second reason is more important. If we used (20), and if A is the matrix of S and B the matrix of T, then we have [using the notation of (1) and (2)]

$$(ST)(x_1, x_2, \ldots, x_n) = (z_1, z_2, \ldots, z_k) \quad \text{if and only if}$$

$$(21) \quad [x_1\, x_2 \ldots x_n] \begin{bmatrix} B_{11} & B_{21} & \ldots & B_{m1} \\ B_{12} & B_{22} & \ldots & B_{m2} \\ \vdots & & & \\ B_{1n} & B_{2n} & \ldots & B_{mn} \end{bmatrix} \begin{bmatrix} A_{11} & A_{21} & \ldots & A_{k1} \\ A_{12} & A_{22} & \ldots & A_{k2} \\ \vdots & & & \\ A_{1m} & A_{2m} & \ldots & A_{km} \end{bmatrix}$$

$$= [z_1\, z_2 \ldots z_k].$$

In other words, the product gets turned around. Our notation corresponds to that used by most authors.

Statement (19) transfers the study of linear transformations to the study of matrix multiplication. Similarly we can transfer the study of systems of equations to the study of matrix equations. The system of equations

$$(22) \quad \begin{aligned} A_{11}x_1 + A_{12}x_2 + \cdots + A_{1n}x_n &= y_1 \\ A_{21}x_1 + A_{22}x_2 + \cdots + A_{2n}x_n &= y_2 \\ \vdots \\ A_{m1}x_1 + A_{m2}x_2 + \cdots + A_{mn}x_n &= y_m \end{aligned}$$

becomes the single equation

$$(23) \quad AX = Y,$$

where A is the matrix of coefficients of (22), and

$$X = \begin{bmatrix} x_1 \\ x_2 \\ \vdots \\ x_n \end{bmatrix}, \qquad Y = \begin{bmatrix} y_1 \\ y_2 \\ \vdots \\ y_m \end{bmatrix}.$$

In this way the methods of Sections 1 and 2 can be interpreted as methods for solving the equation (23) by operating on the rows of A and Y. Clearly (23) is a considerable notational saving over (22).

What are the general laws of matrix multiplication? These derive immediately from the general laws of transformation multiplication given in (44), (45), and (46) of Section 4. Thus if A is $m \times n$, B is $n \times k$, and C is $k \times r$, then $(AB)C = A(BC)$. If A is $m \times n$, B is $n \times k$, and C is $n \times k$, then $A(B + C) = AB + AC$. If A is $m \times n$, B is $n \times k$, and a is a real number, then $a(AB) = (aA)B = A(aB)$.

Now let us specialize to the case when all our matrices are $n \times n$. In this case both AB and BA are defined. In general $AB \neq BA$, e.g.,

$$(24) \quad \begin{bmatrix} 0 & 1 \\ 0 & 0 \end{bmatrix} \begin{bmatrix} 0 & 0 \\ 1 & 0 \end{bmatrix} = \begin{bmatrix} 1 & 0 \\ 0 & 0 \end{bmatrix} \quad \text{and} \quad \begin{bmatrix} 0 & 0 \\ 1 & 0 \end{bmatrix} \begin{bmatrix} 0 & 1 \\ 0 & 0 \end{bmatrix} = \begin{bmatrix} 0 & 0 \\ 0 & 1 \end{bmatrix}.$$

However we can form powers of a matrix. These are defined as follows.

(25) If A is $n \times n$, then $A^2 = AA$, $A^3 = AAA$, etc. In general $A^{k+1} = A^k A$.

Since $(AA)A = A(AA)$, we can write $A^3 = AAA$ and no ambiguity will result.

An $n \times n$ matrix A is the matrix of a linear operator T on R^n. In Section 5 we discussed invertible linear operators. We will now give conditions on A which guarantee that T is invertible. We will also give a method for computing the matrix of T^{-1}.

An $n \times n$ matrix A is said to be *invertible* if A is the matrix of an invertible linear operator T on R^n. From the definition of an invertible linear operator [(7) of Section 5], this is the same as saying that there is an $n \times n$ matrix B such that

$$(26) \qquad\qquad AB = BA = I_n,$$

where B is the matrix of T^{-1} and, as in Section 5, B is uniquely determined by (26). We call B the *inverse* of A and write $B = A^{-1}$. The following are alternative ways to describe this property.

(a) rank $(A) = n$.
(b) column rank $(A) = n$.
(c) nullity $(A) = 0$.
(d) There is an $n \times n$ matrix B such that $BA = I_n$.
(e) There is an $n \times n$ matrix B such that $AB = I_n$.
(27) (f) The rows of A are independent.
(g) $AX = 0$ implies that $X = 0$ for any $n \times 1$ matrix X.
(h) There is an $n \times n$ matrix B such that

$$A \begin{bmatrix} x_1 \\ x_2 \\ \vdots \\ x_n \end{bmatrix} = \begin{bmatrix} y_1 \\ y_2 \\ \vdots \\ y_n \end{bmatrix} \quad \text{if and only if} \quad B \begin{bmatrix} y_1 \\ y_2 \\ \vdots \\ y_n \end{bmatrix} = \begin{bmatrix} x_1 \\ x_2 \\ \vdots \\ x_n \end{bmatrix}.$$

Statements (27a, c, d) are included in Theorem 10. Since rank $(A) =$ column rank (A), (27a, b) are the same. (See the Remarks after Theorem 8.) Part (f) is clearly the same as part (a). Part (g) is the same as part (c), by using (22) and (23). Part (e) follows from:

(28)   If A and B are $n \times n$, then AB is invertible if and only if A and B are invertible. If AB is invertible, then $(AB)^{-1} = B^{-1}A^{-1}$.

This is the matrix analog of (19) of Section 5.

Let us show that (27h) is the same as (26). Let A be invertible and let $B = A^{-1}$. Then if

$$A \begin{bmatrix} x_1 \\ x_2 \\ \vdots \\ x_n \end{bmatrix} = \begin{bmatrix} y_1 \\ y_2 \\ \vdots \\ y_n \end{bmatrix},$$

we can apply A^{-1}. This gives

$$\begin{bmatrix} x_1 \\ x_2 \\ \vdots \\ x_n \end{bmatrix} = (A^{-1}A) \begin{bmatrix} x_1 \\ x_2 \\ \vdots \\ x_n \end{bmatrix} = A^{-1} \begin{bmatrix} y_1 \\ y_2 \\ \vdots \\ y_n \end{bmatrix}.$$

Thus (27h) follows from (26). Let A and B satisfy (27h). Suppose that

$$A \begin{bmatrix} x_1 \\ x_2 \\ \vdots \\ x_n \end{bmatrix} = \begin{bmatrix} 0 \\ 0 \\ \vdots \\ 0 \end{bmatrix}.$$

Then

$$B \begin{bmatrix} 0 \\ 0 \\ \vdots \\ 0 \end{bmatrix} = \begin{bmatrix} x_1 \\ x_2 \\ \vdots \\ x_n \end{bmatrix}.$$

Thus

$$\begin{bmatrix} x_1 \\ x_2 \\ \vdots \\ x_n \end{bmatrix} = \begin{bmatrix} 0 \\ 0 \\ \vdots \\ 0 \end{bmatrix}.$$

We conclude that A satisfies (27g). This shows that (27h) is the same as (26).

Statement (27h) tells us that when A is invertible, the matrix equation

(29)
$$AX = Y,$$

where X and Y are $n \times 1$ matrices, has a unique solution

(30)
$$X = A^{-1}Y.$$

We have reduced the problem of solving (29) to the computation of A^{-1} in the case when A is invertible. We can use (27a) to determine whether A is invertible, so we are left with the question of the computation of A^{-1}. Let us look at an example:

(31)
$$A = \begin{bmatrix} 2 & 1 & 0 \\ 1 & -1 & 1 \\ 0 & 1 & 3 \end{bmatrix}.$$

Then rank $(A) = 3$, so A is invertible. Let

$$A^{-1} = \begin{bmatrix} B_{11} & B_{12} & B_{13} \\ B_{21} & B_{22} & B_{23} \\ B_{31} & B_{32} & B_{33} \end{bmatrix}.$$

Then

(32) $\quad A^{-1}\begin{bmatrix} 1 \\ 0 \\ 0 \end{bmatrix} = \begin{bmatrix} B_{11} \\ B_{21} \\ B_{31} \end{bmatrix}, \qquad A^{-1}\begin{bmatrix} 0 \\ 1 \\ 0 \end{bmatrix} = \begin{bmatrix} B_{12} \\ B_{22} \\ B_{32} \end{bmatrix}, \qquad A^{-1}\begin{bmatrix} 0 \\ 0 \\ 1 \end{bmatrix} = \begin{bmatrix} B_{13} \\ B_{23} \\ B_{33} \end{bmatrix},$

which is the same as [use (27h)]

(33) $\quad A\begin{bmatrix} B_{11} \\ B_{21} \\ B_{31} \end{bmatrix} = \begin{bmatrix} 1 \\ 0 \\ 0 \end{bmatrix}, \qquad A\begin{bmatrix} B_{12} \\ B_{22} \\ B_{32} \end{bmatrix} = \begin{bmatrix} 0 \\ 1 \\ 0 \end{bmatrix}, \qquad A\begin{bmatrix} B_{13} \\ B_{23} \\ B_{33} \end{bmatrix} = \begin{bmatrix} 0 \\ 0 \\ 1 \end{bmatrix}.$

We can solve all three equations of (33) at the same time by forming

(34)
$$\begin{bmatrix} 2 & 1 & 0 & 1 & 0 & 0 \\ 1 & -1 & 1 & 0 & 1 & 0 \\ 0 & 1 & 3 & 0 & 0 & 1 \end{bmatrix}$$

and reducing this matrix to

(35)
$$\begin{bmatrix} 1 & 0 & 0 & \frac{4}{11} & \frac{3}{11} & -\frac{1}{11} \\ 0 & 1 & 0 & \frac{3}{11} & -\frac{6}{11} & \frac{2}{11} \\ 0 & 0 & 1 & -\frac{1}{11} & \frac{2}{11} & \frac{3}{11} \end{bmatrix}.$$

Then

(36)
$$A^{-1} = \tfrac{1}{11} \begin{bmatrix} 4 & 3 & -1 \\ 3 & -6 & 2 \\ -1 & 2 & 3 \end{bmatrix}.$$

The matrix (34) was formed so that we could perform the operations on A and on

$$\begin{bmatrix} 1 \\ 0 \\ 0 \end{bmatrix}, \quad \begin{bmatrix} 0 \\ 1 \\ 0 \end{bmatrix}, \quad \begin{bmatrix} 0 \\ 0 \\ 1 \end{bmatrix}$$

at the same time. The general result is the following theorem.

Theorem 12. Let A be $n \times n$. Then A is invertible if and only if A can be row reduced to I_n. If A is invertible, then A^{-1} is found by applying the same operations, *in the same order*, to I_n as we apply to A in reducing A to I_n.

Proof. That A is invertible if and only if A can be reduced to I_n is a consequence of Theorem 2 and (27c). The computation of A^{-1} is a straightforward generalization of the method given in (32) through (36) and its proof will be omitted. Q.E.D.

Our final topics in this section are concerned with the problem of computation in vector spaces other than R^n. We do this by "choosing coordinates." Let us make this precise.

Let V be a vector space and let $\{X^1, X^2, \ldots, X^n\}$ be a basis for V. Let X be in V. Then since $\{X^1, X^2, \ldots, X^n\}$ spans V, we can write

(37)
$$X = x_1 X^1 + x_2 X^2 + \cdots + x_n X^n.$$

The expression (37) is unique. For suppose that

$$X = y_1 X^1 + y_2 X^2 + \cdots + y_n X^n.$$

Then $0 = (x_1 - y_1)X^1 + (x_2 - y_2)X^2 + \cdots + (x_n - y_n)X^n$. Thus $x_1 = y_1, x_2 = y_2, \ldots, x_n = y_n$, since $\{X^1, X^2, \ldots, X^n\}$ is independent. We call the ordered n-tuple $(x_1, x_2, \ldots, x_n)$ *the coordinates of X with respect to the (ordered) basis* $\{X^1, X^2, \ldots, X^n\}$. As we shall see, all computation in V can be carried out by first expressing each vector in terms of coordinates with respect to an ordered basis, then carrying out the computation in R^n. Before establishing this, we shall define the matrix of a linear operator on V.

Let T be a linear operator on V. Let A be the $n \times n$ matrix whose jth column consists of the coordinates of TX^j with respect to $\{X^1, X^2, \ldots,$

X^n}. A is called *the matrix of T with respect to the (ordered) basis* {X^1, $X^2, \ldots, X^n$}. We have

(38) $TX^j = A_{1j}X^1 + A_{2j}X^2 + \cdots + A_{nj}X^n, \qquad j = 1, 2, \ldots, n.$

The uniqueness of coordinates shows that A is unique.

We can now derive the following, just as we derived (19).

(39) $TX = Y$ if and only if $A \begin{bmatrix} x_1 \\ x_2 \\ \vdots \\ x_n \end{bmatrix} = \begin{bmatrix} y_1 \\ y_2 \\ \vdots \\ y_n \end{bmatrix}$, where A is the matrix

of T and $(x_1, x_2, \ldots, x_n)$ and $(y_1, y_2, \ldots, y_n)$ are the coordinates of X and Y, respectively, all with respect to {$X^1, X^2, \ldots, X^n$}.

We also have the following.

(40)   If S and T are linear operators on V and A is the matrix of S and B the matrix of T, then AB is the matrix of ST, all with respect to {$X^1, X^2, \ldots, X^n$}.

Statement (40) is established in the same fashion as (4). Using these concepts, all computational questions on V are reduced to questions about matrices and coordinates. We now show that this is so.

The equation (37) can be used to define an isomorphism P of V onto R^n. We define P as follows:

(41) $PX = (x_1, x_2, \ldots, x_n)$ if $X = x_1X^1 + x_2X^2 + \cdots + x_nX^n.$

Since the n-tuple $(x_1, x_2, \ldots, x_n)$ is uniquely determined by X (and {$X^1, X^2, \ldots, X^n$}), (41) defines a transformation of V into R^n. If $X = x_1X^1 + x_2X^2 + \cdots + x_nX^n$ and $Y = y_1X^1 + y_2X^2 + \cdots + y_nX^n$, then $aX + bY = (ax_1 + by_1)X^1 + (ax_2 + by_2)X^2 + \cdots + (ax_n + by_n)X^n$. Thus

(42) $\begin{aligned} P(aX + bY) &= (ax_1 + by_1, ax_2 + by_2, \ldots, ax_n + by_n) \\ &= aPX + bPY. \end{aligned}$

In other words, (42) tells us that P is linear. If $PX = 0$, then $x_1 = x_2 = \cdots = x_n = 0$, so that $X = 0$. Thus nullity $(P) = 0$. Therefore, by Theorem 11, P is an isomorphism of V onto R^n.

The key result is given by Theorem 11:

(43)   {$Y^1, Y^2, \ldots, Y^k$} is independent in V if and only if {$PY^1, PY^2, \ldots, PY^k$} is independent in R^n.

Part of (43) was not given in Theorem 11. We have to show that independence of $\{PY^1, PY^2, \ldots, PY^k\}$ gives independence of $\{Y^1, Y^2, \ldots, Y^k\}$. This uses only the fact that P is linear. Suppose that $\{PY^1, PY^2, \ldots, PY^k\}$ is independent, and suppose that $a_1Y^1 + a_2Y^2 + \cdots + a_kY^k = 0$. Apply P. Then $0 = a_1PY^1 + a_2PY^2 + \cdots + a_kPY^k$, so that $a_1 = a_2 = \cdots = a_k = 0$, that is, $\{Y^1, Y^2, \ldots, Y^k\}$ is also independent.

Statement (43) tells us, in precise terms, that all questions about independence (and hence dependence) can be answered in V by expressing the vectors in V in terms of coordinates (with respect to some basis in V), then answering the questions in R^n.

Let us look at an example. Let V be the space of polynomials of degree ≤ 2. Then $\{1, t, t^2\}$ is a basis for V. If

$$f = a_0 + a_1t + a_2t^2,$$

then the coordinates of f, with respect to $\{1, t, t^2\}$, are (a_0, a_1, a_2).

Is the set $\{1 + t + t^2, 1 - 3t + 2t^2, 3 - t + 4t^2\}$ independent in V? The coordinates of $1 + t + t^2$, $1 - 3t + 2t^2$, and $3 - t + 4t^2$ with respect to $\{1, t, t^2\}$ are $(1, 1, 1)$, $(1, -3, 2)$, and $(3, -1, 4)$, respectively. Since

$$\text{rank} \begin{bmatrix} 1 & 1 & 1 \\ 1 & -3 & 2 \\ 3 & -1 & 4 \end{bmatrix} = 2,$$

we conclude that $\{(1, 1, 1), (1, -3, 2), (3, -1, 4)\}$ is dependent, and hence that $\{1 + t + t^2, 1 - 3t + 2t^2, 3 - t + 4t^2\}$ is dependent.

Let T be the linear operator on V defined as follows:

(44)
$$Tf = \frac{d}{dt}(tf).$$

Then

(45)
$$T1 = 1, \qquad Tt = 2t, \qquad Tt^2 = 3t^2.$$

The matrix of T with respect to $\{1, t, t^2\}$ is

(46)
$$\begin{bmatrix} 1 & 0 & 0 \\ 0 & 2 & 0 \\ 0 & 0 & 3 \end{bmatrix}.$$

Statement (39) then gives

(47) $Tf = a_0 + 2a_1t + 3a_2t^2$ if $f = a_0 + a_1t + a_2t^2$.

The matrix of T^r, $r \geq 1$, with respect to $\{1, t, t^2\}$ is [use (38)]

(48)
$$\begin{bmatrix} 1 & 0 & 0 \\ 0 & 2 & 0 \\ 0 & 0 & 3 \end{bmatrix}^r = \begin{bmatrix} 1 & 0 & 0 \\ 0 & 2^r & 0 \\ 0 & 0 & 3^r \end{bmatrix}.$$

Thus

(49)
$$T^r(a_0 + a_1 t + a_2 t^2) = a_0 + 2^r a_1 t + 3^r a_2 t^2.$$

Equation (48) is easy using (40), but is not immediately obvious from (44) because

(50)
$$T^r f = \frac{d}{dt} \left(t \cdot \frac{d}{dt} \left(t \cdot \frac{d}{dt} \cdots \frac{d}{dt} (tf) \right) \cdots \right).$$

Now we turn to the problem of "changing coordinates." Let $\{X^1, X^2, \ldots, X^n\}$ be a basis for V and let $\{Y^1, Y^2, \ldots, Y^n\}$ be another basis for V. Suppose that $X = x_1 X^1 + x_2 X^2 + \cdots + x_n X^n$ and $X = y_1 Y^1 + y_2 Y^2 + \cdots + y_n Y^n$. What is the relation between $(x_1, x_2, \ldots, x_n)$ and $(y_1, y_2, \ldots, y_n)$?

Let $P_0 = (P_{ij})$ be the $n \times n$ matrix defined by

(51) $X^j = P_{1j} Y^1 + P_{2j} Y^2 + \cdots + P_{nj} Y^n$, $j = 1, 2, \ldots, n$.

Then we have

(52)
$$P_0 \begin{bmatrix} x_1 \\ x_2 \\ \vdots \\ x_n \end{bmatrix} = \begin{bmatrix} y_1 \\ y_2 \\ \vdots \\ y_n \end{bmatrix}.$$

This is established by replacing each X^j in $X = x_1 X^1 + x_2 X^2 + \cdots + x_n X^n$ by (51).

Since $X = 0Y^1 + 0Y^2 + \cdots + 0Y^n$ if and only if $X = 0X^1 + 0X^2 + \cdots + 0X^n$, we conclude from (27g) that P_0 is invertible. Thus we have

(53)
$$\begin{bmatrix} x_1 \\ x_2 \\ \vdots \\ x_n \end{bmatrix} = P_0^{-1} \begin{bmatrix} y_1 \\ y_2 \\ \vdots \\ y_n \end{bmatrix}.$$

Let $P_0^{-1} = (Q_{ij})$. Then (53) is the same as

(54) $Y^j = Q_{1j} X^1 + Q_{2j} X^2 + \cdots + Q_{nj} X^n$, $j = 1, 2, \ldots, n$.

Equation (54) is established by computing the coordinates of Y^j with respect to $\{Y^1, Y^2, \ldots, Y^n\}$ to obtain the left-hand side, and with respect to $\{X^1, X^2, \ldots, X^n\}$, using (52), to obtain the right-hand side.

Formulas (52) and (53), along with (51) and (54), give us formulas for "changing coordinates."

Let P be the linear operator on V such that

$$PY^j = X^j, \qquad j = 1, 2, \ldots, n.$$

Then P is invertible by Theorem 20. The formulas (51) state that

(55) P_0 is the matrix of P with respect to $\{Y^1, Y^2, \ldots, Y^n\}$.

Let T be a linear operator on V and let A be the matrix of T with respect to $\{X^1, X^2, \ldots, X^n\}$. Let B be the matrix of T with respect to $\{Y^1, Y^2, \ldots, Y^n\}$. The relation between A and B is given by

(56) $B = P_0 A P_0^{-1}.$

To establish (56) we use (39), (52), and (53). Let $X = x_1 X^1 + x_2 X^2 + \cdots + x_n X^n = x_1' Y^1 + x_2' Y^2 + \cdots + x_n' Y^n$. Let $Z = z_1 X^1 + z_2 X^2 + \cdots + z_n X^n = z_1' Y^1 + z_2' Y^2 + \cdots + z_n' Y^n$. Then

(57) $TX = Z$ if and only if $B \begin{bmatrix} x_1' \\ x_2' \\ \vdots \\ x_n' \end{bmatrix} = \begin{bmatrix} z_1' \\ z_2' \\ \vdots \\ z_n' \end{bmatrix};$

(58) $TX = Z$ if and only if $A \begin{bmatrix} x_1 \\ x_2 \\ \vdots \\ x_n \end{bmatrix} = \begin{bmatrix} z_1 \\ z_2 \\ \vdots \\ z_n \end{bmatrix};$

(59) $\begin{bmatrix} x_1 \\ x_2 \\ \vdots \\ x_n \end{bmatrix} = P_0^{-1} \begin{bmatrix} x_1' \\ x_2' \\ \vdots \\ x_n' \end{bmatrix}, \quad \begin{bmatrix} z_1' \\ z_2' \\ \vdots \\ z_n' \end{bmatrix} = P_0 \begin{bmatrix} z_1 \\ z_2 \\ \vdots \\ z_n \end{bmatrix}.$

Statements (57) and (58) follow from (39). Statement (59) follows from (53) and (52). Putting these together, we have

$$B \begin{bmatrix} x_1' \\ x_2' \\ \vdots \\ x_n' \end{bmatrix} = \begin{bmatrix} z_1' \\ z_2' \\ \vdots \\ z_n' \end{bmatrix} = P_0 \begin{bmatrix} z_1 \\ z_2 \\ \vdots \\ z_n \end{bmatrix} = P_0 A \begin{bmatrix} x_1 \\ x_2 \\ \vdots \\ x_n \end{bmatrix} = P_0 A P_0^{-1} \begin{bmatrix} x_1' \\ x_2' \\ \vdots \\ x_n' \end{bmatrix}.$$

We conclude that (56) holds.

Remarks. These results have a converse. If $P_0 = (P_{ij})$ is an invertible $n \times n$ matrix and $\{Y^1, Y^2, \ldots, Y^n\}$ is a basis for V, then define X^j, $1 \leq j \leq n$, using (51). If $c_1 X^1 + c_2 X^2 + \cdots + c_n X^n = 0$, then
$0 = (P_{11}c_1 + P_{12}c_2 + \cdots + P_{1n}c_n)Y^1 + (P_{21}c_1 + P_{22}c_2 + \cdots + P_{2n}c_n)Y^2 + \cdots + (P_{n1}c_1 + P_{n2}c_2 + \cdots + P_{nn}c_n)Y^n$. From the independence of $\{Y^1, Y^2, \ldots, Y^n\}$ and the invertibility of P_0 we have $c_1 = c_2 = \cdots = c_n = 0$. Therefore $\{X^1, X^2, \ldots, X^n\}$ is a basis for V. This shows that given $\{Y^1, Y^2, \ldots, Y^n\}$, there is a one-to-one correspondence between bases $\{X^1, X^2, \ldots, X^n\}$ and invertible $n \times n$ matrices P_0. Formula (51) gives the relation between $\{X^1, X^2, \ldots, X^n\}$ and P_0.

Suppose that $\mathbf{V}$ is the space of arrows and $\{\mathbf{i}, \mathbf{j}, \mathbf{k}\}$ is a basis for $\mathbf{V}$ consisting of three mutually perpendicular vectors of length 1. Let $\mathbf{i}_1 = \mathbf{i} + \mathbf{j} + \mathbf{k}$, $\mathbf{j}_1 = \mathbf{i} - \mathbf{j} + \mathbf{k}$, and $\mathbf{k}_1 = \mathbf{i} + 2\mathbf{j} - \mathbf{k}$. Then

(60) $\{\mathbf{i}_1, \mathbf{j}_1, \mathbf{k}_1\}$ is a basis for $\mathbf{V}$.

This follows from the fact that

$$\text{rank} \begin{bmatrix} 1 & 1 & 1 \\ 1 & -1 & 1 \\ 1 & 2 & -1 \end{bmatrix} = 3.$$

[Here we have used (43) and the fact that $(1, 1, 1)$, $(1, -1, 1)$, and $(1, 1, -1)$ are the coordinates of $\mathbf{i}_1$, $\mathbf{j}_1$, and $\mathbf{k}_1$ with respect to $\{\mathbf{i}, \mathbf{j}, \mathbf{k}\}$.]

Let $\mathbf{v} = x\mathbf{i} + y\mathbf{j} + z\mathbf{k}$ and let $\mathbf{v} = x_1\mathbf{i}_1 + y_1\mathbf{j}_1 + z_1\mathbf{k}_1$. Then

(61)
$$\begin{bmatrix} x \\ y \\ z \end{bmatrix} = \begin{bmatrix} 1 & 1 & 1 \\ 1 & -1 & 2 \\ 1 & 1 & -1 \end{bmatrix} \begin{bmatrix} x_1 \\ y_1 \\ z_1 \end{bmatrix}.$$

This is formula (53), where P_0^{-1} is computed using (54). ($\{X^1, X^2, \ldots, X^n\}$ has been replaced by $\{\mathbf{i}, \mathbf{j}, \mathbf{k}\}$ and $\{Y^1, Y^2, \ldots, Y^n\}$ has been replaced by $\{\mathbf{i}_1, \mathbf{j}_1, \mathbf{k}_1\}$.) We have (we can use Theorem 12)

(62)
$$\begin{bmatrix} 1 & 1 & 1 \\ 1 & -1 & 2 \\ 1 & 1 & -1 \end{bmatrix}^{-1} = \begin{bmatrix} -\frac{1}{4} & \frac{1}{2} & \frac{3}{4} \\ \frac{3}{4} & -\frac{1}{2} & -\frac{1}{4} \\ \frac{1}{2} & 0 & -\frac{1}{2} \end{bmatrix}.$$

Thus we have

(63)
$$\begin{bmatrix} x_1 \\ y_1 \\ z_1 \end{bmatrix} = \begin{bmatrix} -\frac{1}{4} & \frac{1}{2} & \frac{3}{4} \\ \frac{3}{4} & -\frac{1}{2} & -\frac{1}{4} \\ \frac{1}{2} & 0 & -\frac{1}{2} \end{bmatrix} \begin{bmatrix} x \\ y \\ z \end{bmatrix}.$$

Now we let T be the linear operator on $\mathbf{V}$ defined by

(64) $T(x\mathbf{i} + y\mathbf{j} + z\mathbf{k}) = \dfrac{x + z}{2}\mathbf{i} + (y + z - x)\mathbf{j} + \dfrac{x + z}{2}\mathbf{k}.$

Then the matrix of T with respect to $\{\mathbf{i}, \mathbf{j}, \mathbf{k}\}$ is

(65) $\begin{bmatrix} \frac{1}{2} & 0 & \frac{1}{2} \\ -1 & 1 & 1 \\ \frac{1}{2} & 0 & \frac{1}{2} \end{bmatrix}.$

We can use (56) to find the matrix of T with respect to $\{\mathbf{i}_1, \mathbf{j}_1, \mathbf{k}_1\}$. This is

(66) $\begin{bmatrix} -\frac{1}{4} & \frac{1}{2} & \frac{3}{4} \\ \frac{3}{4} & -\frac{1}{2} & -\frac{1}{4} \\ \frac{1}{2} & 0 & -\frac{1}{2} \end{bmatrix} \begin{bmatrix} \frac{1}{2} & 0 & \frac{1}{2} \\ -1 & 1 & 1 \\ \frac{1}{2} & 0 & \frac{1}{2} \end{bmatrix} \begin{bmatrix} 1 & 1 & 1 \\ 1 & -1 & 2 \\ 1 & 1 & -1 \end{bmatrix} = \begin{bmatrix} 1 & 0 & 0 \\ 0 & 1 & 0 \\ 0 & 0 & 0 \end{bmatrix}.$

We conclude that

(67) $T\mathbf{i}_1 = \mathbf{i}_1, \qquad T\mathbf{j}_1 = \mathbf{j}_1, \qquad \text{and} \qquad T\mathbf{k}_1 = \mathbf{k}_1.$

Remarks. Note the simple form of (67). We shall describe a general method in Chapter 3 for expressing certain types of operators in diagonal form.

The formulas (51) through (54), and (56) are chiefly usable for computation, although (56) has some theoretical importance. We say that two $n \times n$ matrices A and B are *similar* if there is an invertible $n \times n$ matrix P_0 such that

$$B = P_0 A P_0^{-1}.$$

If A is the matrix of T with respect to the basis $\{X^1, X^2, \ldots, X^n\}$, then B is the matrix of T with respect to $\{Y^1, Y^2, \ldots, Y^n\}$, where Y^j is given by (54). Thus two matrices are similar if and only if they are both the matrix of the same operator T with respect to different bases.

The definition of the matrix of T can be extended to the case where T is a linear transformation of V into W. Let $\{X^1, X^2, \ldots, X^n\}$ be a basis for V and let $\{Z^1, Z^2, \ldots, Z^m\}$ be a basis for W. Let A be the $m \times n$ matrix defined by

(68) $TX^j = A_{1j}Z^1 + A_{2j}Z^2 + \cdots + A_{mj}Z^m.$

The matrix A is called the *matrix of T with respect to the ordered bases*

$\{X^1, X^2, \ldots, X^n\}$ and $\{Z^1, Z^2, \ldots, Z^m\}$. Formula (39) becomes

(69) $$TX = Y \quad \text{if and only if} \quad A \begin{bmatrix} x_1 \\ x_2 \\ \vdots \\ x_n \end{bmatrix} = \begin{bmatrix} y_1 \\ y_2 \\ \vdots \\ y_m \end{bmatrix},$$

where

$X = x_1 X^1 + x_2 X^2 + \cdots + x_n X^n$ and $Y = y_1 Z^1 + y_2 Z^2 + \cdots + y_m Z^m$.

Formulas like (56) can also be derived in this case using methods similar to our derivation of (56). Thus if $\{Y^1, Y^2, \ldots, Y^n\}$ is another basis for V and $\{U^1, U^2, \ldots, U^m\}$ is another basis for W, then

(70) $B = Q_0 A P_0^{-1}$, where B is the matrix of T with respect to $\{Y^1, Y^2, \ldots, Y^n\}$ and $\{U^1, U^2, \ldots, U^m\}$. $P_0 = (P_{ij})$ is the matrix given by $X^j = P_{1j} Y^1 + P_{2j} Y^2 + \cdots + P_{nj} Y^n$, $j = 1, 2, \ldots, n$, and $Q_0 = (Q_{ij})$ is given by $U^j = Q_{1j} Z^1 + Q_{2j} Z^2 + \cdots + Q_{mj} Z^m$.

There is no simple way to remember the formulas (51) through (54), (56), (69), and (70). We recommend that the reader carefully study the form of these formulas, and learn how to derive them. An examination of the low-dimensional cases will be helpful.

We have used the concept of coordinates to change questions about V into questions about R^n. How do these concepts agree with the concepts already given for R^n? Let E^i be the vector in R^n whose ith coordinate is one and whose other coordinates are zero. Then $\{E^1, E^2, \ldots, E^n\}$ is a basis for R^n. This basis (in the order given) is called the *standard basis* for R^n. Let $X = (x_1, x_2, \ldots, x_n)$. Then $X = x_1 E^1 + x_2 E^2 + \cdots + x_n E^n$, so that when we talk about coordinates of a vector in R^n we mean coordinates with respect to $\{E^1, E^2, \ldots, E^n\}$. Similarly the matrix of an operator T in R^n is just the matrix of T with respect to $\{E^1, E^2, \ldots, E^n\}$. When we discuss R^n we shall continue to omit mention of $\{E^1, E^2, \ldots, E^n\}$ when no confusion will result.

Note that when $\{Y^1, Y^2, \ldots, Y^n\}$ in (51) is the standard basis for R^n, then P_0 is the matrix whose jth column consists of the coordinates of X^j, with respect to $\{E^1, E^2, \ldots, E^n\}$. This follows easily from (55).

EXERCISES

1. Compute each of the following matrix products.

(a)
$$[2 \quad 1 \quad 3 \quad 1] \begin{bmatrix} -1 & 2 \\ 1 & 1 \\ 2 & 1 \\ 1 & 1 \end{bmatrix}$$

(b)
$$\begin{bmatrix} 3 & -1 & 0 \\ 6 & 1 & 2 \\ 1 & 1 & 1 \end{bmatrix} \begin{bmatrix} -1 & 0 & 0 \\ 2 & 1 & 1 \\ 1 & 0 & 1 \end{bmatrix}$$

(cont.)

(c)
$$\begin{bmatrix} 2 & 1 & \pi & \sqrt{2} \\ 0 & 3 & -\sqrt{2} & 1 \\ 0 & 1 & 1 & 1 \end{bmatrix} \begin{bmatrix} 6 & 1 & 1 & 1 & 1 & 1 \\ 0 & 0 & 0 & 0 & 1 & 1 \\ -1 & 2 & 1 & 0 & 1 & 1 \\ 3 & 1 & 0 & 1 & 0 & 0 \end{bmatrix}$$

(d)
$$\begin{bmatrix} 3 & -1 & 0 \\ 1 & 0 & 1 \\ 1 & 0 & 1 \end{bmatrix} \begin{bmatrix} -1 & 2 \\ -1 & 1 \\ 1 & 0 \end{bmatrix}$$

(e)
$$\begin{bmatrix} 0 & 0 & 1 \\ 0 & 1 & 1 \\ 2 & 2 & 1 \end{bmatrix} \begin{bmatrix} -1 & 1 & 0 \\ 2 & 1 & 0 \\ 1 & 1 & 0 \end{bmatrix}$$

(f)
$$\begin{bmatrix} 3 & -1 & 0 \\ 1 & 0 & 1 \\ 1 & 0 & 1 \end{bmatrix} \begin{bmatrix} 1 \\ 2 \\ 1 \end{bmatrix}$$

(g)
$$\begin{bmatrix} 0 & 0 & 0 & 1 \\ 0 & 0 & 0 & 2 \\ 1 & 2 & 3 & 4 \\ 0 & 1 & 0 & 1 \end{bmatrix} \begin{bmatrix} 0 & 1 & 2 & 3 \\ 0 & 0 & 1 & 2 \\ 0 & 0 & 0 & 1 \\ 1 & 0 & 0 & 0 \end{bmatrix}$$

(h)
$$\begin{bmatrix} 1 & 0 & 0 & 0 & 0 \\ 1 & 0 & 0 & 0 & 0 \\ 0 & 1 & 0 & 0 & 0 \\ 0 & 0 & 1 & 0 & 0 \\ 0 & 0 & 0 & 1 & 0 \end{bmatrix} \begin{bmatrix} 3 & 1 & 1 & 0 & 1 \\ 1 & 2 & 1 & 1 & -1 \\ 0 & 1 & 1 & 1 & 1 \\ 0 & 0 & 1 & 1 & -1 \\ 0 & 0 & 0 & 1 & 1 \end{bmatrix}$$

(i)
$$\begin{bmatrix} -1 & \frac{1}{2} & \frac{2}{3} \\ \frac{1}{4} & \frac{1}{7} & \frac{2}{9} \end{bmatrix} \begin{bmatrix} \frac{1}{3} & \frac{1}{6} \\ \frac{1}{4} & \frac{1}{7} \\ \frac{1}{5} & \frac{1}{8} \end{bmatrix}$$

(j)
$$\begin{bmatrix} -1 & 0.01 & 0.001 \\ 0.002 & 0.01 & 0.003 \\ 2.01 & 0.01 & -0.02 \end{bmatrix} \begin{bmatrix} 0 & 1 \\ 1 & 0 \\ 1 & 1 \end{bmatrix}$$

(k)
$$\begin{bmatrix} 3 & 0 & 0 \\ 0 & 1 & 0 \\ 0 & 0 & 2 \end{bmatrix} \begin{bmatrix} 3 & 2 \\ 1 & 1 \\ -1 & 0 \end{bmatrix}$$

(l)
$$\begin{bmatrix} 0 & 0 & 0 \\ 1 & 2 & 1 \\ 0 & 0 & 0 \end{bmatrix} \begin{bmatrix} 1 & 1 & 0 & 1 \\ 0 & 0 & 0 & 0 \\ 1 & -1 & 0 & 1 \\ 2 & 1 & 1 & 1 \end{bmatrix}$$

(m)
$$\begin{bmatrix} 3 & 1 & 0 \\ 0 & 2 & 0 \\ 0 & 0 & 1 \end{bmatrix} \begin{bmatrix} -1 & 1 & 1 \\ 0 & 1 & 0 \\ 0 & 0 & 0 \end{bmatrix}$$

(n)
$$\begin{bmatrix} 6 & 0 & 0 & 0 \\ 1 & 1 & 0 & 0 \\ -1 & 0 & 1 & 0 \\ 0 & 0 & 1 & 0 \end{bmatrix} \begin{bmatrix} 0 & 0 & 0 & 0 \\ 0 & 2 & 0 & 0 \\ 0 & 1 & 1 & 0 \\ 0 & 0 & 0 & 1 \end{bmatrix}$$

(o)
$$\begin{bmatrix} 3 & 1 & 0 \\ 0 & 1 & 2 \\ 0 & 0 & 1 \end{bmatrix} \begin{bmatrix} 3 & 0 & 0 \\ 1 & 1 & 0 \\ 0 & 2 & 1 \end{bmatrix}$$

(p)
$$\begin{bmatrix} 6 & -1 & 2 & 1 \\ 1 & 0 & 0 & 4 \\ 0 & 3 & 1 & 2 \end{bmatrix} \begin{bmatrix} 3 & 0 & 0 & 0 \\ 0 & 2 & 0 & 0 \\ 0 & 0 & 1 & 0 \\ 0 & 0 & 0 & -1 \end{bmatrix}$$

2. Show that the product AB depends linearly on the rows of A. In other words, if $C = AB$ and $A_{i_0 j} = aD_{i_0 j} + bE_{i_0 j}$, for i_0 fixed and $j = 1$, $2, \ldots, n$, then $C_{ij} = A_{i1}B_{1j} + A_{i2}B_{2j} + \cdots + A_{in}B_{nj}$, for $j = 1$, $2, \ldots, n$, if $i \neq i_0$ and $C_{i_0 j} = a(D_{i_0 1}B_{1j} + D_{i_0 2}B_{2j} + \cdots + D_{i_0 n}B_{nj})$ $+ b(E_{i_0 1}B_{1j} + E_{i_0 2}B_{2j} + \cdots + E_{i_0 n}B_{nj})$.

3. (a) Using the definition (3), establish (10), (17), and (18).

   (b) Using the definition (3), establish the identities $A(BC) = (AB)C$, $A(B + C) = AB + AC$, where A, B, and C are $n \times n$ matrices.

4. A matrix is said to be *strictly upper triangular* if $A_{ij} = 0$ for $i \geq j$.

  (a) Show that if $A_1, A_2, \ldots, A_n$ are strictly upper triangular $n \times n$ matrices, then $A_1 A_2 \ldots A_n = 0$.

  (b) Show that if A and B are $n \times n$, then AB is strictly upper triangular if A is upper triangular and B is strictly upper triangular.

5. Compute each of the following products.

  (a) $\begin{bmatrix} 1 & 0 & 0 \\ 0 & 3 & 0 \\ 0 & 0 & 2 \end{bmatrix}^{10}$

  (b) $\begin{bmatrix} 2 & 1 & 0 \\ -1 & 1 & 0 \\ 0 & 0 & 0 \end{bmatrix}^{2}$

  (c) $\begin{bmatrix} 0 & 1 & 2 & 1 \\ 0 & 0 & 1 & 1 \\ 0 & 0 & 0 & 1 \\ 0 & 0 & 0 & 0 \end{bmatrix}^{6}$

  (d) $\begin{bmatrix} 2 & 1 & 0 & 0 \\ 0 & 2 & 0 & 0 \\ 0 & 0 & 3 & 1 \\ 0 & 0 & 0 & 3 \end{bmatrix}^{3}$

6. Let

$$A = \begin{bmatrix} A_1 & O_1 \\ O_2 & A_2 \end{bmatrix}, \qquad B = \begin{bmatrix} B_1 & O_1 \\ O_2 & B_2 \end{bmatrix},$$

where A_1 and B_1 are $k \times k$, A_2 and B_2 are $(n - k) \times (n - k)$, O_1 is the $k \times (n - k)$ zero matrix, and O_2 is the $(n - k) \times k$ zero matrix. Show that

$$AB = \begin{bmatrix} A_1 B_1 & O_1 \\ O_2 & A_2 B_2 \end{bmatrix}.$$

This is a special case of Exercise 27.

7. Using Theorem 12, determine which of the following matrices are invertible. If the matrix is invertible, use the method of (31) through (36) to find its inverse.

  (a) $\begin{bmatrix} 1 & 2 & 1 & 0 & 1 \\ 1 & -1 & 0 & 1 & 2 \\ 4 & 2 & 8 & 3 & 8 \\ 3 & 1 & 6 & 1 & 3 \\ -1 & 0 & 1 & 1 & 2 \end{bmatrix}$

  (b) $\begin{bmatrix} 1 & 0 & 0 & 0 & 0 \\ 1 & 1 & 0 & 0 & 0 \\ 1 & 1 & 1 & 0 & 0 \\ 1 & 1 & 1 & 1 & 0 \\ 1 & 1 & 1 & 1 & 1 \end{bmatrix}$

  (c) $\begin{bmatrix} 6 & 0 & 6 \\ 0 & -1 & 2 \\ 1 & 2 & 1 \end{bmatrix}$

  (d) $\begin{bmatrix} 1 & 0 & 1 & 0 \\ 0 & 1 & 0 & 1 \\ 1 & 1 & 0 & 2 \\ 3 & -1 & 2 & 0 \end{bmatrix}$

  (e) $\begin{bmatrix} 2 & 1 & 0 & 6 & 1 \\ 1 & 2 & 1 & 0 & 3 \\ 1 & 0 & 0 & 1 & 1 \\ 0 & 1 & 1 & 2 & 1 \\ 3 & 1 & 0 & -1 & 1 \end{bmatrix}$

  (f) $\begin{bmatrix} -1 & 0 & 1 & 0 \\ 1 & 0 & 1 & 0 \\ 2 & 1 & 1 & 1 \\ 0 & -1 & 1 & 1 \end{bmatrix}$

8. For each of the following products, determine if the inverse of the product exists. If it does, find the inverse.

(a) $\begin{bmatrix} 3 & 1 & 0 \\ 0 & 1 & 2 \\ -1 & 0 & 1 \end{bmatrix} \begin{bmatrix} 1 & 0 & 0 \\ 0 & 2 & 0 \\ 0 & 0 & 3 \end{bmatrix} \begin{bmatrix} -1 & 0 & 2 \\ 0 & 1 & 1 \\ 0 & 0 & 3 \end{bmatrix}$

(b) $\begin{bmatrix} 0 & 0 & 1 \\ 0 & 1 & 0 \\ 1 & 0 & 0 \end{bmatrix} \begin{bmatrix} 2 & 0 & 0 \\ 0 & 1 & 0 \\ 0 & 0 & 2 \end{bmatrix} \begin{bmatrix} 1 & 2 & 3 \\ 0 & 1 & 2 \\ 0 & 0 & 1 \end{bmatrix}$

(c) $\begin{bmatrix} 2 & 1 & 3 \\ 0 & 1 & 1 \\ 0 & 1 & -1 \end{bmatrix} \begin{bmatrix} 2 & 0 & 1 \\ -2 & 0 & -1 \\ 1 & 3 & 1 \end{bmatrix} \begin{bmatrix} 2 & 1 & 6 \\ 0 & 1 & 1 \\ 0 & 1 & 0 \end{bmatrix}$

9. Let A be an $n \times n$ upper triangular matrix. Show that A is invertible if and only if $A_{ii} \neq 0$ for $i = 1, 2, \ldots, n$. Show that if A is invertible, then A^{-1} is upper triangular.

10. For which values of the unknowns are the following matrices invertible?

(a) $\begin{bmatrix} a & 1 & 1 & 1 \\ 1 & a & 1 & 1 \\ 1 & 1 & a & 1 \\ 1 & 1 & 1 & a \end{bmatrix}$

(b) $\begin{bmatrix} 1 & 1 & 1 & 1 \\ a & b & c & d \\ a^2 & b^2 & c^2 & d^2 \\ a^3 & b^3 & c^3 & d^3 \end{bmatrix}$

(c) $\begin{bmatrix} \lambda - 1 & 2 & 0 \\ -1 & \lambda + 1 & 0 \\ 0 & 0 & 1 \end{bmatrix}$

(d) $\begin{bmatrix} \lambda - 3 & 2 & 0 \\ 2 & \lambda - 1 & 0 \\ 0 & 0 & \lambda \end{bmatrix}$

11. Let A be an $n \times n$ matrix such that $A^2 + 2A + I = 0$. Show that A is invertible and find an expression for A^{-1}.

12. Let A be a 2×2 matrix such that $AB = BA$ for all 2×2 matrices B. Show that $A = aI$ for some real number a.

13. Let A be a 2×2 matrix such that $AB = BA$ for all *diagonal* 2×2 matrices B. Show that A must be diagonal.

14. An elementary row matrix is a matrix obtained from I by an application of a *single* row operation to I of the type used in Section 1.

(a) Show that the only 2×2 elementary row matrices are of the form

$$\begin{bmatrix} 1 & 0 \\ 0 & a \end{bmatrix}, \quad a \neq 0,$$

or

$$\begin{bmatrix} a & 0 \\ 0 & 1 \end{bmatrix}, \quad a \neq 0,$$

or

$$\begin{bmatrix} 1 & a \\ 0 & 1 \end{bmatrix}, \quad \text{or} \quad \begin{bmatrix} 0 & 1 \\ 1 & 0 \end{bmatrix}.$$

(b) Find the inverse of each of the matrices of part (a).

(c) Show that a row operation on an $m \times n$ matrix A can be accomplished by multiplying on the left of A by the corresponding elementary row matrix.

(d) Show that the inverse of an elementary row matrix is again an elementary row matrix.

(e) Show that a matrix is invertible if and only if it is the product of elementary row matrices. [*Hint:* Use parts (c), (d), and Theorem 12, to show that an invertible matrix is a product of elementary row matrices.]

15. The *trace* of an $n \times n$ matrix is defined to be the sum of the diagonal entries of the matrix. We usually denote this by $tr(A)$. Thus $tr(A) = A_{11} + A_{22} + \cdots + A_{nn}$.

(a) Show that $tr(A + B) = tr(A) + tr(B)$.

(b) Show that $tr(aA) = a tr(A)$.

(c) Show that $tr(AB) = tr(BA)$.

(d) Show that $tr(P_0 A P_0^{-1}) = tr(A)$ if P_0 is invertible.

(e) Show that if we define $tr(T)$ to be $tr(A)$, where T is a linear operator on V (V finite dimensional) and A is the matrix of T with respect to some basis, then $tr(T)$ is independent of the choice of basis.

(f) Show that $AB - BA$ can never equal I.

16. In each of the following spaces V, find the coordinates of the vector X with respect to the given ordered basis D.

(a) V is the space of expressions $ax + by + cz$. (See Exercise 2, Section 3.) $X = 3x + 7y - 6z$, $D = \{x, y, z\}$.

(b) V is the space of 2×2 real matrices. (See Exercise 2, Section 3.)

$$X = \begin{bmatrix} a & b \\ c & d \end{bmatrix},$$

$$D = \left\{ \begin{bmatrix} 1 & 0 \\ 0 & 0 \end{bmatrix}, \begin{bmatrix} 0 & 1 \\ 0 & 0 \end{bmatrix}, \begin{bmatrix} 0 & 0 \\ 1 & 0 \end{bmatrix}, \begin{bmatrix} 0 & 0 \\ 0 & 1 \end{bmatrix} \right\}.$$

(c) V is the space of 3×3 real matrices $A = (A_{ij})$ such that $A_{ij} = A_{ji}$ for $i = 1, 2, 3$ and $j = 1, 2, 3$. (The addition and scalar multiplication in V are given in Section 4.)

$$X = \begin{bmatrix} 1 & 0 & 1 \\ 0 & 1 & 2 \\ 1 & 2 & 1 \end{bmatrix}$$

$$D = \left\{ \begin{bmatrix} 1 & 0 & 0 \\ 0 & 0 & 0 \\ 0 & 0 & 0 \end{bmatrix}, \begin{bmatrix} 0 & 0 & 0 \\ 0 & 1 & 0 \\ 0 & 0 & 0 \end{bmatrix}, \begin{bmatrix} 0 & 0 & 0 \\ 0 & 0 & 0 \\ 0 & 0 & 1 \end{bmatrix}, \begin{bmatrix} 0 & 1 & 0 \\ 1 & 0 & 0 \\ 0 & 0 & 0 \end{bmatrix}, \begin{bmatrix} 0 & 0 & 1 \\ 0 & 0 & 0 \\ 1 & 0 & 0 \end{bmatrix}, \begin{bmatrix} 0 & 0 & 0 \\ 0 & 0 & 1 \\ 0 & 1 & 0 \end{bmatrix} \right\}$$

(*cont.*)

(d) V is the space of 3×3 real matrices $A = (A_{ij})$ such that $A_{ij} = -A_{ji}$, $i = 1, 2, 3$ and $j = 1, 2, 3$. [Addition and scalar multiplication as in part (c).]

$$X = \begin{bmatrix} 0 & -1 & -2 \\ 1 & 0 & -3 \\ 2 & 3 & 0 \end{bmatrix}$$

$$D = \left\{ \begin{bmatrix} 0 & 1 & 0 \\ -1 & 0 & 0 \\ 0 & 0 & 0 \end{bmatrix}, \begin{bmatrix} 0 & 0 & 1 \\ 0 & 0 & 0 \\ -1 & 0 & 0 \end{bmatrix}, \begin{bmatrix} 0 & 0 & 0 \\ 0 & 0 & 1 \\ 0 & -1 & 0 \end{bmatrix} \right\}$$

17. Let V be the space of Exercise 16(c). By choosing coordinates with respect to the basis given there, determine which of the following sets are independent.

(a) $\left\{ \begin{bmatrix} 1 & 2 & 0 \\ 2 & 0 & 0 \\ 0 & 0 & 1 \end{bmatrix}, \begin{bmatrix} 0 & 0 & 1 \\ 0 & 3 & 0 \\ 1 & 0 & 1 \end{bmatrix}, \begin{bmatrix} 1 & -2 & 0 \\ -2 & 0 & 0 \\ 0 & 0 & -1 \end{bmatrix} \right\}$

(b) $\left\{ \begin{bmatrix} 1 & 1 & 1 \\ 1 & 1 & 1 \\ 1 & 1 & 1 \end{bmatrix}, \begin{bmatrix} 1 & -1 & 1 \\ -1 & 1 & 1 \\ 1 & 1 & 1 \end{bmatrix}, \begin{bmatrix} 1 & 1 & -1 \\ 1 & 1 & 1 \\ -1 & 1 & 1 \end{bmatrix}, \begin{bmatrix} 1 & 1 & 1 \\ 1 & 1 & -1 \\ 1 & -1 & 1 \end{bmatrix} \right\}$

(c) $\left\{ \begin{bmatrix} 1 & 1 & 2 \\ 1 & 2 & 3 \\ 2 & 3 & 3 \end{bmatrix}, \begin{bmatrix} 3 & 3 & 2 \\ 3 & 2 & 1 \\ 2 & 1 & 1 \end{bmatrix}, \begin{bmatrix} 2 & 2 & 0 \\ 2 & 0 & -2 \\ 0 & -2 & -2 \end{bmatrix} \right\}$

18. Let V be the space of Exercise 16(d). By choosing coordinates with respect to the basis given there, determine which of the following sets are independent.

(a) $\left\{ \begin{bmatrix} 0 & 1 & 2 \\ -1 & 0 & 0 \\ -2 & 0 & 0 \end{bmatrix}, \begin{bmatrix} 0 & 1 & 0 \\ -1 & 0 & 1 \\ 0 & -1 & 0 \end{bmatrix}, \begin{bmatrix} 0 & 0 & -1 \\ 0 & 0 & 1 \\ 1 & -1 & 0 \end{bmatrix}, \begin{bmatrix} 0 & 3 & 1 \\ -3 & 0 & 0 \\ -1 & 0 & 0 \end{bmatrix} \right\}$

(b) $\left\{ \begin{bmatrix} 0 & 1 & 2 \\ -1 & 0 & 3 \\ -2 & -3 & 0 \end{bmatrix}, \begin{bmatrix} 0 & 1 & -2 \\ -1 & 0 & 3 \\ 2 & -3 & 0 \end{bmatrix}, \begin{bmatrix} 0 & 1 & 2 \\ -1 & 0 & -3 \\ -2 & 3 & 0 \end{bmatrix} \right\}$

19. Let V be the space of Exercise 16(a). Let T be the linear operator on V defined by $T(ax + by + cz) = (a - 3b)x + (b - 2c)y - z$. Find the matrix of T with respect to $\{x, y, z\}$.

20. Let V be the space of Exercise 16(c). Let T be the linear operator on V defined by $TA = AB + BA$, where

$$B = \begin{bmatrix} 1 & 1 & 0 \\ 1 & 2 & 0 \\ 0 & 0 & 3 \end{bmatrix}.$$

Find the matrix of T with respect to the basis given in Exercise 16(c).

21. Let **V** be the space of arrows. Let $\{\mathbf{i}, \mathbf{j}, \mathbf{k}\}$ be a basis for **V** consisting of three mutually perpendicular vectors of length 1.

    (a) Find the coordinates of $3\mathbf{i} + 2\mathbf{j} - \mathbf{k}$ with respect to the basis $\{3\mathbf{i} + \mathbf{j}, \mathbf{j} - \mathbf{k}, \mathbf{i} + \mathbf{j}\}$.

    (b) Let T be the linear operator on V defined by $T\mathbf{i} = 3\mathbf{i}$, $T\mathbf{j} = \mathbf{i} + \mathbf{j}$, $T\mathbf{k} = \mathbf{k}$. Find the matrix of T with respect to $\{\mathbf{i}, \mathbf{j}, \mathbf{k}\}$ and with respect to $\{3\mathbf{i} + \mathbf{j}, \mathbf{j} - \mathbf{k}, \mathbf{i} + \mathbf{j}\}$.

22. (a) Show that the polynomials

$$\frac{(t - 1)(t - 2)(t - 3)}{-6}, \qquad \frac{t(t - 2)(t - 3)}{2},$$

$$\frac{t(t - 1)(t - 3)}{-2}, \qquad \frac{t(t - 1)(t - 2)}{6}$$

are a basis for the space of polynomials of degree ≤ 3. [*Hint:* Find the coordinates of each of these polynomials with respect to $\{1, t, t^2, t^3\}$.]

    (b) Find the coordinates of $1 + t + t^2 + t^3$ with respect to the basis of part (a).

    (c) Let T be the operator defined by

$$Tf = f(0)\,\frac{t(t - 2)(t - 3)}{2} + f(1)\,\frac{(t - 1)(t - 2)(t - 3)}{6}$$

$$+ f(2)\,\frac{t(t - 1)(t - 2)}{6} + f(3)\,\frac{t(t - 1)(t - 3)}{2}.$$

Find the matrix of T with respect to the basis of part (a), and with respect to the basis $\{1, t, t^2, t^3\}$.

23. Using (51) or (52), find the coordinates of each of the following vectors with respect to the basis $\{(1, 0, 0), (1, 1, 0), (1, 1, 1)\}$. [*Hint:* See the last remark following (67).]

    (a) $(3, 2, -1)$ **(b)** $(-1, 1, 2)$

    (c) $(6, 0, -1)$ **(d)** $(0, 0, 1)$

24. Find the matrix of T with respect to the basis of Exercise 23, where [*Hint:* Use (56).]

    (a) $T(x, y, z) = (x - y, z, 0)$

    (b) $T(x, y, z) = (x, x + y, x + y + z)$

    (c) $T(x, y, z) = (2x + y - 3z, 3y - 3z, 0)$

25. Let V be the space of Exercise 16(d), and let W be the space of polynomials of degree ≤ 3. Let T be the linear transformation from V into W defined by

$$T\begin{bmatrix} 0 & a & b \\ -a & 0 & c \\ -b & -c & 0 \end{bmatrix} = at + bt^2 + ct^3.$$

(*cont.*)

(a) Find the matrix of T with respect to the pair of bases

$$\left\{ \begin{bmatrix} 0 & 1 & 0 \\ -1 & 0 & 0 \\ 0 & 0 & 0 \end{bmatrix}, \begin{bmatrix} 0 & 0 & 1 \\ 0 & 0 & 0 \\ -1 & 0 & 0 \end{bmatrix}, \begin{bmatrix} 0 & 0 & 0 \\ 0 & 0 & 1 \\ 0 & -1 & 0 \end{bmatrix} \right\}$$

and

$$\{1, t, t^2, t^3\}.$$

(b) Find the matrix of T with respect to the pair of bases

$$\left\{ \begin{bmatrix} 0 & 1 & 1 \\ -1 & 0 & 1 \\ -1 & -1 & 0 \end{bmatrix}, \begin{bmatrix} 0 & 1 & -1 \\ -1 & 0 & 1 \\ 1 & -1 & 0 \end{bmatrix}, \begin{bmatrix} 0 & 1 & 1 \\ -1 & 0 & -1 \\ -1 & 1 & 0 \end{bmatrix} \right\}$$

and

$$\left\{ \frac{(t-1)(t-2)(t-3)}{-6}, \frac{t(t-2)(t-3)}{2}, \frac{t(t-1)(t-3)}{-2}, \frac{t(t-1)(t-2)}{6} \right\}.$$

26. Let T be a linear transformation from V into W. Let V and W be finite dimensional. Show that there is a basis $\{X^1, X^2, \ldots, X^n\}$ for V and a basis $\{Y^1, Y^2, \ldots, Y^m\}$ for W such that if $A = (A_{ij})$ is the matrix of T with respect to this pair of bases, then $A_{ij} = 0$ if $i \neq j$, and $A_{ii} = 1$ for $i \leq$ rank (T), $A_{ii} = 0$ if $i >$ rank (T). [*Hint:* Use the bases constructed in the proof of Theorem 8.]

27. Suppose that

$$A = \begin{bmatrix} 3 & 1 & 0 \\ 2 & 1 & 0 \\ 1 & 2 & 1 \end{bmatrix} \quad \text{and} \quad B = \begin{bmatrix} 1 & 0 & 3 \\ 0 & 1 & 2 \\ 0 & 0 & 1 \end{bmatrix}.$$

We can simplify the computation of AB by suitably "subdividing" A and B into "submatrices" as follows. Write

$$A = \begin{bmatrix} \begin{bmatrix} 3 & 1 \\ 2 & 1 \end{bmatrix} & \begin{bmatrix} 0 \\ 0 \end{bmatrix} \\ [1 \quad 2] & [1] \end{bmatrix} \quad \text{and} \quad B = \begin{bmatrix} \begin{bmatrix} 1 & 0 \\ 0 & 1 \end{bmatrix} & \begin{bmatrix} 3 \\ 2 \end{bmatrix} \\ [0 \quad 0] & [1] \end{bmatrix}.$$

Then

$$AB = \begin{bmatrix} \begin{bmatrix} 3 & 1 \\ 2 & 1 \end{bmatrix}\begin{bmatrix} 1 & 0 \\ 0 & 1 \end{bmatrix} + \begin{bmatrix} 0 \\ 0 \end{bmatrix}[0 \quad 0] & \begin{bmatrix} 3 & 1 \\ 2 & 1 \end{bmatrix}\begin{bmatrix} 3 \\ 2 \end{bmatrix} + \begin{bmatrix} 0 \\ 0 \end{bmatrix}[1] \\ [0 \quad 0]\begin{bmatrix} 1 & 0 \\ 0 & 1 \end{bmatrix} + [1][1 \quad 2] & [0 \quad 0]\begin{bmatrix} 0 \\ 0 \end{bmatrix} + [1][1] \end{bmatrix}$$

$$= \begin{bmatrix} \begin{bmatrix} 3 & 1 \\ 2 & 1 \end{bmatrix} & \begin{bmatrix} 11 \\ 8 \end{bmatrix} \\ [1 \quad 2] & [8] \end{bmatrix} = \begin{bmatrix} 3 & 1 & 11 \\ 2 & 1 & 8 \\ 1 & 2 & 8 \end{bmatrix}.$$

(The use of "$=$" in the above is not quite correct. For example, A is a matrix whose entries are numbers and

$$\begin{bmatrix} \begin{bmatrix} 3 & 1 \\ 2 & 1 \end{bmatrix} & \begin{bmatrix} 0 \\ 0 \end{bmatrix} \\ [1 \quad 2] & [1] \end{bmatrix}$$

is a matrix whose entries are matrices. This should not cause confusion.) We wrote

$$A = \begin{bmatrix} A'_{11} & A'_{12} \\ A'_{21} & A'_{22} \end{bmatrix} \quad \text{and} \quad B = \begin{bmatrix} B'_{11} & B'_{12} \\ B'_{21} & B'_{22} \end{bmatrix},$$

where

$$A'_{11} = \begin{bmatrix} 3 & 1 \\ 2 & 1 \end{bmatrix}, \quad A'_{12} = \begin{bmatrix} 0 \\ 0 \end{bmatrix}, \quad A'_{21} = [1 \quad 2], \quad A'_{22} = [1],$$

$$B'_{11} = \begin{bmatrix} 1 & 0 \\ 0 & 1 \end{bmatrix}, \quad B'_{12} = \begin{bmatrix} 3 \\ 2 \end{bmatrix}, \quad B'_{21} = [0 \quad 0], \quad B'_{22} = [1].$$

Then

$$AB = \begin{bmatrix} A'_{11}B'_{11} + A'_{12}B'_{21} & A'_{11}B'_{12} + A'_{12}B'_{22} \\ A'_{21}B'_{11} + A'_{22}B'_{21} & A'_{21}B'_{12} + A'_{22}B'_{22} \end{bmatrix}.$$

This method of multiplication is called *block form multiplication* and is particularly useful when simple matrices, such as A'_{12} or B'_{11} in the above, appear. We say that we *partitioned* A between the second and third rows and the second and third columns. This method of multiplication is valid provided that the *column* partitioning of A and the *row* partitioning of B *coincide*. Use this method to partition each of the following matrices and compute the indicated product using block form multiplication

(a) $\begin{bmatrix} 1 & 0 & 0 & 1 \\ 2 & 6 & 1 & 0 \\ 1 & 0 & 3 & 1 \\ 0 & 1 & 0 & 2 \end{bmatrix} \begin{bmatrix} 2 & 1 & 1 & 0 \\ 1 & 1 & 0 & 1 \\ 0 & 0 & 1 & 0 \\ 0 & 0 & 0 & 1 \end{bmatrix}$

(b) $\begin{bmatrix} 1 & 0 & 1 & 3 & 1 \\ 6 & 2 & 0 & 1 & 0 \\ 0 & 0 & 1 & 2 & 1 \\ 0 & 0 & 0 & 1 & 0 \\ 0 & 0 & 0 & 0 & 1 \end{bmatrix} \begin{bmatrix} 2 & 1 & 3 & 0 & -6 \\ 0 & 3 & 1 & 0 & 1 \\ 0 & 0 & 0 & 1 & 0 \\ 0 & 0 & 0 & 1 & 0 \\ 0 & 0 & 0 & 0 & 2 \end{bmatrix}$

(c) $\begin{bmatrix} 0 & 1 & 1 & 1 & 1 & 1 \\ 0 & 0 & 1 & 1 & 1 & 1 \\ 0 & 0 & 0 & 1 & 1 & 1 \\ 0 & 0 & 0 & 0 & 1 & 1 \\ 0 & 0 & 0 & 0 & 0 & 1 \\ 0 & 0 & 0 & 0 & 0 & 0 \end{bmatrix}^2$

28. Write a flow diagram to determine if a 3×3 matrix is invertible and to compute its inverse.

NOTES

The method of reduction given in Sections 1 and 2 is usually called the Gauss elimination method. The adaptation of this method given in Exercise 9, Section 2, is usually called the Crout method. For further discussion of these and other methods, see Faddeeva [8]* and Lanczos [19, Chapter 2]. The row reduced echelon form is discussed in greater detail in Hoffman and Kunze [14, Chapters 1 and 2]. Thorough treatment of vector spaces over arbitrary fields, both finite and infinite dimensional, is given in Jacobson [15]. The study of linear transformations on such spaces is given in Jacobson [15] and Halmos [13, Chapter 2].

We have used matrices to assist in solving systems of equations and in computing on vector spaces. Matrices are also useful in other contexts. For example, see Guillemin [12, Chapter 10] for some of the uses of matrices in circuit theory. For elementary applications to differential equations see Kaplan [16, Chapter 6]; for more advanced questions see Gantmacher [11].

Linear transformations on infinite dimensional spaces arise in many physical problems. For an elementary treatment of one of these, called the Laplace transform, see Churchill [3]. An elementary and very algebraic treatment of ordinary and partial differential equations is given in Erdelyi [7]. A similar and more thorough study is in Friedman [10].

---

* Numbers are keyed to references at the end of the book.

CHAPTER 2

Length, Angle, and Volume

Section 1. THE DOT PRODUCT IN THREE DIMENSIONS

In Chapter 1 we concentrated our discussion on the algebraic properties of vector spaces. We were concerned with solutions to systems of equations, with subspaces, dimension, linear transformations, and matrices. All these topics were treated using the concept of linear combinations of vectors. In this chapter we shall discuss the concepts of length, angle, and volume. Our task in this and the next four sections is to describe a way to treat length and angle in terms of linear concepts. In this section we will study the three-dimensional case. Section 2 will introduce the general theory. Sections 3, 4, and 5 will use the general theory to develop further properties relating to perpendicularity, subspaces, and linear transformations. Sections 6 and 7 will discuss area and volume.

Let $\mathbf{V}$ be our vector space of arrows. Let $\{\mathbf{i}, \mathbf{j}, \mathbf{k}\}$ be a basis for $\mathbf{V}$ consisting of three mutually perpendicular vectors of length 1. (By choosing coordinates in $\mathbf{V}$ with respect to $\{\mathbf{i}, \mathbf{j}, \mathbf{k}\}$, we can extend our results to R^3. This will be done below.) Let $\mathbf{v} = x\mathbf{i} + y\mathbf{j} + z\mathbf{k}$. Then, using the Pythagorean law, we see that the length of $\mathbf{v}$ is $\sqrt{x^2 + y^2 + z^2}$. (See Fig. 1)

We denote the length of $\mathbf{v}$ by $|\mathbf{v}|$, so that we have $|\mathbf{v}| = \sqrt{x^2 + y^2 + z^2}$. The properties of $|\mathbf{v}|$ are

(1)

    (a) $|\mathbf{v}| > 0$ if $\mathbf{v} \neq \mathbf{o}$, $|\mathbf{o}| = 0$,

    (b) $|a\mathbf{v}| = |a|\,|\mathbf{v}|$ for any real number a,

    (c) $|\mathbf{v}_1 + \mathbf{v}_2| \leq |\mathbf{v}_1| + |\mathbf{v}_2|$.

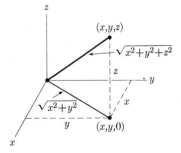

FIGURE 1

Property (1c) is called the "triangle inequality." It states that the diagonal of a parallelogram is not greater in length than the sum of any two adjacent sides, or, in other words, the sum of any two sides of a triangle is not shorter than the third side. (See Fig. 2.) The proof of this inequality will be left to the exercises.

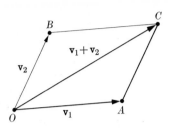

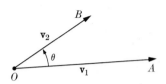

FIG. 2.   *OC* is no longer than *OA* + *AC*.   FIGURE 3

The concept of length is *not* linear; i.e., $|a\mathbf{v}_1 + b\mathbf{v}_2|$ is *not* in general equal to $a|\mathbf{v}_1| + b|\mathbf{v}_2|$. For example, we have

(2) $|\mathbf{v}_1 + \mathbf{v}_2| = |\mathbf{v}_1| + |\mathbf{v}_2|$ if and only if $\mathbf{v}_1 = a\mathbf{v}_2,$ $a \geq 0.$

Let $\mathbf{v}_1$ and $\mathbf{v}_2$ be two nonzero vectors in **V**. We define the *angle between* $\mathbf{v}_1$ *and* $\mathbf{v}_2$ as follows. Let O be the initial point of $\mathbf{v}_1$ and $\mathbf{v}_2$; let A be the terminal point of $\mathbf{v}_1$ and B the terminal point of $\mathbf{v}_2$. Then the angle between $\mathbf{v}_1$ and $\mathbf{v}_2$ is the angle AOB. (See Fig. 3.) We take this angle to be between 0 and π; i.e., if θ is the angle between $\mathbf{v}_1$ and $\mathbf{v}_2$, then $0 \leq \theta \leq \pi$. The following results should be clear.

(3)   If θ is the angle between $\mathbf{v}_1$ and $\mathbf{v}_2$, and θ_1 is the angle between $\mathbf{v}_1$ and $a\mathbf{v}_2$, then $\theta = \theta_1$, if $a > 0$ and $\theta = \pi - \theta_1$ if $a < 0$.

In terms of cosines, statement (3) gives $\cos\theta = \cos\theta_1$ if $a > 0$, and $\cos\theta = -\cos\theta_1$ if $a < 0$. In terms of cosines the following somewhat deeper result holds.

(4)   If θ_1 is the angle between $\mathbf{v}$ and $\mathbf{v}_1$, if θ_2 is the angle between $\mathbf{v}$ and $\mathbf{v}_2$, and if θ_3 is the angle between $\mathbf{v}$ and $\mathbf{v}_1 + \mathbf{v}_2$, then

$$|\mathbf{v}_1 + \mathbf{v}_2| \cos\theta_3 = |\mathbf{v}_1| \cos\theta_1 + |\mathbf{v}_2| \cos\theta_2.$$

The proof of (4) is left as an exercise. Note that (4) is a linear property! Instead of using (4), we use the following concept. If $\mathbf{v}_1$ and $\mathbf{v}_2$ are in **V**, we define the *dot product* of $\mathbf{v}_1$ and $\mathbf{v}_2$ to be the number $|\mathbf{v}_1|\,|\mathbf{v}_2|\cos\theta$, where θ is the angle between $\mathbf{v}_1$ and $\mathbf{v}_2$. We usually denote this by $\mathbf{v}_1 \cdot \mathbf{v}_2$, i.e.,

(5) $\mathbf{v}_1 \cdot \mathbf{v}_2 = |\mathbf{v}_1|\,|\mathbf{v}_2|\cos\theta$, where θ is the angle between $\mathbf{v}_1$ and $\mathbf{v}_2$.

How can we interpret (5) geometrically? $\mathbf{v}_1 \cdot \mathbf{v}_2$ is obtained by projecting $\mathbf{v}_1$ onto $\mathbf{v}_2$ and taking $|\mathbf{v}_2|$ times the length of this projection, with a plus sign if $0 \le \theta < \pi/2$ and with a minus sign if $\pi/2 < \theta \le \pi$. (See Fig. 4.)

If either $\mathbf{v}_1$ or $\mathbf{v}_2$ is $\mathbf{o}$ we take $\mathbf{v}_1 \cdot \mathbf{v}_2$ to be 0. The properties of the dot product are

(6)

(a) $\mathbf{v}_1 \cdot \mathbf{v}_2 = \mathbf{v}_2 \cdot \mathbf{v}_1,$

(b) $\mathbf{v} \cdot (a\mathbf{v}_1 + b\mathbf{v}_2) = a\mathbf{v} \cdot \mathbf{v}_1$
$+ b\mathbf{v} \cdot \mathbf{v}_2,$

(c) $(a\mathbf{v}_1 + b\mathbf{v}_2) \cdot \mathbf{v} = a\mathbf{v}_1 \cdot \mathbf{v}$
$+ b\mathbf{v}_2 \cdot \mathbf{v},$

(d) $\mathbf{v} \cdot \mathbf{v} > 0$ if $\mathbf{v} \ne \mathbf{o}.$

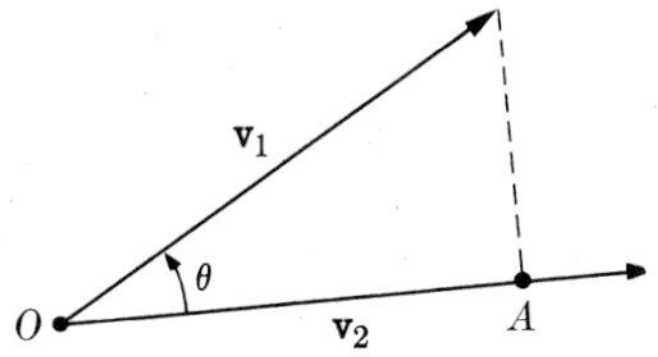

FIG. 4. The length OA is $|\mathbf{v}|\,|\cos \theta|$.

Property (6a) follows from (5), while (6b) and (6c) are consequences of (3), (4), and (5). Property (6d) follows from $\mathbf{v} \cdot \mathbf{v} = |\mathbf{v}|^2 \cos 0 = |\mathbf{v}|^2$.

Property (6b) tells us that $\mathbf{v} \cdot \mathbf{w}$, for $\mathbf{v}$ fixed, is a linear transformation from $\mathbf{V}$ into the real numbers. Property (6c) tells us that $\mathbf{w} \cdot \mathbf{v}$, for $\mathbf{v}$ fixed, is also a linear transformation from $\mathbf{V}$ into the real numbers. Thus the dot product is a real-valued linear transformation of one variable when the other is held fixed. This algebraic property will be essential in our discussions.

Many geometric concepts can be expressed in terms of the dot product. For example,

(7)

(a) $|\mathbf{v}| = (\mathbf{v} \cdot \mathbf{v})^{1/2}.$

(b) The angle between $\mathbf{v}_1$ and $\mathbf{v}_2$ is the angle θ such that

$$0 \le \theta \le \pi \quad \text{and} \quad \cos \theta = \frac{\mathbf{v}_1 \cdot \mathbf{v}_2}{|\mathbf{v}_1|\,|\mathbf{v}_2|}.$$

Thus we can define length and the angle between two vectors in terms of the dot product. Many other geometric properties can be stated succinctly in terms of the dot product.

Suppose that $\mathbf{v}_1$ is perpendicular to $\mathbf{v}_2$. Then the angle between $\mathbf{v}_1$ and $\mathbf{v}_2$ is $\pi/2$. We conclude that $\mathbf{v}_1 \cdot \mathbf{v}_2 = 0$. Conversely, if $\mathbf{v}_1 \cdot \mathbf{v}_2 = 0$, then $|\mathbf{v}_1|\,|\mathbf{v}_2| \cos \theta = 0$. Thus $\mathbf{v}_1 = \mathbf{o}$ or $\mathbf{v}_2 = \mathbf{o}$ or $\theta = \pi/2$. If we establish the convention that $\mathbf{o}$ is perpendicular to any other vector, then we have shown

(8) $\mathbf{v}_1 \cdot \mathbf{v}_2 = 0$ if and only if $\mathbf{v}_1$ and $\mathbf{v}_2$ are perpendicular.

Let θ be the angle between $\mathbf{v}_1$ and $\mathbf{v}_2$ and let d be the distance from the terminal point of $\mathbf{v}_1$ to the terminal point of $\mathbf{v}_2$. The cosine law gives

(9) $$d^2 = |\mathbf{v}_1|^2 + |\mathbf{v}_2|^2 - 2|\mathbf{v}_1|\,|\mathbf{v}_2| \cos \theta.$$

Since $d = |\mathbf{v}_1 - \mathbf{v}_2|$, we can rewrite (9), using (5), as

(10) $|\mathbf{v}_1 - \mathbf{v}_2|^2 = |\mathbf{v}_1|^2 + |\mathbf{v}_2|^2 - 2\mathbf{v}_1 \cdot \mathbf{v}_2.$

This is easily established using (5), (6), and (7a). We have

$$|\mathbf{v}_1 - \mathbf{v}_2|^2 = (\mathbf{v}_1 - \mathbf{v}_2) \cdot (\mathbf{v}_1 - \mathbf{v}_2) = \mathbf{v}_1 \cdot \mathbf{v}_1 - 2\mathbf{v}_1 \cdot \mathbf{v}_2 + \mathbf{v}_2 \cdot \mathbf{v}_2$$
$$= |\mathbf{v}_1|^2 + |\mathbf{v}_2|^2 - 2\mathbf{v}_1 \cdot \mathbf{v}_2.$$

A similar computation establishes

(11) $|\mathbf{v}_1 - \mathbf{v}_2|^2 + |\mathbf{v}_1 + \mathbf{v}_2|^2 = 2|\mathbf{v}_1|^2 + 2|\mathbf{v}_2|^2.$

This says that the sum of the squares of the diagonals of a parallelogram equals the sum of the squares of the sides. For this reason, (11) is usually called the *parallelogram law.*

The dot product can be expressed in terms of length as follows:

(12) $\mathbf{v}_1 \cdot \mathbf{v}_2 = \frac{1}{4}|\mathbf{v}_1 + \mathbf{v}_2|^2 - \frac{1}{4}|\mathbf{v}_1 - \mathbf{v}_2|^2.$

This is called the *polarization identity* and can be established by expressing $|\mathbf{v}_1 + \mathbf{v}_2|^2$ and $|\mathbf{v}_1 - \mathbf{v}_2|^2$ in terms of the dot product.

We can use the dot product to find the projection of one vector upon another. Let $\mathbf{v}$ be a vector of length 1. Then the projection of $\mathbf{v}_1$ onto $\mathbf{v}$ is equal to $(\mathbf{v}_1 \cdot \mathbf{v})\mathbf{v}$. [See Fig. 5. If OB has length 1 and AC is perpendicular to OC, then $\overrightarrow{OC} = (|\overrightarrow{OA}| \cos \theta)\overrightarrow{OB}$.]

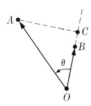   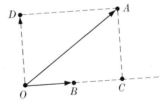

FIGURE 5   FIGURE 6

If $\mathbf{v} \neq \mathbf{o}$, then $\mathbf{v}/|\mathbf{v}|$ has length 1. The projection of $\mathbf{v}_1$ onto $\mathbf{v}$ should not depend upon the length of $\mathbf{v}$. Thus:

(13)   The projection of $\mathbf{v}_1$ onto $\mathbf{v}$ is $\left(\mathbf{v}_1 \cdot \dfrac{\mathbf{v}}{|\mathbf{v}|}\right) \dfrac{\mathbf{v}}{|\mathbf{v}|}.$

Let $\mathbf{w} = \mathbf{v}_1 - \left(\mathbf{v}_1 \cdot \dfrac{\mathbf{v}}{|\mathbf{v}|}\right) \dfrac{\mathbf{v}}{|\mathbf{v}|}.$

Then $\mathbf{w}$ should be perpendicular to $\mathbf{v}$. (See Fig. 6. The vector $\overrightarrow{OD} = \overrightarrow{OA} - \overrightarrow{OC}$ is perpendicular to $\overrightarrow{OB}$.)

Computation shows that $\mathbf{w} \cdot \mathbf{v} = \mathbf{v}_1 \cdot \mathbf{v} - (\mathbf{v}_1 \cdot \mathbf{v}/|\mathbf{v}|)(\mathbf{v}/|\mathbf{v}| \cdot \mathbf{v}) = 0$.
We have shown (see Fig. 6, where $\overrightarrow{OC} + \overrightarrow{OD} = \overrightarrow{OA}$) the following.

(14) If $\mathbf{v} \neq 0$, then $\mathbf{v}_1 = \mathbf{w} + \mathbf{w}_1$, where $\mathbf{w}_1 = (\mathbf{v}_1 \cdot \mathbf{v})\mathbf{v}/|\mathbf{v}|^2$ is parallel to $\mathbf{v}$, and $\mathbf{w} = \mathbf{v}_1 - (\mathbf{v}_1 \cdot \mathbf{v})\mathbf{v}/|\mathbf{v}|^2$ is perpendicular to $\mathbf{v}$.

If $\mathbf{v}_1 = \mathbf{w}_2 + \mathbf{w}_3$, where $\mathbf{w}_3 = a\mathbf{v}$ and $\mathbf{w}_2 \cdot \mathbf{v} = \mathbf{0}$, then $\mathbf{v}_1 \cdot \mathbf{v} = (\mathbf{w}_2 + \mathbf{w}_3) \cdot \mathbf{v} = \mathbf{w}_2 \cdot \mathbf{v} + a\mathbf{v} \cdot \mathbf{v}$.   Thus $a = (\mathbf{v}_1 \cdot \mathbf{v})/|\mathbf{v}_1|^2$, $\mathbf{w}_3 = \mathbf{w}_1$, and $\mathbf{w}_2 = \mathbf{w}$. This shows that $\mathbf{v}_1$ has a unique expression as the sum of a vector perpendicular to $\mathbf{v}$ and a vector parallel to $\mathbf{v}$. The vector $\mathbf{w}_1$ is called the *component* of $\mathbf{v}_1$ parallel to $\mathbf{v}$ and the vector $\mathbf{w}$ is called the *component* of $\mathbf{v}_1$ perpendicular to $\mathbf{v}$.

Now let $\{\mathbf{i}, \mathbf{j}, \mathbf{k}\}$ be a basis for $\mathbf{V}$ consisting of three mutually perpendicular vectors of length 1. If $\mathbf{v}_1 = x_1\mathbf{i} + y_1\mathbf{j} + z_1\mathbf{k}$ and $\mathbf{v}_2 = x_2\mathbf{i} + y_2\mathbf{j} + z_2\mathbf{k}$, then

(15) $$\mathbf{v}_1 \cdot \mathbf{v}_2 = x_1x_2 + y_1y_2 + z_1z_2.$$

This is established using the fact that $\mathbf{i} \cdot \mathbf{i} = \mathbf{j} \cdot \mathbf{j} = \mathbf{k} \cdot \mathbf{k} = 1$, $\mathbf{i} \cdot \mathbf{j} = \mathbf{i} \cdot \mathbf{k} = \mathbf{j} \cdot \mathbf{k} = 0$, and (6).

We can use (15) to define the *dot product* (or *standard inner product*) in R^3. We have

(16) $$(x_1, y_1, z_1) \cdot (x_2, y_2, z_2) = x_1x_2 + y_1y_2 + z_1z_2.$$

We define the dot product (or standard inner product) in R^2 by

(17) $$(x_1, y_1) \cdot (x_2, y_2) = x_1x_2 + y_1y_2.$$

These satisfy the laws

(18)
(a) $X \cdot Y = Y \cdot X$,
(b) $X \cdot (aY + bZ) = aX \cdot Y + bX \cdot Z$,
(c) $(aX + bY) \cdot Z = aX \cdot Z + bY \cdot Z$,
(d) $X \cdot X > 0$ if $X \neq 0$.

In (18), X, Y, and Z represent points in R^3 (or in R^2) with the dot product given by (16) [or by (17)]. We use the dot product on R^3 (or on R^2) to define length and angle in these spaces. For example, if $X = (3, 1, 2)$, then $|X| = (X \cdot X)^{1/2} = (3 \cdot 3 + 1 \cdot 1 + 2 \cdot 2)^{1/2} = 14^{1/2}$. If $Y = (1, 1, -6)$, then θ is the angle between X and Y, where

$$\cos \theta = \frac{X \cdot Y}{|X|\,|Y|} = \frac{3 \cdot 1 + 1 \cdot 1 + 2 \cdot (-6)}{(14)^{1/2}(38)^{1/2}} = \frac{-8}{(14 \cdot 38)^{1/2}}.$$

We say that X^1 is *perpendicular* to X^2 if $X^1 \cdot X^2 = 0$. Thus $(1, -1)$ is perpendicular to $(1, 1)$. The rules (10), (11), and (12), which were proved using (6) and (7a), also hold for these spaces [by using (18) and the definition of $|X|$]. Thus

(19)
$$\text{(a) } |X - Y|^2 = |X|^2 + |Y|^2 - 2X \cdot Y,$$
$$\text{(b) } |X - Y|^2 + |X + Y|^2 = 2|X|^2 + 2|Y|^2,$$
$$\text{(c) } X \cdot Y = \tfrac{1}{4}|X + Y|^2 - \tfrac{1}{4}|X - Y|^2.$$

The *projection* of X onto Y is defined to be $(X \cdot Y)Y/|Y|^2$ which is also called the *component* of X parallel to Y. The component of X *perpendicular* to Y is $X - (X \cdot Y)Y/|Y|^2$.

If $X = (3, 1, 2)$ and $Y = (1, 1, -6)$, then the component of X parallel to Y is

$$[3 \cdot 1 + 1 \cdot 1 + 2 \cdot (-6)] \frac{(1, 1, -6)}{38} = -\tfrac{4}{19}(1, 1, -6),$$

and the component of X perpendicular to Y is

$$X - (-\tfrac{4}{19})(1, 1, -6) = \tfrac{1}{19}(61, 23, 14).$$

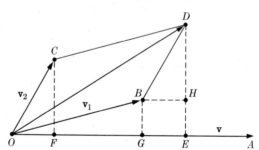

FIGURE 7

EXERCISES

1. (a) Show that the hypotenuse of a right triangle is longer than either leg.
   (b) Prove (1c). [*Hint:* In Fig. 2, drop a perpendicular from C to the line through O and A. Use the Pythagorean law and Exercise 1(a).]
   (c) Prove (2).
   (d) Prove (4). [*Hint:* In Fig. 7, show that $OF = BH = GE$.]
   (e) Prove (11) by writing both sides in terms of the dot product.
   (f) Prove (12).

2. Let $v_1 = 3\mathbf{i} + \mathbf{j}$, $v_2 = \mathbf{i} - \mathbf{j} + \mathbf{k}$, $v_3 = 5\mathbf{i} - 3\mathbf{j} + 2\mathbf{k}$. Find the following.
   (a) $v_1 + v_2$ **(b)** $v_1 \cdot 3v_3$
   (c) $v_2 \cdot (v_1 - v_3)$ **(d)** $v_2 \cdot v_1 - v_2 \cdot v_3$
   (e) The cosine of the angle between $3v_1$ and $v_2 - 2v_1$.

(f) The component of $\mathbf{v}_1$ perpendicular to $\mathbf{v}_2 - \mathbf{v}_3$.

(g) $|\mathbf{v}_2 - \mathbf{v}_1|^2 + |\mathbf{v}_2 + \mathbf{v}_1|^2$ **(h)** $|\mathbf{v}_2|^2 + |\mathbf{v}_1|^2$

(i) The projection of $\mathbf{v}_2$ on $6\mathbf{v}_1$.

(j) The projection of $\mathbf{v}_2$ on $3\mathbf{v}_1$.

(k) Show that $\{\mathbf{v}_1, 5\mathbf{v}_2 - \mathbf{v}_1, 13\mathbf{v}_3 - 18\mathbf{v}_2 + 27\mathbf{v}_1\}$ is a basis consisting of three mutually perpendicular vectors.

3. The physical concept of work can be interpreted as the dot product. If $\mathbf{F}$ is a vector representing a constant force, then the work done in moving an object along $\mathbf{v}$ from the initial to the terminal point of $\mathbf{v}$ is $\mathbf{F} \cdot \mathbf{v}$.

4. (a) Use the dot product to show that the diagonals of a parallelogram are perpendicular if and only if the parallelogram is a rhombus. (A *rhombus* is a parallelogram whose sides have the same length.)

(b) Let $\{\mathbf{i}, \mathbf{j}, \mathbf{k}\}$ be a basis for $\mathbf{V}$ consisting of mutually perpendicular vectors of length 1. Let M be a plane in $\mathbf{V}$, i.e., a parallel translation of a subspace of dimension 2. Let d be the distance from O to M and let $\mathbf{v} = a\mathbf{i} + b\mathbf{j} + c\mathbf{k}$ be a vector perpendicular to M. Write the equation of the plane M in terms of coordinates with respect to $\{\mathbf{i}, \mathbf{j}, \mathbf{k}\}$. (If $\mathbf{v}_1 = x\mathbf{i} + y\mathbf{j} + z\mathbf{k}$ has its terminal point in M, then the projection of $\mathbf{v}_1$ onto $\mathbf{v}$ has length d.)

(c) Let L be a line in $\mathbf{V}$, i.e., a parallel translation of a subspace of dimension 1. Let $\mathbf{v}$ be parallel to L and let $\{\mathbf{i}, \mathbf{j}, \mathbf{k}\}$ be as in (b). The direction cosines of L (in the direction of v) are the cosines of the angles which $\mathbf{v}$ makes with $\mathbf{i}$, $\mathbf{j}$, and $\mathbf{k}$. In terms of coordinates with respect to $\{\mathbf{i}, \mathbf{j}, \mathbf{k}\}$, show that

$$\frac{x - x_0}{l} = \frac{y - y_0}{m} = \frac{z - z_0}{n},$$

where $l^2 + m^2 + n^2 = 1$ is the equation of a line passing through the terminal point of (x_0, y_0, z_0) with direction cosines l, m, and n, respectively.

(d) In terms of coordinates with respect to $\{\mathbf{i}, \mathbf{j}, \mathbf{k}\}$, find the equations of the line through (x_0, y_0, z_0) which is perpendicular to the plane whose equation is

$$Ax + By + Cz = D.$$

(e) In terms of coordinates with respect to $\{\mathbf{i}, \mathbf{j}, \mathbf{k}\}$, write the equations for the distance from (x, y, z) to the line through (x_0, y_0, z_0) and (x_1, y_1, z_1). [*Hint:* Let $\mathbf{v} = (x - x_0)\mathbf{i} + (y - y_0)\mathbf{j} + (z - z_0)\mathbf{k}$ and $\mathbf{v}_1 = (x_1 - x_0)\mathbf{i} + (y_1 - y_0)\mathbf{j} + (z_1 - z_0)\mathbf{k}$. Find the component of $\mathbf{v}$ which is perpendicular to $\mathbf{v}_1$.]

5. Let $\mathbf{v}_1$, $\mathbf{v}_2$, and $\mathbf{v}_3$ be three mutually perpendicular nonzero vectors. Show that $\{\mathbf{v}_1, \mathbf{v}_2, \mathbf{v}_3\}$ is a basis for $\mathbf{V}$.

6. Find the projection of $\mathbf{v}$ onto the subspace spanned by $\mathbf{v}_1$ and $\mathbf{v}_2$.

Section 2.   INNER PRODUCTS ON VECTOR SPACES

In Section 1 we defined the dot product on $\mathbf{V}$ and then described several geometric properties in terms of this product. The dot product was a real-valued function of pairs $\mathbf{v}_1$ and $\mathbf{v}_2$ which satisfied the laws

(1)
$$
\begin{aligned}
&\text{(a)}\ \ \mathbf{v}_1 \cdot \mathbf{v}_2 = \mathbf{v}_2 \cdot \mathbf{v}_1, \\
&\text{(b)}\ \ \mathbf{v} \cdot (a\mathbf{v}_1 + b\mathbf{v}_2) = a\mathbf{v} \cdot \mathbf{v}_1 + b\mathbf{v} \cdot \mathbf{v}_2, \\
&\text{(c)}\ \ (a\mathbf{v}_1 + b\mathbf{v}_2) \cdot \mathbf{v} = a\mathbf{v}_1 \cdot \mathbf{v} + b\mathbf{v}_2 \cdot \mathbf{v}, \\
&\text{(d)}\ \ \mathbf{v} \cdot \mathbf{v} > 0 \quad \text{if} \quad \mathbf{v} \neq \mathbf{0}.
\end{aligned}
$$

These laws are given in (6) of Section 1. The properties (1) were all that we used in defining length, angle, and perpendicularity, and in deriving the various identities of Section 1.

If V is a vector space and we have a function defined for pairs of vectors in V which satisfies laws similar to (1), then we can carry over to V the geometric concepts and identities given in Section 1. We shall do so in this section.

Let V be a vector space. Then an *inner product* on V is a real-valued function, usually denoted by (X, Y), defined for pairs of vectors in V, which has the following properties:

(2)
$$
\begin{aligned}
&\text{(a)}\ \ (X, Y) = (Y, X), \\
&\text{(b)}\ \ (X, aY + bZ) = a(X, Y) + b(X, Z), \\
&\text{(c)}\ \ (aX + bY, Z) = a(X, Z) + b(Y, Z), \\
&\text{(d)}\ \ (X, X) > 0 \quad \text{if} \quad X \neq 0.
\end{aligned}
$$

Remarks. The laws (2) are the same as those of (1) in the case when $V = \mathbf{V}$ and $(\mathbf{v}_1, \mathbf{v}_2) = \mathbf{v}_1 \cdot \mathbf{v}_2$. We use the notation (X, Y) rather than $X \cdot Y$ only because the notation (X, Y) has become standard in most mathematical works. An inner product is also called a *scalar product*, while in the special case given in Section 1 it is usually called a dot product.

Property (2c) is derivable from (2a) and (2b). The properties (2) have suggestive names, (2a) being called the *symmetry* property, (2d) the *positive definite* property. Properties (2b) and (2c) are called the *bilinearity* property, (X, Y) being a linear transformation from V into the reals if X is fixed, from (2b), or if Y is fixed, from (2c).

We will give three examples of inner products and then extend the concepts of Section 1 to the general case.

The *standard inner product* (also called the *dot product*) on R^n is defined by

(3) $(x_1, x_2, \ldots, x_n) \cdot (y_1, y_2, \ldots, y_n) = x_1 y_1 + x_2 y_2 + \cdots + x_n y_n.$

This is an obvious generalization of (16) and (17) of Section 1. The function defined by (3) clearly satisfies (2). An example of an inner product on R^2 which is *not* the standard inner product is

(4) $((x_1, y_1), (x_2, y_2)) = x_1 x_2 + (x_1 + y_1)(x_2 + y_2).$

If we fix (x_2, y_2), then the right-hand side of (4) depends linearly upon (x_1, y_1) so that (2c) holds. Similarly, (2b) holds. We also have $((x_1, y_1), (x_2, y_2)) = x_1 x_2 + (x_1 + y_1)(x_2 + y_2) = x_2 x_1 + (x_2 + y_2) \times (x_1 + y_1) = ((x_2, y_2), (x_1, y_1))$, so that (2a) holds. Property (2d) follows from $((x_1, y_1), (x_1, y_1)) = x_1 x_1 + (x_1 + y_1)(x_1 + y_1) = x_1^2 + (x_1 + y_1)^2.$

Let V be the space of all continuous real-valued functions defined for $0 \le t \le 1$. An inner product of considerable importance is given by

(5) $(f, g) = \int_0^1 f(t)g(t) \, dt.$

That this relation satisfies (2) follows from the properties of the integral. For example, if $f(t_0) \ne 0$ for some t_0, $0 \le t_0 \le 1$, then $f(t)^2 > 0$ for t close enough to t_0. Thus

$$(f, f) = \int_0^1 f(t)^2 \, dt > 0.$$

The exercises will contain other examples of inner products.

Let (X, Y) be an inner product on V. The nonnegative real number $(X, X)^{1/2}$ is called the *length* (or *norm*) of X. We denote this by $|X|$, i.e.,

(6) $|X| = (X, X)^{1/2}.$

We have [compare with (1) of Section 1]

(7)
   (a) $|X| > 0$ if $X \ne 0$,
   (b) $|aX| = |a| \, |X|$ if a is a real number,
   (c) $|X + Y| \le |X| + |Y|.$

Property (7a) is a restatement of (2d) using (6). Property (7b) follows from $|aX| = (aX, aX)^{1/2} = (a^2)^{1/2}(X, X)^{1/2} = |a| \, |X|$. Property (7c) is called the *triangle inequality*. In order to prove this we need another inequality:

(8) $(X, Y)^2 \le |X|^2 |Y|^2.$

This is called the *Schwarz inequality*. We shall prove (8) below, but we will use (8) to establish (7c). We have $|X + Y|^2 = (X + Y, X + Y) = (X, X + Y) + (Y, X + Y) = (X, X) + (X, Y) + (Y, X) + (Y, Y) = |X|^2 + 2(X, Y) + |Y|^2 \leq |X|^2 + 2|X| |Y| + |Y|^2 = (|X| + |Y|)^2$. The first equality uses (6), the second uses (2b), the third uses (2c), the fourth uses (2a) and (6). The inequality comes from (8), and the last equality is simple real number arithmetic. We have shown $|X + Y|^2 \leq (|X| + |Y|)^2$. Taking square roots gives (7c).

The Schwarz inequality also allows us to define the angle between two vectors. If X and Y are not zero, (8) gives

$$(9) \qquad -1 \leq \frac{(X, Y)}{|X| |Y|} \leq 1.$$

There is exactly one real number θ, $0 \leq \theta \leq \pi$, such that $\cos \theta = (X, Y)/|X| |Y|$. This number θ is called the *angle between X and Y*.

The special case when $\theta = \pi/2$ is of interest, for then $(X, Y) = 0$. If we say that 0 is perpendicular to any vector then we can say [see (8) of Section 1]

(10) X and Y are *perpendicular* if and only if $(X, Y) = 0$.

Using the inner product, we have defined the length of a vector, the angle between two vectors, and perpendicularity. We can also define the projection of one vector upon another. [See (13) and (14) of Section 1.] This will be one of our fundamental tools.

Theorem 13. Let (X, Y) be an inner product on V. Let X and Y be in V and $Y \neq 0$. Then we can find a unique vector Z in V and a unique number a such that

(a) $X = aY + Z$,

(b) $(Z, Y) = 0$.

Furthermore $a = (X, Y)/|Y|^2$.

Proof. Suppose that $X = aY + Z$ and $(Z, Y) = 0$. Then $(X, Y) = (aY + Z, Y) = a(Y, Y) + (Z, Y) = a|Y|^2$. Thus $a = (X, Y)/|Y|^2$. Conversely, if $a = (X, Y)/|Y|^2$ and $Z = X - aY$, then $X = aY + Z$ and $(Z, Y) = (X - aY, Y) = (X, Y) - a(Y, Y) = (X, Y) - |Y|^2 \times [(X, Y)/|Y|^2] = 0$. Q.E.D.

The vector aY, where a is given by Theorem 13, is called the *projection of X on Y*, or the *component of X parallel to Y*. The vector Z given in Theorem 13 is called the *component of X perpendicular to Y*.

Remarks. Let us interpret these in our examples. The vectors $(1, 0)$ and $(0, 1)$ are perpendicular and have length 1 with respect to the standard inner product on R^2. With respect to the inner product given by (4) we have $((1, 0), (0, 1)) = 1$; $|(1, 0)| = ((1, 0), (1, 0))^{1/2} = 2^{1/2}$; and $|(0, 1)| = ((0, 1), (0, 1))^{1/2} = 1$. Thus the cosine of the angle θ between $(1, 0)$ and $(0, 1)$, with respect to the inner product of (4), is given by

$$\cos \theta = \frac{((1, 0), (0, 1))}{|(1, 0)|\,|(0, 1)|} = \frac{1}{2^{1/2}},$$

that is, $\theta = \pi/4$. Using this same inner product we have that the components of $(1, 0)$ are

$$\frac{((1, 0), (0, 1))}{|(0, 1)|^2} (0, 1) = (0, 1),$$

parallel to $(0, 1)$, and $(1, 0) - (0, 1) = (1, -1)$, perpendicular to $(0, 1)$.

This example should warn us that all the definitions above are given with respect to a given inner product on V. Another inner product on V gives rise to definitions of length, angle, and projection, which have different meaning. Thus an inner product gives a means of imposing a geometric structure, i.e., a means of using geometric language, upon a vector space. This imposed structure may be unrelated to the "natural" structure which a space might have. The point is that we can use our intuition about spaces like **V** in order to study other spaces. One easy way to do this is through the concept of inner product.

In our example (5), the two functions $\sin 2\pi t$ and $\cos 2\pi t$ are perpendicular, for we have

$$\int_0^1 \sin 2\pi t \cos 2\pi t \, dt = \int_0^1 \frac{\sin 4\pi t}{2} \, dt = 0.$$

The norm of $\sin 2\pi t$ is given by

$$\left(\int_0^1 (\sin 2\pi t)^2 \, dt \right)^{1/2} = \left(\int_0^1 \frac{1 - \cos 4\pi t}{2} \, dt \right)^{1/2} = \frac{1}{2^{1/2}}.$$

The projection of $2 \sin 2\pi t + 4 \sin 4\pi t$ upon $\sin 2\pi t$ is given by

$$(2 \sin 2\pi t + 4 \sin 4\pi t, \sin 2\pi t) \cdot \frac{\sin 2\pi t}{1/2} = 2 \sin 2\pi t.$$

The component of $2 \sin 2\pi t + 4 \sin 4\pi t$ perpendicular to $\sin 2\pi t$ is $4 \sin 4\pi t$.

The identities (10), (11), and (12) of Section 1 extend to the general case. For example,

(11) $$|X - Y|^2 = |X|^2 + |Y|^2 - 2(X, Y).$$

In analogy with (10) of Section 1, this is called the *cosine law*. We have $|X - Y|^2 = (X - Y, X - Y) = (X, X - Y) - (Y, X - Y) = (X, X) - (X, Y) - (Y, X) + (Y, Y) = |X|^2 - 2(X, Y) + |Y|^2$. Similarly we have the *parallelogram law* [see (11) of Section 1]

(12) $$|X - Y|^2 + |X + Y|^2 = 2|X|^2 + 2|Y|^2,$$

and the *polarization identity* [see (12) of Section 1]

(13) $$(X, Y) = \tfrac{1}{4}|X + Y|^2 - \tfrac{1}{4}|X - Y|^2.$$

The proofs of (12) and (13) are left as exercises.

Let us now prove the Schwarz inequality (8). If $Y = 0$, then (8) is trivial. If $Y \neq 0$, let $a = (X, Y)/|Y|^2$. Then $0 \leq |X - aY|^2 = (X - aY, X - aY) = (X, X) - a(Y, X) - a(X, Y) + a^2(Y, Y) = |X|^2 - (X, Y)^2/|Y|^2$. Thus $0 \leq |X|^2 - (X, Y)^2/|Y|^2$. This is the same as (8). To interpret (8) in terms of Theorem 13, let $X = aY + Z$, where $a = (X, Y)/|Y|^2$ and Z is as in Theorem 13. Then $|aY| = |(X, Y)|/|Y|$, so that (8) tells us that the length of the projection of X on Y is no greater than the length of X.

EXERCISES

1. Show that each of the following is an inner product on the given space.

   (a) $V = R^2$: $((x, y), (x_1, y_1)) = xx_1 + 12yy_1 + 3(xy_1 + x_1y)$

   (b) $V = R_3$: $((x, y, z), (x_1, y_1, z_1)) = xx_1 + yy_1 + zz_1 + \tfrac{1}{2}(yz_1 + y_1z)$

   (c) V is the space of polynomials of degree $\leq n$, a and b are real numbers with $a < b$, and $(f, g) = \int_a^b f(t)g(t)\, dt$.

   (d) V is the space of 2×2 matrices with $(A, B) = A_{11}B_{11} + A_{12}B_{12} + A_{21}B_{21} + A_{22}B_{22}$.

   (e) V is the space of $m \times n$ matrices with $(A, B) = A_{11}B_{11} + A_{12}B_{12} + \cdots + A_{1n}B_{1n} + A_{21}B_{21} + \cdots + A_{2n}B_{2n} + \cdots + A_{m1}B_{m1} + A_{m2}B_{m2} + \cdots + A_{mn}B_{mn}$.

   (f) V is the space of expressions of the form $ax^2 + by^2 + cz^2 + dx + ey + fz$ with $(ax^2 + by^2 + cz^2 + dx + ey + fz, a_1x^2 + b_1y^2 + c_1z^2 + d_1x + e_1y + f_1z) = aa_1 + bb_1 + cc_1 + dd_1 + ee_1 + ff_1$.

2. The following is an inner product which is of considerable use in infinite dimensional theory. Let V be the space of sequences $\{x_n\}$ of real numbers such that $\sum_{n=1}^{\infty} |x_n|^2$ converges. The inner product is defined by $(\{x_n\}, \{y_n\}) = \sum_{n=1}^{\infty} x_n y_n$. [This can be shown to converge by using the Schwarz inequality on R^n, i.e., $|\sum_{i=M}^{N} x_i y_i|^2 \leq (\sum_{i=M}^{N} |x_i|^2)(\sum_{i=M}^{N} |y_i|^2)$.]

SEC. 2]   INNER PRODUCTS ON VECTOR SPACES   121

3. Show that each of the following *does not* define an inner product on R^2; i.e., at least one of the properties of (2) fails to hold.

   (a) $\big((x, y), (x_1, y_1)\big) = |xx_1| + yy_1$
   (b) $\big((x_1, y), (x_1, y_1)\big) = xx_1 - yy_1$
   (c) $\big((x, y), (x_1, y_1)\big) = xx_1 + 2xy_1 + 3x_1y + 7yy_1$
   (d) $\big((x, y), (x_1, y_1)\big) = xx_1$

4. Prove (11).

5. Prove (12).

6. Let R^4 have the standard inner product. Let $X = (2, 1, 0, 1)$, $Y = (-3, 0, 1, 2)$, and $Z = (1, 2, 1, 1)$. Compute the following.

   (a) $(X + Y - 3Z, Z)$ **(b)** $(X + Y, X - Y)$ **(c)** $|Z|$
   (d) The projection of Z on $3Y$.
   (e) The projection of X on $-6Y$.
   (f) The components of $3X - Y$ with respect to $Z + Y$.
   (g) The cosine of the angle between X and Z.

7. Let X, Y, and Z be as in Exercise 6. Compute each of the quantities given there, using the inner product $\big((x_1, x_2, x_3, x_4), (y_1, y_2, y_3, y_4)\big) = 2x_1y_1 + (x_1 + x_2)(y_1 + y_2) + (x_1 + x_2 + x_3)(y_1 + y_2 + y_3) + 2x_4y_4$.

8. Let V be the space of polynomials of degree ≤ 5. Let $X = 1 - t$, $Y = 3t + 2t^2$, and $Z = t^5$. Let $(f, g) = \int_0^1 f(t)g(t)\, dt$. Compute the following.

   (a) $(X + Y - 3Z, Z)$ **(b)** $(X + Y, X - Y)$ **(c)** $|Z|$
   (d) The projection of Z on $3Y$.
   (e) The projection of X on $-6Y$.
   (f) The components of $3X - Y$ with respect to $Z + Y$.
   (g) The cosine of the angle between X and Z.

9. Let (X, Y) be an inner product on V. Show that the components of X with respect to Y are independent of the length of Y. [*Hint:* Show that the components of X with respect to aY are the same as the components with respect to bY.]

10. (a) Show that $x^2 + bxy + cy^2 > 0$ for all $(x, y) \neq (0, 0)$ if and only if $b^2 - 4c < 0$. [*Hint:* Complete the square.]
   (b) Use (a) to prove the Schwarz inequality. [*Hint:* Expand $0 \leq |X - aY|^2$ using (2), then use Exercise 10(a).]

11. Let V be the space of (5) with the inner product given there.

   (a) Show that $\sin 2n\pi t$ is orthogonal to $\sin 2m\pi t$ if $n \neq m$.
   (b) Find the components of $f(t) = t$ with respect to $\sin 2\pi t$.

12. Let $\{X^1, X^2, \ldots, X^n\}$ be a basis for V. Let $X = a_1X^1 + a_2X^2 + \cdots + a_nX^n$, and let $Y = b_1X^1 + b_2X^2 + \cdots + b_nX^n$. Define (X, Y) to be $a_1b_1 + a_2b_2 + \cdots + a_nb_n$. Show that (X, Y) is an inner product on V.

13. Suppose R^3 has the standard inner product and let X and Y be vectors in R^3.

(a) Write a flow diagram to find the components of X with respect to Y.

(b) Write a flow diagram to determine if X is perpendicular to Y.

Section 3.   ORTHOGONALITY

In this section we shall discuss the concept of perpendicularity, or, as it is more commonly called, orthogonality. We shall assume that V is an inner product space, i.e., a vector space with an inner product. When we discuss R^n, we shall assume, unless stated otherwise, that this inner product is the standard inner product. We shall give a method for constructing a basis for V (when V is finite dimensional) consisting of mutually perpendicular vectors of length 1.

For ease of reference we list here two examples from Section 2. Let V be the space of continuous real-valued functions defined for $0 \le t \le 1$, with the inner product [see (5) of Section 2]

(1)
$$(f, g) = \int_0^1 f(t)g(t) \, dt.$$

Another inner product which will be helpful in clarifying our ideas is defined on R^2 by [see (4) of Section 2]

(2) $((x_1, y_1), (x_2, y_2)) = x_1 x_2 + (x_1 + y_1)(x_2 + y_2).$

Now let V be a vector space and let (X, Y) be an inner product on V. A set of vectors D contained in V is said to be an *orthogonal set* if $(X, Y) = 0$ for each X and Y in D such that $X \ne Y$. D is said to be *orthonormal* if D is an orthogonal set and $|X| = 1$ for each X in D.

Remarks. The set $\{\mathbf{i}, \mathbf{j}, \mathbf{k}\}$ used in Section 1 is an orthonormal set in **V**. The set $\{(0, 0), (1, 2), (2, -1)\}$ is an orthogonal set but *not* an orthonormal set in R^2 (using the standard inner product). The set $\{\sin \pi t, \sin 2\pi t, \ldots, \sin n\pi t, \ldots\}$ is an orthogonal set in the space of (1). This follows from

(3) $\int_0^1 \sin k\pi t \sin n\pi t \, dt = 0, \qquad n \ne k.$

The set $\{(1, 2), (2, -1), (3, 7)\}$ is *not* orthogonal in R^2 (using the standard inner product). The set $\{(1, 0, 0, 0), (0, 1/\sqrt{2}, 1/\sqrt{2}, 0), (0, 1/\sqrt{2}, -1/\sqrt{2}, 0)\}$ is an orthonormal set in R^4.

Now suppose that R^2 has the inner product given by (2). Then the set $\{(1, 0), (0, 1)\}$ is *not* an orthogonal set, while the set $\{(1, -1), (0, 1)\}$ is an orthonormal set.

Clearly 0 cannot be in an orthonormal set. The definition of orthogonal set, however, does not exclude 0. If D is an orthogonal set, not containing 0, then we can divide each vector in D by its length and obtain an orthonormal set. For example, $\{(2, 1), (1, -2)\}$ is orthogonal but not orthonormal in R^2 (using the standard inner product). The set $\{(2/\sqrt{5}, 1/\sqrt{5}), (1/\sqrt{5}, -2/\sqrt{5})\}$ is an orthonormal set in R^2.

Most of our results can be stated for orthogonal sets or for orthonormal sets. Due to the simplicity obtained when the sets are orthonormal, we shall generally concentrate our attention on such sets. Our first result is geometrically obvious in $\mathbf{V}$ or R^3.

(4) If D is an orthonormal set in V, then D is independent.

For suppose that $c_1 X^1 + c_2 X^2 + \cdots + c_k X^k = 0$, where $\{X^1, X^2, \ldots, X^k\}$ is contained in an orthonormal set D. Then $0 = (0, X^1) = (c_1 X^1 + c_2 X^2 + \cdots + c_k X^k, X^1) = c_1(X^1, X^1) + c_2(X^2, X^1) + \cdots + c_k(X^k, X^1)$. But $(X^1, X^1) = 1$, and $(X^2, X^1) = (X^3, X^1) = \cdots = (X^k, X^1) = 0$. Thus $c_1 = 0$. In general, taking the inner product of $0 = c_1 X^1 + c_2 X^2 + \cdots c_k X^k$ with X^i gives $c_i = 0$, $i = 1, 2, \ldots, k$. This proves (4). For orthogonal sets (4) takes the following form.

(5) If D is an orthogonal set and 0 is not in D, then D is independent.

These results have many corollaries, all easily established using (4) or (5) and the results of Section 3, Chapter 1.

(6) If dim $V = n$, then an orthonormal set D (or an orthogonal set not containing 0) contains at most n vectors.

(7) If dim $V = n$, then an orthonormal set D (or an orthogonal set not containing 0) which contains n vectors, is a basis for V.

An orthonormal set D which is a basis for V is called an *orthonormal basis*. An orthogonal set D which is a basis for V is called an *orthogonal basis*. In terms of an orthonormal basis we can obtain the coordinates of a vector in simple form. Let $\{X^1, X^2, \ldots, X^n\}$ be an orthonormal basis for V [relative to the inner product (X, Y)]. Let X be in V. Then

(8) $$X = (X, X^1)X^1 + (X, X^2)X^2 + \cdots + (X, X^n)X^n.$$

Since $\{X^1, X^2, \ldots, X^n\}$ is a basis for V, we know that $X = a_1 X^1 + a_2 X^2 + \cdots + a_n X^n$. We take the inner product with respect to X^1. Then $(X, X^1) = (a_1 X^1 + a_2 X^2 + \cdots + a_n X^n, X^1) = a_1(X^1, X^1) + a_2(X^2, X^1) + \cdots + a_n(X^n, X^1)$. But $(X^1, X^1) = 1$ and $(X^i, X^1) = 0$ if $i = 2, 3, \ldots, n$. Thus $a_1 = (X, X^1)$. Similarly, $a_i = (X, X^i)$ for $i = 2, 3, \ldots, n$. This establishes (8).

The form (8) makes computation of coordinates very simple. To find the ith coordinate of X with respect to $\{X^1, X^2, \ldots, X^n\}$ [where $\{X^1, X^2, \ldots, X^n\}$ is an orthonormal basis with respect to the inner product (X, Y)] we merely project X onto X^i, obtaining $(X, X^i)X^i$; the ith coordinate is then (X, X^i). Note that if we are given that $\{X^1, X^2, \ldots, X^n\}$ is an orthonormal basis with respect to (X, Y), then the ith coordinate of X depends only on the inner product and X^i.

If $\{X^1, X^2, \ldots, X^n\}$ is an orthogonal basis for V, then (8) takes the form

$$(9) \qquad X = \frac{(X, X^1)}{|X^1|^2} X^1 + \frac{(X, X^2)}{|X^2|^2} X^2 + \cdots + \frac{(X, X^n)}{|X^n|^2} X^n.$$

The basis $\{\mathbf{i}, \mathbf{j}, \mathbf{k}\}$ used in Section 1 for $\mathbf{V}$ is an orthonormal basis for $\mathbf{V}$. So is

$$\left\{ \frac{\mathbf{i} + \mathbf{j}}{\sqrt{2}}, \frac{\mathbf{i} - \mathbf{j}}{\sqrt{2}}, \mathbf{k} \right\}.$$

If $\mathbf{v} = x\mathbf{i} + y\mathbf{j} + z\mathbf{k}$, then

$$\mathbf{v} = \left(\mathbf{v} \cdot \frac{\mathbf{i} + \mathbf{j}}{\sqrt{2}} \right) \frac{\mathbf{i} + \mathbf{j}}{\sqrt{2}} + \left(\mathbf{v} \cdot \frac{\mathbf{i} - \mathbf{j}}{\sqrt{2}} \right) \frac{\mathbf{i} - \mathbf{j}}{\sqrt{2}} + (\mathbf{v} \cdot \mathbf{k})\mathbf{k}$$

$$= \left(\frac{x + y}{\sqrt{2}} \right) \frac{\mathbf{i} + \mathbf{j}}{\sqrt{2}} + \left(\frac{x - y}{\sqrt{2}} \right) \frac{\mathbf{i} - \mathbf{j}}{\sqrt{2}} + z\mathbf{k}.$$

If R^2 has the inner product given by (2), then $\{(1, -1), (0, 1)\}$ is an orthonormal basis. We have

$$(x, y) = ((x, y), (1, -1))(1, -1) + ((x, y), (0, 1))(0, 1)$$
$$= (x + (x + y)(1 - 1))(1, -1) + (x \cdot 0 + (x + y)(0 + 1))(0, 1)$$
$$= x(1, -1) + (x + y)(0, 1).$$

How can we find an orthogonal or orthonormal basis for V? We shall describe a process, which is basically geometric, for constructing such a basis when we are given any basis for V.

The set $\{(1, 2, 2), (-1, 0, 1), (2, 1, 0)\}$ is a basis for R^3 but is clearly not orthonormal with respect to the standard inner product. Let $Y^1 = (1, 2, 2)$. The vector $(-1, 0, 1)$ is *not* perpendicular to Y^1. We can, however, take its component perpendicular to Y^1. Call this Y^2. We have

$$Y^2 = (-1, 0, 1) - \frac{((-1, 0, 1), (1, 2, 2))}{|(1, 2, 2)|^2} (1, 2, 2) = (-\tfrac{10}{9}, -\tfrac{2}{9}, \tfrac{7}{9}).$$

Then Y^1 and Y^2 are perpendicular because of the way we constructed Y^2. $(2, 1, 0)$ is not perpendicular to Y^1 or to Y^2. We project $(2, 1, 0)$ onto

Y^1 and onto Y^2 and subtract these projections from $(2, 1, 0)$. Call this vector Y^3. Then Y^3 is perpendicular to both Y^1 and Y^2. We have

$$Y^3 = (2, 1, 0) - \frac{((2, 1, 0), (1, 2, 2))}{|(1, 2, 2)|^2} (1, 2, 2)$$

$$- \frac{((2, 1, 0), (-\frac{10}{9}, -\frac{2}{9}, \frac{7}{9}))}{|(-\frac{10}{9}, -\frac{2}{9}, \frac{7}{9})|^2} (-\frac{10}{9}, -\frac{2}{9}, \frac{7}{9})$$

$$= (\tfrac{2}{17}, -\tfrac{3}{17}, \tfrac{2}{17}).$$

Thus $\{Y^1, Y^2, Y^3\}$ is an orthogonal set not containing $(0, 0, 0)$ and by (7) is a basis for R^3. By construction, Y^1 is a linear combination of $\{(1, 2, 2)\}$, Y^2 is a linear combination of $\{(1, 2, 2), (-1, 0, 1)\}$, and Y^3 is a linear combination of $\{(1, 2, 2), (-1, 0, 1), (2, 1, 0)\}$. Let

$$Z^1 = \frac{Y^1}{|Y^1|}, \qquad Z^2 = \frac{Y^2}{|Y^2|}, \qquad \text{and} \qquad Z^3 = \frac{Y^3}{|Y^3|}.$$

Then $\{Z^1, Z^2, Z^3\}$ is an orthonormal basis for R^3; Z^1 is a multiple of $(1, 2, 2)$; Z^2 is a linear combination of $\{(1, 2, 2), (-1, 0, 1)\}$; and Z^3 is a linear combination of $\{(1, 2, 2), (-1, 0, 1), (2, 1, 0)\}$. We have

$$Z^1 = (\tfrac{1}{3}, \tfrac{2}{3}, \tfrac{2}{3}), \qquad Z^2 = \frac{9}{\sqrt{153}} (-\tfrac{10}{9}, -\tfrac{2}{9}, \tfrac{7}{9});$$

and

$$Z^3 = \sqrt{17} (\tfrac{2}{17}, -\tfrac{3}{17}, \tfrac{2}{17}).$$

This process is called the *Gram-Schmidt process* and easily generalizes.

Theorem 14. Let (X, Y) be an inner product on V. Let $\{X^1, X^2, \ldots, X^n\}$ be a basis for V. Then there is an orthonormal basis $\{Z^1, Z^2, \ldots, Z^n\}$ for V such that Z^i is a linear combination of $\{X^1, X^2, \ldots, X^i\}$ for each i, $1 \leq i \leq n$.

Proof. We proceed as above. Let

$$Y^1 = X^1,$$

$$Y^2 = X^2 - \frac{(X^2, Y^1)}{|Y^1|^2} Y^1,$$

$$Y^3 = X^3 - \frac{(X^3, Y^2)}{|Y^2|^2} Y^2 - \frac{(X^3, Y^1)}{|Y^1|^2} Y^1, \ldots,$$

$$Y^n = X^n - \frac{(X^n, Y^{n-1})}{|Y^{n-1}|^2} Y^{n-1} - \cdots - \frac{(X^n, Y^1)}{|Y^1|^2} Y^1.$$

For each i, $1 \leq i \leq n$, let M_i be the subspace spanned by $\{X^1, X^2,$ $\ldots, X^i\}$. Then Y^i by construction is in M_i for $1 \leq i \leq n$. X^{i+1} is not in M_i, for $1 \leq i \leq (n-1)$. Clearly $Y^1 \neq 0$. If $Y^{i+1} = 0$, then

$$X^{i+1} = \frac{(X^{i+1}, Y^i)}{|Y^i|^2} Y^i + \cdots + \frac{(X^{i+1}, Y^1)}{|Y^1|^2} Y^1.$$

The right-hand side of this expression is in M_i, while the left-hand side is not in M_i. We conclude that $Y^{i+1} \neq 0$ for $1 \leq i \leq (n-1)$. In other words $Y^i \neq 0$ for $1 \leq i \leq n$.

By construction $\{Y^1, Y^2, \ldots, Y^n\}$ is an orthogonal set and we have shown that $Y^i \neq 0$, for $1 \leq i \leq n$. Let

$$Z^i = \frac{|Y^i|}{Y^i}, \qquad i = 1, 2, \ldots, n.$$

Then $\{Z^1, Z^2, \ldots, Z^n\}$ is an orthonormal set which by (7) is a basis for V. Also Z^i is in M^i, since Y^i is in M_i, for $i = 1, 2, \ldots, n$. Q.E.D.

The fact that Z^i is in M_i has an interesting matrix analog which we will now give. Since $\{Z^1, Z^2, \ldots, Z^i\}$ is in M_i and dim $M_i = i$, we conclude that $\{Z^1, Z^2, \ldots, Z^i\}$ is an orthonormal basis for M_i, for $i = 1, 2, \ldots, n$. In particular we have

(10) X^i is a linear combination of $\{Z^1, Z^2, \ldots, Z^i\}$ for $i = 1, 2, \ldots, n$.

Now let A be an invertible $n \times n$ matrix. Let

$$X^j = \begin{bmatrix} A_{1j} \\ A_{2j} \\ \vdots \\ A_{nj} \end{bmatrix}, \qquad j = 1, 2, \ldots, n.$$

Then considering these as vectors in R^n, we have that $\{X^1, X^2, \ldots, X^n\}$ is a basis for R^n. We apply Theorem 14, obtaining $\{Z^1, Z^2, \ldots, Z^n\}$, an orthonormal basis for R^n. Let U be the $n \times n$ matrix whose jth column is Z^j, $j = 1, 2, \ldots, n$. Then the columns of U are orthonormal when considered as vectors in R^n (using the standard inner product on R^n). Applying (10), gives

(11) $X^i = d_{1i}Z^1 + d_{2i}Z^2 + \cdots + d_{ii}Z^i, \qquad i = 1, 2, \ldots, n.$

Let $\Delta = (d_{ij})$, where $d_{ij} = 0$ if $i > j$ and d_{ij} is given by (11) if $i \leq j$. Then, from (11)

(12) $A = U\Delta.$

We have shown the following.

(13)   If A is an invertible $n \times n$ matrix, then $A = U\Delta$, where the columns of U are orthonormal (when considered as vectors in R^n, using the standard inner product on R^n) and Δ is upper triangular. Furthermore, the entries on the diagonal of Δ are nonzero.

To show that the entries on the diagonal of Δ are nonzero we must show that $d_{ii} \neq 0$, $i = 1, 2, \ldots, n$. If $d_{ii} = 0$ for some i, $1 \leq i \leq n$, then X^i is a linear combination of $\{Z^1, Z^2, \ldots, Z^{i-1}\}$; i.e., X^i is in M_{i-1} (the subspace given in the proof of Theorem 14). This cannot happen since $\{X^1, X^2, \ldots, X^i\}$ is an independent set, and the set $\{X^1, X^2, \ldots, X^{i-1}\}$ is a basis for M_{i-1}. This completes the proof of (13), which is just the matrix analog of Theorem 14.

An example will clarify (13). The matrix

$$\begin{bmatrix} 2 & 1 \\ 2 & 3 \end{bmatrix}$$

is invertible. Thus $\{(2, 2), (1, 3)\}$ is a basis for R^2. Apply Theorem 14 which gives $Z^1 = (1/\sqrt{2}, 1/\sqrt{2})$ and $Z^2 = (-1/\sqrt{2}, 1/\sqrt{2})$. We have, using (8),

$$(2, 2) = 2\sqrt{2}\left(\frac{1}{\sqrt{2}}, \frac{1}{\sqrt{2}}\right)$$

and

$$(1, 3) = 2\sqrt{2}\left(\frac{1}{\sqrt{2}}, \frac{1}{\sqrt{2}}\right) + \sqrt{2}\left(-\frac{1}{\sqrt{2}}, \frac{1}{\sqrt{2}}\right).$$

In matrix terms this is

(14)
$$\begin{bmatrix} 2 & 1 \\ 2 & 3 \end{bmatrix} = \begin{bmatrix} \dfrac{1}{\sqrt{2}} & -\dfrac{1}{\sqrt{2}} \\ \dfrac{1}{\sqrt{2}} & \dfrac{1}{\sqrt{2}} \end{bmatrix} \begin{bmatrix} 2\sqrt{2} & 2\sqrt{2} \\ 0 & \sqrt{2} \end{bmatrix}.$$

The result (13) can be extended to inner products on R^n other than the standard inner product. For example, consider the inner product given by (2). Apply Theorem 14, using this inner product, to $\{(2, 2), (1, 3)\}$. Then

$$|(2, 2)|^2 = ((2, 2), (2, 2)) = 4 + 4 \cdot 4 = 20,$$

$$(1, 3) - \frac{((1, 3), (2, 2))}{|(2, 2)|^2}(2, 2) = (1, 3) - (2 + 4 \cdot 4)\frac{(2, 2)}{20} = (-\tfrac{4}{5}, \tfrac{6}{5}).$$

Thus $Z^1 = (1/\sqrt{5}, 1/\sqrt{5})$ and $Z^2 = (-2/\sqrt{5}, 3/\sqrt{5})$. Using (8) we have

$$
\begin{aligned}
(2, 2) &= \left((2, 2), \left(\frac{1}{\sqrt{5}}, \frac{1}{\sqrt{5}}\right)\right)\left(\frac{1}{\sqrt{5}}, \frac{1}{\sqrt{5}}\right) \\
&\quad + \left((2, 2), \left(-\frac{2}{\sqrt{5}}, \frac{3}{\sqrt{5}}\right)\right)\left(-\frac{2}{\sqrt{5}}, \frac{3}{\sqrt{5}}\right) \\
&= 2\sqrt{5}\left(\frac{1}{\sqrt{5}}, \frac{1}{\sqrt{5}}\right)
\end{aligned}
$$

and

$$
\begin{aligned}
(1, 3) &= \left((1, 3), \left(\frac{1}{\sqrt{5}}, \frac{1}{\sqrt{5}}\right)\right)\left(\frac{1}{\sqrt{5}}, \frac{1}{\sqrt{5}}\right) \\
&\quad + \left((1, 3), \left(-\frac{2}{\sqrt{5}}, \frac{3}{\sqrt{5}}\right)\right)\left(-\frac{2}{\sqrt{5}}, \frac{3}{\sqrt{5}}\right) \\
&= \tfrac{9}{5}\sqrt{5}\left(\frac{1}{\sqrt{5}}, \frac{1}{\sqrt{5}}\right) + \frac{2\sqrt{5}}{5}\left(-\frac{2}{\sqrt{5}}, \frac{3}{\sqrt{5}}\right).
\end{aligned}
$$

[*Remember:* All these computations are made using (2)!] In matrix terms we have

(15)
$$
\begin{bmatrix} 2 & 1 \\ 2 & 3 \end{bmatrix} = \begin{bmatrix} \dfrac{1}{\sqrt{5}} & -\dfrac{2}{\sqrt{5}} \\[2ex] \dfrac{1}{\sqrt{5}} & \dfrac{3}{\sqrt{5}} \end{bmatrix}\begin{bmatrix} 2\sqrt{5} & \dfrac{9\sqrt{5}}{5} \\[2ex] 0 & \dfrac{2\sqrt{5}}{5} \end{bmatrix}.
$$

The generalized version of (13) is the following.

(16) If A is an invertible $n \times n$ matrix, and if (X, Y) is an inner product on R^n, then $A = U\Delta$, where Δ is upper triangular with nonzero diagonal entries, and the columns of U (considered as vectors in R^n) are orthogonal with respect to the inner product (X, Y).

The proof of (16) is the same as that of (13).

EXERCISES

1. Which of the following subsets of R^3 (using the standard inner product) are orthogonal? Which are orthonormal?

   (a) $\{(1, 1, 0), (1, -1, 0), (0, 0, 1), (3, 2, 1)\}$
   (b) $\{(1, 1, 1), (0, -1, 1), (0, 1, 1)\}$
   (c) $\{(\tfrac{3}{5}, \tfrac{4}{5}, 0), (-\tfrac{4}{5}, \tfrac{3}{5}, 0)\}$
   (d) $\{(1, 2, 1), (1, -1, 0), (0, 1, 0)\}$

2. Show that the following is an inner product on R^3 and answer the questions of Exercise 1 for this inner product.

$$((x_1, y_1, z_1), (x_2, y_2, z_2))$$
$$= 2x_1x_2 + \tfrac{1}{2}(y_1y_2 + z_1z_2 - y_1x_2 - x_1y_2 - x_1z_2 - z_1x_2)$$

3. Apply the Gram-Schmidt process to each of the following independent sets to obtain an orthonormal basis for the indicated space V with the indicated inner product.

(a) $V = R^3$ with the standard inner product

$$\{(1, 0, 0), (1, 1, 0), (1, 1, 1)\}.$$

(b) $V = R^4$ with the standard inner product

$$\{(2, 1, -1, 0), (1, 2, 1, 1), (0, 1, 3, 1), (1, 0, 1, 1)\}.$$

(c) V is the space of polynomials of degree ≤ 3, with $(f, g) = \int_0^1 f(t)g(t)\, dt$
$\{1, t, t^2, t^3\}$.

(d) V is the space of 2×2 matrices with $(A, B) = A_{11}B_{11} + A_{12}B_{12} + A_{21}B_{21} + A_{22}B_{22}$;

$$\left\{ \begin{bmatrix} 1 & -1 \\ 1 & 1 \end{bmatrix}, \begin{bmatrix} 1 & -1 \\ 0 & 1 \end{bmatrix}, \begin{bmatrix} 1 & 0 \\ -1 & 1 \end{bmatrix}, \begin{bmatrix} 1 & 2 \\ 3 & 4 \end{bmatrix} \right\}.$$

4. Using (8) or (9) find the coordinates of each of the following vectors with respect to the basis given.

(a) Vectors: $(2, 1, 0)$ and $(3, -1, 2)$

$$\text{Bases: } \left\{ \left(\frac{1}{\sqrt{2}}, -\frac{1}{\sqrt{2}}, 0 \right), \left(\frac{1}{\sqrt{2}}, \frac{1}{\sqrt{2}}, 0 \right), (0, 0, 1) \right\}$$
$$\{(1, 1, 1), (0, -1, 1), (0, 1, 1)\}$$

(b) Vectors: $(3, 1, 2, 1)$ and $(0, 0, 1, 0)$
Basis: $\{(1, 1, 1, 1), (1, 1, 1, -3), (1, -1, 0, 0), (1, 1, -2, 0)\}$

(c) Vectors: $\begin{bmatrix} 2 & 1 \\ 0 & 1 \end{bmatrix}$ and $\begin{bmatrix} 1 & -1 \\ -1 & 1 \end{bmatrix}$

Basis: The orthonormal basis constructed in Exercise 3(d).

(d) Vectors: t and $t^3 + t^2 + t + 1$
Basis: The orthonormal basis constructed in Exercise 3(c).

5. (a) Let V be the space of (1). Show that $\{\sin \pi t, \sin 2\pi t, \sin 3\pi t, \ldots\}$ is an orthogonal set in V.
(b) Let V be the space of continuous real-valued functions defined for $-1 \leq t \leq 1$, with the inner product $(f, g) = \int_{-1}^1 f(t)g(t)\, dt$. Let

$$P_n(t) = \frac{1}{2^n n!} \frac{d^n}{dt^n} ((t^2 - 1)^n), \qquad n = 1, 2, \ldots .$$

Show that $\{P_1, P_2, P_3, \ldots\}$ is an orthogonal set in V. [*Hint:* Integrate by parts.]

6. Let

$$A = \begin{bmatrix} 2 & 1 & 0 \\ 1 & -1 & 1 \\ 0 & 1 & 2 \end{bmatrix}.$$

(a) Using the standard inner product on R^3 find U and Δ as in (13).

(b) Using the inner product on R^3 given in Exercise 2, find U and Δ as in (16).

7. Let (X, Y) be an inner product on V. Let $\{X^1, X^2, \ldots, X^k\}$ be an orthonormal set in V. Show that:

(a) $|X|^2 \geq (X, X^1)^2 + (X, X^2)^2 + \cdots + (X, X^k)^2.$

(b) $|X|^2 = (X, X^1)^2 + (X, X^2)^2 + \cdots + (X, X^k)^2$ if and only if X is a linear combination of $\{X^1, X^2, \ldots, X^k\}$.

(c) $\int_0^1 |f(t)|^2 \, dt \geq a_1^2 + a_2^2 + \cdots + a_k^2$, where f is continuous for $0 \leq t \leq 1$ and $a_r = 2\int_0^1 f(t) \sin r\pi t \, dt$ for $r = 1, 2, \ldots$. [*Hint:* To prove 7(a) and 7(b), compute the square of the length of $X - (X, X^1)X^1 - (X, X^2)X^2 - \cdots - (X, X^k)X^k$.   Use 7(a) and 5(a) to establish 7(c). Exercise 7(a) is called *Bessel's inequality*.)

8. Let (X, Y) be an inner product on V and let $\{X^1, X^2, \ldots, X^k\}$ be an orthonormal set. Let $Y = X - c_1X^1 - c_2X^2 - \cdots - c_kX^k$. Show that $|Y|^2$ assumes its smallest value when and only when $c_i = (X, X^i)$ for all i, $1 \leq i \leq k$. [*Hint:* Show that $|Y|^2 = |X|^2 - ((X, X^1)^2 + (X, X^2)^2 + \cdots + (X, X^k)^2) + (c_1 - (X, X^1))^2 + (c_2 - (X, X^2))^2 + \cdots + (c_k - (X, X^k))^2.$]

9. Suppose that A is an invertible $n \times n$ matrix. Show that there is an $n \times n$ matrix U whose *rows* are orthogonal and a *lower* triangular matrix Δ such that $A = \Delta U$. Also, the diagonal entries of Δ are nonzero.

10. Suppose that R^3 has the standard inner product. Write a flow diagram to apply the Gram-Schmidt process to a set of three vectors.

Section 4.   SUBSPACES AND COMPLEMENTS

In this section we shall use our results on inner products to study subspaces of a vector space and certain kinds of linear transformations on vector spaces. Let us begin with an example in R^3. We shall use the standard inner product as our inner product on R^3.

Let f be the real-valued function on R^3 defined by

$$(1) \qquad\qquad f(x, y, z) = x - y + z.$$

Clearly then f is linear and

$$(2) \qquad\qquad \text{Rank } (f) = 1.$$

The null space of f is the set of all triples (x, y, z) such that $f(x, y, z) = 0$. From (2) this subspace is of dimension 2 and is obviously the plane determined by $x - y + z = 0$. In the proof of Theorem 6 we found a means for constructing a basis for this subspace. Using this, we see that $\{(1, 1, 0), (-1, 0, 1)\}$ is a basis for the null space of f. The vector $(1, 1, 1)$ is *not* in this subspace, so that by Lemma 2, the set $\{(1, 1, 0), (-1, 0, 1), (1, 1, 1)\}$ is independent and hence is a basis for R^3. Applying the Gram-Schmidt process to this basis, we obtain

$$\left\{ \left(\frac{1}{\sqrt{2}}, \frac{1}{\sqrt{2}}, 0 \right), \left(-\frac{1}{\sqrt{6}}, \frac{1}{\sqrt{6}}, \frac{2}{\sqrt{6}} \right), \left(\frac{1}{\sqrt{3}}, -\frac{1}{\sqrt{3}}, \frac{1}{\sqrt{3}} \right) \right\},$$

which is an orthonormal basis for R^3. Since $(1/\sqrt{2}, 1/\sqrt{2}, 0)$ and $(-1/\sqrt{6}, 1/\sqrt{6}, 2/\sqrt{6})$ are linear combinations of $\{(1, 1, 0), (-1, 0, 1)\}$, they are in the null space of f. Therefore $\{(1/\sqrt{2}, 1/\sqrt{2}, 0), (-1/\sqrt{6}, 1/\sqrt{6}, 2/\sqrt{6})\}$ is an orthonormal basis for the null space of f. The vector $(1/\sqrt{3}, -1/\sqrt{3}, 1/\sqrt{3})$ is perpendicular to $(1/\sqrt{2}, 1/\sqrt{2}, 0)$ and $(-1/\sqrt{6}, 1/\sqrt{6}, 2/\sqrt{6})$ and is therefore perpendicular to any linear combination of them; i.e., $(1/\sqrt{3}, -1/\sqrt{3}, 1/\sqrt{3})$ is perpendicular to any vector in the null space of f. Clearly any multiple of $(1/\sqrt{3}, -1/\sqrt{3}, 1/\sqrt{3})$ is also perpendicular to any vector in the null space of f. The converse of this statement is true. For if X is a vector which is perpendicular to the null space of f, then the projection of X onto both $(1/\sqrt{2}, 1/\sqrt{2}, 0)$ and $(-1/\sqrt{6}, 1/\sqrt{6}, 2/\sqrt{6})$ is zero. We know from (8) of Section 3 that X is the sum of its projections onto $(1/\sqrt{2}, 1/\sqrt{2}, 0)$, $(-1/\sqrt{6}, 1/\sqrt{6}, 2/\sqrt{6})$, and $(1/\sqrt{3}, -1/\sqrt{3}, 1/\sqrt{3})$. Thus X is a multiple of $(1/\sqrt{3}, -1/\sqrt{3}, 1/\sqrt{3})$. To summarize

(3)

    (a) $\{(1/\sqrt{2}, 1/\sqrt{2}, 0), (-1/\sqrt{6}, 1/\sqrt{6}, 2/\sqrt{6}), (1/\sqrt{3}, -1/\sqrt{3}, 1/\sqrt{3})\}$ is an orthonormal basis for R^3.

    (b) $\{(1/\sqrt{2}, 1/\sqrt{2}, 0), (-1/\sqrt{6}, 1/\sqrt{6}, 2/\sqrt{6})\}$ is an orthonormal basis for the null space of f.

    (c) The subspace spanned by $(1/\sqrt{3}, -1/\sqrt{3}, 1/\sqrt{3})$ consists of all vectors which are perpendicular to each vector in the null space of f.

Now let X be an arbitrary vector in R^3. Then $X = a(1/\sqrt{2}, 1/\sqrt{2}, 0) + b(-1/\sqrt{6}, 1/\sqrt{6}, 2/\sqrt{6}) + c(1/\sqrt{3}, -1/\sqrt{3}, 1/\sqrt{3})$. We apply f to X and use the linearity of f:

$$f(X) = af\left(\frac{1}{\sqrt{2}}, \frac{1}{\sqrt{2}}, 0 \right) + bf\left(-\frac{1}{\sqrt{6}}, \frac{1}{\sqrt{6}}, \frac{2}{\sqrt{6}} \right)$$

$$+ cf\left(\frac{1}{\sqrt{3}}, -\frac{1}{\sqrt{3}}, \frac{1}{\sqrt{3}} \right)$$

$$= cf\left(\frac{1}{\sqrt{3}}, -\frac{1}{\sqrt{3}}, \frac{1}{\sqrt{3}} \right) = \frac{3c}{\sqrt{3}}.$$

We know the value of c:

$$c = \left(X, \left(\frac{1}{\sqrt{3}}, -\frac{1}{\sqrt{3}}, \frac{1}{\sqrt{3}}\right)\right),$$

by (8) of Section 3. This gives

(4) $f(X) = \dfrac{3}{\sqrt{3}}\left(X, \left(\dfrac{1}{\sqrt{3}}, -\dfrac{1}{\sqrt{3}}, \dfrac{1}{\sqrt{3}}\right)\right) = (X, (1, -1, 1)).$

Of course, equation (4) can be directly obtained from (1) without considering (2) or (3). We have derived (4) in a fashion which can be generalized easily.

Suppose that V is a vector space and (X, Y) is an inner product on V. Let M be a subspace of V. Then the *orthogonal complement* of M consists of all vectors in V which are perpendicular to each vector in M. We denote the orthogonal complement of M by $M^\perp$ (usually read "M perpendicular"). In our example, if M is the null space of f, then $M^\perp$ is the subspace spanned by $(1/\sqrt{3}, -1/\sqrt{3}, 1/\sqrt{3})$ as given in (3c). In general we have

(5) $M^\perp$ is a subspace of V.

For if X and Y are in $M^\perp$, then $(X, Z) = (Y, Z) = 0$ for all Z in M. Therefore $(aX + bY, Z) = a(X, Z) + b(Y, Z) = 0$ for all Z in M. Clearly 0 is in $M^\perp$. Therefore $M^\perp$ is a subspace.

In our example, the null space of f, and its orthogonal complement, determine R^3.

(6)   If X is in R^3, then X can be uniquely expressed in the form $X = Y + Z$, where Y is in the null space of f and Z is in the orthogonal complement of the null space of f.

We know from (3) that $X = a(1/\sqrt{2}, 1/\sqrt{2}, 0) + b(-1/\sqrt{6}, 1/\sqrt{6}, 2/\sqrt{6}) + c(1/\sqrt{3}, -1/\sqrt{3}, 1/\sqrt{3})$. Let $Y = a(1/\sqrt{2}, 1/\sqrt{2}, 0) + b(-1/\sqrt{6}, 1/\sqrt{6}, 2/\sqrt{6})$ and $Z = c(1/\sqrt{3}, -1/\sqrt{3}, 1/\sqrt{3})$. Then Y and Z satisfy (6). We shall now generalize (6). The following will be useful.

(7) M and $M^\perp$ have only the zero vector in common.

For if X is in M and X is in $M^\perp$, then $(X, X) = 0$, i.e., $X = 0$. Our result is a generalization of (6) as well as of Theorem 13.

Theorem 15. If V is finite dimensional and M is a subspace of V, then each vector X in V can be uniquely expressed in the form $X = Y + Z$, where Y is in M and Z is in $M^\perp$.

Proof. Let $\{X^1, X^2, \ldots, X^k\}$ be a basis for M. Expand to a basis $\{X^1, X^2, \ldots, X^n\}$ for V. Apply the Gram-Schmidt process. This gives an orthonormal basis $\{Z^1, Z^2, \ldots, Z^n\}$ for V such that Z^i is a linear combination of $\{X^1, X^2, \ldots, X^i\}$. We conclude that $\{Z^1, Z^2, \ldots, Z^k\}$ is contained in M and is therefore a basis for M. We claim that $\{Z^{k+1}, Z^{k+2}, \ldots, Z^n\}$ is a basis for $M^\perp$. Let X be in V. Then $X = (X, Z^1)Z^1 + (X, Z^2)Z^2 + \cdots + (X, Z^n)Z^n$ by (8) of Section 3. If X is in $M^\perp$, then $(X, Z^1) = (X, Z^2) = \cdots = (X, Z^k) = 0$. Conversely if $(X, Z^1) = (X, Z^2) = \cdots = (X, Z^k) = 0$, then X is perpendicular to any linear combination of $\{Z^1, Z^2, \ldots, Z^k\}$, i.e., any vector in M. Therefore to say that X is in $M^\perp$ is the same as saying that $(X, Z^1) = (X, Z^2) = \cdots = (X, Z^k) = 0$, which is the same as saying that $X = (X, Z^{k+1})Z^{k+1} + (X, Z^{k+2})Z^{k+2} + \cdots + (X, Z^n)Z^n$. Therefore $\{Z^{k+1}, Z^{k+2}, \ldots, Z^n\}$ spans $M^\perp$ and, being orthonormal, is independent; i.e., $\{Z^{k+1}, Z^{k+2}, \ldots, Z^n\}$ is a basis for $M^\perp$.

If X is in V, then $X = (X, Z^1)Z^1 + (X, Z^2)Z^2 + \cdots + (X, Z^k)Z^k + (X, Z^{k+1})Z^{k+1} + (X, Z^{k+2})Z^{k+2} + \cdots + (X, Z^n)Z^n$. Let $Y = (X, Z^1)Z^1 + (X, Z^2)Z^2 + \cdots + (X, Z^k)Z^k$, and $Z = (X, Z^{k+1})Z^{k+1} + (X, Z^{k+2})Z^{k+2} + \cdots + (X, Z^n)Z^n$. Then Y is in M, Z is in $M^\perp$, and $X = Y + Z$. If $X = Y^1 + Z^1$, where Y^1 is in M and Z^1 is in $M^\perp$, then subtraction gives $Y - Y^1 = Z^1 - Z$. The left-hand side is in M; the right-hand side is in $M^\perp$. From (7) we conclude that $Y = Y^1$ and $Z = Z^1$. Q.E.D.

Remarks. The proof of Theorem 15 is a straightforward generalization of the proofs of (3) and (6). The vector Y is called the *projection* of X on M, and Z is called the *projection* of X on $M^\perp$. This terminology corresponds to the obvious geometric fact that in R^3, using the standard inner product, we obtain Y and Z by projecting X onto each of the subspaces M and $M^\perp$. (The reader should check this with a few diagrams.) In Chapter 3 we shall study the concept of projection in terms of linear operators.

In the above proof we have established two other results. We showed that if dim $M = k$ and dim $V = n$, then dim $M^\perp = n - k$; i.e.,

$$(8) \qquad \dim V = \dim M + \dim M^\perp.$$

The second result we established is

$$(9) \qquad (M^\perp)^\perp = M;$$ i.e., the orthogonal complement of the orthogonal complement of M is M.

For we showed that if $\{Z^1, Z^2, \ldots, Z^n\}$ is a basis for V which is orthonormal and such that $\{Z^1, Z^2, \ldots, Z^k\}$ is a basis for M, then

$\{Z^{k+1}, Z^{k+2}, \ldots, Z^n\}$ is a basis for $M^\perp$. We conclude that if $\{Z^1, Z^2, \ldots, Z^n\}$ is an orthonormal basis for V such that $\{Z^{k+1}, Z^{k+2}, \ldots, Z^n\}$ is a basis for $M^\perp$, then $\{Z^1, Z^2, \ldots, Z^k\}$ is a basis for $(M^\perp)^\perp$. Putting these two statements together gives (9).

Property (9) tells us that we can describe M by describing $M^\perp$; i.e., M is the collection of all X in V such that $(X, Y) = 0$ for each Y in $M^\perp$. Therefore if we are given an inner product on V (V finite dimensional), then we can describe a subspace M of V by giving a basis for M or a basis for $M^\perp$. We essentially established this result for R^n in Chapter 1, where we showed that a subspace of R^n can be described as the null space of a matrix or as the row space of a matrix. (See Section 3 of Chapter 1.)

Another consequence of Theorem 15 is the following.

(10)   The projection of X on M is that unique vector in M which is closest to X in terms of the distance defined in V by the inner product.

Let Y be the projection of X on M, and Z the projection of X on $M^\perp$. Then $X = Y + Z$. Let Y^1 be any vector in M. Then $(Z, Y) = (Z, Y^1) = 0$. Suppose that $Y \neq Y^1$. Then $|Y - Y^1|^2 > 0$, and $|X - Y^1|^2 = |X - Y + Y - Y^1|^2 = (X - Y + Y - Y^1, X - Y + Y - Y^1) = (Z + Y - Y^1, Z + Y - Y^1) = (Z, Z) + 2(Z, Y - Y^1) + (Y - Y^1, Y - Y^1) = |Z|^2 + |Y - Y^1|^2 > |Z|^2 = |X - Y|^2$. This proves (10). It is possible to give a direct proof of (10) and use this to prove Theorem 15.

Our final result in this section will be a generalization of (4). Let f be a real-valued linear transformation defined on V. Then

(11) $\text{Rank}(f) \leq 1$.

If $f(X) = 0$ for all X in V, then rank $(f) = 0$. So suppose that $f(X) = a \neq 0$ for some X in V. Let b be any real number. Then

$$f((b/a)X) = (b/a)f(X) = (b/a)a = b.$$

This proves (11). Let M be the null space of f, and suppose that V is finite dimensional. Then, by Theorem 8, we have

(12)   if $f \neq 0$, then nullity $(f) = \dim M = \dim V - 1$.

Now suppose that V has an inner product (X, Y), and let $M^\perp$ be the orthogonal complement of M.

(13)   If $f \neq 0$, then $\dim M^\perp = 1$.

This follows from (12) and (8).

Let X^1 be in $M^\perp$, $X^1 \neq 0$. Then $f(X^1) \neq 0$, for otherwise X^1 would be in M, contradicting (7). Let

$$Y^1 = \frac{f(X^1)X^1}{|X^1|^2}.$$

Then Y^1 is in $M^\perp$. Let X be any vector in V. Then we can write $X = Y + Z$, where Y is in M and Z is in $M^\perp$. Since Z is in $M^\perp$, which is one dimensional, we know that $Z = aX^1$. What is a? We have $X = Y + aX^1$. Take the inner product of this with X^1 and use the fact that $(X^1, Y) = 0$. This gives

$$a = \frac{(X, X^1)}{|X^1|^2},$$

which gives

$$X = Y + \frac{(X, X^1)}{|X^1|^2} X^1.$$

Apply f and use the fact that Y is in M. Thus

$$f(X) = f(Y) + \frac{(X, X^1)}{|X^1|^2} f(X^1)$$

$$= \frac{(X, X^1)}{|X^1|^2} f(X^1)$$

$$= \left(X, \frac{f(X^1)}{|X^1|^2} X \right) = (X, Y^1).$$

(14)   Therefore there is a vector Y^1 such that $f(X) = (X, Y^1)$ for all X in V.

This result is so fundamental that we shall state it as a theorem.

Theorem 16. If V is finite dimensional, if f is a real-valued linear transformation on V, and if (X, Y) is an inner product on V, then there is a unique vector Y^1 in V such that $f(X) = (X, Y^1)$ for all X in V.

Proof. If $f = 0$, choose $Y^1 = 0$. If $f \neq 0$, then (14) shows the existence of Y^1. Suppose that $(X, Y^1) = (X, Y^2)$ for all X in V. Then subtraction gives $(X, Y^1 - Y^2) = 0$ for all X in V. In particular $(Y^1 - Y^2, Y^1 - Y^2) = 0$ so that $Y^1 = Y^2$. This shows the uniqueness of Y^1. Q.E.D.

Remarks. This is a direct generalization of (4), where $Y^1 = (1, -1, 1)$. The key to the proof lies in (13); i.e., the dimension of the orthogonal complement of the null space of f is 1. We then used Theorem 15. We could use Theorem 14 directly to conclude that

$$X = Y + \frac{(X, X^1)}{|X^1|^2} X^1,$$

where Y is perpendicular to X^1; i.e., Y is in M. With this we can remove the restriction of finite dimensionality, as follows.

(15)   Let (X, Y) be an inner product on V. Let f be a real-valued linear transformation on V such that the orthogonal complement of the null space of f has dimension 1. Then there is a unique vector Y^1 in V such that $f(X) = (X, Y^1)$ for all X in V.

In the exercises of the following section, we shall show that Theorem 16 is not true if V is not finite dimensional, unless we make some further restriction such as that given in (15).

A word of caution about Theorem 16. The Y^1 given there depends upon the choice of inner product on V. If $\langle X, Y \rangle$ is another inner product on V, then we can find a unique Y^2 such that $f(X) = \langle X, Y^2 \rangle$ for all X in V. In general $Y^2 \neq Y^1$. An example of this will be given in the exercises.

In the special case when $V = R^n$ and (X, Y) is the standard inner product on R^n, we can obtain Theorem 16 more directly. We shall do this for the case $n = 3$. Let f be a real-valued linear transformation defined on R^3, and A the matrix of f. Then A is 3×1, and $A_{11} = f(1, 0, 0)$, $A_{12} = f(0, 1, 0)$, and $A_{13} = f(0, 0, 1)$. Thus $f(x, y, z) = f(x(1, 0, 0) + y(0, 1, 0) + z(0, 0, 1)) = xf(1, 0, 0) + yf(0, 1, 0) + zf(0, 0, 1) = A_{11}x + A_{12}y + A_{13}z = ((x, y, z), (A_{11}, A_{12}, A_{13}))$. Therefore (A_{11}, A_{12}, A_{13}) is the vector Y^1 given in Theorem 16. In other words, when $V = R^3$ and (X, Y) is the standard inner product, then the Y^1 given in Theorem 16 is just the matrix of f considered as a vector in R^3! The same result holds for R^n. The statement and proof of Theorem 16 give this result in noncoordinate form.

In the literature of mathematics, a real-valued linear transformation defined on V is called a *linear functional* or *linear form* on V. The collection of all linear functionals on V is often denoted by V^*. We can equip V^* with a vector space structure by defining $\{f + g\} X = fX + gX$ and $\{af\} X = a(fX)$ for f and g in V^* and a a real number. With this structure V^* is called the *dual (adjoint, conjugate) space* of V. Theorem 16 tells us that, with respect to an inner product on V, we can "represent" each f in V^* by a vector Y^1 in V (assuming that V is finite dimensional). This "representation" is fundamental in most of our work. Due, however, to the confusion which the study of V^* usually causes for the beginning student, we shall omit a discussion of V^*.

EXERCISES

1. Find the orthogonal complement of each of the following subspaces M of R^n, using the standard inner product on R^n.

   (a) M is the subspace of R^3 spanned by $\{(1, 0, 1), (2, -1, 1)\}$.

   (b) M is the subspace of R^4 consisting of all vectors of the form (x, y, z, w), where $x + y - z + w = 0$ and $2x = y$.

   (c) M is the subspace of R^n consisting of all vectors of the form $(x_1, x_2, \ldots, x_n)$, where $x_1 + x_2 + \cdots + x_n = 0$.

   (d) M is the subspace of R^4 spanned by $\{(1, 0, 1, 1), (1, 0, -1, 1)\}$.

   (e) M is the null space of

   $$\begin{bmatrix} 3 & 0 & 1 & 2 \\ 1 & 0 & 1 & 1 \end{bmatrix}.$$

2. Find an orthonormal basis for M and for $M^\perp$ where M is a subspace of R^3, and R^3 has the standard inner product.

   (a) M is the null space of

   $$\begin{bmatrix} 3 & 0 & 1 \\ 1 & -1 & 2 \\ 2 & 1 & -1 \end{bmatrix}.$$

   (b) M is the subspace spanned by $\{(1, 1, 1)\}$.

   (c) M is the collection of all (x, y, z) such that $x + 2y + 3z = 0$.

3. A method for computing the projection of a vector onto a subspace is given in the proof of Theorem 15. Use this method to find the projection of $(1, -1, 0)$ on each of the subspaces M of Exercise 2, using the standard inner product on R^3.

4. Let R^3 have the inner product defined by $((x_1, y_1, z_1), (x_2, y_2, z_2)) = x_1 x_2 + (x_1 + y_1)(x_2 + y_2) + (x_1 + y_1 + z_1)(x_2 + y_2 + z_2)$. Using this inner product, find an orthonormal basis for the orthogonal complement of each of the subspaces of Exercise 2.

5. Using the inner product on R^3 given in Exercise 4, find the projection of $(1, -1, 0)$ on each of the subspaces M of Exercise 2.

6. Let f be the real-valued linear transformation defined on R^3 by $f(x, y, z) = 3x - y$.

   (a) If (X, Y) is the standard inner product, find a vector Y in R^3 such that $f(X) = (X, Y)$.

   (b) If (X, Y) is the inner product given in Exercise 4, find a vector Y in R^3 such that $f(X) = (X, Y)$. [*Hint:* A method for finding such a Y is given in the proof of Theorem 16.]

7. Let V be the space of polynomials of degree ≤ 2. Let (f, g) be the inner product on V defined by $(f, g) = \int_0^1 f(t)g(t)\,dt$.

   (a) Find an orthonormal basis for the orthogonal complement of the subspace spanned by $\{1 + t\}$.

   (cont.)

(b) Project t^2 onto each of the subspaces of (a).

(c) Let T be the linear transformation on V defined by $Tf = f(2)$. Find a vector g in V such that $Tf = (f, g)$.

8. Let (X, Y) be an inner product on V.

(a) Show that $V^\perp = \{0\}$ and $\{0\}^\perp = V$.

(b) We can extend the definition of orthogonal complement as follows. Let M be any subset of V (not necessarily a subspace). Then $M^\perp$ is the collection of all X in V such that $(X, Y) = 0$ for all Y in M. Show that $M^\perp$ is a subspace of V.

(c) Let V be finite dimensional and let M be a subset of V. Show that $(M^\perp)^\perp$ is the subspace spanned by M. [*Hint:* Let M_1 be the subspace spanned by M. Show that $M_1^\perp = M^\perp$, and use (9).]

9. Let (X, Y) be an inner product on V.

(a) Establish the identity
$$2|X - \tfrac{1}{2}(Y + Z)|^2 + \tfrac{1}{2}|Y - Z|^2 = |X - Y|^2 + |X - Z|^2.$$

(b) Let the distance from X to Y be the same as the distance from X to Z. Show that if $Y \neq Z$, then the point $\tfrac{1}{2}(Y + Z)$ is closer to X than either Y or Z. [*Hint:* Use the identity in (a).]

(c) Let M be a convex set in V. Let X be a point in V which is not in M. Show that there is at most one point in M closest to X. [*Hint:* Use (b).]

10. Let M be a convex set in V. A point X in M is called an *extreme point* *of* M if X is not the midpoint of a line segment contained in M, i.e., if $X = \tfrac{1}{2}(Y + Z)$ for Y and Z in M implies that $X = Y$ and $X = Z$. A subset D of M is called an *extremal subset of* M if $X = \tfrac{1}{2}(Y + Z)$ for X in D, and Y and Z in M implies that Y and Z are in D; i.e., points in D cannot be midpoints of lines in M which are not in D.

(a) Find the extreme points of the set of all points (x, y) in R^2 such that $x^2 + y^2 \leq 1$.

(b) Let M be the convex set consisting of all points (x, y) in R^2 such that $-1 \leq x \leq 1$ and $0 \leq y \leq 3$. Find the extremal subsets of M.

(c) Let M be a convex set in V. Let f be a real-valued linear transformation defined on V. Suppose that f has a maximum value on M; i.e., there is a point X_0 in M such that $fX_0 \geq fX$ for all X in M. Let $\delta = fX_0$. Show that the collection of all points Y in M such that $fY = \delta$ is an extremal subset of M.

(d) Let $f(x, y) = 3x + 2y$ and let $g(x, y) = 6y$. Let M be the convex set given in (b). Find the points (x, y) in M where f, g, and $g - 3f$ have their maximum values on M.

11. Suppose that $\{X^1, X^2, \ldots, X^k\}$ is a collection of vectors in V. The *convex polyhedron* determined by $\{X^1, X^2, \ldots, X^k\}$ is the collection of all $X = x_1 X^1 + x_2 X^2 + \cdots + x_k X^k$ such that $x_i \geq 0$ for $1 \leq i \leq k$ and $x_1 + x_2 + \cdots + x_k = 1$.

(a) Show that the convex polyhedron determined by $\{X^1, X^2, \ldots, X^k\}$ is a convex set.

(b) Draw a diagram illustrating the convex polyhedron determined by $\{(1, 1), (\frac{1}{2}, 2), (-1, 2), (-2, -4), (\frac{1}{4}, -5), (\frac{3}{4}, -1)\}$.

(c) Let M be the convex polyhedron determined by $\{X^1, X^2, \ldots, X^k\}$. Show that X is an extreme point of M if and only if $X = X^i$ for some i, $1 \leq i \leq k$.

(d) Let M be as in part (c), and let f be a real-valued linear transformation on V. Show that the maximum value of f on M is attained for some X^i, $1 \leq i \leq k$. [*Hint:* If $f(X^1) \geq f(X^i)$ for $i \geq 1$ and $X = x_1 X^1 + x_2 X^2 + \cdots + x_k X^k$ with $x_i \geq 0$ and $x_1 + x_2 + \cdots + x_k = 1$, then can $f(X) > f(X^1)$? This result is central to the so-called *simplex method* in linear programming.]

(e) Let M be the set in part (b). Using part (d), find the maximum and minimum values of $f(x, y) = 3x - y$ and $g(x, y) = 3y$ on M.

Section 5. THE ADJOINT OF AN OPERATOR

In this section we shall use Theorem 16 as a tool for the study of linear operators. We shall show that a linear operator on a vector space V with an inner product defines a new linear operator, called the "adjoint." This new operator has a simple matrix description and is of considerable computational and theoretical interest. Let us begin with a two-dimensional example.

Let T be a linear operator on R^2 and let

$$A = \begin{bmatrix} a & b \\ c & d \end{bmatrix}$$

be the matrix of T. Then

(1) $T(x, y) = (x', y')$ if and only if $\begin{bmatrix} a & b \\ c & d \end{bmatrix}\begin{bmatrix} x \\ y \end{bmatrix} = \begin{bmatrix} x' \\ y' \end{bmatrix}$.

An operator which is closely connected with T is the operator T^* defined by

(2) $T^*(x, y) = (x', y')$ if and only if $\begin{bmatrix} a & c \\ b & d \end{bmatrix}\begin{bmatrix} x \\ y \end{bmatrix} = \begin{bmatrix} x' \\ y' \end{bmatrix}$.

The matrix of T^* is obtained from A by interchanging both the rows and columns of A. (This can also be described by saying that the matrix of T^* is obtained from A by reflection in the diagonal of A.) We shall examine the relationship between T and T^*.

Let $((x, y), (x_1, y_1))$ be the standard inner product on R^2. Then we have the following identity:

(3) $\big(T(x_1, y_1), (x_2, y_2)\big) = \big((x_1, y_1), T^*(x_2, y_2)\big)$.

This can be established using (1) and (2). We have: $T(x_1, y_1) = (ax_1 + by_1, cx_1 + dy_1)$ and $T^*(x_2, y_2) = (ax_2 + cy_2, bx_2 + dy_2)$. Since $((ax_1 + by_1, cx_1 + dy_1), (x_2, y_2)) = ax_1x_2 + by_1x_2 + cx_1y_2 + dy_1y_2 = ((ax_2 + cy_2, bx_2 + dy_2), (x_1, y_1))$, we conclude that (3) is valid.

To make computation easier let us denote vectors in R^2 by capital letters and use (X, Y) to denote the standard inner product on R^2. Then (3) becomes

(4) $\qquad (TX, Y) = (X, T^*Y)$ for all X and Y in R^2.

One consequence of (4) is the following.

(5) $\quad$ Let M be the null space of T. Then $M^\perp$ is the range of T^*.

To establish (5) let Y^1 be in the range of T^* and choose Y in R^2 such that $T^*Y = Y^1$. Let X be in the null space of T. Then $TX = 0$. Equation (4) tells us that $(TX, Y) = (X, T^*Y)$. Thus $0 = (0, Y) = (TX, Y) = (X, T^*Y) = (X, Y^1)$. This shows that each vector in the range of T^* is perpendicular to each vector in the null space of T; i.e., the range of T^* is contained in $M^\perp$. From a remark after Theorem 8 we know that rank (T) = rank (T^*). [See (28) of Section 4, Chapter 1.] We also know from Theorem 8 that rank (T) = dim R^2 − dim M. From (8) of Section 4 we have that rank (T) = dim $M^\perp$. Thus rank T^* = dim $M^\perp$. Since the range of T^* is included in $M^\perp$ and has the same dimension, we conclude that (5) holds.

Some of the consequences of the definition (2) are

(6)
- (a) $(T^*)^* = T$,
- (b) $(S + T)^* = S^* + T^*$,
- (c) $(aT)^* = aT^*$, where a is a real number,
- (d) $(ST)^* = T^*S^*$.

Each of these can be established using (2). Let us establish (6d). Let

$$\begin{bmatrix} a & b \\ c & d \end{bmatrix}$$

be the matrix of T and

$$\begin{bmatrix} a_1 & b_1 \\ c_1 & d_1 \end{bmatrix}$$

the matrix of S. Then the matrix of ST is

$$\begin{bmatrix} a_1a + b_1c & a_1b + b_1d \\ c_1a + d_1c & c_1b + d_1d \end{bmatrix}$$

so that the matrix of $(ST)^*$ is

$$\begin{bmatrix} a_1 a + b_1 c & c_1 a + d_1 c \\ a_1 b + b_1 d & c_1 b + d_1 d \end{bmatrix} = \begin{bmatrix} a & c \\ b & d \end{bmatrix} \begin{bmatrix} a_1 & c_1 \\ b_1 & d_1 \end{bmatrix},$$

which is the matrix of T^* times the matrix of S^*. This proves (6d).

By suitably choosing coordinates in V, each of these results can be generalized. Instead of this we shall use (4) in order to define T^* and to obtain its properties. This will lead to simple proofs and less cumbersome statements.

Suppose that V is a finite dimensional vector space and (X, Y) is an inner product on V. Let T be a linear operator on V. Let Y be fixed and let $fX = (TX, Y)$. Then f is a real-valued linear transformation on V. That f is linear is shown by $f(aX^1 + bX^2) = (T(aX^1 + bX^2), Y) = (aTX^1 + bTX^2, Y) = a(TX^1, Y) + b(TX^2, Y) = afX^1 + bfX^2$. We can now apply Theorem 16 to f and conclude that there is a unique vector Y^1 in V such that

(7) $$f(X) = (X, Y^1) \text{ for all } X \text{ in } V.$$

Since Y^1 is uniquely determined by f (which depends upon Y and T), we have defined a transformation from V into V. We usually denote this transformation by T^* (read "T-star," or "T-adjoint"), which is called the *adjoint* of T relative to the inner product (X, Y). T^*Y is, by definition, the vector Y^1, which is uniquely determined by the condition that $(TX, Y) = (X, Y^1)$ for all X in V. In other words T^*Y is defined by the condition

(8) $$(TX, Y) = (X, T^*Y) \text{ for all } X \text{ and } Y \text{ in } V.$$

Let us show that T^* is linear. We want to show that $T^*(aY^2 + bY^3) = aT^*Y^2 + bT^*Y^3$, for any Y^2 and Y^3 in V and any real numbers a and b. $T^*(aY^2 + bY^3)$ is that vector in V such that $(X, T^*(aY^2 + bY^3)) = (TX, aY^2 + bY^3)$. Since $(TX, aY^2 + bY^3) = a(TX, Y^2) + b(TX, Y^3)$; $(TX, Y^2) = (X, T^*Y^2)$; and $(TX, Y^3) = (X, T^*Y^3)$; we conclude that $(X, T^*(aY^2 + bY^3)) = (X, aT^*Y^2 + bT^*Y^3)$ for all X in V. Thus $T^*(aY^2 + bY^3) = aT^*Y^2 + bT^*Y^3$. This shows that T^* is linear.

Formally, (8) is just a means of shifting the effect of T in an inner product. Anytime we move T from one side of the inner product to another, we just change it into T^*. Let us demonstrate this process by establishing some of the following. [Compare with (6).]

(9)

    (a) $(T^*)^* = T$

    (b) $(S + T)^* = S^* + T^*$

    (c) $(aT)^* = aT^*$, where a is a real number

    (d) $(ST) = T^*S^*$

We have $(TX, Y) = (X, T^*Y)$ for all X and Y in V. We also have $(X, T^*Y) = (T^*Y, X)$, and using (8): $(T^*Y, X) = (Y, (T^*)^*X)$. Thus $(TX, Y) = (Y, (T^*)^*X) = ((T^*)^*X, Y)$ for all X and Y in V. To conclude that $T = (T^*)^*$ we use the following.

(10)   If T_1 and T_2 are linear operators on V such that $(T_1X, Y) = (T_2X, Y)$ for all X and Y in V, then $T_1 = T_2$.

The condition $(T_1X, Y) = (T_2X, Y)$ is the same as

$$((T_1 - T_2)X, Y) = 0$$

for all X and Y in V. Let $Y = (T_1 - T_2)X$. Then $|(T_1 - T_2)X|^2 = ((T_1 - T_2)X, (T_1 - T_2)X) = 0$ for all X in V. Thus $T_1X = T_2X$ for all X in V. This establishes (10), from which (9a) follows.

The proofs of (9b) and (9c) are left to the exercises. Let us prove (9d). We have $(X, (ST)^*Y) = ((ST)X, Y) = (S(TX), Y) = (TX, S^*Y) = (X, T^*(S^*Y)) = (X, (T^*S^*)Y)$ for all X and Y in V. We conclude from (10) that $(ST)^* = T^*S^*$, which is (9d).

The relation between the matrix of T and that of T^* has a simple form with respect to an orthonormal basis. This is analogous to the relation between (1) and (2). Let $\{X^1, X^2, \ldots, X^n\}$ be an orthonormal basis for V. Let A be the matrix of T, and B the matrix of T^*, with respect to $\{X^1, X^2, \ldots, X^n\}$. Then $TX^j = A_{1j}X^1 + A_{2j}X^2 + \cdots + A_{nj}X^n$ for $j = 1, 2, \ldots, n$; while (8) of Section 3 gives $TX^j = (TX^j, X^1)X^1 + (TX^j, X^2)X^2 + \cdots + (TX^j, X^n)X^n$ for $j = 1, 2, \ldots, n$. This gives

(11)   If $\{X^1, X^2, \ldots, X^n\}$ is an orthonormal basis for V and A is the matrix of T with respect to $\{X^1, X^2, \ldots, X^n\}$, then $A_{ij} = (TX^j, X^i)$ for $i = 1, 2, \ldots, n$ and $j = 1, 2, \ldots, n$.

Let us apply (11) to B, the matrix of T^* with respect to $\{X^1, X^2, \ldots, X^n\}$. We have: $B_{ij} = (T^*X^j, X^i) = (X^j, TX^i) = (TX^i, X^j) = A_{ji}$; i.e., B is obtained from A by interchanging the rows and columns of A. B has a name. In general, if A is an $m \times n$ real matrix, then the $n \times m$ matrix B defined by $B_{ij} = A_{ji}$, $i = 1, 2, \ldots, n$ and $j = 1, 2, \ldots, m$, is called the *transpose* of A. We shall denote this matrix B by A^t (read "A-transpose"). In this terminology our result is as follows.

(12)   If A is the matrix of T with respect to an orthonormal basis, then A^t is the matrix of T^* with respect to the same basis.

The general form of (5) is as follows.

Theorem 17. Suppose that V is finite dimensional and (X, Y) is an inner product on V. Let T be a linear operator on V. Let M be the null space of T and N the range of T^*. Then $M^{\perp} = N$.

Proof. The proof is similar to the proof of (5) with some modifications. Let Y^1 be in N and choose Y in V such that $T^*Y = Y^1$. Let X be in M. Then $TX = 0$. Thus $0 = (0, Y) = (TX, Y) = (X, T^*Y) = (X, Y^1)$. This shows that N is contained in $M^\perp$. To show that $N = M^\perp$ we can use the following.

(13) Let V be as in Theorem 17. Let M_1 and M_2 be subspaces of V. Suppose that M_1 is contained in M_2. If $M_1 \neq M_2$, then there is a vector X^2 in M_2 such that X^2 is in $M_1^\perp$ and $X^2 \neq 0$.

To prove (13) let X be a vector in M_2 which is not in M_1. Thus $X \neq 0$ and $X = X^1 + X^2$, where X^1 is in M_1 and X^2 is in $M_1^\perp$. Therefore $X^2 \neq 0$ (otherwise X would be in M_1) and X^2 is in M_2 (since $X^2 = X - X^1$ which is in M_2). This establishes (13).

If $N \neq M^\perp$, choose X^2 in $M^\perp$ such that $X^2 \neq 0$ and X^2 is in $N^\perp$. Therefore $(X^2, T^*Y) = 0$ for all Y in V. We have, however, that $(X^2, T^*Y) = (TX^2, Y)$, so that $(TX^2, Y) = 0$ for all Y in V. In particular $(TX^2, TX^2) = 0$, that is, $TX^2 = 0$. Thus X^2 is in N. This is a contradiction. We conclude that $N = M^\perp$. Q.E.D.

Theorem 17 gives us a proof of the following, which could also be established using (12).

(14)   Rank (T) = rank (T^*).

We have, using the notation of Theorem 17, Rank $(T) = \dim V - \dim M = \dim M^\perp = \dim N = $ rank (T^*).

Remarks. In computation, (12) is generally more useful than (8). For some computations and for theoretical use (8) is easier to use than (12). Sometimes, particularly when T is defined geometrically, (8) gives simple descriptions of T^*. For example let T be a counterclockwise rotation in R^2 through an angle θ. Then T^* (using the standard inner product) is easily seen from (8) to be a counterclockwise rotation through the angle $-\theta$. In this case $T^*T = I$, i.e., $T^* = T^{-1}$.

An operator T such that $T^* = T^{-1}$ is called an *orthogonal operator*. These will be studied in Chapter 4. An operator T such that $T^* = T$ is called a *symmetric operator*. An operator T such that $T^* = -T$ is called *skew symmetric*. We use this same terminology for matrices: A is *orthogonal* if $A^t = A^{-1}$; A is *symmetric* if $A^t = A$; and A is *skew symmetric* if $A^t = -A$. Symmetric operators will be studied in Chapter 3. Meanwhile the following result is of some interest.

(15) $T = T_1 + T_2$, where $T_1 = T_1^*$ and $T_2 = -T_2^*$. This expression for T is unique.

The proof of (15) is left to the exercises.

We used (13) to complete the proof of Theorem 17. We could establish (14) by using (12) and (28) of Section 4, Chapter 1. Then we could use (14) to complete the proof of Theorem 17. [Then the proof would duplicate the proof of (5).]

The definition, (8) has been given when V is finite dimensional. When V is infinite dimensional, (7) may not be valid. In many important cases, however, (7) may be valid. We say that if there is a linear operator T^* on V such that (8) holds, then T has an adjoint, namely T^*. The exercises will give some examples of the infinite dimensional case.

EXERCISES

1. Let R^3 have the standard inner product. For each of the following operators T, describe T^*. By choosing bases for the subspaces involved, verify that Theorem 17 holds for each of these operators.

   (a) $T(x, y, z) = (x, x + y, x + y + z)$
   (b) T is a rotation about the y-axis through the angle $\pi/4$.
   (c) T reflects all points through the xz-plane.
   (d) T projects onto the plane $y = x$.
   (e) $T(x, y, z) = (y + 2z, -x + 3z, -2x - 3y)$

2. Let R^2 have the inner product defined by $((x_1, y_1), (x_2, y_2)) = x_1x_2 + (x_1 + y_1)(x_2 + y_2)$. For each of the operators T, describe T^*. [Equation (8) is probably easiest to use.]

   (a) $T(x, y) = (x - y, y)$
   (b) $T(x, y) = (0, x + y)$

3. Let V be the space of polynomials of degree ≤ 2. Let V have the inner product given by $(f, g) = \int_0^1 f(t)g(t)\, dt$. Find the adjoint of each of the following operators. [*Hint:* Use integration by parts and Exercise 7(c) of Section 4.]

   (a) $(T_1f)(t) = (d/dt)f(t)$ (b) $(T_2f)(t) = t\,(d/dt)f(t)$
   (c) $(T_3f)(t) = (d/dt)tf(t)$ (d) $(T_4f)(t) = (1/t)\int_0^t f(u)\, du$
   (e) $(T_5f)(t) = \int_0^1 (t + u)^3 f(u)\, du$

4. Find the matrix of each operator of Exercise 2 with respect to an orthonormal basis (using the inner product given in Exercise 2). Do the same for the adjoint of those operators.

5. Let V, (f, g), and T_1, T_2, T_3, T_4, and T_5 be as in Exercise 3. Describe each of the following.

   (a) $T_1^*T_2$ (b) $T_1(T_2)^*$
   (c) $(T_1T_2)^*$ (d) $(T_1T_2T_3T_4T_5)^*$
   (e) $T_5^* + T_5$

6. Let V be the space of 2×2 matrices with the inner product defined by $(A, B) = A_{11}B_{11} + A_{12}B_{12} + A_{21}B_{21} + A_{22}B_{22}$. Find the adjoint of each of the following. [*Hint:* These can be computed using (8). A simpler method would be to note that $(A, B) = tr(B^t A)$ and use Exercise 15 of Section 6, Chapter 1.]

   (a) $TA = CA$, where C is a 2×2 matrix.
   (b) $TA = AC - CA$, where C is a 2×2 matrix.
   (c) $TA = AC + CA$, where C is a 2×2 matrix.

7. Let V be finite dimensional and let T be a linear operator on V. Show that T is invertible if and only if T^* is invertible. Also show that $(T^*)^{-1} = (T^{-1})^*$. [*Hint:* Theorem 17, (9d), and Theorem 10 are useful.]

8. (a) Prove (9b) and (9c).
   (b) Prove (15). [*Hint:* Show that $T_1 = (T + T^*)/2$ and $T_2 = (T - T^*)/2$.]

9. (a) Which of the operators of Exercise 1 are symmetric? Which are skew symmetric? Which are orthogonal? Express each as the sum of a symmetric and a skew-symmetric operator.
   (b) Express each operator in Exercise 2 as the sum of a symmetric and a skew-symmetric operator with respect to the inner product given there.

10. Let V be the space of real-valued continuous functions f defined for $0 \le t \le 1$ with the inner product defined by $(f, g) = \int_0^1 f(t)g(t)\, dt$. Let T be the linear operator on V defined by $(Tf)(t) = \int_0^1 K(t, s)f(s)\, ds$, where $K(t, s)$ is a real-valued continuous function defined for $0 \le t \le 1$ and $0 \le s \le 1$.

   (a) Show that if T^* is defined by $(T^*f)(t) = \int_0^1 K(s, t)f(s)\, ds$, then T^* is the adjoint of T.
   (b) Show that T is symmetric if and only if $K(t, s) = K(s, t)$.

11. Let V be the space of polynomials with the inner product defined by $(f, g) = \int_0^1 f(t)g(t)\, dt$.

   (a) Let F be the real-valued linear transformation defined on V by $F(f) = f(1)$. Show that there is *no* vector g in V such that $F(f) = (f, g)$ for all f in V. [*Hint:* If there is a g in V such that $F(f) = (f, g)$, then $(f, g) = 0$ for all f such that $f(1) = 0$. Since $F(1) \ne 0$, $g \ne 0$. But $((1 - t)^2 g, g) = 0$ so that $(1 - t)g = 0$.]
   (b) Let T be the linear operator on V defined by $(Tf)(t) = (d/dt)f(t)$. Show that the adjoint of T does *not* exist. [*Hint:* If T^* exists, then integration by parts shows that $(f, T^*g) = f(1)g(1) - f(0)g(0) = (f, Tg)$, i.e., $(f, (T + T^*)g) = f(1)g(1) - f(0)g(0)$ for all f and g in V. Let $g(t) = t$ and use part (a).]

12. Let R^2 have the inner product of Exercise 2 and let T be a linear operator on R^2. Write a flow diagram to find the matrix of T^*.

SPECIAL EXERCISE

Let A and B be $n \times n$ matrices. Show that the following are equivalent.

(a) A and B can be reduced to the same row reduced echelon matrix.

(b) A and B have the same row space.

(c) A and B have the same null space.

(d) $A = P_0 B$ where P_0 is invertible.

[*Hints:* To show that (a) implies (b) use (36) of Section 3, Chapter 1. To show that (b) implies (c) use the fact that A^t and B^t have the same column space. Then use Theorem 17 and the remarks after Theorem 8. To show that (c) implies (d), let $\{X^1, X^2, \ldots, X^k, X^{k+1}, \ldots, X^n\}$ be a basis for R^n such that $\{X^1, X^2, \ldots, X^k\}$ is a basis for the null space of A (and B). Let S be the operator whose matrix is A, and T the operator whose matrix is B. In the proof of Theorem 8 the set $\{TX^{k+1}, TX^{k+2}, \ldots, TX^n\}$ was shown to be independent. Let $\{Z^1, Z^2, \ldots, Z^k, TX^{k+1}, \ldots, TX^n\}$ be a basis for R^n. Let P be the linear operator defined by $PZ^i = Z^i, i = 1, 2, \ldots, k$ and $P(TX^j) = SX^j, j = k+1, \ldots, n$. Show that P is invertible and that if P_0 is the matrix of P, then $A = P_0 B$. To show that (d) implies (a), use Exercise 14 of Section 6, Chapter 1.]

Section 6. THE DETERMINANT

This section is devoted to the development of the theory of determinants. The determinant is a useful computational tool in low dimensions and a powerful theoretical tool in higher dimensions. For this reason we shall concentrate on obtaining the properties of the determinant. We begin with a discussion of area in R^2 and its relation to the 2×2 determinant. We will obtain the properties of the determinant geometrically and then generalize these properties.

The plane R^2 can be considered as a vector space of arrows with initial point at $(0, 0)$; i.e., a point (a, b) in R^2 corresponds to the arrow **X** whose initial point is $(0, 0)$ and whose terminal point is (a, b). For convenience we shall write X instead of **X**, and also write $X = (a, b)$ to indicate that X is the arrow whose initial point is $(0, 0)$ and whose terminal point is (a, b).

Let $X = (a, b)$ and $Y = (c, d)$ be independent vectors in R^2; i.e., $(0, 0)$, (a, b), and (c, d) are not collinear. Then X and Y form two sides of a parallelogram P whose vertices are $(0, 0)$, (a, b), (c, d), and $(a + c, b + d) = X + Y$. We denote the area of P by $|A|$. Let θ be the angle, measured counterclockwise, between X and Y. (See Fig. 1).

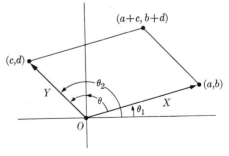

FIGURE 1

We shall adopt the following convention.

(1) The *oriented area* A of the parallelogram P is $\pm|A|$, where we take the plus sign if $0 < \theta < \pi$ and the minus sign if $\pi < \theta < 2\pi$. (Since $\{X, Y\}$ is an independent set, $\theta = 0$, π, or 2π cannot occur.)

This convention will give us a concept of signed area which is very helpful when we deal with problems requiring an orientation. Note that the oriented area of P depends not only on P, but also on the *order* we have chosen for the sides X, Y.

(2) The oriented area of the parallelogram determined by X and Y is the negative of the oriented area of the parallelogram determined by Y and X.

We shall determine the oriented area A in terms of (a, b) and (c, d). We know that $|A|$ is the base times the altitude of P and $\sin \theta > 0$ when $A > 0$, $\sin \theta < 0$ when $A < 0$. Let θ_1 be the angle between $(1, 0)$ and X, and let θ_2 be the angle between $(1, 0)$ and Y. Then $\theta = \theta_2 - \theta_1$ and $(a, b) = \sqrt{a^2 + b^2}\,(\cos \theta_1, \sin \theta_1)$; $(c, d) = \sqrt{c^2 + d^2}\,(\cos \theta_2, \sin \theta_2)$. (See Fig. 1.)

Let $|X|$ be the length of X, and $|Y|$ the length of Y. Then $A = |X|\,|Y| \sin \theta = \sqrt{a^2 + b^2}\,\sqrt{c^2 + d^2}\, \sin(\theta_2 - \theta_1) = \sqrt{a^2 + b^2}\,\sqrt{c^2 + d^2}$ $(\sin \theta_2 \cos \theta_1 - \cos \theta_2 \sin \theta_1) = (\sqrt{a^2 + b^2}\,\cos \theta_1)(\sqrt{c^2 + d^2}\,\sin \theta_2) - (\sqrt{a^2 + b^2}\,\sin \theta_1)(\sqrt{c^2 + d^2}\,\cos \theta_2) = ad - bc$. This shows

(3) The oriented area of the parallelogram determined by (a, b) and (c, d) is $ad - bc$.

and

(4) $ad - bc$ is positive when $0 < \theta < \pi$ and negative when $\pi < \theta < 2\pi$.

If (a, b) and (c, d) are dependent, then we say that they determine a parallelogram with zero area. This is consistent with (3), since $\{(a, b), (c, d)\}$ is dependent if and only if $ad = bc$. (See Exercise 7 of Section 2, Chapter 1.)

Now let T be a linear operator on R^2. We define the *determinant* of T, denoted by $\det(T)$, as follows.

(5) $\det(T)$ is the *ratio* of the oriented area of the parallelogram determined by $T(a, b)$ and $T(c, d)$ to the oriented area of the parallelogram determined by (a, b) and (c, d).

This definition of course requires that $\{(a, b), (c, d)\}$ be independent. This definition of determinant gives us a quantity without physical or geometric dimensions. It should be clear geometrically that $\det(T)$

does not depend on the choice of (a, b) and (c, d), except that they be independent, or even on the choice of distance and angle. We shall establish this algebraically at the end of this section.

Let

$$A = \begin{bmatrix} A_{11} & A_{12} \\ A_{21} & A_{22} \end{bmatrix}$$

be the matrix of T. Then $T(a, b) = (A_{11}a + A_{12}b, A_{21}a + A_{22}b)$ and $T(c, d) = (A_{11}c + A_{12}d, A_{21}c + A_{22}d)$. Thus the oriented area of the parallelogram determined by $T(a, b)$ and $T(c, d)$ is, using (3), $(A_{11}a + A_{12}b)(A_{21}c + A_{22}d) - (A_{21}a + A_{22}b)(A_{11}c + A_{12}d) = (A_{11}A_{22} - A_{12}A_{21})(ad - bc)$.

Since the oriented area of the parallelogram determined by (a, b) and (c, d) is $ad - bc$, we have

(6) $\det(T) = A_{11}A_{22} - A_{12}A_{21}.$

We use (6) to define the determinant of a 2×2 matrix. Thus if

$$A = \begin{bmatrix} A_{11} & A_{12} \\ A_{21} & A_{22} \end{bmatrix},$$

then the *determinant* of A is denoted by $\det(A)$ and is given by

(7) $\det(A) = A_{11}A_{22} - A_{12}A_{21}.$

With this definition we have that $\det(T) = \det(A)$, where A is the matrix of T. In order to generalize $\det(T)$ to n dimensions, we shall list the properties of (7) and then generalize these properties. We have that $\det(A)$ is a real-valued function defined for 2×2 matrices. The function $\det(A)$ has the following properties.

(8)
   (a) If A' is obtained from A by an interchange of two rows of A, then $\det(A') = -\det(A)$.
   (b) If A' is obtained from A by multiplying one row of A by a real number p, then $\det(A') = p \det(A)$.
   (c) If A' is obtained from A by multiplying one row of A by a number and adding to another row, then $\det(A') = \det(A)$.
   (d) $\det(I) = 1$.

The properties (8) follow easily from the definition (7). Each of the properties (8) can be given a geometric interpretation. This will be left to the exercises. The importance of (8) is that the properties given in (8) completely characterize $\det(A)$. For suppose that $d(A)$ is another real-valued function of 2×2 matrices with the properties (8); that is, $d(A') =$

$-d(A)$, if A' is as in (8a); $d(A') = p\,d(A)$, if A' is as in (8b); $d(A') = d(A)$ if A' is as in (8c); and $d(I) = 1$.

Let $g(A) = d(A) - \det(A)$. The function g has the following properties.

(9)
  (a) If A' is as in (8a), then $g(A') = g(A)$.
  (b) If A' is as in (8b), then $g(A') = pg(A)$.
  (c) If A' is as in (8c), then $g(A') = g(A)$.
  (d) $g(I) = 0$.

We shall show that $g(A) = 0$ for all 2×2 matrices A. If A is invertible, then by using the operations given in (8), with $p \neq 0$ in (8b), we can reduce A to I. From (9a, b, c), $g(A)$ is a nonzero multiple of $g(I)$. From (9d) we conclude that $g(A) = 0$. If A is noninvertible, then the rows of A are dependent. Suppose that $(A_{11}, A_{12}) = a(A_{21}, A_{22})$. Let

$$B = \begin{bmatrix} A_{11} & A_{12} \\ 0 & 0 \end{bmatrix}.$$

Then from (9c) we have $g(A) = g(B)$, since B is obtained from A by multiplying row one of A by $-a$ and adding to row two of A. Since

$$B = \begin{bmatrix} A_{11} & A_{12} \\ 0 \cdot 0 & 0 \cdot 0 \end{bmatrix},$$

we have from (9b) that $g(B) = 0g(B) = 0$. Thus $g(A) = 0$. We have shown that $g(A) = 0$ for all 2×2 matrices A. Thus $d(A) = \det(A)$ for all 2×2 matrices A, so that the properties (8) completely determine the determinant on 2×2 matrices.

(10) The function defined by (7) is the only real-valued function defined on 2×2 matrices which satisfies (8).

We could at this point construct the $n \times n$ determinant and show that it satisfies the properties (8). We wish, however, to stress the properties and not the computation of the determinant. For this reason we shall use the properties (8) to define the determinant.

A *determinant function* on $n \times n$ matrices A is a real-valued function, denoted by $\det(A)$, which satisfies the properties (8). As we shall see, there is exactly one function with the properties (8). Meanwhile, let $\det(A)$ be any function on $n \times n$ matrices which satisfies (8).

(11) If one row of A consist entirely of zeros; then $\det(A) = 0$.

For suppose that the ith row of A consists of zeros. Let A' be the matrix obtained from A by multiplying row i by 0. Then $A' = A$ and det $(A') = 0$ det $(A) = 0$, using (8b). Thus det $(A) = 0$ so that (11) is established. Another property of det (A) is the following.

(12)   If A is not invertible, then det $(A) = 0$.

If A is not invertible, we can reduce A, using the operations given in (8), where $p \neq 0$ in (8b), to a matrix B with a row of zeros. Then det (A) is a nonzero multiple of det (B) and det $(B) = 0$ so that det $(A) = 0$. This proves (12). The proof of (11) and (12) used only the fact that det (A) satisfied (8a, b, c), which are the same as (9a, b, c). Thus we have shown the following.

(13)   If $g(A)$ is a real-valued function of $n \times n$ matrices which satisfies (9a, b, c), then $g(A) = 0$ if A is not invertible.

We can now use (13) to generalize (10).

(14)   There is *at most* one determinant function defined on $n \times n$ matrices.

For suppose that det (A) and $d(A)$ both satisfy (8). Let $g(A) =$ det $(A) - d(A)$. Then $g(A)$ satisfies (9). If A is not invertible, then (13) shows that $g(A) = 0$. If A is invertible, then we can reduce A to I, using the operations of (8), with $p \neq 0$ in (8b). Thus $g(A)$ is a nonzero multiple of $g(I)$ so that $g(A) = 0$. Thus $g(A) = 0$ for all $n \times n$ matrices A which establishes (14).

In the proof of (14) we also established the following.

(15)   If det (A) is a determinant function on $n \times n$ matrices, then det $(A) \neq 0$ if and only if A is invertible.

Property (13) shows that if det $(A) \neq 0$, then A must be invertible. If A is invertible, then we can reduce A to I using the operations of (8), with $p \neq 0$ in (8b). Thus det (A) is a nonzero multiple of det (I) and det $(I) = 1$. This proves (15).

Most of the properties of the determinant can be easily deduced from (8) and (14). We shall exhibit some of these. Let det (A) be a determinant function on $n \times n$ matrices. Then

(16)   det $(AB) =$ det (A) det (B).

If B is not invertible, then AB is not invertible. [See (28) of Section 6, Chapter 1.] In this case det $(AB) = 0$ and det $(B) = 0$ from (11), so that (16) holds. If B is invertible, then det $(B) \neq 0$ from (15). Let $d(A)$ be defined by $d(A) =$ det $(AB)/$det (B). Then $d(A)$ satisfies (8). For example, let A' be obtained from A by multiplying row i of A by p. Then $A'B$ is obtained from AB by multiplying row i of AB by p. [If $C = AB$, then $C_{ij} = A_{i1}B_{1j} + A_{i2}B_{2j} + \cdots + A_{in}B_{nj}$, so that $pC_{ij} = (pA_{i1})B_{1j} + (pA_{i2})B_{2j} + \cdots + (pA_{in})B_{nj}$.] Thus det $(A'B) = p$ det (AB)

so that $d(A') = pd(A)$. The other parts of (8) are also easily shown to hold for $d(A)$. From (14) we conclude that $d(A) = \det(A)$, that is, $\det(AB)/\det(B) = \det(A)$. This is (16).

We can use (8) and (14) to show that (8a, b, c) can be extended to column operations. We have the following.

(17)
> (a) If A' is obtained from A by interchanging two columns of A, then $\det(A') = -\det(A)$.
> (b) If A' is obtained from A by multiplying one column of A by p, then $\det(A') = p\det(A)$.
> (c) If A' is obtained from A by multiplying one column of A by a number and adding to another column, then $\det(A') = \det(A)$.

We shall indicate a method for establishing (17). Let A' be obtained from A by interchanging columns j and k. Let $d(A) = -\det(A')$. Let B be obtained from A by interchanging rows r and s, and let B' be obtained from B by interchanging columns j and k. Then B' is obtained from A' by interchanging rows r and s of A'. Thus $\det(B') = -\det(A')$. Therefore $d(B) = -\det(B') = \det(A') = -d(A)$. This shows that $d(A)$ satisfies (8a). The proof that $d(A)$ satisfies (8b) and (8c) is equally straightforward. Let I' be obtained from I by interchanging columns i and j. Then I can be obtained from I' by interchanging *rows* i and j! Thus $d(I) = -\det(I') = \det(I) = 1$. Hence $d(A)$ is a determinant function so that $d(A) = \det(A)$; i.e., $\det(A) = -\det(A')$ which is (17a).

To prove (17b) suppose that $p \neq 0$ and define $d(A)$ to be $\det(A')/p$, where A' is as in (17b). Then it is easy to show that $d(A)$ is a determinant function, i.e., $d(A)$ satisfies (8), so that from (14), $d(A) = \det(A)$. Thus $p\det(A) = \det(A')$. If $p = 0$, then column rank $(A') \leq (n-1)$, so that rank $(A') \leq (n-1)$. Thus A' is not invertible. We conclude from (12) that $\det(A') = 0 = 0 \det(A) = p\det(A)$. This proves (17b). To prove (17c) let A' be as in (17c) and let $d(A) = \det(A')$. Again $d(A)$ is a determinant function so that $d(A) = \det(A)$. This is (17c).

A consequence of (17) is

(18) $\det(A^t) = \det(A)$, where A^t is the transpose of A.

To prove (18) let $d(A) = \det(A^t)$. Then a row operation on A gives a column operation on A^t, so that from (17) $d(A)$ is a determinant function. Thus $d(A) = \det(A)$, which is (18).

The method of proof used to establish (16), (17), and (18) is as follows. We define a function $d(A)$ and show that $d(A)$ is a determinant function, i.e., satisfies (8). [To prove (16) we let $d(A) = \det(AB)/\det(B)$; to prove (18) we let $d(A) = \det(A^t)$; etc.] The exercises will contain further results which can be established using this method of proof. Most of the standard properties of the determinant can be easily obtained in this manner.

The following result is useful in constructing the determinant.

(19) Let A be an $n \times n$ matrix. Let s be a fixed integer with $1 \leq s \leq n$. Suppose that $A_{sj} = b_{sj} + c_{sj}$ for $j = 1, 2, \ldots, n$. Let B and C be the $n \times n$ matrices defined by $B_{ij} = C_{ij} = A_{ij}$ for $j = 1, 2, \ldots, n$, if $i \neq s$; $B_{sj} = b_{sj}, j = 1, 2, \ldots, n$; and $C_{sj} = c_{sj}, j = 1, 2, \ldots, n$. Then $\det(A) = \det(B) + \det(C)$.

This result combined with (8c) tells us that $\det(A)$ is a linear function of row s when the other rows of A are fixed. To prove (19), let $c_{s1}, c_{s2}, \ldots, c_{sn}$ be fixed and let $d(B) = \det(A) - \det(C)$, where the rows of B, A, and C are the same except for row s; $C_{sj} = c_{sj}, j = 1, 2, \ldots, n$; $A_{sj} = B_{sj} + C_{sj}, j = 1, 2, \ldots, n$. The proof that $d(B)$ is a determinant function is straightforward and will be left to the exercises. Thus $d(B) = \det(B)$, which gives (19).

Let us now construct the $n \times n$ determinant. We shall do this inductively; i.e., we shall show how to obtain the $n \times n$ determinant from the $(n-1) \times (n-1)$ determinant. Thus the 7×7 determinant is constructed from the 6×6 determinant which is constructed from the 5×5 determinant. We obtain the 5×5 from the 4×4, the 4×4 from the 3×3, and the 3×3 from the 2×2, which is given by (7). This will give one method for evaluating the determinant, and the exercises will give others. We begin with the 3×3 case. Let A be a 3×3 matrix. We define $\det(A)$ by

$$(20) \quad \det(A) = A_{11} \det \begin{bmatrix} A_{22} & A_{23} \\ A_{32} & A_{33} \end{bmatrix} - A_{21} \det \begin{bmatrix} A_{12} & A_{13} \\ A_{32} & A_{33} \end{bmatrix} + A_{31} \det \begin{bmatrix} A_{12} & A_{13} \\ A_{22} & A_{23} \end{bmatrix}.$$

To show that this definition satisfies (8) is easy. For example, let us show that (8c) holds. Let

$$A' = \begin{bmatrix} A_{11} - aA_{21} & A_{12} - aA_{22} & A_{13} - aA_{23} \\ A_{21} & A_{22} & A_{23} \\ A_{31} & A_{32} & A_{33} \end{bmatrix}.$$

Then

$$\det(A') = (A_{11} - aA_{21}) \det \begin{bmatrix} A_{22} & A_{23} \\ A_{32} & A_{33} \end{bmatrix} - A_{21} \det \begin{bmatrix} A_{12} - aA_{22} & A_{13} - aA_{23} \\ A_{32} & A_{33} \end{bmatrix} + A_{31} \det \begin{bmatrix} A_{12} - aA_{22} & A_{13} - aA_{23} \\ A_{22} & A_{23} \end{bmatrix}.$$

From (19) and (8b) we have

$$\det\begin{bmatrix} A_{12} - aA_{22} & A_{13} - aA_{23} \\ A_{32} & A_{33} \end{bmatrix}$$

$$= \det\begin{bmatrix} A_{12} & A_{13} \\ A_{32} & A_{33} \end{bmatrix} + \det\begin{bmatrix} -aA_{22} & -aA_{23} \\ A_{32} & A_{33} \end{bmatrix}$$

$$= \det\begin{bmatrix} A_{12} & A_{13} \\ A_{32} & A_{33} \end{bmatrix} - a\det\begin{bmatrix} A_{22} & A_{23} \\ A_{32} & A_{33} \end{bmatrix}.$$

From (8c) we have

$$\det\begin{bmatrix} A_{12} - aA_{22} & A_{13} - aA_{23} \\ A_{22} & A_{23} \end{bmatrix} = \det\begin{bmatrix} A_{12} & A_{13} \\ A_{22} & A_{23} \end{bmatrix}.$$

Thus

$$\det(A') = (A_{11} - aA_{21})\det\begin{bmatrix} A_{22} & A_{23} \\ A_{32} & A_{33} \end{bmatrix} - A_{21}\det\begin{bmatrix} A_{12} & A_{13} \\ A_{32} & A_{33} \end{bmatrix}$$

$$+ aA_{21}\det\begin{bmatrix} A_{22} & A_{23} \\ A_{32} & A_{33} \end{bmatrix} + A_{31}\det\begin{bmatrix} A_{12} & A_{13} \\ A_{22} & A_{23} \end{bmatrix} = \det(A).$$

A similar calculation applies for other row operations so that (8c) holds.

From (14) we conclude that (20) defines *the* determinant function on 3×3 matrices. A similar calculation shows that if $d(A)$ and $d_1(A)$ are defined by

$$(21) \qquad d(A) = -A_{12}\det\begin{bmatrix} A_{21} & A_{23} \\ A_{31} & A_{33} \end{bmatrix} + A_{22}\det\begin{bmatrix} A_{11} & A_{13} \\ A_{31} & A_{33} \end{bmatrix}$$

$$- A_{32}\det\begin{bmatrix} A_{11} & A_{13} \\ A_{21} & A_{23} \end{bmatrix}$$

and

$$(22) \qquad d_1(A) = A_{13}\det\begin{bmatrix} A_{21} & A_{22} \\ A_{31} & A_{32} \end{bmatrix} - A_{23}\det\begin{bmatrix} A_{11} & A_{12} \\ A_{31} & A_{32} \end{bmatrix}$$

$$+ A_{33}\det\begin{bmatrix} A_{11} & A_{12} \\ A_{21} & A_{22} \end{bmatrix},$$

then $d(A)$ and $d_1(A)$ both satisfy (8). Uniqueness tells us that $d(A) = d_1(A) = \det(A)$.

This construction generalizes. Let A be an $n \times n$ matrix. Suppose that the $(n - 1) \times (n - 1)$ determinant is known. Let $A(i, j)$ denote the determinant of the $(n - 1) \times (n - 1)$ matrix obtained by omitting the ith row and jth column of A. $A(i, j)$ is called the i, j *minor* of A. Let

j be fixed. Then the function det (A) defined by

$$(23) \quad \det (A) = (-1)^{j+1}A_{1j}A(1, j) + (-1)^{j+2}A_{2j}A(2, j) + \cdots \\ + (-1)^{j+n}A_{nj}A(n, j)$$

is the determinant on $n \times n$ matrices. The proof that the function defined by (23) satisfies (8) is similar to the proof that (20) satisfies (8) and will be left to the exercises. The rule given in (23) is called the *Laplace expansion of the determinant along the jth column*. Note that (23) does not depend on j; i.e., any fixed j, $1 \leq j \leq n$, will give the same value. This is, of course, a consequence of (14).

The rule (23) is not very satisfactory for computation. In computation, (8) is much more useful. This will be shown in Exercise 4.

We can use (18) to give an expansion by rows. Let i be fixed. Then we have

$$(24) \quad \det (A) = (-1)^{i+1}A_{i1}A(i, 1) + (-1)^{i+2}A_{i2}A(i, 2) + \cdots \\ + (-1)^{i+n}A_{in}A(i, n).$$

This follows from (23) by taking the transpose and using (18).

In the proof of (14) we actually established the following.

(25) If $g(A)$ is a real-valued function of $n \times n$ matrices satisfying (8), then $g(A) = 0$ for all A.

This result can be used to establish a useful formula for the inverse of a matrix. Let A be 3×3 and let $g(A) = -A_{11}A(1, 2) + A_{21}A(2, 2) - A_{31}A(3, 2)$. Then g satisfies (9) so that $g(A) = 0$ for all A. The general result is as follows.

(26) If A is $n \times n$ and $k \neq j$ (or $i \neq r$), then the function $g(A)$ defined by $g(A) = (-1)^{k+1}A_{1j}A(1, k) + (-1)^{k+2}A_{2j}A(2, k) + \cdots + (-1)^{k+n}A_{nj}A(n, k)$, or by $g(A) = (-1)^{r+1}A_{i1}A(r, 1) + (-1)^{r+2}A_{i2}A(r, 2) + \cdots + (-1)^{r+n}A_{in}A(r, n)$, satisfies the conditions of (9), so that $g(A) = 0$ for all A.

The proof of (26) is again straightforward and will be left to the exercises. We can combine (23), (24), and (26) as follows.

(27) If $\delta_{st} = 0$ when $s \neq t$ and $\delta_{ss} = 1$, then we have $(-1)^{k+1}A_{1j}A(1, k) + (-1)^{k+2}A_{2j}A(2, k) + \cdots + (-1)^{k+n}A_{nj}A(n, k) = \delta_{jk} \det (A)$, and $(-1)^{r+1}A_{i1}A(r, 1) + (-1)^{r+2}A_{i2}A(r, 2) + \cdots + (-1)^{r+n}A_{in} \times A(r, n) = \delta_{ir} \det (A)$.

Let B be the $n \times n$ matrix given by $B_{st} = (-1)^{s+t}A(t, s)$ for $1 \leq s \leq n, 1 \leq t \leq n$. B is called the *classical adjoint* of A. (B has no relation to the adjoint of Section 5.) We can restate (27) as follows.

(28) $$AB = BA = (\det (A))I.$$

Thus A is invertible if and only if $\det (A) \neq 0$ [see (15)], and

(29)   If $\det (A) \neq 0$, then $A^{-1} = (1/\det (A))B$, where B is the classical adjoint of A.

From the rule (16) and (8d), we have that $1 = \det (I) = \det (AA^{-1}) = \det (A) \det (A^{-1})$. Since $B = (\det (A))A^{-1}$ we have the following:

(30) $$\det (A^{-1}) = 1/\det (A),$$

(31) $\det (B) = \det (A)^{n-1}$, where B is the classical adjoint of A.

Statement (31) is a special case of the following.

(32)   If A is $n \times n$, then $\det (aA) = a^n \det (A)$.

The proof of (32) is obtained by n applications (one for each row) of (8b).

Now let T be a linear operator on V, where $\dim V = n$. We then define $\det (T)$ to be the determinant of a matrix of T with respect to a basis for V. This is not dependent upon the choice of basis. For suppose that A is the matrix of T with respect to one basis and B the matrix of T with respect to another basis. Then we can find an invertible $n \times n$ matrix P_0 such that $B = P_0AP_0^{-1}$. [See (56) of Section 6, Chapter 1.] Thus $\det (B) = \det (P_0AP_0^{-1}) = \det (P_0) \det (A) \det (P_0^{-1}) = \det (P_0) \times \det (P_0^{-1}) \det (A) = \det (A)$. The final equality in this uses (29).

The general form of (4) is as follows. If T is a linear operator on R^n and $\{X^1, X^2, \ldots, X^n\}$ is a basis for R^n, let C be the $n \times n$ matrix whose ith row is X^i and let D be the $n \times n$ matrix whose ith row is TX^i, $i = 1$, $2, \ldots, n$. Let A be the matrix of T. Then $CA^t = D$. [See (20) of Section 6, Chapter 1.] We have

(33) $$\det (T) = \frac{\det (D)}{\det (C)},$$

since

$$\det (T) = \det (A) = \det (A^t)$$

$$= \frac{\det (C) \det (A^t)}{\det (C)} = \frac{\det (CA^t)}{\det (C)} = \frac{\det (D)}{\det (C)}.$$

Therefore if we define $\det (C)$ to be the oriented n-dimensional volume of the n-dimensional parallelopiped determined by $\{X^1, X^2, \ldots, X^n\}$, then det (T) is the ratio of the oriented n-dimensional volume of the n-dimensional parallelopiped determined by $\{TX^1, TX^2, \ldots, TX^n\}$ to the oriented n-dimensional volume of the n-dimensional parallelopiped determined by $\{X^1, X^2, \ldots, X^n\}$. This shows that det (T) is independent of the choice of basis $\{X^1, X^2, \ldots, X^n\}$.

We shall show in the next section that when $n = 3$, then the determinant of C does give the volume of the parallelopiped determined by the rows of C. This justifies the use of the word "volume" in the above.

EXERCISES

1. **(a)** Show using (7) that the properties (8) hold for the 2×2 determinant.

   (b) If

   $$A = \begin{bmatrix} a & b \\ c & d \end{bmatrix},$$

   then det (A) is the oriented area of the parallelogram determined by (a, b) and (c, d). Using this interpretation of the determinant, describe each of the properties (8) geometrically. [For example, (8d) says that the oriented area of the parallelogram determined by $(1, 0)$ and $(0, 1)$ is 1.]

   (c) Interpret (11), (12), and (15) geometrically for 2×2 matrices. For linear operators on R^2 using (4).

   (d) Let S and T be linear operators on R^2. Let det (S) and det (T) be defined as in (4). Interpret (16) geometrically for S and T.

   (e) Interpret (19) geometrically for 2×2 matrices.

2. Using (7) or (23), find the determinant of each of the following matrices. [*Note:* In parts (d), (e), and (f) careful choice of the column for expansion leads to simpler computation.]

   (a) $\begin{bmatrix} 2 & 1 \\ 6 & 0 \end{bmatrix}$

   (b) $\begin{bmatrix} 3 & -1 \\ 2 & \sqrt{2} \end{bmatrix}$

   (c) $\begin{bmatrix} 4 & 1 & 0 \\ 2 & -1 & 1 \\ 1 & 2 & 1 \end{bmatrix}$

   (d) $\begin{bmatrix} 3 & 1 & 2 \\ 1 & 0 & -1 \\ 1 & 0 & 1 \end{bmatrix}$

   (e) $\begin{bmatrix} 3 & 1 & 2 & 1 \\ 1 & 1 & 0 & 1 \\ 2 & 0 & 0 & 1 \\ 1 & 3 & 0 & 1 \end{bmatrix}$

   (f) $\begin{bmatrix} 1 & 0 & 2 & 1 & 1 \\ 0 & 0 & 1 & 1 & 0 \\ 1 & 0 & 0 & 0 & 0 \\ 0 & 3 & 0 & 1 & 0 \\ 0 & 1 & 0 & 2 & 0 \end{bmatrix}$

3. Show that if A is an upper triangular $n \times n$ matrix, then det $(A) = A_{11}A_{22} \ldots A_{nn}$. [*Hint:* Use (23).]

4. Using row operations of the type given in (8a) and (8c), we can reduce an $n \times n$ matrix to upper triangular form and then use Exercise 3 to evaluate the determinant. Evaluate each of the determinants in Exercise 2, parts (c) through (f), in this manner. [Remember that the use of (8a) gives a change of sign.]

5. Exercise 3 can be generalized in many ways. We shall give one generalization. Let A be $n \times n$, let B be $k \times k$, let C be $n \times k$, and let O be the $k \times n$ zero matrix. Let

$$D = \begin{bmatrix} A & C \\ O & B \end{bmatrix},$$

that is,

$$D = \begin{bmatrix}
A_{11} & A_{12} \ldots A_{1n} & C_{11} & C_{12} \ldots C_{1k} \\
A_{21} & A_{22} \ldots A_{2n} & C_{21} & C_{22} \ldots C_{2k} \\
\vdots & & \vdots & \\
A_{n1} & A_{n2} \ldots A_{nn} & C_{n1} & C_{n2} \ldots C_{nk} \\
0 & 0 \ldots 0 & B_{11} & B_{12} \ldots B_{1k} \\
0 & 0 \ldots 0 & B_{21} & B_{22} \ldots B_{2k} \\
\vdots & & \vdots & \\
0 & 0 \ldots 0 & B_{k1} & B_{k2} \ldots B_{kk}
\end{bmatrix}.$$

Show that det (D) = det (A) det (B). [*Hint:* Show that if A is not invertible, then D is not invertible, and use (12). If A is invertible, let A and C be fixed and define $d(B)$ = det (D)/det (A). Show that $d(B)$ satisfies (8). Then use (14).]

6. Use Exercise 5 to evaluate the determinant of the following.

(a) $\begin{bmatrix} 2 & 1 & 0 & 0 \\ 0 & 1 & 1 & 1 \\ 0 & 0 & 3 & 1 \\ 0 & 0 & 2 & 0 \end{bmatrix}$
(b) $\begin{bmatrix} 4 & 1 & 7 & 1 & 3 & 2 \\ 2 & 1 & 6 & 2 & 1 & 1 \\ 0 & 0 & 2 & 1 & 1 & -1 \\ 0 & 0 & 1 & 1 & 1 & 1 \\ 0 & 0 & 0 & 1 & -1 & 3 \\ 0 & 0 & 0 & 0 & 1 & 2 \\ 0 & 0 & 0 & 0 & 1 & 3 \end{bmatrix}$

7. Using (15) determine which of the following matrices is invertible. If the matrix is invertible, use (28) to find its inverse.

(a) $\begin{bmatrix} 3 & 1 & 0 \\ 1 & 2 & -1 \\ -4 & -3 & 1 \end{bmatrix}$
(b) $\begin{bmatrix} 6 & 1 & 0 \\ 2 & -1 & 1 \\ 0 & 1 & 3 \end{bmatrix}$

(c) $\begin{bmatrix} 1 & 0 & 1 & 2 \\ -1 & 1 & 2 & 1 \\ 1 & 0 & 1 & 1 \\ 3 & 1 & 0 & 2 \end{bmatrix}$

8. (a) Establish (19) in the 3×3 case.
   (b) By computing directly, using (7), show that (20), (21), and (22) give the same value.
   (c) Verify that (26) holds in the 3×3 case.

9. (a) Complete the proof of (19) by showing that the function $d(B)$ defined in (19) ff is a determinant function.
   (b) Prove that (23) satisfies (8).
   (c) Establish (26) by showing that $g(A)$ has the properties of (9).

10. Let A be an $n \times n$ matrix such that $\det (A) \neq 0$. Let

$$X = \begin{bmatrix} x_1 \\ x_2 \\ \vdots \\ x_n \end{bmatrix} \quad \text{and} \quad Y = \begin{bmatrix} y_1 \\ y_2 \\ \vdots \\ y_n \end{bmatrix}.$$

Let C_j be the matrix obtained from A by replacing the jth column of A by Y. Show that the equation $AX = Y$ has a unique solution X given by: $x_j = \det (C_j)/\det (A)$ for $j = 1, 2, \ldots, n$. [This is called *Cramer's rule*. To establish Cramer's rule, use (29) to write

$$x_j = \left(\frac{1}{\det (A)} \right)$$

$$\times \left((-1)^{j+1} A(1, j) y_1 + (-1)^{j+2} A(2, j) y_2 + \cdots + (-1)^{j+n} A(n, j) y_n \right)$$

and show, using a Laplace expansion along the jth column that $\det (C_j) = (-1)^{j+1} A(1, j) y_1 + (-1)^{j+2} A(2, j) y_2 + \cdots + (-1)^{j+n} A(n, j) y_n.$]

11. By using Cramer's rule (see Exercise 10), solve each of the following systems of equations.

   (a) $3x - 2y = 1$ **(b)** $x + 2y - z = 1$ **(c)** $3x - y - z = 1$
          $x + y = 3$ $3x - 2y + z = 0$ $x + y = 1$
                                   $2x + y + z = 2$ $y - z = 1$

12. Let A be an $n \times n$ matrix. An *r-rowed minor* of A is obtained by taking the determinant of a matrix obtained from A by omitting $n - r$ rows and $n - r$ columns. The *determinant rank* of A is defined to be r if all k-rowed minors of A vanish for $k > r$ and if there is at least one r-rowed minor of A which does not vanish. Show that if A is 3×3, then rank (A) is the same as the determinant rank of A. (This result also holds when A is $n \times n$.)

13. An alternative form of the determinant can be obtained using the theory of permutations. A *permutation of degree n* is an n-tuple of the form $(\sigma_1, \sigma_2, \ldots, \sigma_n)$, where each σ_i is an integer such that $1 \leq \sigma_i \leq n$ for $1 \leq i \leq n$ and $\sigma_i \neq \sigma_j$ if $i \neq j$. We shall write $\sigma = (\sigma_1, \sigma_2, \ldots, \sigma_n)$. It should be clear that by a succession of interchanges of adjacent pairs of σ we can obtain the n-tuple $(1, 2, \ldots, n)$. The number of interchanges required for a given σ is always even or always odd, and we say that the sign of σ is $+1$ if the number is even, and -1 if the number is odd.

(a) Show that the number of interchanges of adjacent pairs of σ needed to obtain $(1, 2, \ldots, n)$ is always even or always odd. [*Hint:* Let E_σ be the $n \times n$ matrix whose ith row is the σ_ith row of I_n. Show that the sign of σ is equal to det (E_σ).]

(b) Show that det $(A) = \Sigma_\sigma (\text{sgn } \sigma) A_{\sigma_1 1} A_{\sigma_2 2} \ldots A_{\sigma_n n}$. [This means that for each permutation σ of degree n, form the product $A_{\sigma_1 1} A_{\sigma_2 2} \ldots A_{\sigma_n n}$, multiply by sgn σ ($=$ the sign of σ) and add, with one term for each σ. To show this, show that the right-hand side defines a determinant function, i.e., satisfies (8).]

14. Let V be the space of 2×2 matrices and let T be the linear operator defined on V by $TA = AB$, where B is a fixed 2×2 matrix. Show that det $(T) = \bigl(\det (B)\bigr)^2$. [*Hint:* Find a basis for V such that

$$\begin{bmatrix} B_{11} & B_{12} & 0 & 0 \\ B_{21} & B_{22} & 0 & 0 \\ 0 & 0 & B_{11} & B_{12} \\ 0 & 0 & B_{21} & B_{22} \end{bmatrix}$$

is the matrix of T.]

15. Let A be a 4×4 matrix.

(a) Show that the maximum number of multiplications needed to find det (A) using either Exercise 4 or (23) is 72. (A product $abcd$ consists of *three* multiplications.)

(b) Show that the maximum number of multiplications and divisions needed to solve $AX = Y$ using Cramer's rule (see Exercise 10) is 364.

(c) Find the maximum number of multiplications and divisions needed to solve $AX = Y$ using the method of row reduction in Chapter 1. Is Cramer's rule an efficient method for solving systems of equations?

16. Let A be $n \times n$ and let t be a real number. Show that det $(tI - A)$ is a polynomial of degree n with leading coefficient 1. [*Hint:* Use Exercise 14, or use induction and (23).]

Section 7.   THE CROSS PRODUCT IN THREE DIMENSIONS

In this section we shall study the geometry of R^3. Our chief tools will be the determinant and a closely related concept called the *cross product*. The space R^3 will be considered as a vector space of arrows with initial point at $(0, 0, 0)$; i.e., a point (x_1, x_2, x_3) in R_3 corresponds to the arrow $\mathbf{X}$ whose initial point is $(0, 0, 0)$ and whose terminal point is (x_1, x_2, x_3).

For convenience we shall write X instead of $\mathbf{X}$ and also write $X = (x_1, x_2, x_3)$ to indicate that X is the arrow whose initial point is $(0, 0, 0)$ and whose terminal point is (x_1, x_2, x_3). We shall assume that R^3 has the standard inner product and will use the notation (X, Y) to indicate this inner product. Vector length and the angle between two vectors will be computed using this inner product.

We assign an orientation to R^3 as follows. If $X = (x_1, x_2, x_3)$, $Y = (y_1, y_2, y_3)$, and $Z = (z_1, z_2, z_3)$, then we say that the ordered triple $\{X, Y, Z\}$ is a *positive triple* if

$$\det \begin{bmatrix} x_1 & x_2 & x_3 \\ y_1 & y_2 & y_3 \\ z_1 & z_2 & z_3 \end{bmatrix} > 0$$

and a *negative triple* if

$$\det \begin{bmatrix} x_1 & x_2 & x_3 \\ y_1 & y_2 & y_3 \\ z_1 & z_2 & z_3 \end{bmatrix} < 0.$$

(1) Let $\{X, Y, Z\}$ be a positive triple. Then $\{Y, Z, X\}$ and $\{Z, X, Y\}$ are positive triples, and $\{X, Z, Y\}$, $\{Z, Y, X\}$, and $\{Y, X, Z\}$ are negative triples.

(2) If $\{X, Y, Z\}$ is a positive triple, then $\{X + aY, Y, Z\}$, $\{X + aZ, Y, Z\}$, $\{X, Y + aX, Z\}$, $\{X, Y + aZ, Z\}$, $\{X, Y, Z + aX\}$, and $\{X, Y, Z + aY\}$ are all positive triples, where a is any real number.

(3) Let $a > 0$ and let $\{X, Y, Z\}$ be a positive triple. Then $\{aX, Y, Z\}$, $\{X, aY, Z\}$, and $\{X, Y, aZ\}$ are all positive triples.

(4) Let $a < 0$ and let $\{X, Y, Z\}$ be a positive triple. Then $\{aX, Y, Z\}$, $\{X, aY, Z\}$, and (X, Y, aZ) are all negative triples.

(5) The triple $\{(1, 0, 0), (0, 1, 0), (0, 0, 1)\}$ is a positive triple.

These are consequences of (8) of Section 6. Now let $X = (x_1, x_2, x_3)$ and $Y = (y_1, y_2, y_3)$ be two independent vectors. Let $Z = (z_1, z_2, z_3)$ be defined by the following conditions.

(6)   (a) $|Z| = |X|\,|Y| \sin \theta$, where θ is the angle between X and Y.
      (b) $(Z, X) = (Z, Y) = 0$.
      (c) $\{X, Y, Z\}$ is a positive triple.

There is precisely one vector with these three properties. Condition (6a) tells us the length of Z. Condition (6b) gives us only two choices for Z, and condition (6c) eliminates one of these. We call Z the *cross product* of X and Y, and we write $Z = X \times Y$. (See Fig. 1.)

If X and Y are dependent, then we define $X \times Y$ to be 0. This is consistent with (6a), since $\theta = 0$ or π if $\{X, Y\}$ is dependent. The converse of this holds; i.e., if $\theta = 0$ or π, then X and Y are dependent. Thus, from (6a), we have

(7) $X \times Y = 0$ if and only if X and Y are dependent.

Since

$$\sin^2 \theta = 1 - \cos^2 \theta$$

$$= 1 - \left(\frac{(X, Y)}{|X|\,|Y|} \right)^2,$$

condition (6a) can be restated as

(8) $|X \times Y|^2 = |X|^2 |Y|^2 - (X, Y)^2$

We have the following identities.

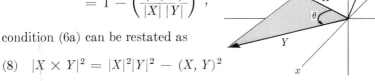

FIGURE 1

(9) $X \times Y = -Y \times X.$

(10) $a(X \times Y) = (aX) \times Y = X \times (aY)$ for any real number a.

(11) $(X + aY) \times Y = X \times (Y + aX) = X \times Y$ for any real number a.

Property (9) is an immediate consequence of (6c) and (1). We show that $a(X \times Y) = (aX) \times Y$. Let $Z^1 = a(X \times Y)$ and $Z^2 = (aX) \times Y$. We shall show that Z^1 satisfies the same conditions as Z^2. If $a = 0$, then clearly $Z^1 = Z^2 = 0$. If $a \neq 0$, then $|Z^2|^2 = |aX|^2 |Y|^2 - (aX, Y)^2 = a^2 (|X|^2 |Y|^2 - (X, Y)^2) = |Z^1|^2$. Thus $|Z^1| = |Z^2|$. Since Z^1 is perpendicular to both X and Y, Z^1 must also be perpendicular to aX and Y. Clearly $\{X, Y\}$ is dependent if and only if $\{aX, Y\}$ is dependent. So we can suppose that $\{X, Y\}$ is independent. Then $\{X, Y, X \times Y\}$ is a positive triple. If $a > 0$, then two applications of (3) show that $\{aX, Y, Z^1\}$ is a positive triple. If $a < 0$, then two applications of (4) show that $\{aX, Y, Z^1\}$ is a positive triple. Thus Z^1 satisfies the same conditions as Z^2. Therefore $Z^1 = Z^2$. The equality $a(X \times Y) = X \times (aY)$ is established in a similar manner.

Let us show that $(X + aY) \times Y = X \times Y$. The other identity of (11) then follows from this and (9). Since two vectors are dependent if and only if they are collinear with $(0, 0, 0)$, we know that $\{X + aY, Y\}$ is dependent if and only if $\{X, Y\}$ is dependent. In this case both $(X + aY) \times Y$ and $X \times Y$ are 0. So we suppose that $\{X, Y\}$ is independent. Hence

$\{X + aY, Y\}$ is independent. We have, using (8), $|(X + aY) \times Y|^2 = |X + aY|^2|Y|^2 - (X + aY, Y)^2 = (|X|^2 + 2a(X, Y) + |Y|^2)|Y|^2 - (X, Y)^2 - 2a(X, Y)|Y|^2 - a^2(Y, Y)^2 = |X|^2|Y|^2 - (X, Y)^2.$ Thus $(X + aY) \times Y$ has the same length as $X \times Y$. Since $(X + aY) \times Y$ is perpendicular to $X + aY$ and to Y, we know that $(X + aY) \times Y$ is perpendicular to X and to Y. We know that $\{X + aY, Y, (X + aY) \times Y\}$ is a positive triple. From (2) we know that $\{X, Y, (X + aY) \times Y\}$ is a positive triple. Thus $(X + aY) \times Y$ satisfies the same conditions as does $X \times Y$. We conclude that $(X + aY) \times Y = X \times Y$. This completes the proof of (11).

The cross product can be interpreted as area. From (6a) we see that $|X \times Y|$ is the area of the parallelogram determined by X and Y. (See Fig. 2.)

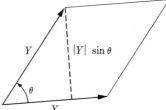

Y $|Y| \sin \theta$

θ

FIGURE 2 X

Now let $\{X, Y\}$ be an independent set and let $aX + bY + c(X \times Y) = 0$. Then $0 = (0, X \times Y) = a(X, X \times Y) + b(Y, X \times Y) + c(X \times Y, X \times Y) = c|X \times Y|^2$. This last equality uses (6b). From (6a), $|X \times Y|^2 > 0$. Thus $c = 0$. Therefore $aX + bY = 0$. We conclude that $\{X, Y, X \times Y\}$ is an independent set and is therefore a basis for R^3. Let W be any vector in R^3. Then $W = aX + bY + c(X \times Y)$. We have, using (6b),

$$(12) \qquad\qquad (X \times Y, W) = c|X \times Y|^2.$$

Let ϕ be the angle between $X \times Y$ and W. Then (12) tells us that $0 \le \phi \le \pi/2$ if $c \ge 0$ and $\pi/2 < \phi \le \pi$ if $c < 0$. From (2), $\{X, Y, W\}$ is a positive triple if and only if $\{X, Y, c(X \times Y)\}$ is a positive triple. Since $\{X, Y, X \times Y\}$ is a positive triple, we have that $\{X, Y, c(X \times Y)\}$ is a positive triple if and only if $c > 0$. Combining these results we have the following.

(13)   Let ϕ be the angle between W and $X \times Y$. Then $0 \le \phi < \pi/2$ if and only if $\{X, Y, W\}$ is a positive triple and $\pi/2 < \phi \le \pi$ if and only if $\{X, Y, W\}$ is a negative triple.

Let θ be the angle between X and Y. Suppose that $\theta \ne 0$ or π, and $\phi \ne \pi/2$. Then $|(X \times Y, W)| = \big||X|\,|Y|\,|W| \sin\theta \cos\phi\big|$, which is just

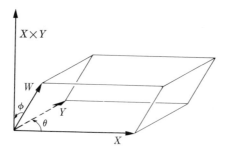

FIGURE 3

the volume of the parallelopiped determined by X, Y, and W. (See Fig. 3.) Thus, using (13), we have the following.

(14) $(X \times Y, W) = \pm$ the volume of the parallelopiped determined by X, Y, and W, with a plus sign if $\{X, Y, W\}$ is a positive triple, and a minus sign if $\{X, Y, W\}$ is a negative triple.

If $\{X, Y, W\}$ is a dependent set, then we define the volume of the parallelopiped determined by X, Y, and W to be zero. This is consistent with (14). For if $\{X, Y, W\}$ is dependent, then either $\{X, Y\}$ is dependent, (hence $X \times Y = 0$) or W is a linear combination of X and Y, (in which case W is perpendicular to $X \times Y$).

Since the volume of the parallelopiped determined by X, Y, and W is the same as the volume of the parallelopiped determined by Y, W, and X, and $\{X, Y, W\}$ is a positive triple if and only if $\{Y, W, X\}$ is a positive triple [see (1)], we must have

(15) $$(X \times Y, W) = (Y \times W, X).$$

We are now in a position to give a formula for computation of $(X \times Y, W)$ and $X \times Y$ in terms of coordinates.

If $X = (x_1, x_2, x_3)$, $Y = (y_1, y_2, y_3)$, and $W = (w_1, w_2, w_3)$, then

(16) $$(X \times Y, W) = \det \begin{bmatrix} x_1 & x_2 & x_3 \\ y_1 & y_2 & y_3 \\ w_1 & w_2 & w_3 \end{bmatrix}.$$

To prove (16) let

$$A = \begin{bmatrix} x_1 & x_2 & x_3 \\ y_1 & y_2 & y_3 \\ w_1 & w_2 & w_3 \end{bmatrix}$$

and let $d(A) = (X \times Y, W)$. We shall show that $d(A)$ is a determinant function. Let A' be obtained from A by interchanging two rows of A. If these are the first and second row, then $d(A') = -d(A)$ from (9). Suppose that these are the first and third rows. Then, using (16) and (9), we have $d(A') = (W \times Y, X) = (Y \times X, W) = -(X \times Y, W) = -d(A)$. If we interchange the second and third rows, then a similar proof shows that $d(A') = -d(A)$. This shows that (8a) of Section 6 holds for $d(A)$.

Since $a(X \times Y, W) = (X \times Y, aW) = (a(X \times Y), W) = ((aX) \times Y, W) = (X \times (aY), W)$, by using (10) and the properties of the inner product, we see that (8b) of Section 6 holds for $d(A)$. The fact that $d(A)$ satisfies (8c) of Section 6 is a consequence of (11) and (15). Its proof is left as an exercise.

Let $X^1 = (1, 0, 0)$, $X^2 = (0, 1, 0)$, and $X^3 = (0, 0, 1)$. Then, using (6), we have that $X^1 \times X^2 = X^3$, so that $(X^1 \times X^2, X^3) = 1$. Since $d(I) = (X^1 \times X^2, X^3)$ we see that (8d) of Section 6 is valid. Therefore $d(A)$ is a determinant function. Since there is only one such function on 3×3 matrices, we must have $d(A) = \det(A)$. This completes the proof of (16).

The result (16) has many consequences. We have [see (19) of Section 6]

(17) $(X \times Y, W)$ is a linear function of one variable with the other two fixed; i.e., $((aX^1 + bX^2) \times Y, W) = a(X^1 \times Y, W) + b(X^2 \times Y, W)$; $(X \times (aY^1 + bY^2), W) = a(X \times Y^1, W) + b(X \times Y^2, W)$; and $(X \times Y, aW^1 + bW^2) = a(X \times Y, W^1) + b(X \times Y, W^2)$.

Let $\{X^1, X^2, X^3\}$ be the standard basis. Then

(18) $X \times Y = (X \times Y, X^1)X^1 + (X \times Y, X^2)X^2 + (X \times Y, X^3)X^3$,

so that if $X = (x_1, x_2, x_3)$ and $Y = (y_1, y_2, y_3)$, then, using the Laplace expansion along the third row, we obtain

$$(X \times Y, X^1) = \det \begin{bmatrix} x_1 & x_2 & x_3 \\ y_1 & y_2 & y_3 \\ 1 & 0 & 0 \end{bmatrix} = \det \begin{bmatrix} x_2 & x_3 \\ y_2 & y_3 \end{bmatrix},$$

$$(X \times Y, X^2) = \det \begin{bmatrix} x_1 & x_2 & x_3 \\ y_1 & y_2 & y_3 \\ 0 & 1 & 0 \end{bmatrix} = -\det \begin{bmatrix} x_1 & x_3 \\ y_1 & y_3 \end{bmatrix},$$

$$(X \times Y, X^3) = \det \begin{bmatrix} x_1 & x_2 & x_3 \\ y_1 & y_2 & y_3 \\ 0 & 0 & 1 \end{bmatrix} = \det \begin{bmatrix} x_1 & x_2 \\ y_1 & y_2 \end{bmatrix}.$$

These give

(19) $X \times Y = (x_2 y_3 - x_3 y_2, x_3 y_1 - x_1 y_3, x_1 y_2 - x_2 y_1)$.

Remarks. The result (16), combined with the result (15), gives full justification for calling det (A) the oriented n-dimensional volume of the n-dimensional parallelopiped determined by the rows of A.

We could have derived (19) directly from (6), and could use (19) to derive the properties of the cross product. We have chosen to derive (19) last as this procedure stresses the geometrical properties of the cross product and its relation to orientation in R^3.

The notation $\mathbf{i} = (1, 0, 0)$, $\mathbf{j} = (0, 1, 0)$, and $\mathbf{k} = (0, 0, 1)$ is common. Using this we have the following mnemonic form of (19):

$$(20) \qquad X \times Y = \det \begin{bmatrix} \mathbf{i} & \mathbf{j} & \mathbf{k} \\ x_1 & x_2 & x_3 \\ y_1 & y_2 & y_3 \end{bmatrix}.$$

We then obtain $X \times Y$ by taking a Laplace expansion along the first row of

$$\begin{bmatrix} \mathbf{i} & \mathbf{j} & \mathbf{k} \\ x_1 & x_2 & x_3 \\ y_1 & y_2 & y_3 \end{bmatrix}.$$

This formula is not quite legitimate, since $\mathbf{i}$, $\mathbf{j}$, and $\mathbf{k}$ are not numbers. It does give us, however, a simple form for remembering (19). From (20) we have

$$(21) \quad \begin{aligned} \mathbf{i} \times \mathbf{j} &= \mathbf{k} = -\mathbf{j} \times \mathbf{i}; \quad & \mathbf{i} \times \mathbf{k} &= -\mathbf{j} = -\mathbf{k} \times \mathbf{i}; \\ \mathbf{j} \times \mathbf{k} &= \mathbf{i} = -\mathbf{k} \times \mathbf{j}; \quad & \mathbf{i} \times \mathbf{i} &= \mathbf{j} \times \mathbf{j} = \mathbf{k} \times \mathbf{k} = 0. \end{aligned}$$

These can also be derived directly from (6).

A second cross product can be obtained by replacing (6c) by the condition

$$(22) \qquad \{X, Y, Z\} \text{ is a negative triple.}$$

Let us denote this by $X \otimes Y$. Then $X \otimes Y = Y \times X$. There is no particular reason for preferring (6c) over (22). In physics we often use the so-called "right-hand rule" or "left-hand rule" to distinguish which of the cross products we use. We say that $\{\mathbf{i}, \mathbf{j}, \mathbf{k}\}$ is oriented by the "right-hand rule" if we can point the index finger of the right hand in the direction of $\mathbf{i}$, the middle finger of the right hand in the direction of $\mathbf{j}$, and the thumb of the right hand in the direction of $\mathbf{k}$. If we say that $\{\mathbf{i}, \mathbf{j}, \mathbf{k}\}$ is oriented by the "right-hand rule" and use (6c), then we say that $\{X, Y, X \times Y\}$ is also oriented by the "right-hand rule," and call $X \times Y$ the "right-hand" cross product of X and Y. These concepts are helpful, but they are also difficult to use in proofs.

The use of the standard inner product in defining $X \times Y$ is also arbitrary. If $(X, Y)_1$ is another inner product, then we can use (6) to define the cross product with respect to $(X, Y)_1$. When we do this the concepts of length and angle used in (6) must, of course, be given in terms of $(X, Y)_1$.

The cross product does not easily generalize to higher dimensions. On R^4, for example, the conditions (6a) and (6b) only describe a circle; i.e., those vectors of length given by (6a) and satisfying (6b) have their terminal points on a circle in the two-dimensional subspace which is the orthogonal complement of $\{X, Y\}$. There is no simple condition like (6c) which allows us to pick a unique vector from this circle.

EXERCISES

1. This exercise shows how certain geometric properties can be easily treated using the cross product. We assume that R^3 has been identified with V as in the first paragraph of this section. The drawing of figures may be helpful.

   (a) Show that the area of the triangle whose vertices are X, Y, and Z is $\frac{1}{2}|(X - Z) \times (Y - Z)|$.

   (b) Show that the volume of a tetrahedron whose vertices are X, Y, Z, and W is $\frac{1}{6}|((X - W) \times (Y - W), Z - W)|$.

   (c) Show that the perpendicular distance from X to the line through Y and Z is
   $$\frac{|(X - Z) \times (Y - Z)|}{|Y - Z|}.$$

   (d) Show that the perpendicular distance from X to the plane through Y, Z, and W is
   $$\frac{|((X - W) \times (Y - W), Z - W)|}{|(Y - W) \times (Z - W)|}.$$

   (e) Show that the distance between the line through X and Y, and the line through Z and W is given by
   $$\frac{|((X - Y) \times (Z - W), X - Z)|}{|(X - Y) \times (Z - W)|}.$$

2. Several geometric figures can be easily described using vector notation. Show that each of the following is true.

   (a) A sphere with center at Y and radius r is the collection of all vectors X such that $|X - Y| = r$.

   (b) The plane perpendicular to Y, and passing through Z is the collection of all vectors X such that $(X - Z, Y) = 0$.

   (c) The line through Y parallel to the line through Z and 0 is the collection of all vectors X such that $(X - Y) \times Z = 0$. [*Hint:* Use (7).]

3. Determine the geometric nature of each of the following collections of vectors in R^3.

   (a) The collection of all X such that $X \times Y = Z$, where Y and Z are fixed.

   (b) The collection of all X such that $(X \times Y, Z) = 0$, where Y and Z are fixed.

   (c) The collection of all X such that $(X \times Y, X \times Z) = 0$, where Y and Z are fixed.

4. Let $X = (1, 0, 1)$, $Y = (0, 1, 1)$, $Z = (1, 1, 1)$, $W = (1, 2, 3)$. Find the following.

   (a) $(X \times Y, Z)$

   (b) $(3X - 2Y + Z) \times W$

   (c) $X \times Y + 3Z \times Y$

   (d) $(X \times Y) \times (Y \times Z)$

   (e) $(((X \times Y) \times W) \times Z) \times W$

   (f) The area of the triangle whose vertices are X, Y, and W.

   (g) The volume of the tetrahedron whose vertices are X, $X + Y$, Z, $Z + W$.

   (h) The perpendicular distance from Y to the line through X and Z.

   (i) The distance between the line through X and Y and the line through Z and W.

   (j) The perpendicular distance from W to the plane through X, Y, and Z.

5. Complete the proof of (16) by showing that $d(A)$ satisfies (8c) of Section 6.

6. Let $\{Y^1, Y^2, Y^3\}$ be an orthonormal basis for R^3, using the standard inner product. Show that $Y^1 \times Y^2 = \pm Y^3$ and that if $Y^1 \times Y^2 = Y^3$, then $Y^1 \times Y^3 = -Y^2$ and $Y^2 \times Y^3 = Y^1$. [*Hint:* Use (6a) and (6b) to show that $Y^1 \times Y^2 = \pm Y^3$, that $Y^1 \times Y^3 = \pm Y^2$ and that $Y^2 \times Y^3 = \pm Y^1$. Then use (14) and (2).]

7. Show that $(X \times Y) \times Z = (X, Z)Y - (Y, Z)X$. [*Hint:* Establish the result where X, Y, and Z are any one of $\mathbf{i} = (1, 0, 0)$, $\mathbf{j} = (0, 1, 0)$, or $\mathbf{k} = (0, 0, 1)$. Then use (17) to establish the result when X is arbitrary and Y and Z are any one of $\mathbf{i}$, $\mathbf{j}$, or $\mathbf{k}$. Apply (17) twice more.]

8. Using Exercise 7, establish each of the following.

   (a) $(X \times Y) \times Z + (Z \times X) \times Y + (Y \times Z) \times X = 0$.

   (b) Suppose that $\{X, Z\}$ is independent. Then $(X \times Y) \times Z = X \times (Y \times Z)$ if and only if $(Y, Z) = 0$.

9. (a) Establish (17) directly by using (15) and the fact that $(X \times Y, aW^1 + bW^2) = a(X \times Y, W^1) + b(X \times Y, W^2)$ for all X, Y, W^1, and W^2 and all real numbers a and b. This gives an alternative proof of (19) of Section 6.

   (b) Show that $(aX^1 + bX^2) \times Y = a(X^1 \times Y) + b(X^2 \times Y)$.

10. Let R^3 have the standard inner product. Let T be a skew-symmetric linear operator on R^3, that is, $T^* = -T$. Show that there is a unique vector Y in R^3 such that $TX = Y \times X$. [*Hint:* The matrix of T is of the form

$$\begin{bmatrix} 0 & a & b \\ -a & 0 & c \\ -b & -c & 0 \end{bmatrix}.$$

Let $Y = (-c, b, -a)$.]

11. Let $\{X, Y, Z\}$ be independent and let T be a linear operator on R^3. Show that $\det(T) = (TX \times TY, TZ)/(X \times Y, Z)$. [*Hint:* Use (16) and (33) of Section 6.]

NOTES

We have given only a small number of the many applications of linear algebra to geometry. Robinson [22] gives further elementary applications to geometry. An older, thorough, and highly readable treatment of algebra and geometry is given in Klein [18].

A certain class of infinite dimensional spaces, called Hilbert spaces, possess inner products. An introduction to the theory of these spaces is given in Berberian [2]. For applications of inner products and orthogonality in Fourier series see Tolstov [25, Chapter 2]. An inner product gives rise to a concept of length, which enables the study of approximation. For an elegant treatment of this subject using linear algebra, see Nickerson, *et al.* [21, Chapters 6–8].

The adjoint of Section 5 and the determinant are useful in differential equations. For example, see Kaplan [16]. More results about determinants can be found in Aitken [1]. Many integral equations can be solved using an infinite dimensional analog of Cramer's rule. For example, see Lovitt [20, Chapter 3]. For various applications of the cross product see Kaplan [17]. The cross product is not available in dimensions other than 3. For a related concept, called the tensor product, see Smirnov [24, Chapter 3] and Jacobson [15, Chapter 7].

The exercises of Section 4 contain results of use in linear programming. For an introduction to one of the central tools in this important new field, see Ficken [9].

Introduction to the
Theory of a Single Linear Operator

Section 1. DIAGONALIZABLE OPERATORS: I

In many applications of linear algebra we are concerned with various properties of a single linear operator. This has led to a considerable collection of literature confined to the study of a single operator. This chapter gives an introduction to some of these results. If T is a linear operator on V, many questions about T arise. In Chapter 1 we showed how to find a matrix expression for T. We then showed how to find the rank and nullity of T using the matrix expression. We could also use this matrix expression and the theory of matrix multiplication in order to find T^2, and other powers of T. When dim V is large, many of these computations are very tedious. If we were restricted to a single matrix expression for T, this would be a serious hindrance. We may be able, however, by a clever choice of a basis for V, to find a "simple" matrix expression for T. As we saw in Chapter 1, matrix multiplication is easiest for diagonal matrices.

In this chapter we shall give answers to the following questions. Can we find a basis for V such that the matrix of T is diagonal? If so, what kind of questions about T can we answer? As we shall see, the answer to the first question is not always affirmative, but fortunately, it is affirmative for a large class of operators. This section will discuss the case where T does have a diagonal matrix representation. We will also show that questions about diagonal representations lead naturally to questions about roots of certain polynomials. In Sections 2 and 3 we shall discuss polynomials, then apply the theory of polynomials in Section 4 to the question of diagonal matrix representations. The most important result in this chapter is given in Section 4. It states that a symmetric operator always has at least one diagonal matrix representation. Chapter 4 will contain applications of the results of this chapter. We begin with an example.

Let T be the linear operator on R^2 such that

$$(1) \qquad T(x, y) = (x', y') \quad \text{if and only if} \quad \begin{bmatrix} 3 & -1 \\ -1 & 3 \end{bmatrix} \begin{bmatrix} x \\ y \end{bmatrix} = \begin{bmatrix} x' \\ y' \end{bmatrix}.$$

Compute the matrix of T with respect to the basis $\{(1, 1), (1, -1)\}$. This gives

$$\begin{bmatrix} 3 & -1 \\ -1 & 3 \end{bmatrix}\begin{bmatrix} 1 \\ 1 \end{bmatrix} = \begin{bmatrix} 2 \\ 2 \end{bmatrix} = 2\begin{bmatrix} 1 \\ 1 \end{bmatrix}$$

and

$$\begin{bmatrix} 3 & -1 \\ -1 & 3 \end{bmatrix}\begin{bmatrix} 1 \\ -1 \end{bmatrix} = \begin{bmatrix} 4 \\ -4 \end{bmatrix} = 4\begin{bmatrix} 1 \\ -1 \end{bmatrix}$$

so that

(2) $T(1, 1) = 2(1, 1)$ and $T(1, -1) = 4(1, -1)$.

Thus the matrix of T with respect to $\{(1, 1), (1, -1)\}$ is the matrix

$$\begin{bmatrix} 2 & 0 \\ 0 & 4 \end{bmatrix}.$$

This is a diagonal matrix.

Let us list some of the computations we can carry out easily for T by using this matrix. We have if k is an integer ≥ 1, that the matrix of T^k with respect to $\{(1, 1), (1, -1)\}$ is

(3) $$\begin{bmatrix} 2^k & 0 \\ 0 & 4^k \end{bmatrix}.$$

T is invertible, since

$$\begin{bmatrix} 2 & 0 \\ 0 & 4 \end{bmatrix}$$

is invertible, and the matrix of T^{-1} with respect to $\{(1, 1), (1, -1)\}$ is

(4) $$\begin{bmatrix} \frac{1}{2} & 0 \\ 0 & \frac{1}{4} \end{bmatrix}.$$

If λ is a real number, then the equation

$$TX = Y + \lambda X$$

is the same as the equation

$$TX = Y + \lambda IX.$$

This equation is the same as the equation

(5) $(T - \lambda I)X = Y.$

The matrix of $T - \lambda I$ with respect to $\{(1, 1), (1, -1)\}$ is

$$\begin{bmatrix} 2 - \lambda & 0 \\ 0 & 4 - \lambda \end{bmatrix}$$

so that (5) has a unique solution X for each Y if and only if this matrix is invertible; i.e., if and only if $\lambda \neq 2$ and $\lambda \neq 4$.

Does T have a square root? In other words, is there an operator S on R^2 such that $S^2 = T$? The simple form of

$$\begin{bmatrix} 2 & 0 \\ 0 & 4 \end{bmatrix}$$

allows us to answer this easily. Let S be the linear operator on R^2 whose matrix with respect to $\{(1, 1),\ (1, -1)\}$ is

$$\begin{bmatrix} \sqrt{2} & 0 \\ 0 & 2 \end{bmatrix}.$$

Then since

$$\begin{bmatrix} \sqrt{2} & 0 \\ 0 & 2 \end{bmatrix}^2 = \begin{bmatrix} 2 & 0 \\ 0 & 4 \end{bmatrix}$$

we see that $S^2 = T$.

Let k be any integer ≥ 1 and let R be the linear operator on R^2 whose matrix with respect to $\{(1, 1),\ (1, -1)\}$ is

$$\begin{bmatrix} 2^{1/k} & 0 \\ 0 & 4^{1/k} \end{bmatrix}.$$

Then

(6) $R^k = T.$

This follows from the fact that

$$\begin{bmatrix} 2^{1/k} & 0 \\ 0 & 4^{1/k} \end{bmatrix}^k = \begin{bmatrix} 2 & 0 \\ 0 & 4 \end{bmatrix}.$$

We shall now generalize these results. Let V be a finite dimensional vector space, and let T be a linear operator on V. We say that T is *diagonalizable* if there is a basis $\{X^1, X^2, \ldots, X^n\}$ for V such that the matrix of T with respect to $\{X^1, X^2, \ldots, X^n\}$ is a diagonal matrix. Thus the operator given in (1) is a diagonalizable operator on R^2.

Let T be a diagonalizable operator on V and let $\{X^1, X^2, \ldots, X^n\}$ be a basis for V such that the matrix of T with respect to this basis is diagonal. Let A be the matrix of T with respect to $\{X^1, X^2, \ldots, X^n\}$. Then

(7) $A = \begin{bmatrix} d_1 & 0 & 0 \ldots 0 \\ 0 & d_2 & 0 \ldots 0 \\ \vdots & & \\ 0 & 0 & 0 \ldots d_n \end{bmatrix}.$

We have

(8) $\det (T) = d_1 d_2 \ldots d_n.$

This tells us that T is invertible if and only if $d_i \neq 0$ for $i = 1, 2, \ldots, n$. T^{-1} is easily described in terms of $\{X^1, X^2, \ldots, X^n\}$ for the matrix of T^{-1} with respect to this basis is A^{-1}, and

$$
(9) \qquad A^{-1} = \begin{bmatrix} \dfrac{1}{d_1} & 0 & \cdots & 0 \\ 0 & \dfrac{1}{d_2} & \cdots & 0 \\ \vdots & & & \\ 0 & 0 & \cdots & \dfrac{1}{d_n} \end{bmatrix} \quad \text{if} \quad d_i \neq 0, \qquad i = 1, 2, \ldots, n.
$$

Let k be an integer ≥ 1. Then the matrix of T^k with respect to $\{X^1, X^2, \ldots, X^n\}$ is A^k, where

$$
(10) \qquad A^k = \begin{bmatrix} d_1^k & 0 & \ldots & 0 \\ 0 & d_2^k & \ldots & 0 \\ \vdots & & & \\ 0 & 0 & \ldots & d_n^k \end{bmatrix}.
$$

Suppose that $d_i \geq 0$ for $i = 1, 2, \ldots, n$ and let k be an integer ≥ 1. Let R be the linear operator on V whose matrix with respect to $\{X^1, X^2, \ldots, X^n\}$ is

$$
(11) \qquad B = \begin{bmatrix} d_1^{1/k} & 0 & \ldots & 0 \\ 0 & d_2^{1/k} & \ldots & 0 \\ \vdots & & & \\ 0 & 0 & \ldots & d_n^{1/k} \end{bmatrix}.
$$

Then $B^k = A$ so that

$$
(12) \qquad\qquad\qquad R^k = T.
$$

If λ is a real number, then

$$
(13) \qquad TX = Y + \lambda X \quad \text{if and only if} \quad (T - \lambda I)X = Y.
$$

The matrix of $T - \lambda I$ with respect to $\{X^1, X^2, \ldots, X^n\}$ is

$$
(14) \qquad C = \begin{bmatrix} d_1 - \lambda & 0 & \ldots & 0 \\ 0 & d_2 - \lambda & \ldots & 0 \\ \vdots & & & \\ 0 & 0 & \ldots & d_n - \lambda \end{bmatrix}.
$$

Thus $TX = Y + \lambda X$ has a unique solution X for each Y in V if and only if $\det (C) \neq 0$, that is, $\lambda \neq d_i$ for $i = 1, 2, \ldots, n$.

From these examples the ease of computation with a diagonalizable operator should be clear. In the exercises and in subsequent sections we will give further examples of the simplicity obtained when T is diagonalizable. Thus the important question is: How can we determine whether an operator is diagonalizable? There is no simple answer to this question. In this section we shall give a condition which guarantees that an operator is diagonalizable. In Section 4 we shall characterize diagonalizable operators and then show that if T is symmetric with respect to some inner product, then T is diagonalizable.

Let A be the matrix of T with respect to the basis $\{X^1, X^2, \ldots, X^n\}$. Suppose that A is diagonal so that A has the form (7). Then from the definition of A we have

$$(15) \qquad\qquad TX^i = d_i X^i, \qquad i = 1, 2, \ldots, n.$$

The equation $TX^i = d_i X^i$ is the same as the equation

$$(d_i I - T)X^i = 0.$$

Since $X^i \neq 0$, we know that $d_i I - T$ is *not* invertible, i.e.,

$$\det (d_i I - T) = 0 \qquad \text{for} \qquad i = 1, 2, \ldots, n.$$

Let us introduce some new terminology.

Let T be a linear operator on V. A real number c is called a *(real) characteristic value* of T if $cI - T$ is *not* invertible. Suppose that V is finite dimensional. Then the following are equivalent.

(16)
    (a) c is a characteristic value of T.
    (b) nullity $(cI - T) \neq 0$.
    (c) There is a vector $X \neq 0$ such that $TX = cX$.
    (d) $\det (cI - T) = 0$.

The proof of (16) follows from Theorem 10 and (15) of Section 6, Chapter 2. A vector $X \neq 0$ such that $TX = cX$ is called a *characteristic vector* (of T) *belonging to* c. If c is a characteristic value of T, then the null space of $cI - T$ is called the *characteristic subspace* belonging to c.

In terms of these concepts we have the following.

(17) T is diagonalizable if and only if there is a basis for V consisting of characteristic vectors for T.

Suppose that T is diagonalizable and let $\{X^1, X^2, \ldots, X^n\}$ be a basis for V such that (15) holds. Using (16c) we have that d_i is a characteristic value of T and that X^i is a characteristic vector belonging to d_i, $i = 1, 2, \ldots, n$. Thus $\{X^1, X^2, \ldots, X^n\}$ is a basis for V consisting of characteristic vectors for T. Conversely, if $\{X^1, X^2, \ldots, X^n\}$ is a basis for V such that X^i is a characteristic vector belonging to d_i, $i = 1, 2, \ldots,$ n, then equations (15) hold so that the matrix of T with respect to $\{X^1, X^2, \ldots, X^n\}$ is diagonal. This establishes (17).

The problem of determining whether T is diagonalizable is reduced to the problem of finding real numbers c such that $\det (cI - T) = 0$ and to the problem of finding "enough" characteristic vectors for such c. The equation $\det (cI - T) = 0$ is called the *characteristic equation* of T. As we shall see, T will fail to be diagonalizable when $\det (cI - T) = 0$ fails to have "enough" real roots or when a given characteristic value fails to have "enough" characteristic vectors. Let us look at some examples.

Let T be the operator on R^2 defined by

$$(18) \qquad T(x, y) = (x', y') \quad \text{if and only if} \quad \begin{bmatrix} 1 & -2 \\ 1 & -1 \end{bmatrix} \begin{bmatrix} x \\ y \end{bmatrix} = \begin{bmatrix} x' \\ y' \end{bmatrix}.$$

Then, from (16c), c is a characteristic value of T if and only if

$$(19) \qquad \det \begin{bmatrix} c - 1 & 2 \\ -1 & c + 1 \end{bmatrix} = 0.$$

We have, however, that

$$\det \begin{bmatrix} c - 1 & 2 \\ -1 & c + 1 \end{bmatrix} = c^2 + 1,$$

and the equation $c^2 + 1 = 0$ has no real roots. Thus T has no real characteristic values so that T cannot be diagonalizable.

Let T be the operator on R^2 defined by

$$(20) \qquad T(x, y) = (x', y') \quad \text{if and only if} \quad \begin{bmatrix} 1 & 1 \\ 0 & 1 \end{bmatrix} \begin{bmatrix} x \\ y \end{bmatrix} = \begin{bmatrix} x' \\ y' \end{bmatrix}.$$

Then c is a characteristic value of T if and only if

$$(21) \qquad \det \begin{bmatrix} c - 1 & -1 \\ 0 & c - 1 \end{bmatrix} = (c - 1)^2 = 0.$$

Thus $c = 1$ is the only real characteristic value of T. Therefore, if T is diagonalizable, then, from (17), we must have at least two independent solutions to $T(x, y) = (x, y)$, i.e., nullity $(I - T) = 2$. Since the matrix of $I - T$ is

$$\begin{bmatrix} 0 & -1 \\ 0 & 0 \end{bmatrix},$$

we see that nullity $(I - T) = 1$. Thus T is *not* diagonalizable.

If $T = I$, then

$$\det (cI - T) = \det \begin{bmatrix} c - 1 & 0 \\ 0 & c - 1 \end{bmatrix} = (c - 1)^2.$$

The identity is clearly diagonalizable. We see from this that I and the operator of (20) have the same characteristic equation, yet I is diagonalizable and the operator of (20) is not. We conclude that the characteristic equation, even if it has real roots, does not *in general* give us enough information to determine if T is diagonalizable. In spite of this, there is one situation in which the characteristic equation does give us enough information.

(22) If $\det (cI - T) = 0$ has n distinct real roots $d_1, d_2, \ldots, d_n$ [i.e., $d_i \neq d_j$ if $i \neq j$ and $\det (d_iI - T) = 0$ for $i = 1, 2, \ldots, n$], where $n = \dim V$, then T is diagonalizable.

This is a consequence of the following.

Lemma 3. Let $d_1, d_2, \ldots, d_k$ be distinct real numbers such that $\det (d_iI - T) = 0$ for $i = 1, 2, \ldots, k$. Let X^i be a characteristic vector of T belonging to d_i for $i = 1, 2, \ldots, k$. Then $\{X^1, X^2, \ldots, X^k\}$ is an independent set.

Proof. We have $TX^i = d_iX^i$, where $X^i \neq 0$ for $i = 1, 2, \ldots, k$. Suppose that $a_1X^1 + a_2X^2 + \cdots + a_kX^k = 0$. Let $S_1 = (d_2I - T)(d_3I - T) \ldots (d_kI - T)$. Then

(23) $$a_1S_1X^1 + a_2S_1X^2 + \cdots + a_kS_1X^k = 0.$$

Compute S_1X^i, $i = 1, 2, \ldots, k$. We have

$$S_1X^k = (d_2I - T)((d_3I - T) \cdots ((d_{k-1}I - T)((d_kI - T)X^k)) \cdots).$$

Since $TX^k = d_kX^k$, we know that $(d_kI - T)X^k = 0$. Thus $S_1X^k = 0$. Also

$$S_1X^{k-1}$$
$$= (d_2I - T)((d_3I - T) \cdots ((d_{k-1}I - T)((d_kI - T)X^{k-1})) \cdots).$$

Since $TX^{k-1} = d_{k-1}X^{k-1}$, we have that

$$(d_kI - T)X^{k-1} = (d_k - d_{k-1})X^{k-1}.$$

Thus $(d_{k-1}I - T)(d_kI - T)X^{k-1} = (d_k - d_{k-1})(d_{k-1}I - T)X^{k-1} = 0$, that is, $S_1X^{k-1} = 0$. In the same fashion we have that $S_1X^i = 0$ for

$i = 2, 3, \ldots, k$, and $S_1 X^1 = (d_2 - d_1)(d_3 - d_1) \cdots (d_k - d_1) X^1$. This shows that (23) is reduced to

$$(24) \qquad a_1(d_2 - d_1)(d_3 - d_1) \cdots (d_k - d_1) X^1 = 0.$$

Since $X^1 \neq 0$ and $d_1 \neq d_i$ for $i = 2, 3, \ldots, k$, we must have $a_1 = 0$. Let $S_2 = (d_1 I - T)(d_3 I - T) \cdots (d_k I - T)$; that is, S_2 is the product of the factors $(d_i I - T)$ for $i \neq 2$. Then $a_1 X^1 + a_2 X^2 + \cdots + a_k X^k = 0$ gives

$$(25) \qquad a_1 S_2 X^1 + a_2 S_2 X^2 + \cdots + a_k S_2 X^k = 0.$$

In the same manner that we obtained (24) from (23), we have

$$(26) \qquad a_2(d_1 - d_2)(d_3 - d_2) \cdots (d_k - d_2) X^2 = 0.$$

Since $X^2 \neq 0$ and $d_2 \neq d_i$ for $i \neq 2$, we must have $a_2 = 0$. Repetition of this process gives $a_i = 0$ for $i = 1, 2, \ldots, k$. This shows that $\{X^1, X^2, \ldots, X^k\}$ is an independent set. Q.E.D.

Remarks. The general form of Lemma 3 is given in Theorems 20 and 21 in the proofs of which we shall use operators like S_1 and S_2.

Let T_1 be the linear operator on R^2 defined by

$$(27) \qquad T_1(x, y) = (x', y') \quad \text{if and only if} \quad \begin{bmatrix} 1 & 1 \\ 0 & 2 \end{bmatrix} \begin{bmatrix} x \\ y \end{bmatrix} = \begin{bmatrix} x' \\ y' \end{bmatrix}.$$

Since

$$\det \begin{bmatrix} c - 1 & -1 \\ 0 & c - 2 \end{bmatrix} = (c - 1)(c - 2),$$

we see that $c = 1$ and $c = 2$ are characteristic values for T_1. Thus T_1 is diagonalizable by (22). A basis for R^2 consisting of characteristic vectors for T_1 is obtained by solving the equations

$$(28) \qquad \begin{bmatrix} 1 & 1 \\ 0 & 2 \end{bmatrix} \begin{bmatrix} x \\ y \end{bmatrix} = \begin{bmatrix} x \\ y \end{bmatrix} \quad \text{and} \quad \begin{bmatrix} 1 & 1 \\ 0 & 2 \end{bmatrix} \begin{bmatrix} x \\ y \end{bmatrix} = 2 \begin{bmatrix} x \\ y \end{bmatrix}.$$

This yields $\{(1, 0), (1, 1)\}$ as one basis for R^2 consisting of characteristic vectors for T_1. [We have $T_1(1, 0) = (1, 0)$, and $T_1(1, 1) = 2(1, 1)$.]

Let T be the operator on R^2 defined by (1). Then the matrix of TT_1 with respect to the standard basis is

$$\begin{bmatrix} 3 & -1 \\ -1 & 3 \end{bmatrix} \begin{bmatrix} 1 & 1 \\ 0 & 2 \end{bmatrix} = \begin{bmatrix} 3 & 1 \\ -1 & 5 \end{bmatrix}.$$

We have

$$\det (cI - TT_1) = \det \begin{bmatrix} c - 3 & -1 \\ 1 & c - 5 \end{bmatrix} = c^2 - 8c + 16 = (c - 4)^2.$$

Therefore, $c = 4$ is the only characteristic value of TT_1. Since nullity

$$(4I - TT_1) = \text{nullity} \begin{bmatrix} 1 & -1 \\ 1 & -1 \end{bmatrix} = 1,$$

we conclude that TT_1 is *not* diagonalizable. Yet both T and T_1 are diagonalizable.

Let T_2 be the linear operator on R^2 defined by

(29) $T_2(x, y) = (x', y')$ if and only if $\begin{bmatrix} 1 & 100 \\ 0 & 2 \end{bmatrix} \begin{bmatrix} x \\ y \end{bmatrix} = \begin{bmatrix} x' \\ y' \end{bmatrix}.$

Then $c = 1$ and $c = 2$ are characteristic values for T_2 so that T_2 is diagonalizable, using (22). If T is the operator given by (1), then the matrix of $T + T_1$ with respect to the standard basis is

$$\begin{bmatrix} 3 & -1 \\ -1 & 3 \end{bmatrix} + \begin{bmatrix} 1 & 100 \\ 0 & 2 \end{bmatrix} = \begin{bmatrix} 4 & 99 \\ -1 & 5 \end{bmatrix}.$$

We have

$$\det [cI - (T + T_1)] = \det \begin{bmatrix} c - 4 & -99 \\ 1 & c - 5 \end{bmatrix} = c^2 - 9c + 118.$$

Using the quadratic formula we conclude that $T + T_1$ has no real characteristic values.

In Chapter 4 we shall give a condition which will guarantee that $S + T$ and ST are diagonalizable whenever S and T are diagonalizable.

The phrase "characteristic value" has many synonyms. Some of these are *eigenvalue, latent root, spectral value, proper value*. A comparable terminology is used for "characteristic vector" and "characteristic subspace." Some authors say that T is of *spectral type*, or *completely reducible*, if T is diagonalizable. Equation (16d) is also called the *secular equation*.

The definition of characteristic value is the same when V is *not* finite dimensional. In this case we can have $cI - T$ not invertible even if nullity $(cI - T) = 0$. Because of this many authors distinguish between at least two types of characteristic values, i.e., those for which nullity $(cI - T) \neq 0$ and those for which nullity $(cI - T) = 0$.

We could generalize Lemma 3 and obtain a characterization of diagonalizable operators. Instead we shall follow a different path which uses several elementary facts about polynomials. These facts will be presented in Sections 2 and 3.

One minor matter needs attention. Let T be a diagonalizable operator on V. Let $\{Y^1, Y^2, \ldots, Y^n\}$ be a basis for V, and let A be the matrix of T with respect to $\{Y^1, Y^2, \ldots, Y^n\}$. We know that there is some basis for V, say $\{X^1, X^2, \ldots, X^n\}$, such that the matrix of T, say B, with respect to $\{X^1, X^2, \ldots, X^n\}$ is a diagonal matrix. As we have seen, many computations with T are greatly simplified using B. It may be, however, that we wish our results stated in terms of A, i.e., in terms of $\{Y^1, Y^2, \ldots, Y^n\}$, rather than $\{X^1, X^2, \ldots, X^n\}$. The relationship between A and B is given in (56) of Section 6, Chapter 1. We can use this to state our results in terms of A.

In (1), let

$$A = \begin{bmatrix} 3 & -1 \\ -1 & 3 \end{bmatrix} \quad \text{and} \quad B = \begin{bmatrix} 2 & 0 \\ 0 & 4 \end{bmatrix}.$$

Then A is the matrix of T with respect to $\{(1, 0), (0, 1)\}$ and B is the matrix of T with respect to $\{(1, 1), (1, -1)\}$. [See (2).] Let

$$P_0 = \begin{bmatrix} 1 & 1 \\ 1 & -1 \end{bmatrix}.$$

Then, using (56) of Section 6, Chapter 1, or by direct computation we have

(30) $$P_0^{-1} \begin{bmatrix} 3 & -1 \\ -1 & 3 \end{bmatrix} P_0 = \begin{bmatrix} 2 & 0 \\ 0 & 4 \end{bmatrix},$$

or, equivalently

(31) $$\begin{bmatrix} 3 & -1 \\ -1 & 3 \end{bmatrix} = P_0 \begin{bmatrix} 2 & 0 \\ 0 & 4 \end{bmatrix} P_0^{-1}.$$

Our results (3) through (6) were stated for B, that is, in terms of the basis $\{(1, 1), (1, -1)\}$. These results can be given for A by using P_0. For example, the matrix of T^k with respect to $\{(1, 0), (0, 1)\}$ is A^k and with respect to $\{(1, 1), (1, -1)\}$ is B^k. Thus, using (56) of Section 6, Chapter 1, we have

(32) $$P_0^{-1} A^k P_0 = B^k,$$

or, equivalently

(33) $$A^k = P_0 B^k P_0^{-1}.$$

To compute A^k directly if k is large is no easy task. The computation of B^k is trivial. Thus the formula (33) greatly reduces computation. The results (4) and (6) can also be given in terms of A. We have

(34) $$A^{-1} = P_0 B^{-1} P_0^{-1}.$$

(35) If $D = \begin{bmatrix} 2^{1/k} & 0 \\ 0 & 4^{1/k} \end{bmatrix}$ and $C = P_0 D P_0^{-1}$, then $C^k = A$.

If A and B are $n \times n$ matrices, we say that A is *similar* to B if there is an invertible $n \times n$ matrix P_0 such that $B = P_0 A P_0^{-1}$. (Note that if $B = P_0 A P_0^{-1}$, then $A = P_0^{-1} B P_0$, so that B is similar to A.) We say that A is *diagonalizable* if A is similar to a diagonal matrix. From (56) of Section 6, Chapter 1, we see that A is diagonalizable if and only if A is the matrix of a diagonalizable operator T on R^n (or on V, where dim $V = n$) with respect to some basis.

EXERCISES

1. Find at least one characteristic value and a corresponding characteristic vector for each of the following operators on R^3.
   (a) T is reflection in the plane $x = z$.
   (b) T is rotation about the line $x = y = z$ through the angle θ, where $0 < \theta < \pi$.
   (c) T is projection onto the plane $z = 0$.
   (d) $T(x, y, z) = (4x - y, x - y + z, 3x - z)$.
   (e) $T(x, y, z) = (3x + y + z, 2y + z, z)$.

2. Show that each of the following linear operators T on the indicated vector space V is diagonalizable.
   (a) $V = R^3$; $T(x, y, z) = (x, 2x + 2y, 3x + 3y + 3z)$
   (b) $V = R^3$; $T(x, y, z) = (3x - y, -x + 3y, z)$
   (c) $V = R^3$; $T(x, y, z) = (x + y + z, x + y + z, x + y + z)$
   (d) V is the space of polynomials of degree ≤ 2; $(Tf)(t) = (1/t) \int_0^t f(u)\, du$.
   (e) V is the space of 2×2 matrices; $TA = BA$, where
   $$B = \begin{bmatrix} 1 & 0 \\ 0 & -3 \end{bmatrix}.$$
   (f) V is the space of 2×2 matrices; $TA = BA$, where
   $$B = \begin{bmatrix} 1 & 1 \\ 0 & 2 \end{bmatrix}.$$

3. Which of the following operators on R^2 is diagonalizable?
   (a) $T(x, y) = (x - y, x + y)$
   (b) T is counterclockwise rotation about $(0, 0)$ through an angle θ, where $0 < \theta < \pi$.
   (c) T is reflection through the line $y = x$.
   (d) $T(x, y) = (x - y, x + 4y)$

4. (a) For each of the operators T of Exercise 2, give a description of T^k for $k \geq 1$.
   (b) For which of the operators T of Exercise 2 can you find an operator R such that $R^2 = T$ as in (12)?
   (c) For each of the operators T of Exercise 2, give a description of the values of λ for which $TX = Y + \lambda X$ has a unique solution X for each Y.

5. This exercise gives a complete description of the 2×2 case. Let T be a linear operator on V (dim $V = 2$) whose matrix with respect to some basis is

$$\begin{bmatrix} a & b \\ c & d \end{bmatrix}.$$

(a) Show that the characteristic equation for T is det $(tI - T) = t^2 - (a + d)t + ad - bc = 0$.
(b) Show that if $(a - d)^2 + 4bc < 0$, then T has no real characteristic values. [*Hint:* $(a + d)^2 - 4(ad - bc) = (a - d)^2 + 4bc.$]
(c) Show that if $(a - d)^2 + 4bc > 0$, then T is diagonalizable. [*Hint:* Use Lemma 3.]
(d) Suppose that $(a - d)^2 + 4bc = 0$. Show that T is diagonalizable if and only if $T = ((a + d)/2)I$.
(e) Suppose that $b = c$. Show that T is diagonalizable. [*Hint:* Show that (c) holds, or that $a = d$ and $b = 0$.]

6. Let T be a linear operator on R^3 defined by $T(x, y, z) = (ax + by, cx + dy, z)$. Show that T is diagonalizable if and only if

$$\begin{bmatrix} a & b \\ c & d \end{bmatrix}$$

is similar to a diagonal matrix. [*Hint:* Show that 1 is a characteristic value of T and that

$$\begin{bmatrix} a & b \\ c & d \end{bmatrix}\begin{bmatrix} x \\ y \end{bmatrix} = t\begin{bmatrix} x \\ y \end{bmatrix}$$

if and only if $T(x, y, 0) = t(x, y, 0).$]

7. Let

$$A = \begin{bmatrix} B & 0 \\ 0 & C \end{bmatrix},$$

where B is $n \times n$, C is $k \times k$, and each 0 represents a zero matrix of appropriate size. Show that A is similar to a diagonal matrix if and only B and C are each similar to diagonal matrices. This generalizes Exercise 6.

8. Let A be an upper triangular $n \times n$ matrix. Suppose that $A_{ii} \neq A_{jj}$ for $i \neq j$. Show that A is similar to a diagonal matrix. [*Hint:* Show that det $(tI - A) = (t - A_{11})(t - A_{22}) \cdots (t - A_{nn}).$]

9. Which of the following matrices is similar to a diagonal matrix? [*Hint:* Exercises 5 through 8 may be helpful.]

(a) $\begin{bmatrix} 2 & 1 & 0 & 0 \\ 1 & 1 & 0 & 0 \\ 0 & 0 & 3 & 1 \\ 0 & 0 & 1 & 0 \end{bmatrix}$ (b) $\begin{bmatrix} 7 & 0 & 0 & 0 & 0 \\ 1 & 6 & 0 & 0 & 0 \\ 2 & 1 & 5 & 0 & 0 \\ 1 & 1 & 1 & 4 & 0 \\ 0 & 1 & 1 & 1 & 3 \end{bmatrix}$

(c) $\begin{bmatrix} 2 & 1 & 0 & 0 \\ -1 & 1 & 0 & 0 \\ 0 & 0 & 3 & 1 \\ 0 & 0 & 1 & 0 \end{bmatrix}$

(d) $\begin{bmatrix} 2 & 1 & 0 & 0 \\ -1 & -1 & 0 & 0 \\ 0 & 0 & 1 & 1 \\ 0 & 0 & 1 & 1 \end{bmatrix}$

(e) $\begin{bmatrix} 0 & 1 & 0 \\ 0 & 0 & 2 \\ 0 & 0 & 0 \end{bmatrix}$

(f) $\begin{bmatrix} 6 & 1 & 0 & 0 & 0 & 0 & 0 \\ 1 & 2 & 0 & 0 & 0 & 0 & 0 \\ 0 & 0 & 4 & 1 & 0 & 0 & 0 \\ 0 & 0 & 0 & 2 & 0 & 0 & 0 \\ 0 & 0 & 0 & 0 & 2 & 1 & 0 \\ 0 & 0 & 0 & 0 & 0 & 1 & 1 \\ 0 & 0 & 0 & 0 & 0 & 0 & 3 \end{bmatrix}$

10. Show that if T is diagonalizable, then there is an operator S such that $S^3 = T$.

11. Find A^{23}, where

$$A = \tfrac{1}{4} \begin{bmatrix} -1 & 3 & 2 \\ 3 & -1 & 2 \\ 1 & 1 & 2 \end{bmatrix}.$$

12. Let V be finite dimensional and let (X, Y) be an inner product on V. Let T be a linear operator on V.

(a) Show that c is a characteristic value of T if and only if c is a characteristic value of T^*. [*Hint:* $(cI - T)^* = cI - T^*$. Use Theorem 17.]

(b) Show that if $c_1 \neq c_2$ and if $TX^1 = c_1 X^1$ and $T^*X^2 = c_2 X^2$, then $(X^1, X^2) = 0$. [*Hint:* Show that $(c_1 - c_2)(X^1, X^2) = 0$.]

(c) Show that if $T^* = -T$ and if c is a characteristic value of T, then $c = 0$. [*Hint:* If $TX = cX$, show that $(TX, X) = 0$.]

13. Let $Y(t) = (y_1(t), y_2(t), \ldots, y_n(t))$ be defined for $0 \leq t \leq c$. Let us denote

$$\left(\frac{d}{dt} y_1(t), \frac{d}{dt} y_2(t), \ldots, \frac{d}{dt} y_n(t) \right)$$

by $(d/dt)Y(t)$. Let T be a diagonalizable operator on R^n. Let $\{X^1, X^2, \ldots, X^n\}$ be a basis for R^n such that $TX^i = c_i X^i$ for $i = 1, 2, \ldots, n$. Show that the differential equation

$$\frac{d}{dt} Y(t) = T(Y(t))$$

has a solution $Y(t)$ such that $Y(0) = X = a_1 X^1 + a_2 X^2 + \cdots + a_n X^n$. Show that this solution is given by $Y(t) = a_1 e^{c_1 t} X^1 + a_2 e^{c_2 t} X^2 + \cdots + a_n e^{c_n t} X^n$. [*Hint:* In terms of coordinates with respect to $\{X^1, X^2, \ldots, X^n\}$, $(d/dt)Y(t) = T(Y(t))$, and $Y(0) = X$ become $(d/dt)Z_i(t) = c_i Z_i(t)$ and $Z_i(0) = a_i$, $1 \leq i \leq n$, where $Y(t) = Z_1(t)X^1 + Z_2(t)X^2 + \cdots + Z_n(t)X^n$.]

14. Using the method of Exercise 13, describe the solutions to the system of equations

$$\frac{dy_1}{dt} = 3y_1 - y_2 \qquad \frac{dy_2}{dt} = -y_1 + 3y_2$$

where $y_1(0) = 1$, $y_2(0) = 3$.

15. Let V be the vector space of continuous real-valued functions $f(t)$ defined for $0 \le t \le 1$. Let T be the linear operator on V defined by $Tf(t) = tf(t)$.

   (a) Show that if c is a real number and if $Tf = cf$, then $f(t) = 0$ for all t.

   (b) Show that if c is a real number such that $0 \le c \le 1$, then $cI - T$ is not invertible. [*Hint:* Show that $|t - c|^{1/2}$ is not in the range of $cI - T$.]

   (c) Show that if $c < 0$ or $c > 1$, then $cI - T$ is invertible by giving an explicit expression for $(cI - T)^{-1}$.

16. Write a flow diagram to determine if a 2×2 matrix is diagonalizable. [*Hint:* Use Exercise 5.]

Section 2.   POLYNOMIAL THEORY

In order to characterize diagonalizable operators we need a few results on polynomials. This section will sketch the results on polynomials which we will use.

A polynomial is a formal expression of the form

$$(1) \qquad f = a_0 + a_1 t + a_2 t^2 + \cdots + a_n t^n.$$

If each a_i is a real number, we call this expression a *real* polynomial. [If each a_i is a complex number, we call (1) a *complex* polynomial. If each a_i is a rational number, we call (1) a *rational* polynomial.] Unless otherwise qualified the word "polynomial" will mean "real polynomial." Most of our results, however, carry over without change to complex or rational polynomials.

If $a_n \ne 0$ in (1), then we call n the *degree* of the polynomial f and denote this by $\deg f$; we also call a_n the *leading coefficient* of f. If $f = 0$, then we do *not* define the degree of f.

For example, if $f = 8 + 7t + t^3$, then $\deg f = 3$; and if $g = 4$, then $\deg g = 0$.

When f and g are polynomials, we define the *sum* $f + g$ to be the polynomial obtained by adding the coefficients of like powers of t. For example, if $f = a_0 + a_1 t + a_2 t^2 + \cdots + a_n t^n$ and $g = b_0 + b_1 t + b_2 t^2 + \cdots + b_k t^k$ with $k \le n$, then $f + g = (a_0 + b_0) + (a_1 + b_1)t + (a_2 + b_2)t^2 + \cdots + (a_k + b_k)t^k + a_{k+1} t^{k+1} + \cdots + a_n t^n$. If a is a real number, then we denote the polynomial $(aa_0) + (aa_1)t + (aa_2)t^2 + \cdots + (aa_n)t^n$ by af. The collection of all polynomials with these definitions is a vector space.

The following is a consequence of these definitions.

(2)   If $f + g \neq 0$, then $\deg (f + g) \leq$ the maximum of the degrees of f and g. If $\deg f > \deg g$, then $\deg (f + g) = \deg f$.

One consequence of (2) is that the polynomials of degree $\leq n$ form a subspace of the space of all polynomials.

If $f = a_0 + a_1 t + a_2 t^2 + \cdots + a_n t^n$ and $g = b_0 + b_1 t + b_2 t^2 + \cdots + b_k t^k$, then we call the polynomial $(a_0 b_0) + (a_0 b_1 + a_1 b_0)t + (a_0 b_2 + a_1 b_1 + a_2 b_0)t^2 + \cdots + a_n b_k t^{n+k}$, the *product* of f and g and denote this by fg. The following are consequences of this definition.

(3) $fg = gf, \quad (af)g = a(fg), \quad f(g + h) = fg + fh.$

(4)   If $f \neq 0$ and $g \neq 0$, then $fg \neq 0$ and $\deg (fg) = \deg f + \deg g$.

From (4) we have the following.

(5)   If $fg = fh$ and $f \neq 0$, then $g = h$.

This is sometimes called the *cancellation law*. If $fg = fh$, then $f(g - h) = 0$, so that (4) tells us that either $f = 0$ or $g = h$.

We can also divide with polynomials. This is contained in the following result, called the *division algorithm* or *remainder theorem*. This result is merely a precise statement of the familiar long division.

(6)   If f and g are polynomials with $g \neq 0$, then there are *unique* polynomials q and r such that $f = gq + r$, where $r = 0$ or $\deg r < \deg g$.

We usually call q the *quotient* and r the *remainder*. The proof of (9) is straightforward. We merely apply long division, dividing f by g until we either have no remainder or a remainder of smaller degree than g. If we also have $f = gq_1 + r_1$, where $r_1 = 0$ or $\deg r_1 < \deg g$, then we must show that $r_1 = r$ and $q_1 = q$. Subtraction gives $0 = gq + r - (gq_1 + r_1) = g(q - q_1) + r - r_1$. Thus $r - r_1 = g(q_1 - q)$. If $q_1 - q \neq 0$, then (4) gives $\deg (r - r_1) = \deg g + \deg (q_1 - q) \geq \deg g$. From (2) and the conditions on r and r_1 we know that $r = r_1$ or $\deg (r - r_1) < \deg g$. We conclude that $q_1 = q$ and that $r_1 = r$. This proves (6).

As examples of (6) we have

(7)
$$t^4 + 7t^3 - 6t = (t^2 + 1)(t^2 + 7t - 1) + (1 - 13t),$$
$$t^3 + 3t^2 - 4 = (t - 1)(t^2 + 4t + 4) + 0,$$
$$t^2 + 7 = (t^4 + 7) \cdot 0 + (t^2 + 7).$$

The remainder theorem will be a helpful tool in our polynomial study. We may not be able to divide one polynomial by another and obtain a polynomial, but we can always find a quotient and a remainder.

A real number c is called a *real root* (or *real zero*) of the polynomial f if $f(c) = 0$. Here $f(c)$ is the number: $f(c) = a_0 + a_1c + a_2c^2 + \cdots + a_nc^n$, where f is given by (1). The following result is a consequence of the remainder theorem and is often called the *factor-root theorem*.

(8)   If $\deg f > 0$, then c is a real root of f if and only if $f = (t - c)q$, that is, if and only if $t - c$ "divides" f.

We have $f = (t - c)q + r$, where $r = 0$ or $\deg r < \deg (t - c) = 1$. In either case $r = d$, where d is a real number. Thus $f(c) = (c - c)q(c) + r(c) = d$. Therefore $f(c) = 0$ if and only if $d = 0$, that is, if and only if $f = (t - c)q$. This is (8). From (8) we have the following.

(9)   If $\deg f = n$, then f has at most n roots.

Let $c_1, c_2, \ldots, c_m$ be roots of f. Then an application of (8) m times yields $f = (t - c_1)(t - c_2) \ldots (t - c_m)g$. From (4) we have $\deg f = \deg (t - c_1) + \deg (t - c_2) + \cdots + \deg (t - c_m) + \deg g \geq m$. Thus $\deg f = n$ implies that $m \leq n$. This proves (9).

We use these results to construct a collection of polynomials of degree $(n - 1)$ which form a basis for the space of all polynomials of degree $\leq (n - 1)$. Let $c_1, c_2, \ldots, c_n$ be n distinct real numbers, that is, $c_i \neq c_j$ if $i \neq j$. Define

(10) $P_i = \dfrac{(t - c_1)(t - c_2) \ldots (t - c_{i-1})(t - c_{i+1}) \ldots (t - c_n)}{(c_i - c_1)(c_i - c_2) \ldots (c_i - c_{i-1})(c_i - c_{i+1}) \ldots (c_i - c_n)},$

$i = 1, 2, \ldots, n.$

In other words P_i is obtained by taking a product of all the factors $t - c_j$, omitting the factor $t - c_i$, then dividing by the product of the factors $c_i - c_j$, omitting the factor $c_i - c_i$. Then P_i is a polynomial of degree $(n - 1)$ and

(11) $P_i(c_j) = 0$ if $i \neq j$ and $P_i(c_i) = 1$, $i = 1, 2, \ldots, n.$

Let f be a polynomial of degree $\leq (n - 1)$, and let $g = f - f(c_1)P_1 - f(c_2)P_2 - \cdots - f(c_n)P_n$. If $g \neq 0$, then $\deg g \leq (n - 1)$. We have

$g(c_1)$
$= f(c_1) - f(c_1)P_1(c_1) - f(c_2)P_2(c_1) - f(c_3)P_3(c_1) - \cdots - f(c_n)P_n(c_1).$

Using (11) we have $P_1(c_1) = 1$ and $P_i(c_1) = 0$ if $i > 1$. Thus $g(c_1) = 0$. Similarly $g(c_2) = g(c_3) = \cdots = g(c_n) = 0$. The polynomial g has n

roots, and if $g \neq 0$, $\deg g \leq (n - 1)$. This contradicts (9). We conclude that $g = 0$. We have shown the following theorem.

Theorem 18. Let $c_1, c_2, \ldots, c_n$ be n distinct real numbers. Let P_i be defined by (10) for $i = 1, 2, \ldots, n$. Let f be a real polynomial such that $f = 0$ or $\deg f \leq (n - 1)$. Then

$$(12) \qquad f = f(c_1)P_1 + f(c_2)P_2 + \cdots + f(c_n)P_n.$$

The polynomials P_i are called the *Lagrange interpolation polynomials* for the numbers $c_1, c_2, \ldots, c_n$. The formula in (12) is called the *Lagrange interpolation formula*. Theorem 18 tells us that $\{P_1, P_2, \ldots, P_n\}$ spans the space of polynomials of degree $\leq (n - 1)$. Since this space has dimension n, we know that $\{P_1, P_2, \ldots, P_n\}$ is a basis for the space and that the expression for f given in (12) is unique.

The following special case of Theorem 18 will be useful in Section 4.

If $n \geq 2$, then

$$
\begin{aligned}
1 &= P_1 + P_2 + \cdots + P_n \\
t &= c_1 P_1 + c_2 P_2 + \cdots + c_n P_n \\
t^2 &= c_1^2 P_1 + c_2^2 P_2 + \cdots + c_n^2 P_n \\
&\vdots \\
t^{n-1} &= c_1^{n-1} P_1 + c_2^{n-1} P_2 + \cdots + c_n^{n-1} P_n.
\end{aligned}
$$

(13)

As we saw in Section 1 we need to find the roots of the characteristic equation to determine the characteristic values of an operator. The following results will be helpful in finding the nature of these roots.

Let $f = t^2 + bt + c$, where b and c are real numbers. Then f has a real root if and only if $b^2 - 4c \geq 0$. If $b - 4c \geq 0$, then the (14)   roots of f are given by

$$t = \frac{-b \pm \sqrt{b^2 - 4c}}{2}.$$

This is the well-known *quadratic formula*. A proof is given in Exercise 10(a), Section 2, Chapter 2. From (14) we conclude that $t^2 + 1$ has *no real* roots. The following result, known as the *fundamental theorem of algebra* is true.

(15)   If f is a real (or complex) polynomial of degree ≥ 1, then f has a complex root; i.e., there is a complex number α such that $f(\alpha) = 0$.

The proof of (15) is most easily given using the theory of integration of complex functions. As such a theory would lead us too far astray, we shall omit a proof. The form in which (15) is most useful is the following.

If f is a nonzero real polynomial, then we can write $f = dq_1q_2 \cdots q_r$,
(16)   where each q_i is a nonzero real polynomial of degree 1 or 2 with leading coefficient 1, and d is a real number.

We shall prove (16). If $\deg f = 0$, then (16) is obvious. If $\deg f > 0$,
let $\alpha = a + ib$ be a complex root of f. Then if $f = a_0 + a_1t + a_2t^2 + \cdots$
$+ a_nt^n$, we have $a_0 + a_1(a + ib) + a_2(a + ib)^2 + \cdots + a_n(a + ib)^n = 0$.
Computation gives $a_0 + a_1(a - ib) + a_2(a - ib)^2 + \cdots + a_n(a - ib)^n = 0$.
This gives

(17) $f(a + ib) = 0$ if and only if $f(a - ib) = 0$.

We also have

(18) $\big(t - (a + ib)\big)\big(t - (a - ib)\big) = t^2 - 2at + a^2 + b^2$.

Thus if $\alpha = a + ib$ is a root of f, then either $b = 0$, in which case
$f = q_1g_1$, where q_1 and g_1 are nonzero real polynomials such that $\deg q_1 = 1$
(where $q_1 = t - a$), or $b \neq 0$. If $b \neq 0$ let $q_1 = t^2 - 2at + a^2 + b^2$ and
write $f = q_1g_1 + r$, where $r = 0$ or $\deg r < \deg q_1$. Thus $r = d$ or $r =$
$c(t - d)$, where c and d are real numbers. Since $q_1(\alpha) = 0$ and $f(\alpha) = 0$,
we must have $r(\alpha) = 0$. Therefore if $r = d$, then $d = 0$, and if $r =$
$c(t - d)$, then $r(\alpha) = c((a + ib) - d) = ca - cd + icb = 0$. Since a,
b, c, and d are real numbers, we must have $cb = 0$, that is, $c = 0$. This
shows that $r = 0$. We have shown that $f = q_1g_1$, where q_1 has leading
coefficient 1, and $\deg q_1 = 1$ (if $b = 0$) or $\deg q_1 = 2$ (if $b \neq 0$). If
$\deg g_1 = 0$, let $d = g_1$. Otherwise we apply this same process to g_1 obtaining $g_1 = q_2g_2$, where q_2 has leading coefficient 1, has degree 1 or 2,
and both q_2 and g_2 are real polynomials. If $\deg g_2 = 0$, let $d = g_2$.
Otherwise continue in the same manner, applying this process until f is
factored as in (16).

The fundamental usefulness of polynomials in linear algebra resides
in the following concept. Let T be a linear operator on V and let $f = a_0 +$
$a_1t + a_2t^2 + \cdots + a_nt^n$. We denote the operator $a_0I + a_1T + a_2T^2 +$
$\cdots + a_nT^n$ by $f(T)$, that is,

(19) $f(T) = a_0I + a_1T + a_2T^2 + \cdots + a_nT^n$.

This gives a new and powerful notation for treating operators like
$a_0I + a_1T + a_2T^2 + \cdots + a_nT^n$. For example, if $f = 0$, then $f(T) = 0$,
the zero operator, for any T. If $f = t$, then $f(T) = T$. If $f = 1 + t +$
t^3, then $f(T) = I + T + T^3$. The rules for computation with this notation are

         (a) $(f + g)T = f(T) + g(T)$,
(20)   (b) $(af)(T) = af(T)$,
         (c) $(fg)(T) = f(T)g(T) = g(T)f(T)$.

The proofs of these rules use only the definitions of sum, scalar multiple, and product of polynomials and the new definition (19). An example will clarify this. Let $V = R^2$ and let T be the operator defined by

$$(21) \qquad\qquad T(x, y) = (2x - y, x + y).$$

Let $f = 2 + 3t$ and $g = t + t^2$. Because $T^2(x, y) = T(T(x, y)) = T(2x - y, x + y) = (3x - 3y, 3x)$ and because $f(T) = 2I + 3T$ and $g(T) = T + T^2$, we have

$$(22) \qquad f(T)(x, y) = 2(x, y) + 3T(x, y) = (8x - 3y, 3x + 5y),$$

$$(23) \qquad g(T)(x, y) = T(x, y) + T^2(x, y) = (5x - 4y, 4x + y).$$

Since $g = t(1 + t)$, we also have that $g(T) = T(I + T)$, that is, $g(T)(x, y) = T(I + T)(x, y) = T((I + T)(x, y)) = T((x, y) + (2x - y, x + y)) = T(3x - y, x + 2y) = (5x - 4y, 4x + y)$. This is the same as (23), which it should be, from (20c).

Let A be an $n \times n$ matrix and let $f = a_0 + a_1 t + a_2 t^2 + \cdots + a_n t^n$. We define $f(A)$ to be $a_0 I + a_1 A + a_2 A^2 + \cdots + a_n A^n$. Therefore if A is the matrix of T with respect to some basis, then $f(A)$ is the matrix of $f(T)$ with respect to that same basis. Let B be the matrix of T with respect to another basis and let P_0 be such that $B = P_0^{-1} A P_0$. [See (56) of Section 6, Chapter 1.] Since $f(B)$ is the matrix of $f(T)$ with respect to the second basis we have $f(B) = P_0^{-1} f(A) P_0$, that is,

$$(24) \qquad\qquad f(P_0^{-1} A P_0) = P_0^{-1} f(A) P_0.$$

The formula (24) can also be verified directly using (19).
In (21) let

$$A = \begin{bmatrix} 2 & -1 \\ 1 & 1 \end{bmatrix},$$

so that A is the matrix of T. Then (22) and (23) show us that

$$(25) \qquad f(A) = \begin{bmatrix} 8 & -3 \\ 3 & 5 \end{bmatrix}, \qquad g(A) = \begin{bmatrix} 5 & -4 \\ 4 & 1 \end{bmatrix}.$$

The results (25) can also be verified directly. For example,

$$g(A) = A + A^2 = \begin{bmatrix} 2 & -1 \\ 1 & 1 \end{bmatrix} + \begin{bmatrix} 2 & -1 \\ 1 & 1 \end{bmatrix}^2$$

$$= \begin{bmatrix} 2 & -1 \\ 1 & 1 \end{bmatrix} + \begin{bmatrix} 3 & -3 \\ 3 & 0 \end{bmatrix} = \begin{bmatrix} 5 & -4 \\ 4 & 1 \end{bmatrix}.$$

The rules (20) extend to the matrix case.

The computation of $f(T)$ when T is diagonalizable is very simple. Let $\{X^1, X^2, \ldots, X^n\}$ be a basis for V such that if D is the matrix of T with respect to this basis; then

$$
(26) \qquad D = \begin{bmatrix} d_1 & 0 & \ldots & 0 \\ 0 & d_2 & \ldots & 0 \\ \vdots & & & \\ 0 & 0 & \ldots & d_n \end{bmatrix}.
$$

Let $f = a_0 + a_1 t + a_2 t^2 + \cdots + a_n t^n$. Then $f(D) = a_0 I + a_1 D + a_2 D^2 + \cdots + a_n D^n$. We have

$$
(27) \qquad f(D) = \begin{bmatrix} f(d_1) & 0 & \ldots & 0 \\ 0 & f(d_2) & \ldots & 0 \\ \vdots & & & \\ 0 & 0 & \ldots & f(d_n) \end{bmatrix}.
$$

This is the matrix of $f(T)$ with respect to $\{X^1, X^2, \ldots, X^n\}$.

EXERCISES

1. For each of the polynomials f and g, find polynomials q and r such that $f = gq + r$ and $r = 0$ or $\deg r < \deg g$.
   (a) $f = t^5 + t^4 + t^3 - t^2 - t - 1$, $g = t^3 - 1$
   (b) $f = t^7 + 3t^6 + 5t^5 + 1$, $g = t^4 + t^2 + 1$
   (c) $f = 7t^6 + 3t^3 + 7$, $g = 6t^8 + 1$
   (d) $f = (1 + i)t^2 - (\sqrt{3} + 2i)t + i$, $g = it$
   (e) $f = t^3 - 6it + (2 + 3i)$, $g = it^4 - 7it^2 + (6 + 2i)$

2. Show that $(1 - t)(1 + t + t^2 + \cdots + t^n) = (1 - t^{n+1})$.

3. Verify that if $a_0 + a_1(a + ib) + a_2(a + ib)^2 + \cdots + a_n(a + ib)^n = 0$, where $a_0, a_1, a_2, \ldots, a_n$, a and b are real numbers, then $a_0 + a_1(a - ib) + a_2(a - ib)^2 + \cdots + a_n(a - ib)^n = 0$. [*Hint:* If $\alpha = x + iy$, where x and y are real, denote $x - iy$ by $\bar{\alpha}$. Verify that $\overline{(\alpha + \beta)} = \bar{\alpha} + \bar{\beta}$, $\overline{\alpha\beta} = \bar{\alpha}\,\bar{\beta}$, and that α is real if and only if $\alpha = \bar{\alpha}$. Use this to compute $\overline{a_0 + a_1(a + ib) + a_2(a + ib)^2 + \cdots + a_n(a + ib)^n}$.]

4. Show that if f is a real polynomial of *odd* degree, then there is a real number c such that $f(c) = 0$. [*Hint:* If the leading coefficient of f is >0, show that $\lim_{a \to \infty} f(a) = \infty$ and $\lim_{a \to -\infty} f(a) = -\infty$ by using L'hopital's rule. Then use the intermediate value theorem to establish the desired result.]

5. Let f be a real polynomial and let c be a real root of f. Show that c is a repeated root of f; i.e., $(t - c)^k$ divides f for some $k > 1$, if and only if $(df/dt)(c) = 0$.

6. (a) Give the Lagrange interpolation polynomials for 1, 2, 3, 4, 5.

    (b) Show that if c_1, c_2, ..., c_n are distinct real numbers and if b_1, b_2, ..., b_n are any real numbers, then there is exactly one real polynomial f such that $f(c_i) = b_i$ and $\deg f \leq (n - 1)$. [*Hint:* Express f in terms of the Lagrange interpolation polynomials for c_1, c_2, ..., c_n.]

    (c) Find a polynomial f of degree ≤ 4 such that $f(1) = 0$, $f(2) = 3$, $f(3) = -1$, $f(4) = 2$, $f(5) = 0$.

7. Let c_1, c_2, ..., c_n be distinct real numbers. Show that the matrix

$$A = \begin{bmatrix} 1 & 1 & \ldots 1 \\ c_1 & c_2 & \ldots c_n \\ c_1^2 & c_2^2 & \ldots c_n^2 \\ \vdots & & \\ c_1^{n-1} & c_2^{n-1} & \ldots c_n^{n-1} \end{bmatrix}$$

is invertible. [*Hint:* Use (13) and the fact that $\{1, t, t^2, \ldots, t^{n-1}\}$ is a basis for the space of polynomials of degree $\leq (n - 1)$.]

8. Let T be the linear operator on R^3 defined by

$$T(x, y, z) = (3x - y, 2x + 7y + z, x + z).$$

Let $f = 2t^2 + 7t - 1$; $g = t - (-7 + \sqrt{41})/4$, $h = t - (-7 - \sqrt{41})/4$, $k = 3t^3 + 6t$. Find the following.

(a) $f(T)$ **(b)** $g(T)h(T)$ **(c)** $(f(T))^2$ **(d)** $k(T)$ **(e)** $(3f + 7k)(T)$

9. Let $f(t) = 6t^4 + t^3 + 6t + 1$, $g = 3t^2 + 1$, $q = 2t^2 + t/3 - \frac{2}{3}$, $r = (17t + 5)/3$. For each of the matrices A given below find $f(A)$, $g(A)$, $q(A)$, $r(A)$, and $(gq + r)(A)$. [*Hint:* If possible show that A is diagonalizable.]

(a) $A = \begin{bmatrix} 1 & 1 \\ 0 & 1 \end{bmatrix}$ **(b)** $A = \begin{bmatrix} 1 & 1 \\ 0 & 2 \end{bmatrix}$

(c) $A = \begin{bmatrix} 0 & 1 \\ 0 & 0 \end{bmatrix}$ **(d)** $A = \begin{bmatrix} 3 & -1 & 0 & 0 \\ -1 & 3 & 0 & 0 \\ 0 & 0 & 1 & 1 \\ 0 & 0 & 0 & 2 \end{bmatrix}$

10. Let

$$A = \begin{bmatrix} 3 & 1 & 0 \\ 0 & 2 & 0 \\ 0 & 0 & 1 \end{bmatrix}$$

and let $f = t^{16} + 7t^2 + 1$. Find $f(A)$.

11. Show that if

$$A = \begin{bmatrix} B & 0 \\ 0 & C \end{bmatrix},$$

where B is $n \times n$, C is $k \times k$, and 0 represents a zero matrix of appropriate size, then

$$f(A) = \begin{bmatrix} f(B) & 0 \\ 0 & f(C) \end{bmatrix}.$$

12. Show that if V has an inner product and f is a real polynomial, then $f(T)^* = f(T^*)$.

13. (a) Write out a proof of (20c).
   (b) Verify directly that (24) holds. [*Hint:* Show that $(P_0^{-1}AP_0)^k = P_0^{-1}A^kP_0$ for any integer $k \geq 1$.]

SPECIAL EXERCISE

All polynomials in this exercise will be *rational* polynomials; i.e., the coefficients are of the form p/q, where p and q are integers with $q \neq 0$. A polynomial is said to be *monic* if its leading coefficient is 1. A polynomial f is said to be *reducible* if we can write $f = gq$, where g and q are polynomials of positive degree. If f is not reducible, then we say that f is *irreducible*. If f is monic, irreducible, and deg $f \geq 1$, we say that f is *prime*.

Show that if f is a monic polynomial such that deg $f \geq 1$, then $f = q_1q_2 \ldots q_r$, where $q_i \neq q_j$ if $i \neq j$ and each q_i is a prime. Show, furthermore, that if $f = p_1p_2 \ldots p_k$, where $p_i \neq p_j$ if $i \neq j$ and each p_i is a prime, then $k = r$ and we can reorder the p_i so that $q_i = p_i$. [*Hint:* The existence of such an expression for f is easy. To show uniqueness first establish that if p is a prime and p divides gh, then p divides g, or p divides h. To establish this result show that if p does not divide g, then there are polynomials g_1 and g_2 such that $1 = pg_1 + gg_2$. To establish this result show that if r is a polynomial of least degree among the polynomials of the form $pg_1 + gg_2$, where g_1 and g_2 are arbitrary, then r divides p.]

Section 3. THE CHARACTERISTIC AND MINIMUM POLYNOMIALS

In this section we shall describe two polynomials which are closely related to a linear operator. The first of these is the *characteristic polynomial*. Let V be finite dimensional and let $\Delta(t) = \det(tI - T)$. Then Δ is a polynomial of degree equal to the dimension of V. (See Exercise 16, Section 6, Chapter 2.) Δ is called the *characteristic polynomial* of T. [See Section 1 where the equation (16d) is called the characteristic equation. This is just the equation $\Delta(c) = 0$.] The roots of the characteristic polynomial are just the characteristic values of T. If A is an $n \times n$ matrix, then we call $\Delta(t) = \det(tI - A)$ the characteristic polynomial of A.

In order to compute Δ we can choose a basis for V. Let A be the matrix of T with respect to this basis. Then since the matrix of $tI - T$ is just $tI - A$, we have

(1) $$\Delta = \det (tI - A).$$

The formula (1) does not depend on the choice of basis. This follows from the fact that if B is the matrix of T with respect to a second basis, then $tI - B$ is the matrix of $tI - T$ with respect to this second basis. For each t, $\det (tI - T)$ does not depend on the choice of basis. Thus we must have $\det (tI - A) = \det (tI - B)$. Since $B = P_0^{-1}AP_0$, the following identities give an alternative proof of this fact:

$$\det (tI - B) = \det (tP_0^{-1}P_0 - P_0^{-1}AP_0) = \det (P_0^{-1}(tI - A)P_0)$$
$$= \det (P_0^{-1}) \det (tI - A) \det (P_0) = \det (tI - A).$$

The characteristic polynomial does not always give us enough information to determine if T is diagonalizable. [See (21) ff and (22) of Section 1.] We shall describe a second polynomial, closely related to Δ, which will enable us to determine the diagonalizability of T. The following result, while not central for our purposes, will help us to define this second polynomial:

(2) $$\Delta(T) = 0.$$

This is known as the *Cayley-Hamilton theorem*. The 0 on the right-hand side of (2) means the zero operator. We shall prove (2) for the case, where dim $V = 2$ and leave the general proof as a special exercise. Suppose that dim $V = 2$ and let

$$A = \begin{bmatrix} a_{11} & a_{12} \\ a_{21} & a_{22} \end{bmatrix}$$

be the matrix of T with respect to some basis. Let B be the classical adjoint of $tI - A$. (See Section 6, Chapter 2.) Then

(3) $$B = \begin{bmatrix} t - a_{22} & a_{12} \\ a_{21} & t - a_{11} \end{bmatrix} = tI - \begin{bmatrix} a_{22} & -a_{12} \\ -a_{21} & a_{11} \end{bmatrix}$$

and [see (28) of Section 6, Chapter 2]

(4) $$\Delta(t)I = (tI - A)B.$$

Since $t^2I - A^2 = (tI - A)(tI + A)$ and $\Delta(t) = t^2 - (a_{11} + a_{22})t + a_{11}a_{22} - a_{21}a_{12}$, we have $\Delta(t)I - \Delta(A) = (t^2I - (a_{11} + a_{22})tI + (a_{11}a_{22} - a_{21}a_{12})I) - (A^2 - (a_{11} + a_{22})A + (a_{11}a_{22} - a_{21}a_{12})I) = (t^2I - A^2) - (a_{11} + a_{22})(tI - A) = (tI - A)(tI + A - (a_{11} + a_{22})I).$

This gives

(5) $\Delta(t)I = \Delta(A) + (tI - A)(tI + A - (a_{11} + a_{22})I)$.

Equate (4) and (5) and solve for $\Delta(A)$:

(6) $\Delta(A) = (tI - A)C$, where $C = B - tI - A + (a_{11} + a_{22})I$.

Using (3) we see that $C = 0$. This gives (2).

A polynomial p is said to be *monic* if its leading coefficient is 1. For example, Δ is monic. The second polynomial we want is given in the following.

Theorem 19. Let V be finite dimensional and let T be a linear operator on V. Then there is a unique monic polynomial p with the following properties.

(7)   (a) $p(T) = 0$.
       (b) If $g(T) = 0$, then p divides g.

Furthermore $1 \le \deg p \le \dim V$. The polynomial p is called the *minimum polynomial* of T.

Proof. There is at least one monic polynomial g of positive degree such that $g(T) = 0$. For example, Δ is such a polynomial. Let p be a monic polynomial of positive degree such that $p(T) = 0$ and such that p has the smallest degree among those monic polynomials g of positive degree such that $g(T) = 0$. By choice, p satisfies (7a). We shall show that p satisfies (7b) and that p is the only monic polynomial satisfying (7a) and (7b).

Let g be any polynomial such that $g(T) = 0$. If $g = 0$, then certainly p divides g. If $g \ne 0$, let $g = pq + r$, where $r = 0$ or $\deg r < \deg p$. Since $g(T) = 0$ and $p(T) = 0$, we have

$$0 = g(T) = p(T)q(T) + r(T) = r(T).$$

If $r \ne 0$, then cr is monic for some real number $c \ne 0$. But $\deg (cr) = \deg r < \deg p$, and $cr(T) = c(r(T)) = 0$. This contradicts the choice of p. Thus $cr = 0$, $r = 0$, and p divides g. This shows that p satisfies (7b).

Let p_1 be another monic polynomial satisfying (7). Since p_1 is monic, $p_1 \ne 0$. Since $p(T) = 0$, we know that p_1 divides p, i.e., $p = p_1 q$. Thus $\deg p = \deg p_1 + \deg q$. Thus $\deg p_1 \le \deg p$. From the definition of p we must have $\deg p_1 = \deg p$. Therefore $\deg q = 0$. Since both p and p_1 are monic, we have $q = 1$, which shows that $p = p_1$.

The definition of p shows that $\deg p \ge 1$. Since $\Delta(T) = 0$ and p divides Δ, we know that $\deg p \le \deg \Delta = \dim V$. Q.E.D.

The computation of p is in general not very easy. We shall give a method below, which is useful in low-dimensional cases. For some operators, the construction of p is simple. If $T = I$, then p is clearly $t - 1$. If $T^k = 0$ for some $k > 0$, then $g(T) = 0$, where $g = t^k$. From (7b) we know that p divides g. Thus $p = t^r$, where $1 \leq r \leq k$. If $T = 0$, then p is clearly t. The following result gives us further information about p.

(8)   Let p be the minimum polynomial of T. Then c is a characteristic value of T if and only if $p(c) = 0$.

If $p(c) = 0$, then $t - c$ divides p. Since p divides Δ, we know that $t - c$ divides Δ. Thus $\Delta(c) = 0$; that is, c is a characteristic value of T. Conversely, suppose that c is a characteristic value of T. Let $p = (t - c)g + r$, where $r = 0$ or deg $r <$ deg $(t - c) = 1$. Then $r = d$, where d is a real number.

We have $0 = p(T) = (T - cI)g(T) + dI$. This gives: $(T - cI)g(T) = -dI$. If $d \neq 0$, then $g(T)/-d$ would be an inverse for $T - cI$. Since c is a characteristic value of T, we have that $cI - T$ is not invertible. Therefore $T - cI$ is not invertible, so that $d = 0$. This shows that $p(c) = 0$ and completes the proof of (8).

The following result is useful in computing p.

(9)   Let q be a real polynomial such that deg $q = 2$, q divides Δ, and q has no real roots. Then q divides p.

The proof of (9) can be given by considering complex roots of Δ. As this will lead us astray we shall omit a proof. Using (8) and (9) we can give the following method for computing p. First, factor Δ as follows:

$$(10) \qquad \Delta = q_1^{k_1} q_2^{k_2} \ldots q_l^{k_l},$$

where $q_i \neq q_j$ if $i \neq j$, $k_i \geq 1$, and each q_i is a real monic polynomial of degree 1 or of degree 2. If deg $q_i = 2$, then we assume that q_i has no real roots.

From (8) and (9) we know that

$$(11) \qquad p = q_1^{s_1} q_2^{s_2} \ldots q_l^{s_l},$$

where $1 \leq s_i \leq k_i$ for $i = 1, 2, \ldots, l$.

We now test each of the polynomials of the form $g = q_1^{t_1} q_2^{t_2} \ldots q_l^{t_l}$, where $1 \leq t_i \leq k_i$ for $i = 1, 2, \ldots, l$, to see if $g(T) = 0$ and find the smallest values of $t_1, t_2, \ldots, t_l$ such that $g(T) = 0$. This gives p.

If A is an $n \times n$ matrix, then the minimum polynomial of A is that monic polynomial p of least degree among monic polynomials g such that $g(A) = 0$. Therefore if A is the matrix of T, then the minimum polynomial of A is just the minimum polynomial of T.

Some examples will clarify the above discussion. Δ and p will denote the characteristic and minimum polynomials of the matrix under consideration.

Let

$$A = \begin{bmatrix} 3 & -1 \\ -1 & 3 \end{bmatrix}.$$

Then $\Delta = (t - 2)(t - 4)$, so that from (8), $p = (t - 2)(t - 4)$. Let

$$A = \begin{bmatrix} 1 & 1 \\ 0 & 2 \end{bmatrix}.$$

Then $\Delta = (t - 1)(t - 2)$, so that, again using (8), $p = (t - 1)(t - 2)$. Let

$$A = \begin{bmatrix} 1 & -2 \\ 1 & -1 \end{bmatrix}.$$

Then $\Delta = t^2 + 1$, so that, from (9), $p = t^2 + 1$. Let

$$A = \begin{bmatrix} 1 & 1 \\ 0 & 1 \end{bmatrix}.$$

Then $\Delta = (t - 1)^2$. In this case $p = t - 1$ or $p = (t - 1)^2$. Since $A \neq I$, we have that $A - I \neq 0$, that is, $p \neq t - 1$. Thus $p = (t - 1)^2$.

Let

$$A = \begin{bmatrix} 0 & 1 & 0 & 0 \\ 0 & 0 & 0 & 0 \\ 0 & 0 & 1 & -2 \\ 0 & 0 & 1 & -1 \end{bmatrix}.$$

Then $\Delta = t^2(t^2 + 1)$. Thus $p = t(t^2 + 1)$ or $p = t^2(t^2 + 1)$. Computation shows that $A(A^2 + I) \neq 0$. Thus $p = t^2(t^2 + 1)$.

Let

$$A = \begin{bmatrix} 3 & 1 & 0 & 0 \\ 0 & 3 & 0 & 0 \\ 0 & 0 & 2 & 1 \\ 0 & 0 & 1 & 2 \end{bmatrix}.$$

Then $\Delta = (t - 3)^3(t - 1)$. Thus $p = (t - 3)(t - 1)$, or $p = (t - 3)^2(t - 1)$, or $p = (t - 3)^3(t - 1)$. Computation shows that $(A - 3I)(A - I) \neq 0$ and that $(A - 3I)^2(A - I) = 0$. Thus $p = (t - 3)^2(t - 1)$.

The computation of p is quite easy when T is diagonalizable. Let $\{X^1, X^2, \ldots, X^n\}$ be a basis for V and let D be the matrix of T with respect to this basis. Suppose that D is diagonal, i.e.,

$$(12) \qquad D = \begin{bmatrix} d_1 & 0 & \dots & 0 \\ 0 & d_2 & \dots & 0 \\ \vdots & & & \\ 0 & 0 & \dots & d_n \end{bmatrix}.$$

Then $\Delta = (t - d_1)(t - d_2) \dots (t - d_n)$. Let us suppose that the order of $\{X^1, X^2, \dots, X^n\}$ is chosen so that $d_1 = d_2 = \cdots = d_{r_1} = c_1$, $d_{(r_1+1)} = d_{(r_1+2)} = \cdots = c_2, \dots, d_{(r_{k-1}+1)} = d_{(r_{k-1}+2)} = \cdots = d_n = c_k$, and $c_1, c_2, \dots, c_k$ are distinct. Then we have

(13) $p = (t - c_1)(t - c_2) \dots (t - c_k)$ is the minimum polynomial of T.

If c is a characteristic value of T, then $\Delta(c) = 0$. Thus $c = d_i$ for some i, i.e., $c = c_j$ for some j. Thus if p is the polynomial of (13), then $p(c) = 0$. Since

$$D = \begin{bmatrix} c_1 & 0 & \dots & 0 & 0 & 0 & \dots & & & & 0 \\ 0 & c_1 & & & & & & & & & \\ \vdots & & \ddots & & & & & & & & \\ 0 & 0 & \dots & c_1 & & & & & & & \\ 0 & 0 & \dots & 0 & c_2 & 0 & \dots & 0 & & & 0 \\ & & & & 0 & c_2 & \dots & 0 & & & \\ \vdots & & & & \vdots & & \ddots & & & & \\ & & & & 0 & 0 & \dots & c_2 & & & \\ & & & & & & & & \ddots & & \\ & & & & & & & c_k & 0 & \dots & 0 \\ & & & & & & & 0 & c_k & \dots & 0 \\ & & & & & & & \vdots & & \ddots & \\ 0 & 0 & \dots & & & & & 0 & 0 & \dots & c_k \end{bmatrix}$$

computation shows that $p(D) = 0$. Therefore the minimum polynomial divides p. Since the minimum polynomial must contain each distinct linear factor of Δ, we conclude that (13) is true.

EXERCISES

1. Find the characteristic polynomial for each of the following operators T on the given space V.

   (a) $V = R^3$, $T(x, y, z) = (x + 3y, y + 3z, 3z + x)$.
   (b) $V = R^2$, T is rotation in a counterclockwise direction about $(0, 0)$ through the angle θ.
   (c) $V = R^3$, T is projection onto plane $x = y$.   (cont.)

(d) V is the space of 2×2 matrices and $TA = AB$, where

$$B = \begin{bmatrix} 1 & 1 \\ 2 & 1 \end{bmatrix}.$$

(e) V is the space of polynomials of degree ≤ 2 and $Tf(t) = t(d/dt)f$.

(f) $V = R^4$, $T(x, y, z, w) = (x + y + z + w, y + z + w, z + w, w)$.

2. Find the characteristic polynomial of each of the following matrices.

(a) $\begin{bmatrix} 0 & 1 & 1 \\ 0 & 0 & 1 \\ 0 & 0 & 0 \end{bmatrix}$ **(b)** $\begin{bmatrix} 3 & 1 & 2 \\ 1 & 0 & 1 \\ 1 & 1 & 1 \end{bmatrix}$

(c) $\begin{bmatrix} 4 & 1 & 0 & 0 \\ 1 & 1 & 0 & 0 \\ 0 & 0 & 1 & 2 \\ 0 & 0 & 1 & 1 \end{bmatrix}$ **(d)** $\begin{bmatrix} 2 & 1 & 2 & 1 & 3 & 1 \\ 0 & 1 & 2 & 1 & 0 & 1 \\ 0 & 0 & 1 & 0 & 1 & 1 \\ 0 & 0 & 0 & 1 & 0 & 0 \\ 0 & 0 & 0 & 0 & 1 & 1 \\ 0 & 0 & 0 & 0 & 0 & 1 \end{bmatrix}$

3. Show that if $f = a_0 + a_1 t + a_2 t^2 + \cdots + a_n t^n$, where $a_0 \neq 0$ and if $f(T) = 0$, then T is invertible. Compute T^{-1}.

4. **(a)** Find the minimum polynomial of each of the operators of Exercise 1.
   (b) Find the minimum polynomial of each of the matrices of Exercise 2.

5. Let

$$A = \begin{bmatrix} B & 0 \\ 0 & C \end{bmatrix},$$

where B is $n \times n$, C is $k \times k$, and 0 represents a zero matrix of appropriate size. Let Δ be the characteristic polynomial of A, Δ_1 the characteristic polynomial of B, and Δ_2 the characteristic polynomial of C. Let p be the minimum polynomial of A, p_1 the minimum polynomial of B, and p_2 the minimum polynomial of C.

(a) Show that $\Delta = \Delta_1 \Delta_2$.   **(b)** Show that p divides $p_1 p_2$.
(c) Give an example to show that p may *not* be equal to $p_1 p_2$.

6. **(a)** Show that if T is diagonalizable and $T^k = 0$ for some $k \geq 1$, then $T = 0$. [*Hint:* Find the minimum polynomial of T and use (13).]
   (b) Show that if $T^k = 0$ and dim $V = n$, then $T^n = 0$.

7. Let V be the space of all real polynomials. Let W be a subspace of V such that fg is in W whenever f is in V and g is in W. Show that there is a unique monic polynomial p such that h is in W if and only if p divides h. [*Hint:* Let p be a monic polynomial of minimal degree in W. As in the proof of Theorem 19, repeated use of the remainder theorem will give this result.]

8. Find the minimum polynomial of each of the following matrices.

(a) $\begin{bmatrix} 1 & 1 & 1 & 0 & 1 & 0 \\ 0 & 1 & 1 & 0 & 1 & 0 \\ 0 & 0 & 1 & 0 & 1 & 0 \\ 0 & 0 & 0 & 1 & 1 & 0 \\ 0 & 0 & 0 & 0 & 1 & 0 \\ 0 & 0 & 0 & 0 & 0 & 1 \end{bmatrix}$

(b) $\begin{bmatrix} 2 & 1 & 0 & 0 & 0 & 0 \\ 1 & 0 & 0 & 0 & 0 & 0 \\ 0 & 0 & 2 & 1 & 0 & 0 \\ 0 & 0 & -2 & 1 & 0 & 0 \\ 0 & 0 & 0 & 0 & 4 & 8 \\ 0 & 0 & 0 & 0 & -1 & -1 \end{bmatrix}$

(c) $\begin{bmatrix} 1 & -1 & 1 & 0 \\ 2 & 1 & 0 & 0 \\ 0 & 0 & 1 & -1 \\ 0 & 0 & 2 & 1 \end{bmatrix}$

9. (a) Let A be 3×3. Show that

$$\Delta = t^3 - (A_{11} + A_{22} + A_{33})t^2$$

$$+ \left(\det \begin{bmatrix} A_{11} & A_{12} \\ A_{21} & A_{22} \end{bmatrix} + \det \begin{bmatrix} A_{11} & A_{13} \\ A_{31} & A_{33} \end{bmatrix} + \det \begin{bmatrix} A_{22} & A_{23} \\ A_{32} & A_{33} \end{bmatrix} \right) t$$

$$- \det (A).$$

(b) Let A be $n \times n$. Let $\Delta = t^n + a_{n-1}t^{n-1} + \cdots + a_1 t + a_0$ be the characteristic polynomial of A. Show that A is invertible if and only if $a_0 \neq 0$. If A is invertible, show that

$$A^{-1} = (A^{n-1} + a_{n-1}A^{n-2} + \cdots + a_2 A + a_1 I)/-a_0.$$

[*Hint:* A is invertible if and only if 0 is *not* a root of Δ. This result is often used on computers.]

(c) If A and Δ are as in (b) show that $a_{n-1} = -(A_{11} + A_{22} + \cdots + A_{nn})$. [*Hint:* Use Exercise 13, Section 6, Chapter 2.]

10. Show that if A is upper triangular, then $\Delta = (t - A_{11})(t - A_{22}) \ldots (t - A_{nn})$.

11. Show without using (2) that if A is $n \times n$, then there is a polynomial q of degree $\leq n^2$ such that $q(A) = 0$. [*Hint:* In the vector space of $n \times n$ matrices, can the set $\{I, A, A^2, \ldots, A^{n^2}\}$ be independent?]

12. Write a flow diagram to compute the inverse of a 3×3 matrix using the method of Exercise 9(b).

SPECIAL EXERCISE

Prove (2). [*Hint:* Let f be a polynomial with matrix coefficients; i.e., $f = A_0 + A_1 t + A_2 t^2 + \cdots + A_k t^k$, where $A_0, A_1, A_2, \ldots, A_k$ are $n \times n$ matrices. If $A_k \neq 0$, we say that A_k is the leading coefficient of f and that $\deg f = k$. Show that if $\deg f = k$ and $\deg g = l$, where the leading coefficient of f is invertible, then $\deg (fg) = \deg f + \deg g$. Let A be $n \times n$ and let Δ be the characteristic polynomial of A. Let B be the classical adjoint of $tI - A$. Show that B is a polynomial with matrix coefficients of degree $\leq (n - 1)$. Then use $\Delta(t)I = (tI - A)B$ and the fact that for each integer $k \geq 1$, $t^k I - A^k = (tI - A)(t^{k-1}I + t^{k-2}A + \cdots + tA^{k-2} + A^{k-1})$. This will give an expression like (6), i.e., $\Delta(A) = (tI - A)C$. If $C \neq 0$, then the right-hand side is a polynomial in t with matrix coefficients and positive degree, while the left-hand side is either 0 or a polynomial in t with matrix coefficients of degree 0.]

Section 4. DIAGONALIZABLE OPERATORS: II

In this section we shall show that we can describe those operators which are diagonalizable by means of a simple condition on the minimum polynomial. This description will enable us to show that a symmetric operator is diagonalizable. We begin by looking at the simplest example of a diagonalizable operator.

Let E be the operator on R^3 which projects each vector perpendicularly onto the x, y plane, i.e., $E(x, y, z) = E(x, y, 0)$. Then the matrix of E is

$$\begin{bmatrix} 1 & 0 & 0 \\ 0 & 1 & 0 \\ 0 & 0 & 0 \end{bmatrix}.$$

The following properties of E are easily verified geometrically.

(1)
    (a) $E^2 = E$.
    (b) E is diagonalizable.
    (c) The range of E consists of all X such that $EX = X$.
    (d) The null space of E consists of all X in the range of $I - E$.

Property (1b) follows from the above matrix expression for E, (1c) is geometrically clear, and (1d) follows from the fact that $(I - E)(x, y, z) = (0, 0, z)$. As we shall see, (1b, c, d) are consequences of (1a).

Let E be a linear operator on V such that $E^2 = E$. Then E is called a *projection* on V. Let X be in the range of E. Then $X = EY$ for some Y. Apply E and use $E^2 = E$. Thus $EX = E^2Y = EY = X$, that is, $EX = X$. Conversely if $EX = X$, then X is certainly in the range of E. This shows the following.

(2) If $E^2 = E$, then the range of E consists of all vectors X such that $EX = X$.

If $E^2 = E$, then $(I - E)^2 = I - 2E + E^2 = I - 2E + E = I - E$.

(3) If E is a projection, then $I - E$ is a projection.

From (2) we have the following.

(4) If E is a projection, then the range of $I - E$ consists of all vectors X such that $(I - E)X = X$.

The equation $(I - E)X = X$ is the same as $EX = 0$. Thus (4) gives:

(5) If E is a projection, then the null space of E is the range of $I - E$.

Let X be in V. Then $X = EX + X - EX = EX + (I - E)X$, so that X is the sum of a vector in the range of E and a vector in the range of $I - E$. Suppose that $X = Y + Z$, where Y is in the range of E and Z is in the range of $I - E$. Then from (2) and (4) we have $Y = EY$ and $Z = (I - E)Z$. Thus $X = EY + (I - E)Z$. Applying E gives $EX = E^2Y + E(I - E)Z = EY + EZ - E^2Z = EY + EZ - EZ = EY = Y$. Similarly $Z = (I - E)X$. This gives the following.

(6) If E is a projection on V, then each vector X in V has a unique expression $X = Y + Z$, where Y is in the range of E, and Z is in the range of $I - E$. Furthermore $Y = EX$ and $Z = (I - E)X$.

Now let $D_1 = \{X^1, X^2, \ldots, X^k\}$ be a basis for the range of E and let $D_2 = \{X^{k+1}, X^{k+2}, \ldots, X^n\}$ be a basis for the range of $I - E$. If $X = Y + Z$ as in (6), then Y has a unique expression in terms of D_1 and Z has a unique expression in terms of D_2. Thus X has a unique expression in terms of $\{X^1, X^2, \ldots, X^k, X^{k+1}, X^{k+2}, \ldots, X^n\}$. We conclude that $\{X^1, X^2, \ldots, X^k, X^{k+1}, X^{k+2}, \ldots, X^n\}$ is a basis for V. Let $T = c_1E + c_2(I - E)$. Then $TX^1 = c_1EX^1 + c_2(I - E)X^1$. Since X^1 is in the range of E we have, using (2), $X^1 = EX^1$. Thus $(I - E)X^1 = (I - E)EX^1 = (E - E^2)X^1 = (E - E)X^1 = 0$. Thus $TX^1 = c_1X^1$. Similarly we have $TX^i = c_1X^i$ for $1 \leq i \leq k$ and $TX^i = c_2X^i$ for $(k + 1) \leq i \leq n$. Since $\{X^1, X^2, \ldots, X^k, X^{k+1}, X^{k+2}, \ldots, X^n\}$ is a basis for V we have the following.

(7) If E is a projection and $T = c_1E + c_2(I - E)$, then T is diagonalizable.

The case where $c_1 = 1$ and $c_2 = 0$ gives the following.

(8) If E is a projection, then E is diagonalizable.

We have shown that (1b, c, d) are consequences of (1a). In the process we have obtained much more information about projections. The general form of (7) is as follows.

Theorem 20. Let V be finite dimensional. Let T be a linear operator on V. Let $E_1, E_2, \ldots, E_r$ be nonzero projections on V with the following properties.

(9)
(a) $I = E_1 + E_2 + \cdots + E_r$.
(b) $E_iE_j = 0$ if $i \neq j$.
(c) $T = c_1E_1 + c_2E_2 + \cdots + c_rE_r$.

Then T is diagonalizable.

Proof. Let X be in the range of E_1. Then from (2), $X = E_1X$. If $i > 1$, then $E_iX = E_iE_1X = 0$, because of (9b). Apply T and use (9c). Then $TX = c_1E_1X + c_2E_2X + \cdots + c_rE_rX$. Since $E_1X = X$ and $E_iX = 0$ for $i > 1$, we have $TX = c_1X$. Similarly, if X is in the range of E_i, then $TX = c_iX$, for $i = 2, 3, \ldots, r$. Thus:

(10)   If X is a nonzero vector in the range of E_i, then X is a characteristic vector of T belonging to c_i, for $i = 1, 2, \ldots, r$.

Let X be any vector in V. Then (9a) gives $X = E_1X + E_2X + \cdots + E_rX$. Furthermore, E_iX is in the range of E_i for $i = 1, 2, \ldots, r$. This expression for X is unique. For suppose that $X = Y^1 + Y^2 + \cdots + Y^r$, where Y^i is in the range of E_i for $i = 1, 2, \ldots, r$. Then $Y^i = E_iY^i$ for $1 \le i \le r$, from (2). Therefore $E_1X = E_1Y^1 + E_1Y^2 + \cdots + E_1Y^r = E_1Y^1 + E_1(E_2Y^2) + E_1(E_3Y^3) + \cdots + E_1(E_rY^r)$. Property (9b) gives $E_1E_i = 0$ if $i > 1$. Thus $E_1X = E_1Y^1 = Y^1$. Similarly $Y^i = E_iX$ for $i = 2, 3, \ldots, r$. We have shown the next result.

(11)   If X is in V, then X has a unique expression in the form $X = Y^1 + Y^2 + \cdots + Y^r$, where Y^i is in the range of E_i for $i = 1, 2, \ldots, r$. Furthermore $Y^i = E_iX$ for $i = 1, 2, \ldots, r$.

This is the general form of (6). In the same fashion that we deduced (7) from (6) we can deduce Theorem 20 from (11). Let $D_i = \{X_i^1, X_i^2, \ldots, X_i^{k_i}\}$ be a basis for the range of E_i, $i = 1, 2, \ldots, r$. Let $D = \{X_1^1, X_1^2, \ldots, X_1^{k_1}, X_2^1, X_2^2, \ldots, X_2^{k_2}, \ldots, X_r^1, X_r^2, \ldots, X_r^{k_r}\}$. Each X in V has a unique expression as $X = Y^1 + Y^2 + \cdots + Y^r$, where Y^i is in the range of E_i and each Y^i has a unique expression in terms of D_i, $i = 1, 2, \ldots, r$. Thus each X in V has a unique expression in terms of D. This tells us that D is a basis for V. The result (10) tells us that each vector in D is a characteristic vector of T. Therefore T is diagonalizable. Q.E.D.

Using Theorem 18 and Theorem 20 we are now in a position to establish the following theorem.

Theorem 21. Let V be finite dimensional and let T be a linear operator on V. Let p be the minimum polynomial of T. Then T is diagonalizable if and only if p factors into distinct *real* linear factors, i.e., if and only if $p = (t - c_1)(t - c_2) \ldots (t - c_r)$, where $c_1, c_2, \ldots, c_r$ are distinct real numbers.

Proof. In (13) of Section 3 we showed that if T is diagonalizable, then p has the form given in Theorem 21. To prove Theorem 21 we have only to show that if p has the form given in the theorem, then T is diagonalizable. Before showing this let us note the relation between Theorem 21 and our previous results. In (22) of Section 1 we showed that if Δ (the characteristic polynomial of T) has n *distinct* real roots, where dim $V = n$, then T is diagonalizable. In this case $p = \Delta$ because of (8) of Section 3. We established Theorem 21 for the case dim $V = 2$ in the exercises of Section 1.

Let $p = (t - c_1)(t - c_2) \ldots (t - c_r)$, where $c_1, c_2, \ldots, c_r$ are distinct real numbers. Let p be the minimum polynomial of T. We shall show that the conditions of Theorem 20 hold. Thus we want to construct projections $E_1, E_2, \ldots, E_r$ such that (9) holds.

To understand the construction of these projections, let us suppose that we have nonzero projections $E_1, E_2, \ldots, E_r$ such that (9) holds. Let $D_1, D_2, \ldots, D_r$, and D be the bases constructed in the proof of Theorem 20. Let A be the matrix of T with respect to D. Then

(12)
$$A = \begin{bmatrix} c_1 & 0 \ldots 0 & 0 & 0 \ldots & & & & 0 \\ 0 & c_1 & & & & & & \\ \vdots & & \ddots & & & & & \vdots \\ 0 & 0 \ldots c_1 & & & & & & \\ 0 & 0 \ldots 0 & c_2 & 0 \ldots 0 & & & & 0 \\ & & 0 & c_2 \ldots 0 & & & & \\ \vdots & & \vdots & & \ddots & & & \\ & & 0 & 0 \ldots c_2 & & \ddots & & \\ & & & & & c_r & 0 \ldots 0 & \\ & & & & & 0 & c_r \ldots 0 & \\ & & & & & \vdots & & \ddots \\ 0 & 0 \ldots & & & & 0 & 0 \ldots c_r \end{bmatrix}.$$

In this representation we have that the number of c_i's for a given i is rank (E_i). Let Q_i be the matrix of E_i with respect to D, for $1 \leq i \leq r$. Let us suppose that $c_1, c_2, \ldots, c_r$ are distinct. Then

(13) $Q_i = \Big[\dfrac{(A - c_1 I)(A - c_2 I) \ldots (A - c_{i-1} I)(A - c_{i+1} I)}{(c_i - c_1)(c_i - c_2) \ldots (c_i - c_{i-1})(c_i - c_{i+1})}$

$\dfrac{\ldots (A - c_r I)}{\ldots (c_i - c_r)} \Big], \qquad i = 1, 2, \ldots, r.$

The verification of (13) is left to the exercises. From (13) we see that if $P_1, P_2, \ldots, P_r$ are the Lagrange interpolation polynomials [see (10) of Section 2] for $c_1, c_2, \ldots, c_r$, then

(14) $Q_i = P_i(A), \qquad i = 1, 2, \ldots, r.$

Thus

(15) $E_i = P_i(T), \qquad i = 1, 2, \ldots, r.$

Now suppose that $p = (t - c_1)(t - c_2) \ldots (t - c_r)$ is the minimum polynomial for T, where $c_1, c_2, \ldots, c_r$ are distinct real numbers. If $r = 1$, then $T = c_1 I$, which is clearly diagonalizable. If $r > 1$, then (15) suggests a means for constructing the projections of Theorem 20. Let $P_1, P_2, \ldots, P_r$ be the Lagrange interpolation polynomials for $c_1, c_2, \ldots, c_r$. Then we have [see (13) of Section 2]

(16)
$$1 = P_1 + P_2 + \cdots + P_r$$
$$t = c_1 P_1 + c_2 P_2 + \cdots + c_r P_r.$$

Since P_i contains each factor of p except $t - c_i$ for $i = 1, 2, \ldots, r$ we see that

(17)   if $i \neq j$, then p divides $P_i P_j$.

Let $E_i = P_i(T)$ for $i = 1, 2, \ldots, r$. Then (16) and (17) give

(18)
(a) $I = E_1 + E_2 + \cdots + E_r$,
(b) $T = c_1 E_1 + c_2 E_2 + \cdots + c_r E_r$,
(c) $E_i E_j = 0$ if $i \neq j$.

From (18a) we have $E_1 = E_1 I = E_1(E_1 + E_2 + \cdots + E_r) = E_1^2 + E_1 E_2 + E_1 E_3 + \cdots + E_1 E_r$. From (18c) we have $E_1 E_2 = E_1 E_3 = \cdots = E_1 E_r = 0$. Thus $E_1 = E_1^2$. An analogous proof shows that $E_i^2 = E_i$ for $i > 1$. Thus each E_i is a projection. If $E_i = 0$ for some i, $1 \leq i \leq r$, then $P_i(T) = 0$. Since p does not divide P_i, this cannot be so. We conclude that $E_1, E_2, \ldots, E_r$ satisfies the conditions of Theorem 20. Q.E.D.

Remarks. If $c_1, c_2, \ldots, c_r$ are distinct, then (15) shows that the projections given by Theorem 20 are uniquely determined by the conditions (9). If T is diagonalizable, then p satisfies the conditions of Theorem 21. We can then apply the construction (16), (17), and (18) so that T satisfies the conditions of Theorem 20. Since the projections E_i are uniquely determined by the conditions (9), in the case where $c_1, c_2, \ldots, c_r$ are distinct, we call them the _spectral projections_ of T. Since computations with projections are relatively simple, the form given in (9) is so easy to use that often we do not bother finding a diagonal matrix expression for T.

In (10) we showed that if $E_1, E_2, \ldots, E_r$ are as in (9), then the range of E_i is contained in the characteristic subspace of T belonging to c_i for $i = 1, 2, \ldots, r$. The following results are related to this.

(19)   If T is as in (9), then c is a characteristic value of T if and only if $c = c_i$ for some i, $1 \leq i \leq r$. If $c_1, c_2, \ldots, c_r$ are distinct, then the range of E_i is precisely the characteristic subspace of T belonging to c_i for $i = 1, 2, \ldots, r$.

The matrix form (12) shows that c is a characteristic value if and only if $c = c_i$ for some i, $1 \leq i \leq r$, since det $(cI - A) = (c - c_1)^{k_1}(c - c_2)^{k_2}$ $\ldots (c - c_r)^{k_r}$, where k_i is the number of c_i's on the diagonal of A for $1 \leq i \leq r$. Now let $c = c_1$, and let k_1 be the number of c_1's on the diagonal of A. Then the column matrix X is in the null space of $c_1 I - A$ if and only if the entries below row k_1 of X are zero. This is the same condition as the condition that $Q_1 X = 0$, where Q_1 is given in (13). This proves (19) for $i = 1$. The proof for $i > 1$ is similar.

We have defined $f(T)$ for f a polynomial and T a linear operator. Let $T = c_1 E_1 + c_2 E_2 + \cdots + c_r E_r$, where $E_i E_j = 0$ if $i \neq j$ and $E_i^2 = E_i$ for $i = 1, 2, \ldots, r$. Then

$$(20) \qquad f(T) = f(c_1)E_1 + f(c_2)E_2 + \cdots + f(c_r)E_r.$$

To establish (20), let $f = a_0 + a_1 t + a_2 t^2 + \cdots + a_n t^n$. Then if $T^k = c_1^k E_1 + c_2^k E_2 + \cdots + c_r^k E_r$ for $1 \leq k \leq n$, formula (20) will follow by linearity. We have $T^2 = (c_1 E_1 + c_2 E_2 + \cdots + c_r E_r)(c_1 E_1 + c_2 E_2 + \cdots + c_r E_r) = c_1^2 E_1 + c_2^2 E_2 + \cdots + c_r^2 E_r$, since $E_i E_j = 0$ if $i \neq j$ and $E_i^2 = E_i$ for $1 \leq i \leq r$. An analogous proof establishes $T^k = c_1^k E_1 + c_2^k E_2 + \cdots + c_r^k E_r$ for $k > 2$. This gives (20).

We can extend (20) to functions which are not polynomials. Let f be any real-valued function such that $f(c_i)$ is defined for $1 \leq i \leq r$. Then we define $f(T)$ to be $f(c_1)E_1 + f(c_2)E_2 + \cdots + f(c_r)E_r$. As in the polynomial case this is really nothing new; the symbol $f(T)$ is merely a convenient, suggestive symbol for $f(c_1)E_1 + f(c_2)E_2 + \cdots + f(c_r)E_r$. This symbol satisfies the following:

$$(21) \qquad \begin{array}{ll} \text{(a)} & (f + g)(T) = f(T) + g(T), \\ \text{(b)} & (af)(T) = af(T), \\ \text{(c)} & (fg)(T) = f(T)g(T) = g(T)f(T). \end{array}$$

These properties follow easily from the definition of $f(T)$. Suppose that $c_i \neq 1$ for $1 \leq i \leq r$. Let $f(t) = 1/(1 - t)$ and $g(t) = 1 - t$. Then

$$f(T) = \frac{1}{1 - c_1} E_1 + \frac{1}{1 - c_2} E_2 + \cdots + \frac{1}{1 - c_r} E_r$$

and $g(T) = (1 - c_1)E_1 + (1 - c_2)E_2 + \cdots + (1 - c_r)E_r$. Property (20c) gives $f(T)g(T) = I$. This can be verified directly, using the relations $E_i^2 = E_i$, $1 \leq i \leq r$, and $E_i E_j = 0$ if $i \neq j$.

The spectral projections of T can be computed using (15). Let us give an example. Let T be the operator on R^3 whose matrix is

$$(22) \qquad A = \begin{bmatrix} 1 & 0 & -1 \\ 0 & 1 & 0 \\ 0 & 0 & 3 \end{bmatrix}.$$

We have $\Delta = (t - 1)^2(t - 3)$. Let p be the minimum polynomial for T. Computation shows that $(A - I)(A - 3I) = 0$, so that $p = (t - 1)(t - 3)$. Thus T is diagonalizable. Let P_1 and P_2 be the Lagrange interpolation polynomials for 1 and 3. Let $E_1 = P_1(T)$, $E_2 = P_2(T)$. Let Q_1 be the matrix of E_1 and Q_2 the matrix of E_2. Since

$$P_1 = \frac{t - 3}{-2} \quad \text{and} \quad P_2 = \frac{t - 1}{2},$$

we have $Q_1 = (A - 3I)/(-2)$, $Q_2 = (A - I)/2$. Thus $A = Q_1 + 3Q_2$ and

$$(23) \qquad Q_1 = \begin{bmatrix} 1 & 0 & \frac{1}{2} \\ 0 & 1 & 0 \\ 0 & 0 & 0 \end{bmatrix}, \qquad Q_2 = \begin{bmatrix} 0 & 0 & -\frac{1}{2} \\ 0 & 0 & 0 \\ 0 & 0 & 1 \end{bmatrix}.$$

We survey our results. Let T be a linear operator on the finite dimensional space V. Let Δ be the characteristic polynomial of T and let p be the minimum polynomial of T. If Δ has a quadratic factor q without real roots, then so does p. [See (9) of Section 3.] Therefore T is not diagonalizable. If $\Delta = (t - c_1)^{k_1}(t - c_2)^{k_2} \cdots (t - c_r)^{k_r}$, where $k_i \geq 1$, $i = 1$, $2, \ldots, r$ and $c_1, c_2, \ldots, c_r$ are distinct real numbers, then $p = (t - c_1)^{s_1}(t - c_2)^{s_2} \ldots (t - c_r)^{s_r}$, where $1 \leq s_i \leq k_i$, $i = 1, 2, \ldots, r$. [See (8) of Section 3.] Then T is diagonalizable if and only if $s_i = 1$ for $i = 1, 2, \ldots, r$.

The problem of determining whether p has the desired form is in general very difficult. Fortunately there is one case where we know in advance that p has the desired form. This is given in the next theorem.

Theorem 22. Suppose that V is finite dimensional and (X, Y) is an inner product on V. Let T be a symmetric linear operator on V; i.e., $T = T^*$, where T^* is computed using (X, Y). Then T is diagonalizable.

Proof. There are several ways to prove this theorem. We shall give a two-dimensional proof which generalizes rather easily to the n-dimensional case. In Chapter 4 we shall give another proof, and in a special exercise at the end of this section we shall outline a proof which generalizes to infinite dimensions and which also gives a method for computing the characteristic values.

Let $\dim V = 2$ and let A be the matrix of T with respect to an orthonormal basis. Then $A = A^t$, so that

$$A = \begin{bmatrix} a & b \\ b & c \end{bmatrix}.$$

Therefore

(24) $\Delta = \det \begin{bmatrix} t - a & -b \\ -b & t - c \end{bmatrix} = t^2 - (a + c)t + ac - b^2.$

We shall show that Δ factors into real factors. We know that $t^2 + \beta t + \gamma$ factors into real factors if $\beta^2 - 4\gamma \geq 0$. These factors are distinct if $\beta^2 - 4\gamma > 0$ and equal if $\beta^2 - 4\gamma = 0$. [See (14) of Section 2.] In our case $\beta = -(a + c)$ and $\gamma = ac - b^2$. Thus $\beta^2 - 4\gamma = (a + c)^2 - 4(ac - b^2) = (a - c)^2 + 4b^2$. Therefore $\beta^2 - 4\gamma \geq 0$ so that Δ factors into real factors. If $\beta^2 - 4\gamma > 0$, then we have

(25) $\Delta = (t - d)(t - e),   d \neq e.$

If p is the minimum polynomial for T, then $p = (t - d)(t - e)$ and T is diagonalizable by Theorem 21. If $\beta^2 - 4\gamma = 0$, then $a = c$ and $b = 0$. Therefore

$$A = \begin{bmatrix} a & 0 \\ 0 & a \end{bmatrix},$$

so that again T is diagonalizable.

Now let dim V be arbitrary and let p be the minimum polynomial for T. We shall show that p factors into *distinct real* linear factors. Suppose that p does not so factor. Then two cases can result: either

(26) $p = (t - a)^2 q,$

that is, a repeated root, or

(27) $p = gq$, where $g = t^2 + \beta t + \gamma$ and $\beta^2 - 4\gamma < 0,$

that is, a quadratic factor without real roots. [See (16) of Section 2.]

We shall show that both (26) and (27) lead to contradictions. Assume that (26) holds. Let $h = (t - a)q$ and let $S = h(T)$. Then $S \neq 0$, since p does not divide h. Let X be in V such that $SX \neq 0$. Since $SX \neq 0$, we know that $(SX, SX) > 0$. Therefore

$$0 < (SX, SX) = ((T - aI)q(T)X, (T - aI)q(T)X)$$
$$= ((T - aI)^2 q(T)X, q(T)X) = (p(T)X, q(T)X) = 0.$$

This is a contradiction, so that (26) cannot hold.

Suppose that (27) holds. Let $S = g(T)$ and let W be the null space of S. We know that $q(T) \neq 0$, since p does not divide q, so let X be in V such that $q(T)X \neq 0$. Then $Sq(T)X = g(T)q(T)X = p(T)X = 0$. Therefore $q(T)X$ is in W; i.e., W is *not* the zero subspace. Restrict T to W; i.e., let T_1 be the linear operator on W defined by $T_1 X = TX$ for X

in W. We must show that T_1 is actually an operator on W (i.e., *not* just a linear transformation from W into some *other* subspace of V.) But X is in W if and only if $g(T)X = 0$. Thus if X is in W, then $g(T)TX = Tg(T)X = 0$; that is, TX is also in W. Therefore T_1 is a linear operator on W. If X and Y are in W, then $(T_1X, Y) = (TX, Y) = (X, TY) = (X, T_1Y)$; i.e., the operator T_1 defined on W is symmetric. Since $g(T_1)X = g(T)X = SX = 0$, if X is in W, we see that $g(T_1)$ is the zero operator on W. Therefore the minimum polynomial for T_1 divides g. But g has no real factors. Thus the minimum polynomial for T_1 must be g. We have shown the following.

(28)   If (27) holds, we can find a subspace W of V and a linear operator T_1 on W such that $T_1 = T_1^*$ and such that g is the minimum polynomial for T_1.

Therefore $T_1^2 + \beta T_1 + \gamma I_W = 0$, where I_W is the identity operator on W. Therefore $T_1^2X + \beta T_1X + \gamma X = 0$ for all X in W. Take the inner product of this with X. We have

(29) $(T_1^2X, X) + \beta(T_1X, X) + \gamma(X, X) = 0$ for all X in W.

Solve (29) for $\beta(T_1X, X)$ and square both sides:

(30) $$\beta^2(T_1X, X)^2 = ((T_1^2X, X) + \gamma(X, X))^2.$$

Use the fact that $(T_1X, X)^2 \le |T_1X|^2|X|^2$ (the Schwarz inequality) and $(T_1^2X, X) = (T_1X, T_1X) = |T_1X|^2$; $(X, X) = |X|^2$. This gives

(31) $$(|T_1X|^2 + \gamma|X|^2)^2 \le \beta^2|T_1X|^2|X|^2.$$

Since $g \ne t$, $T_1 \ne 0$. Hence we can find X in W such that $T_1X \ne 0$. Therefore $|T_1X| > 0$ and $|X| > 0$. Let us use this X in (31) along with the condition $\beta^2 - 4\gamma < 0$ of (27). This gives

(32) $$(|T_1X|^2 + \gamma|X|^2)^2 < 4\gamma|T_1X|^2|X|^2.$$

Note that (32) is the same as

(33) $$(|T_1X|^2 - \gamma|X|^2)^2 < 0,$$

which is nonsense. Thus (27) leads to a contradiction. Q.E.D.

Remarks. Theorem 22 is certainly the deepest theorem in this book. We suggest that the reader study this proof with considerable care as it contains many ideas which can lead to many further results. The reader might try giving a direct proof for the 3×3 case, so that the difficulties involved can be seen. The key to our proof lies in the deduction of (28) from (27). Once we know (28), the remainder of the proof is a simple application of the Schwarz inequality and the quadratic theorem.

The general ideas behind the deduction of (28) are the following. If T is a linear operator on V and W is a subspace such that TX is in W for all X in W, then we say that W is an *invariant subspace* for T. If W is an invariant subspace for T, then we can restrict T to W and obtain a linear operator on W; i.e., the linear transformation T_1 defined by $T_1 X = TX$, X in W, is a linear operator on W. The proof of (28) can be used to show the following.

(34)   If g is a quadratic factor, without real roots, of the minimum polynomial of the linear operator T, then we can find an invariant subspace for T such that the restriction of T to this invariant subspace has g as its minimum polynomial.

The general problem of finding roots for Δ is very difficult. In the case where T is symmetric, many methods have been developed for finding the characteristic values for T. We shall indicate one such method in the special exercise below.

Let T be symmetric and let p be the minimum polynomial for T. Then we know that $p = (t - c_1)(t - c_2) \ldots (t - c_r)$, where $c_1, c_2, \ldots, c_r$ are distinct real numbers. Let $E_1, E_2, \ldots, E_r$ be the spectral projections of T. Then E_i is a real polynomial in T, from (15), so that $E_i^* = E_i$. (See Exercise 12, Section 2.) A linear operator E such that $E^2 = E = E^*$ is called an *orthogonal projection*. This terminology arises from the following.

(35)   If E is an orthogonal projection, then the range of E is the orthogonal complement of the null space of E.

Let X be in the range of E and Y in the null space of E. Then $X = EX$, from (2), so that $(X, Y) = (EX, Y) = (X, EY) = 0$. Since $\dim V = \operatorname{rank}(E) + \operatorname{nullity}(E)$ and $\dim V = \operatorname{nullity}(E) +$ the dimension of the orthogonal complement of the null space of E, we conclude that (35) holds.

When T is symmetric we have:

(36)   (a) $T = c_1 E_1 + c_2 E_2 + \cdots + c_r E_r$, where $c_1, c_2, \ldots, c_r$ are distinct real numbers.
              (b) $I = E_1 + E_2 + \cdots + E_r$.
              (c) $E_i E_j = 0$ if $i \neq j$.
              (d) $E_i^2 = E_i^* = E_i \neq 0$.

The range of the projection E_i is precisely the characteristic subspace belonging to c_i, $1 \leq i \leq r$. This follows from (36a) and (19). The following result is a consequence of this and of (36c) and (36d). We shall give a direct proof.

(37)   If $T = T^*$ and if $TX = cX$, $TY = dY$, where $c \neq d$, then $(X, Y) = 0$. In other words, the characteristic subspace belonging to c is perpendicular to the characteristic subspace belonging to d if $c \neq d$.

We have $(c - d)(X, Y) = (cX, Y) - (X, dY) = (TX, Y) - (X, TY) = 0$. The final equation results from the fact that $T = T^*$. Since $c - d \neq 0$ we must have $(X, Y) = 0$.

We can choose an orthonormal basis for the range of each spectral projection E_i and put these together as in the proof of Theorem 20 to obtain a basis for V, consisting of characteristic vectors for T. From (37) this basis is automatically an orthonormal basis. Since computation is easier with orthonormal bases, this is a very useful result. Restating this result we have the following sharpened form of Theorem 22.

(38)   If $T = T^*$, then V has an orthonormal basis consisting of characteristic vectors for T.

Remarks. Let $\{X_1, X^2, \ldots, X^n\}$ be an orthonormal basis for V. Let A be the matrix of T. Assume that $T = T^*$, so that (38) applies. Suppose that $\{Y^1, Y^2, \ldots, Y^n\}$ is an orthonormal basis for V consisting of characteristic vectors for T, and B is the matrix of T with respect to $\{Y^1, Y^2, \ldots, Y^n\}$. Then B is a diagonal matrix.

Let P be the linear operator on V defined by $PX^i = Y^i$ for $i = 1, 2, \ldots, n$ and let P_0 be the matrix of P with respect to $\{X^1, X^2, \ldots, X^n\}$. Using (55) and (56) of Section 6, Chapter 1, we have

$$(39) \qquad\qquad B = P_0^{-1} A P_0.$$

The condition that $\{X^1, X^2, \ldots, X^n\}$ and $\{Y^1, Y^2, \ldots, Y^n\}$ are both orthonormal gives us further information about P and P_0. Let

$$X = x_1 X^1 + x_2 X^2 + \cdots + x_n X^n.$$

Then $(X, P^*Y^i) = (PX, Y^i) = (x_1 PX^1 + x_2 PX^2 + \cdots + x_n PX^n, Y^i) = (x_1 Y^1 + x_2 Y^2 + \cdots + x_n Y^n, Y^i) = x_i(Y^i, Y^i) = x_i = (X, X^i)$. Since this holds for any X we have

$$(40) \qquad\qquad P^*Y^i = X^i, \qquad i = 1, 2, \ldots, n.$$

Since $P^{-1}Y^i$ is also X^i for $i = 1, 2, \ldots, n$, we know from Theorem 9 that

(41) $$P^* = P^{-1}.$$

The matrix of P^* with respect to $\{X^1, X^2, \ldots, X^n\}$ is P_0^t, while the matrix of P^{-1} with respect to this basis is P_0^{-1}. We conclude that

(42) $$P_0^t = P_0^{-1},$$

so that (39) becomes

(43) $$B = P_0^t A P_0.$$

A linear operator P is said to be *orthogonal* if $P^* = P^{-1}$. A matrix P_0 is *orthogonal* if $P_0^t = P_0^{-1}$. By letting $\{X^1, X^2, \ldots, X^n\}$ be the standard basis in R^n we have shown the following.

(44) If A is a symmetric $n \times n$ matrix, then there is an orthogonal matrix P_0 such that $P_0^t A P_0$ is a diagonal matrix.

Let us look at an example:

(45) $$A = \begin{bmatrix} \frac{4}{3} & \sqrt{2}/6 & -\sqrt{6}/6 \\ \sqrt{2}/6 & \frac{7}{6} & -\sqrt{3}/6 \\ -\sqrt{6}/6 & -\sqrt{3}/6 & \frac{3}{2} \end{bmatrix}.$$

Then [Exercise 9(a) of Section 3 gives this quickly]

(46) $$\det(tI - A) = t^3 - 4t^2 + 5t - 2 = (t - 1)^2(t - 2).$$

Since A is symmetric, it must be diagonalizable. Thus its minimum polynomial must be $(t - 1)(t - 2)$. The null space of $(I - A)$ is spanned by $\{(\sqrt{2}, 1, \sqrt{3}), (\sqrt{2}, -2, 0)\}$. The null space of $(2I - A)$ is spanned by $\{(2\sqrt{2}, 2, -2\sqrt{3})\}$. These vectors are mutually orthogonal. Therefore $\{(1/\sqrt{3}, 1/\sqrt{6}, 1/\sqrt{2}), (1/\sqrt{3}, -2/\sqrt{6}, 0), (2/\sqrt{3}, 2/\sqrt{6}, -2/\sqrt{2})\}$ is an orthonormal basis for R^3 consisting of characteristic vectors for A. If

$$P_0 = \begin{bmatrix} 1/\sqrt{3} & 1/\sqrt{3} & 2/\sqrt{3} \\ 1/\sqrt{6} & -2/\sqrt{6} & 2/\sqrt{6} \\ 1/\sqrt{2} & 0 & -2/\sqrt{2} \end{bmatrix},$$

then

$$P_0^t = P_0^{-1} \quad \text{and} \quad \begin{bmatrix} 1 & 0 & 0 \\ 0 & 1 & 0 \\ 0 & 0 & 2 \end{bmatrix} = P_0^t A P_0.$$

The remainder of this book will study various applications of the theorems of this section.

EXERCISES

1. Which of the following linear operators E, defined on the given space V, are projections?

   (a) $V = R^2$; $E(x, y) = (y, 0)$

   (b) $V = R^3$; $E(x, y, z) = (3x + y + z, -3x - y - z, -3x - y - z)$

   (c) $V = R^3$;
   $$E(x, y, z) = (6x + 10y + 5z, -x - y - z, -4x - 8y - 3z)$$

   (d) $V = R^4$; $E(x, y, z, w) = (x + 3w, y - z, 0, 0)$

   (e) $V = R^4$; $E(x, y, z, w) = (y, z, w, 0)$

   (f) V is the space of 2×2 matrices, $EA = BA$, where

   $$B = \begin{bmatrix} 1 & 0 \\ 0 & 0 \end{bmatrix}.$$

   (g) V is the space of 2×2 matrices, $EA = BA - AB$, where

   $$B = \begin{bmatrix} 1 & 0 \\ 0 & 0 \end{bmatrix}.$$

   (h) V is the space of polynomials of degree ≤ 2; $Ef = f(0)g$, where g is a polynomial such that $g(0) = 1$.

   (i) V is the space of polynomials of degree ≤ 2; $Ef = f(0)g + f(1)h$, where g and h are polynomials such that $g(0) = h(0) = g(1) = h(1) = 1$.

   (j) V is the space of all real-valued continuous functions f defined for $0 \leq t \leq 1$; $Ef = f(0)e^{-t}$.

2. Show that each of the following linear operators E, defined on the given space V, is a projection. Describe the range of E and the null space of E.

   (a) $V = R^2$; $E(x, y) = (x, x)$ (b) $V = R^3$; $E(x, y, z) = (x, y, y)$

   (c) $V = R^3$; $E(x, y, z) = (-y, y, x + y + z)$

   (d) V is the space of 2×2 matrices; $EA = BAB$, where $B^2 = B$.

   (e) V is the space of 2×2 matrices; $EA = (A + A^t)/2$.

   (f) V is the space of all polynomials; $Ef = f(0) + f'(0)t$, where $f'(0) = (df/dt)(0)$.

   (g) V is the space of all real-valued continuous functions f defined for $0 \leq t \leq 1$; $Ef(t) = f(t)$ for $0 \leq t \leq \frac{1}{2}$ and $Ef(t) = f(\frac{1}{2})$ for $\frac{1}{2} < t \leq 1$.

3. On the given space V, find a projection E whose range is the subspace M. [*Hint:* Choose a basis for V which contains a basis for M.]

   (a) $V = R^2$; M is the subspace spanned by $(1, 2)$.

   (b) $V = R^3$; M is the subspace spanned by $\{(1, 1, 1), (1, 1, 0)\}$.

   (c) V is the space of polynomials of degree ≤ 2 and M is the subspace spanned by $\{1 + t + t^2, 1 + t + 2t^2\}$.

   (d) V is the space of 2×2 matrices and M is the subspace spanned by

   $$\begin{bmatrix} 0 & 1 \\ -1 & 0 \end{bmatrix}.$$

4. On the given space V, find a projection E whose range is the given space M and whose null space is the given space N. [*Hint:* Choose a basis for V by choosing a basis for M and for N.]

(a) $V = R^2$; M is the line $y = 2x$ and N is the line $y = \frac{1}{2}x$.

(b) $V = R^3$; M is the plane $x = -2z$ and N is the line $x = y = z$.

5. Let $V = R^2$. Find two different projections whose range is the x-axis.

6. Let E be a projection on V and let T be a linear operator on V. Show that $T = ET + (I - E)T = TE + T(I - E) = ETE + ET(I - E) + (I - E)TE + (I - E)T(I - E)$.

7. Let E and F be projections on V. Show that $E + F$ is a projection on V if and only if $EF = FE = 0$. [*Hint:* Compute $(E + F)^2$.]

8. Let E be an $n \times n$ matrix such that $E^2 = E$. Show that $tr(E) = \operatorname{rank}(E)$. [*Hint:* Use (8) to write E in diagonal form. Since $E^2 = E$ what must these diagonal entries be? Then use Exercise 15, Section 6, Chapter 1.]

9. (a) Show that if $E \neq 0$, $E \neq I$ and $E^2 = E$, then the minimum polynomial for E must be $(t - 1)t$. [*Hint:* $E^2 = E$ is the same as $E^2 - E = 0$.]

(b) Show that if $E^2 = E$, then the characteristic polynomial for E is $t^k(1 - t)^{n-k}$, where $n = \dim V$, $n - k = \operatorname{rank}(E)$, and $k = $ nullity (E). [*Hint:* Use (8).]

(c) Show that if $E \neq I$ and $E^2 = E$, then E is *not* invertible.

10. Let A be an $n \times n$ matrix with the following properties: $A_{i(i+1)} = 1$, $i = 1, 2, \ldots, (n - 1)$; $A_{ij} = 0$ if $i \neq n$ and $j \neq i + 1$. Let Δ be the characteristic polynomial of A. Show that $\Delta = t^n - A_{nn}t^{n-1} - A_{n(n-1)}t^{n-2} - \cdots - A_{n2}t - A_{n1}$. [*Hint:* Use a Laplace expansion along the nth row of $tI - A$.]

11. Show that each of the following matrices is diagonalizable. Find the spectral projections of these matrices, i.e., the projections given by (14).

(a) $\begin{bmatrix} 1 & 1 & 1 \\ 0 & 2 & 1 \\ 0 & 0 & 3 \end{bmatrix}$ (b) $\begin{bmatrix} 0 & 1 & 0 \\ 0 & 0 & 1 \\ 6 & -11 & 6 \end{bmatrix}$

(c) $\begin{bmatrix} 0 & 1 & 0 & 0 \\ -2 & 3 & 0 & 0 \\ 0 & 0 & 0 & 1 \\ 0 & 0 & -3 & 4 \end{bmatrix}$ (d) $\begin{bmatrix} 0 & 1 & 1 & 2 \\ -2 & 3 & 1 & 1 \\ 0 & 0 & 0 & 1 \\ 0 & 0 & -3 & 4 \end{bmatrix}$

(e) $\begin{bmatrix} 1 & 1 & 0 & 0 \\ 0 & 2 & 0 & 0 \\ 0 & 0 & 1 & 1 \\ 0 & 0 & 0 & 2 \end{bmatrix}$ (f) $\begin{bmatrix} 1 & 1 & 1 & 1 \\ 1 & 1 & 1 & 1 \\ 1 & 1 & 1 & 1 \\ 1 & 1 & 1 & 1 \end{bmatrix}$ (*cont.*)

(g) $\begin{bmatrix} 2 & 1 & 0 & 0 \\ 1 & 4 & 0 & 0 \\ 0 & 0 & 1 & 2 \\ 0 & 0 & 2 & 1 \end{bmatrix}$
(h) $\begin{bmatrix} 2 & 1 & 3 & 1 \\ 1 & 4 & 0 & 2 \\ 0 & 0 & 1 & 2 \\ 0 & 0 & 2 & 1 \end{bmatrix}$

12. Let A be 2×2. Let A' be obtained from A by interchanging the rows of A. Let A'' be obtained from A by multiplying the second row by a and adding to the first row of A.

(a) Give an example to show that A may be diagonalizable while A' is not.

(b) Give an example to show that A may be diagonalizable while A'' is not.

13. Which of the following projections on R^3 is an orthogonal projection with respect to the standard inner product? Which is an orthogonal projection with respect to the inner product defined by $((x_1, y_1, z_1), (x_2, y_2, z_2)) = x_1 x_2 + (x_1 + y_1)(x_2 + y_2) + (x_1 + y_1 + z_1)(x_2 + y_2 + z_2)$?

(a) $E(x, y, z) = \left(\dfrac{x + y + z}{3}, \dfrac{x + y + z}{3}, \dfrac{x + y + z}{3} \right)$

(b) $E(x, y, z) = (x, x, 0)$

(c) $E(x, y, z) = (x, -x, 0)$

14. For each of the following matrices A find an orthogonal matrix P_0 such that $P_0^{-1} A P_0$ is diagonal.

(a) $\begin{bmatrix} 6 & 1 \\ 1 & 1 \end{bmatrix}$

(b) $\begin{bmatrix} \frac{11}{6} & -\frac{2}{3} & -\frac{1}{6} \\ -\frac{2}{3} & \frac{7}{3} & -\frac{2}{3} \\ -\frac{1}{6} & -\frac{2}{3} & \frac{11}{6} \end{bmatrix}$

(c) $\begin{bmatrix} 4 & 6 & 0 & 0 \\ 6 & 1 & 0 & 0 \\ 0 & 0 & 1 & -1 \\ 0 & 0 & -1 & 0 \end{bmatrix}$

15. Let R^3 have the inner product $((x_1, y_1, z_1), (x_2, y_2, z_2)) = x_1 x_2 + (x_1 + y_1)(x_2 + y_2) + (x_1 + y_1 + z_1)(x_2 + y_2 + z_2)$. Let T be the linear operator defined by $T(x, y, z) = (x, x + 2y, x + y + 3z)$. Show that T is symmetric with respect to the given inner product and find the spectral projections of T. Verify that these projections are also symmetric with respect to the given inner product.

16. (a) Show that if A and P_0 are $n \times n$, then $(P_0^t A P_0)^t = P_0^t A^t P_0$.

(b) Show that if P_0 is orthogonal and A is symmetric, then $P_0^t A P_0$ is symmetric.

(c) Show that if P_0 is orthogonal and $P_0^t A P_0$ is diagonal, then A is symmetric. [This shows that symmetry is also a necessary condition for (44) to hold.]

17. Let (X, Y) be an inner product on V. Let E be an orthogonal projection with respect to (X, Y). Show that if $P = 2E - I$, then P is an orthogonal transformation, which is also symmetric.

18. Show that if rank $(T) = 1$, then either T is diagonalizable or $T^k = 0$ for some integer $k > 1$, but not both.

19. Let q be a polynomial with distinct real roots; i.e.,

$$q = a(t - c_1)(t - c_2) \dots (t - c_k),$$

where $c_i \neq c_j$ if $i \neq j$ and a is a nonzero real number. Suppose that $q(T) = 0$. Show that T is diagonalizable. [*Hint:* What form must the minimum polynomial of T have?]

20. Let T be a linear operator on R^n. Let Δ be the characteristic polynomial of T and let p be the minimum polynomial. Suppose that the matrix of T is as given in Exercise 10. Show that $p = \Delta$. [*Hint:* Let $X = (1, 0, 0, \cdot, 0)$. Show that $\{X, TX, T^2X, \dots, T^kX\}$ is an independent set in R^n for $k \leq (n - 1)$. Deduce from this that deg $p \geq n$.]

21. Let T be diagonalizable and let f be any real-valued function such that $f(c)$ is defined for any characteristic value c of T. What are the characteristic values of $f(T)$?

22. Let $f(t) = e^t$. Let V have the inner product (X, Y). Let $T = T^*$. Show that

$$(f(T)X, Y) = (X, Y) + \sum_{n=1}^{\infty} \frac{(T^nX, Y)}{n!}.$$

[*Hint:* Use the fact that $f(t) = \sum_{n=0}^{n=\infty} (t^n/n!)$ and establish the result first in the case when X and Y belong to an orthogonal basis consisting of characteristic vectors for T.]

23. (a) Show that if c is a characteristic value of T and if P is invertible, then c is a characteristic value of $P^{-1}TP$.

(b) Show that if E is a projection and P is invertible, then $P^{-1}EP$ is a projection.

(c) Show that if T is diagonalizable and P is invertible, then $P^{-1}TP$ is diagonalizable.

(d) Show that if T is diagonalizable, if P is invertible, and if f is any function such that $f(T)$ is defined, then $f(P^{-1}TP)$ is defined and $f(P^{-1}TP) = P^{-1}f(T)P$.

(e) Show that if T is diagonalizable, then $ST = TS$ if and only if $SE = ES$ for each spectral projection E of T. [*Hint:* The spectral projections are polynomials in T.]

(f) Show that if T is diagonalizable, and if f is any function such that $f(T)$ is defined, then $f(T)S = Sf(T)$ for any operator S such that $ST = TS$. [*Hint:* Use (e).]

24. Let $f(t) = \log t$, $t > 0$ and $g(t) = t^{5/2}$. Find $f(A)$ and $g(A)$, where

$$A = \begin{bmatrix} 1 & 1 & 1 \\ 0 & 2 & 1 \\ 0 & 0 & 3 \end{bmatrix}.$$

[*Hint:* Find P_0 such that $P_0^{-1} A P_0$ is diagonal and use Exercise 23(d).]

25. Let (X, Y) be an inner product on the finite dimensional space V. Let $T = T^*$ and let c be the largest characteristic value of T. Let $TX^1 = cX^1$ with $(X^1, X^1) = 1$. Show that if $(X, X) \le 1$, then $(TX, X) \le c$. [*Hint:* Choose $X^2, X^3, \ldots, X^k$ such that $\{X^1, X^2, \ldots, X^n\}$ is a basis for V consisting of characteristic vectors of T. Express X in terms of $\{X^1, X^2, \ldots, X^n\}$.]

26. Let T be the linear operator on R^3 defined by $T(x, y, z) = (-2x + y + 2z, -4x + 3y + 2z, -5x + y + 5z)$. Let M be the subspace spanned by $\{(1, 1, 1), (1, 2, 1)\}$.

(a) Show that M is invariant for T.

(b) Let T_1 be the operator on M defined by $T_1 X = TX$ if X is in M. Find the matrix of T_1 with respect to $\{(1, 1, 1), (1, 2, 1)\}$.

27. (a) Let T be the linear operator on R^2 whose matrix is

$$\begin{bmatrix} 1 & 5 \\ -1 & -1 \end{bmatrix}.$$

Show that if M is a subspace invariant for T, then M is R^2 or $M = \{(0, 0)\}$.

(b) Let T be rotation on R^2 about $(0, 0)$ through the angle θ, where $0 < \theta < \pi/2$. Show that if M is a subspace invariant for T, then $M = R^2$ or $M = \{(0, 0)\}$.

(c) Let T be reflection on R^2 in the x-axis. What subspaces of R^2 are invariant for T?

28. Let D be the linear operator on the space of all real polynomials defined by $Df = (d/dt)f$. Let M be the subspace consisting of all polynomials of degree $\le n$. Show that M is invariant for D.

29. Show that if $T = T^*$ and M is invariant under T, then $M^\perp$ is also invariant for T. [*Hint:* What is the condition that X belong to $M^\perp$?]

30. Prove (34). [*Hint:* Let p be the minimum polynomial of T. Suppose that $p = gq$, where g is as in (34). Let W be the null space of $q(T)$.]

31. Let c be a characteristic value of T. Let M be the characteristic subspace belonging to c. Show that M is invariant for T.

32. Suppose that $\dim V > 2$ and T is a linear operator on V. Show that there is a nonzero subspace M such that $\dim M < \dim V$ and M is invariant for T. [*Hint:* Use (16) of Section 2 and Exercises 30 and 31.]

33. Suppose that A is a 2×2 symmetric matrix.

    (a) Write a flow diagram to find the spectral projections of A.

    (b) Write a flow diagram to find an invertible matrix P_0 such that $P_0^{-1} A P_0$ is diagonal.

SPECIAL EXERCISE

Suppose that V is finite dimensional and that (X, Y) is an inner product on V. Let T be a symmetric linear operator on V and let $S = T^2$.

    (a) Show that there is a number $K \geq 0$ such that $|TX| \leq K$ if $|X| \leq 1$. [*Hint:* See Exercise 25.]

Let K_0 be the greatest lower bound of the numbers K in part (a).

    (b) Show that $|TX| \leq K_0$ if $|X| \leq 1$ and there is a vector X^1 such that $|X^1| \leq 1$ and $|TX^1| = K_0$. [*Hint:* Let c be the characteristic value of T of largest absolute value. Proceed as in Exercise 25.]

Parts (a) and (b) can be proved directly, i.e., without using Theorem 22, by using the methods of advanced calculus. The remainder of this exercise will give a proof of Theorem 22 using parts (a) and (b).

    (c) Show that $|SX| \leq K_0^2$ if $|X| \leq 1$ and $|SX^1| = K_0^2$. [*Hint:* $|SX^1| = |T^2 X^1| = K_0 |T(TX^1/K_0)| \leq K_0^2 = |TX^1|^2 = (T^2 X^1, X^1) \leq |T^2 X^1| = |SX^1|$.]

    (d) Show that $(SX^1, X^1) = K_0^2$. [*Hint:* $(SX^1, X^1) = (TX^1, TX^1)$.]

    (e) Show that $SX^1 = K_0^2 X^1$. [*Hint:* Let $Z = SX^1 - K_0^2 X^1$ and use parts (c) and (d) to compute $|Z|^2$.]

    (f) Show that K_0 or $-K_0$ is a characteristic value of T. [*Hint:* $S - K_0^2 I = (T - K_0 I)(T + K_0 I)$ and $S - K_0^2 I$ is not invertible.]

    (g) Suppose that c is a real characteristic value of T. [From part (f) T has at least one real characteristic value.] Let $TZ^1 = cZ^1$, $|Z^1| = 1$. Let M_1 be the orthogonal complement of the subspace spanned by $\{Z^1\}$. Show that M_1 is invariant for T.

    (h) Complete the proof of Theorem 22 by restricting T to M_1 and applying parts (a) through (g) to this restriction, etc.

NOTES

Theorems 20, 21, and 22 give us a canonical form for operators of a certain type. As we have seen, the diagonal form greatly simplifies many questions. In Hoffman and Kunze [14, Chapter 7] and Jacobson [15, Chapter 3] a more general form, called the Jordan form, is given. Every operator on a finite dimensional space is shown to have such a form.

A systematic discussion of polynomial theory including a proof of the Cayley-Hamilton theorem is given in Hoffman and Kunze [14, Chapters 4 and 6]. A proof of the Fundamental Theorem of Algebra can be found in Churchill

[4, p. 96]. Many numerical methods for finding roots of polynomials and characteristic values can be found in Lanczos [19, Chapters 1 and 2].

The results of this chapter can be rather easily extended to a certain class of symmetric integral equations. (See Exercise 10 of Section 5, Chapter 2.) Such an extension can be found in Lovitt [20, Chapter 5]. Further discussion and many other applications of linear methods can be found in Courant and Hilbert [5].

Parts (a) and (b) of the special exercise of Section 4 are consequences of a general theorem about continuous functions and maximum values. This is given in Rudin [23, pp. 30 and 67]. Rudin [23, Chapter 9] also derives several major theorems in analysis using the techniques of linear algebra.

CHAPTER 4

Miscellaneous Results and the Complex Case

Section 1. COMMUTING OPERATORS

In Chapter 3 we introduced the concept of diagonalizable operator. We showed the simplicity with which we can answer questions about T when T has a diagonal matrix representation.   In some applications of linear algebra we wish to answer questions about the relationships among two or more operators.   Suppose that S and T are linear operators on V. Let A be the matrix of S and B the matrix of T with respect to a basis for V. If we had some way of knowing that we could choose this basis so that *both* A and B are diagonal, then most questions involving both S and T could be easily answered.   This clearly requires that both S and T be diagonalizable.   In this section we will give a simple criterion which guarantees that we can find a basis for V such that both A and B are diagonal.

If A and B are diagonal $n \times n$ matrices, then many computations with A and B are particularly simple.   For example, if

$$A = \begin{bmatrix} 2 & 0 \\ 0 & 4 \end{bmatrix} \quad \text{and} \quad B = \begin{bmatrix} -1 & 0 \\ 0 & 2 \end{bmatrix},$$

then

$$AB = \begin{bmatrix} -2 & 0 \\ 0 & 8 \end{bmatrix},$$

$$A^2 + 3AB^2 - B^{-1} = \begin{bmatrix} 4 & 0 \\ 0 & 8 \end{bmatrix} - 3\begin{bmatrix} 2 & 0 \\ 0 & 4 \end{bmatrix}\begin{bmatrix} 1 & 0 \\ 0 & 4 \end{bmatrix} - \begin{bmatrix} -1 & 0 \\ 0 & \frac{1}{2} \end{bmatrix}$$

$$= \begin{bmatrix} -1 & 0 \\ 0 & -40\frac{1}{2} \end{bmatrix},$$

$$A^{-3/2} - B^2 + I = \begin{bmatrix} \sqrt{2}/4 & 0 \\ 0 & -2\frac{7}{8} \end{bmatrix}.$$

Now let S and T be linear operators on V.   We say that S and T are *simultaneously diagonalizable* if and only if there is a basis $\{X^1, X^2, \ldots, X^n\}$ such that if A is the matrix of S and B of T with respect to that basis, then *both* A and B are diagonal matrices. In this case, computations with S and T are quite simple, as the above examples show.

Clearly S and T are simultaneously diagonalizable if and only if there is a basis for V consisting of characteristic vectors for *both* S and T. Suppose that S and T are simultaneously diagonalizable. Let $\{X^1, X^2, \ldots, X^n\}$ be a basis for V such that

(1) $$SX^i = a_i X^i, \qquad i = 1, 2, \ldots, n,$$

(2) $$TX^i = b_i X^i, \qquad i = 1, 2, \ldots, n.$$

Let

$$A = \begin{bmatrix} a_1 & 0 & \ldots & 0 \\ 0 & a_2 & \ldots & 0 \\ \vdots & & & \\ 0 & 0 & \ldots & a_n \end{bmatrix} \quad \text{and} \quad B = \begin{bmatrix} b_1 & 0 & \ldots & 0 \\ 0 & b_2 & \ldots & 0 \\ \vdots & & & \\ 0 & 0 & \ldots & b_n \end{bmatrix}.$$

Then A is the matrix of S and B of T with respect to the given basis. We have

(3) $$AB = BA,$$

so that

(4) $$ST = TS.$$

Also

$$AB = \begin{bmatrix} a_1 b_1 & 0 & \ldots & 0 \\ 0 & a_2 b_2 & \ldots & 0 \\ \vdots & & & \\ 0 & 0 & \ldots & a_n b_n \end{bmatrix},$$

so that ST is also diagonalizable. Since $aA + bB$ is diagonal for any a and b, we have that $aS + bT$ is diagonalizable.

(5) If S and T are simultaneously diagonalizable, then ST and $aS + bT$ are diagonalizable.

As we shall see below, the condition (4) is the important property. We say that two operators S and T *commute* if $ST = TS$. Let us study this concept a little further. We have the following.

(6) If S and T commute and if f is a polynomial, then S and $f(T)$ commute.

For we have $ST^2 = (ST)T = (TS)T = T(ST) = T(TS) = T^2 S$. More generally we have $ST^k = T^k S$ for any integer $k \geq 1$. Thus if $f = c_0 + c_1 t + c_2 t^2 + \cdots + c_n t^n$, then $Sf(T) = S(c_0 I + c_1 T + c_2 T^2 + \cdots + c_n T^n) = c_0 SI + c_1 ST + c_2 ST^2 + \cdots + c_n ST^n = c_0 IS + c_1 TS + c_2 T^2 S + \cdots + c_n T^n S = f(T)S$.

We note that aI commutes with every operator, and that if f and g are polynomials, then [see (20) of Section 2]

(7) $$f(T)g(T) = g(T)f(T).$$

Suppose that E and F are projections.

(8) If $EF = FE$, then EF is a projection.

This follows from $(EF)^2 = (EF)(EF) = E(FE)F = E(EF)F = E^2F^2 = EF$. The exercises will give an example showing that the converse of (8) is false.

We can use the results obtained thus far to prove the following theorem.

Theorem 23. Let V be finite dimensional. Let S and T be diagonalizable. Suppose that $ST = TS$. Then S and T are simultaneously diagonalizable.

Proof. Let $c_1, c_2, \ldots, c_r$ be distinct real numbers and let $E_1, E_2, \ldots, E_r$ be nonzero projections such that (see Theorem 20 and the Remarks after Theorem 21)

(9)
  (a) $I = E_1 + E_2 + \cdots + E_r$,
  (b) $E_iE_j = 0$ if $i \neq j$,
  (c) $S = c_1E_1 + c_2E_2 + \cdots + c_rE_r$.

Similarly, let $d_1, d_2, \ldots, d_k$ be distinct real numbers and let $F_1, F_2, \ldots, F_k$ be nonzero projections such that

(10)
  (a) $I = F_1 + F_2 + \cdots + F_k$,
  (b) $F_iF_j = 0$ if $i \neq j$,
  (c) $T = d_1F_1 + d_2F_2 + \cdots + d_kF_k$.

Substitute (9a) in (10c) and (10a) in (9c). This gives

(11)
  (a) $S = c_1E_1F_1 + c_1E_1F_2 + \cdots + c_1E_1F_k + c_2E_2F_1 + c_2E_2F_2 + \cdots + c_2E_2F_k + \cdots + c_rE_rF_1 + c_rE_rF_2 + \cdots + c_rE_rF_k,$
  (b) $T = d_1F_1E_1 + d_1F_1E_2 + \cdots + d_1F_1E_r + d_2F_2E_1 + d_2F_2E_2 + \cdots + d_2F_2E_r + \cdots + d_kF_kE_1 + d_kF_kE_2 + \cdots + d_kF_kE_r.$

To simplify notation let $C_{ij} = E_iF_j$ and $D_{ij} = F_jE_i$ for $1 \leq i \leq r$, $1 \leq j \leq k$. We note that E_i is a polynomial in S and F_j is a polynomial in T for $1 \leq i \leq r$, $1 \leq j \leq k$. [See (15) of Section 4.] Thus from two applications of (6) we have that E_i and F_j commute, that is, $C_{ij} = D_{ij}$. From (8) we conclude that each C_{ij} is a projection.

We also have

(12) $\qquad C_{ij}C_{ls} = 0 \quad \text{if} \quad i \neq l \quad \text{or if} \quad j \neq s.$

For we have $C_{ij}C_{ls} = E_i(F_jE_l)F_s = E_iE_lF_jF_s$. Using (9b) or (10b), this is 0 if $i \neq l$ or $j \neq s$.

Substitution of (10a) in (9a) and (9a) in (10a) yields

(a) $\begin{aligned} I =\ & E_1F_1 + E_1F_2 + \cdots + E_1F_k + E_2F_1 + E_2F_2 \\ & + \cdots + E_2F_k + \cdots + E_rF_1 + E_rF_2 \\ & + \cdots + E_rF_k, \end{aligned}$

(13)

(b) $\begin{aligned} I =\ & F_1E_1 + F_1E_2 + \cdots + F_1E_r + F_2E_1 + F_2E_2 \\ & + \cdots + F_2E_r + \cdots + F_kE_1 + F_kE_2 \\ & + \cdots + F_kE_r. \end{aligned}$

If we omit those C_{ij} in (11), (12), and (13) which are 0, we have that (11a), (12), and (13a) are the same conditions (with notation changes) as in Theorem 20 for S. Similarly (11b), (12), and (13b) are the same as in Theorem 20 for T. We showed in the proof of Theorem 20 that we could find a basis for V consisting of characteristic vectors for S by choosing a basis for the range of each C_{ij} for which $C_{ij} \neq 0$. Since $C_{ij} = D_{ij}$, the same proof shows that this basis consists of characteristic vectors of T. Q.E.D.

The matrix formulation of this theorem is immediate. Let A and B be $n \times n$ matrices, each of which is similar to a diagonal matrix.

(14) If $AB = BA$, then there is an invertible matrix P_0 such that both $P_0^{-1}AP_0$ and $P_0^{-1}BP_0$ are diagonal.

To prove (14) let A be the matrix of S and B the matrix of T with respect to the same basis for R^n. Then apply Theorem 23 and (56) of Section 6, Chapter 1.

Theorem 23 also extends to the symmetric case as follows.

(15) Let $S = S^*$, $T = T^*$, and $ST = TS$. Then there is an orthonormal basis for V consisting of characteristic vectors for both S and T.

In the case where $S = S^*$ and $T = T^*$, we know that $E_i = E_i^*$ and $F_j = F_j^*$ for $i = 1, 2, \ldots, r$, $j = 1, 2, \ldots, k$, where E_i and F_j are given by (9) and (10). As in the proof of Theorem 23 we have $E_iF_j = F_jE_i$ and $(E_iF_j)^2 = E_iF_j$. Thus $(E_iF_j)^* = F_j^*E_i^* = F_jE_i = E_iF_j$. This shows that E_iF_j is an orthogonal projection for each i and j. As in the proof of (38) of Section 4 we can now conclude (15) from (11), (12), and (13) combined with the condition

(16) $\qquad (E_iF_j)^* = E_iF_j, \quad 1 \leq i \leq r, \quad 1 \leq j \leq k.$

We can use this to extend (14) to the following sharper form.

(17)   If A and B are symmetric $n \times n$ matrices and $AB = BA$, then there is an orthogonal matrix P_0 such that both $P_0^{-1}AP_0$ and $P_0^{-1}BP_0$ are diagonal.

The proof of (17) follows from (15) just as (44) followed from (38) in Section 4.

The construction of P_0 can be carried out using (11). Choose a basis for the range of $E_i F_j$ for each i and j and put these together to give a basis for R^n. Say this basis is $\{Y^1, Y^2, \ldots, Y^n\}$. Then P_0 is the matrix whose rth column is Y^r for $r = 1, 2, \ldots, n$. [See (55) of Section 6, Chapter 1.] If $\{Y^1, Y^2, \ldots, Y^n\}$ is orthonormal, then P_0 is orthogonal.

EXERCISES

1. For each of the following operators S and T, defined on the given space V, determine whether S and T commute.

   (a) $V = R^2$; $S(x, y) = (2x + y, x - y)$ and $T(x, y) = (x - 3y, y)$
   (b) $V = R^2$; $S(x, y) = (x + 2y, y)$ and $T(x, y) = (x + 4y, y)$
   (c) $V = R^3$; $S(x, y, z) = (3x - y, z, 2x + y)$ and
   $$T(x, y, z) = (3x - 7y - z, 2x + y - 2z, 2x - 4y + z)$$
   (d) $V = R^3$; $S(x, y, z) = (3x, 2y, z)$ and
   $$T(x, y, z) = (x, x + y, x + y + z)$$
   (e) $V = R^3$; $S(x, y, z) = (x, y, x + y + z)$ and
   $$T(x, y, z) = (x + y, x + y, 6x - y + 2z)$$
   (f) V is the space of polynomials of degree ≤ 2;

   $$Sf = \frac{d}{dt}f \quad \text{and} \quad Tf = \frac{1}{t}\int_0^t f(u)\,du.$$

   (g) V is the space of all real polynomials; $Sf(t) = tf(t)$ and $Tf(t) = (d/dt)f$.
   (h) V is the space of real-valued continuous functions $f(t)$ defined for $0 \leq t \leq 1$; $Sf(t) = tf(t)$ and $Tf(t) = \sqrt{1 - t^2}\,f(t)$.
   (i) V is the space of real-valued continuous functions, $f(t)$ defined for $0 \leq t \leq 1$; $Sf(t) = \int_0^1 e^{-tu}f(u)\,du$ and $Tf(t) = tf(t)$.

2. For each of the following operators S and T, defined on the given space V, show that S and T are simultaneously diagonalizable. [*Hint*: Use Theorem 23.]

   (a) $V = R^2$; $S(x, y) = (x + 2y, 2x - y)$ and $T(x, y) = (-y, -x + y)$
   (b) $V = R^2$; $S(x, y) = (13x - 2y, -3x + 8y)$ and
   $$T(x, y) = (5x - 4y, -6x - 5y)$$
   (c) $V = R^3$; $S(x, y, z) = (-2x + y + 2z, -4x + 3y + 2z, -5x + y + 5z)$
   and $T(x, y, z) = (-2x + 2y, -4x + 4y, -2x + 2y)$
   (d) $V = R^3$; $S(x, y, z) = (x + 2y + z, 2x + 6y - z, x - y)$ and
   $$T(x, y, z) = (-6x + y - 7z, x - y + 2z, -7x + 2y - 4z)$$
   (cont.)

(e) V is the space of polynomials of degree ≤ 2;

$$Sf(t) = \frac{d}{dt}(tf) \quad \text{and} \quad Tf(t) = \frac{1}{t}\int_0^t f(u)\, du.$$

3. For each of the following operators S and T defined on R^3, find a basis for R^3 such that the matrices of S and T with respect to the basis are diagonal.

   (a) $S(x, y, z) = (-2x + y + 2z, -4x + 3y + 2z, -5x + y + 5z)$
       $T(x, y, z) = (-2x + 2y, -4x + 4y, -2x + 2y)$
   (b) $S(x, y, z) = (x + 2y, 2x - y, z)$
       $T(x, y, z) = (-y, -x + y, z)$

4. Let

$$A = \begin{bmatrix} 1 & 1 \\ 0 & 2 \end{bmatrix} \quad \text{and} \quad B = \begin{bmatrix} 3 & -1 \\ 0 & 4 \end{bmatrix}.$$

   Find $(A + B)^{10}$, $(AB)^{16}$ and $f(A + B)$, where $f(t) = e^t$. [*Hint:* Find P_0 such that $P_0^{-1}AP_0$ and $P_0^{-1}BP_0$ are diagonal.]

5. (a) Let S and T both be diagonalizable. Let $f(t) = e^t$. Show that if $ST = TS$, then $f(S + T) = f(S)f(T)$. [*Hint:* Express S and T as in (11).]

   (b) Let

$$A = \begin{bmatrix} 2 & 0 \\ 2 & 1 \end{bmatrix} \quad \text{and} \quad B = \begin{bmatrix} 3 & 0 \\ 1 & 1 \end{bmatrix},$$

   so that

$$A + B = \begin{bmatrix} 5 & 0 \\ 3 & 2 \end{bmatrix}.$$

   Show that A, B, and $A + B$ are diagonalizable, yet if $f(t) = e^t$, then $f(A + B) \neq f(A)f(B)$. [*Hint:* To compute $f(A)$ and $f(B)$ it is easiest to find the spectral projections of A and B.]

6. (a) Show that if S and T are symmetric, then ST is symmetric if and only if S and T commute.

   (b) Let E and F be orthogonal projections. Show that EF is an orthogonal projection if and only if $EF = FE$.

7. (a) Let

$$A = \begin{bmatrix} 1 & 0 \\ 0 & 0 \end{bmatrix} \quad \text{and} \quad B = \begin{bmatrix} 1 & 0 \\ -1 & 0 \end{bmatrix}.$$

   Show that $A^2 = A$, $B^2 = B$, $(AB)^2 = AB$, $(BA)^2 = BA$, and $AB \neq BA$.

   (b) Let

$$A = \begin{bmatrix} 0 & 1 \\ 0 & 1 \end{bmatrix} \quad \text{and} \quad B = \begin{bmatrix} 1 & 1 \\ 0 & 0 \end{bmatrix}.$$

   Show that $A^2 = A$, $B^2 = B$, $(AB)^2 = AB$, and $(BA)^2 \neq BA$.

(c) Let

$$A = \begin{bmatrix} 1 & 0 \\ 0 & 0 \end{bmatrix} \quad \text{and} \quad B = \begin{bmatrix} \frac{1}{2} & \frac{1}{2} \\ \frac{1}{2} & \frac{1}{2} \end{bmatrix}.$$

Show that $A^2 = A$, $B^2 = B$, $(AB)^2 \neq AB$, and $(BA)^2 \neq BA$.

(d) Let E and F be projections on R^2 whose matrices are given by

$$A = \begin{bmatrix} 1 & 0 \\ 0 & 0 \end{bmatrix} \quad \text{and} \quad B = \begin{bmatrix} 1 & 0 \\ -1 & 0 \end{bmatrix},$$

respectively. Draw a diagram indicating the range and null spaces of E and F. Draw lines from (x, y) to $E(x, y)$, $F(x, y)$, $EF(x, y)$, and $FE(x, y)$. Do the same when

$$A = \begin{bmatrix} 0 & 1 \\ 0 & 1 \end{bmatrix} \quad \text{and} \quad B = \begin{bmatrix} 1 & 1 \\ 0 & 0 \end{bmatrix}$$

and when

$$A = \begin{bmatrix} 1 & 0 \\ 0 & 0 \end{bmatrix} \quad \text{and} \quad B = \begin{bmatrix} \frac{1}{2} & \frac{1}{2} \\ \frac{1}{2} & \frac{1}{2} \end{bmatrix}.$$

8. Let dim $V = n$ and let S and T be commuting diagonalizable operators on V. Suppose that both S and T have n distinct characteristic values. Show that X is a characteristic vector of S if and only if X is a characteristic vector of T. [*Hint:* Choose a basis consisting of characteristic vectors for both S and T. Express X in terms of coordinates with respect to this basis.]

9. (a) Let E be a projection on V and let M be the range of E. Show that M is an invariant subspace for T, if and only if $TE = ETE$. [*Hint:* X is in M if and only if $X = EX$.]

(b) Suppose that E is an orthogonal projection in V. Let M be the range of E and N the null space of E. Show that $N = M^{\perp}$. [*Hint:* If $EX = 0$, then $(X, EY) = 0$.]

(c) Suppose that E is an orthogonal projection in V. Then T commutes with E if and only if the range and the null space of E are invariant for T.

Section 2.   POSITIVE DEFINITE OPERATORS

As we have seen, a vector space possesses many inner products. In this section we shall discuss the relationships among inner products on a vector space. We begin with an example.

We shall denote the standard inner product on R^2 by $X \cdot Y$, so that if $X = (x_1, x_2)$ and $Y = (y_1, y_2)$, then

(1)
$$X \cdot Y = x_1 y_1 + x_2 y_2.$$

If we define (X, Y) by

(2) $$(X, Y) = 4x_1y_1 - x_2y_1 - x_1y_2 + 2x_2y_2,$$

where $X = (x_1, x_2)$ and $Y = (y_1, y_2)$, then (X, Y) is an inner product on R^2. The expression (2) shows clearly that $(X, Y) = (Y, X)$ and that (X, Y) is linear in X for fixed Y and linear in Y for fixed X. If $X \neq 0$ and $X = (x_1, x_2)$, then $(X, X) = 4x_1^2 - 2x_1x_2 + 2x_2^2 = 2(x_2^2 - x_1x_2 + 2x_1^2) = 2(x_2^2 - x_1x_2 + \frac{1}{4}x_1^2 + \frac{7}{4}x_1^2) = 2((x_2 - \frac{1}{2}x_1)^2 + \frac{7}{4}x_1^2)$. This final expression is a sum of squares so it is ≥ 0. If $2((x_2 - \frac{1}{2}x_1)^2 + \frac{7}{4}x_1^2) = 0$, then x_1 must be zero so that x_2 must also be zero. This shows that (2) defines an inner product on R^2.

To find the relation between (X, Y) and $X \cdot Y$, let $X^1 = (1, 0)$ and $X^2 = (0, 1)$. Form the matrix

(3) $$A = \begin{bmatrix} (X^1, X^1) & (X^2, X^1) \\ (X^1, X^2) & (X^2, X^2) \end{bmatrix} = \begin{bmatrix} 4 & -1 \\ -1 & 2 \end{bmatrix}.$$

We can then rewrite (2) as

(4) $$(X, Y) = (y_1 \ y_2) \begin{bmatrix} 4 & -1 \\ -1 & 2 \end{bmatrix} \begin{bmatrix} x_1 \\ x_2 \end{bmatrix}.$$

Let P be the linear operator on R^2 whose matrix (with respect to $\{X^1, X^2\}$) is A. Then we can rewrite (4) as

(5) $$(X, Y) = PX \cdot Y.$$

This follows from the fact that $PX = Z$, where $X = (x_1, x_2)$ and $Z = (z_1, z_2)$ if and only if

$$A \begin{bmatrix} x_1 \\ x_2 \end{bmatrix} = \begin{bmatrix} z_1 \\ z_2 \end{bmatrix}, \quad \text{and that} \quad Z \cdot Y = (y_1 \ y_2) \begin{bmatrix} z_1 \\ z_2 \end{bmatrix}.$$

We have shown that the inner product (X, Y) can be expressed in terms of $X \cdot Y$ by using the operator P as in (5), or the matrix A as in (4). As we shall see below, each inner product on R^n gives rise to an operator P such that (5) holds. Before giving this result, we examine the properties of P.

Since $A = A^t$, we see that $P = P^*$ (where P^* is computed using $X \cdot Y$), so that P is symmetric with respect to $X \cdot Y$. From (5) and the fact that (X, Y) is an inner product, we have

(6) $$PX \cdot X > 0 \quad \text{if} \quad X \neq 0.$$

This follows from the fact that $PX \cdot X = (X, X)$, which is >0 if $X \neq 0$. Computation using (3) shows that the characteristic values of P

are $3 + \sqrt{2}$ and $3 - \sqrt{2}$. Both of these numbers are > 0. This can also be established using (6). Let c be a characteristic value of P and let $PX = cX$ with $X \neq 0$. Then $(X, X) > 0$ and $X \cdot X > 0$. Also $(X, X) = PX \cdot X = cX \cdot X$. We conclude that $c > 0$, i.e.,

(7)   The characteristic values of P are positive.

We can use (2), (6), or (7) to conclude that

(8) P is invertible.

Using (36) of Section 4, Chapter 3, we have

(9)
(a) $P = (3 + \sqrt{2})E_1 + (3 - \sqrt{2})E_2$,
(b) $I = E_1 + E_2$,
(c) $E_1E_2 = E_2E_1 = 0$,
(d) $E_i^2 = E_i^* = E_i \neq 0$, $i = 1, 2$.   (E_i^* is computed using $X \cdot Y$.)

Let $Q = \sqrt{3 + \sqrt{2}}\, E_1 + \sqrt{3 - \sqrt{2}}\, E_2$. Then $Q = Q^*$ (with respect to $X \cdot Y$) and $Q^2 = P$. This shows that P has a square root. We have shown more than this; Q is symmetric (with respect to $X \cdot Y$) and the characteristic values of Q, which are $\sqrt{3 + \sqrt{2}}$ and $\sqrt{3 - \sqrt{2}}$, are > 0. Thus:

(10)   There is a symmetric operator Q (with respect to $X \cdot Y$) whose characteristic values are > 0, and $Q^2 = P$.

We should note that P (as well as Q) is symmetric with respect to (X, Y) also. For we have $(PX, Y) = P(PX) \cdot Y = PX \cdot PY = (X, PY)$. The first and third of these equalities use (5), while the second equality uses the fact that P is symmetric with respect to $X \cdot Y$.

Now suppose that P_1 is another operator such that $(X, Y) = P_1X \cdot Y$ for all X and Y in R^2. From (10) of Section 5, Chapter 2, we conclude that $P_1 = P$. This gives

(11) P is uniquely determined by the condition (5).

In order to derive the general results it is somewhat inconvenient to use (2), which depends on the choice of basis for R^2. As we shall see, Theorem 16 will provide us with the tools needed to describe the general case.

Now let V be an arbitrary finite dimensional vector space with an inner product. For convenience we shall denote this inner product by $X \cdot Y$. All statements about adjoint and symmetry will refer to the inner product $X \cdot Y$.

A linear operator P on V is called a *positive definite* linear operator if P is symmetric and $PX \cdot X > 0$ if $X \neq 0$. We shall use the shorter phrase "positive operator" instead of "positive definite linear operator."

As we shall see, the results (7) through (10) can be extended to the general case.

Suppose that P is a positive operator on V and suppose that c is a characteristic value of P. Suppose that $PX = cX$ with $X \neq 0$. Then $PX \cdot X = cX \cdot X$. Since $PX \cdot X > 0$ and $X \cdot X > 0$, we must have $c > 0$. This establishes the following result.

(12)   If P is a positive operator on V, then all the characteristic values of P are > 0.

This result has a partial converse. We could prove this directly by choosing an orthonormal basis for V and expressing $X \cdot Y$ in terms of coordinates. Instead let us derive the general form of (10) and use this to prove the converse of (12).

Suppose that $P = P^*$ and that the characteristic values of P are positive. Since $P = P^*$, we know from (36) of Section 4, Chapter 3 that we have

(13)
(a) $P = c_1 E_1 + c_2 E_2 + \cdots + c_r E_r$,
(b) $I = E_1 + E_2 + \cdots + E_r$,
(c) $E_i E_j = 0$, $i \neq j$,
(d) $E_i^2 = E_i^* = E_i \neq 0$, $i = 1, 2, \ldots, r$.

The numbers c_i are the characteristic values of P so that $c_i > 0$ for $i = 1, 2, \ldots, r$. Let $f(t) = \sqrt{t}$ and let $Q = f(P)$. Then $Q = \sqrt{c_1} E_1 + \sqrt{c_2} E_2 + \cdots + \sqrt{c_r} E_r$, $Q = Q^*$, and $Q^2 = P$. Also the numbers $\sqrt{c_1}$, $\sqrt{c_2}, \ldots, \sqrt{c_r}$ are the characteristic values of Q. [See (19) of Section 4, Chapter 3.] We know that $c_i > 0$ and $\sqrt{c_i} > 0$ for $i = 1, 2, \ldots, r$. Thus 0 is not a characteristic value of P and is also not a characteristic value of Q. Therefore

(14) P and Q are both invertible.

Let $X \neq 0$. Then $PX \cdot X = Q^2 X \cdot X = QX \cdot QX > 0$. The fact that $QX \cdot QX > 0$ follows from the fact that $QX \neq 0$. We have shown that P is a positive operator, that is,

(15)   If $P = P^*$, then P is a positive operator if and only if the characteristic values of P are positive.

We also have:

(16) P is a positive operator if and only if $P = Q^2$, where Q is a positive operator.

For if we let Q be defined as above, then $Q = Q^*$, $Q^2 = P$, and the characteristic values of Q are positive. From (15) we conclude that Q is a positive operator. Conversely if Q is a positive operator and $P = Q^2$, then $P = P^*$. Since Q is a positive operator, Q is invertible. Therefore if $X \neq 0$, $QX \neq 0$ so that $PX \cdot X = Q^2 X \cdot X = QX \cdot QX > 0$. This establishes (16).

The Q of (16) is uniquely determined by P. To see this let P be expressed as in (13). In the expression (13) we can suppose that $c_i \neq c_j$ if $i \neq j$. Suppose that $P = Q_1^2$, where Q_1 is a positive operator. Then

(17)
(a) $Q_1 = d_1 F_1 + d_2 F_2 + \cdots + d_k F_k$,
(b) $I = F_1 + F_2 + \cdots + F_k$,
(c) $F_i F_j = 0$, $\quad i \neq j$,
(d) $F_i^2 = F_i^* = F_i \neq 0$, $\quad i = 1, 2, \ldots, k$.

In the expression (17) we can suppose that $d_i \neq d_j$ if $i \neq j$. Then $Q_1^2 = d_1^2 F_1 + d_2^2 F_2 + \cdots + d_k^2 F_k = P$. We know that $d_i > 0$ for $i = 1, 2, \ldots, k$, so that $d_i^2 \neq d_j^2$, if $i \neq j$. Since the spectral projections are unique, we conclude that $k = r$ and that we can reorder so that $d_i^2 = c_i$, $F_i = E_i$ for $i = 1, 2, \ldots, r$. Thus $Q = Q_1$. This proves the following.

(18)   If P is a positive operator, then there is a *unique* positive operator Q such that $Q^2 = P$.

Q is called the *positive square root* of P. Suppose that P is a positive operator on V. Then P gives rise to another inner product which we shall denote by (X, Y). We define (X, Y) by $(X, Y) = PX \cdot Y$. Since $PX \cdot Y = X \cdot PY = PY \cdot X$, we see that $(X, Y) = (Y, X)$. Clearly (X, Y) is linear in X for fixed Y and linear in Y for fixed X, since $X \cdot Y$ has these properties, and P is linear. If $X \neq 0$, then $(X, X) = PX \cdot X > 0$ so that (X, Y) is an inner product on V. This result has a converse.

Suppose that (X, Y) is an inner product on V. Let X be fixed and define $f(Y)$ by $f(Y) = X \cdot Y$. Then f is a real-valued linear transformation on V, so that from Theorem 16 there is a unique vector X' such that $f(Y) = X' \cdot Y$ for all Y in V. X' is uniquely determined by X so that if PX is defined to be X', then P is a transformation from V into V. We have

(19) $(X, Y) = PX \cdot Y$ for all X and Y in V.

From (19) we have $(aX^1 + bX^2, Y) = P(aX^1 + bX^2) \cdot Y = a(X^1, Y) + b(X^2, Y) = aPX^1 \cdot Y + bPX^2 \cdot Y$. This gives $(P(aX^1 + bX^2) - (aPX^1 + bPX^2)) \cdot Y = 0$ for all Y in V. In particular if $Y = P(aX^1 + bX^2) - aPX^1 - bPX^2$, this shows that $P(aX^1 + bX^2) - aPX^1 - bPX^2 = 0$. We conclude that P is linear. Because $(X, Y) = (Y, X)$, we have that $PX \cdot Y = PY \cdot X = X \cdot PY$ so that P is symmetric with respect to $X \cdot Y$. The fact that $(X, X) > 0$ if $X \neq 0$ and $(X, X) = PX \cdot X$ shows that P is a positive operator on V.

If P_1 is another operator on V such that $(X, Y) = P_1 X \cdot Y$, then $(PX - P_1 X) \cdot Y = 0$ for all X and Y in V. Thus $(PX - P_1 X) \cdot (PX - P_1 X) = 0$, that is, $PX = P_1 X$ for all X in V. We have shown the following.

(20)   If $X \cdot Y$ and (X, Y) are two inner products on V, then there is a unique linear operator P on V such that $(X, Y) = PX \cdot Y$ for all X and Y in V. Furthermore P is positive with respect to either $X \cdot Y$ or (X, Y). Conversely if $X \cdot Y$ is an inner product on V and if P is a positive operator with respect to $X \cdot Y$, then $(X, Y) = PX \cdot Y$ defines an inner product on V.

We have not yet shown that P is positive with respect to (X, Y). Since P is positive with respect to $X \cdot Y$, we see from (14) that P is invertible. Thus if $X \neq 0$, $PX \neq 0$, so that $(PX, X) = P^2 X \cdot X = PX \cdot PX > 0$.

See (10) ff for the proof that P is symmetric with respect to (X, Y).

——————————

Remarks. We can translate these results into matrix form as follows. Let $X \cdot Y$ denote the standard inner product on R^n. If we consider R^n as column matrices we have $X \cdot Y = Y^t X$. A symmetric $n \times n$ matrix A is called a *positive definite* matrix if $AX \cdot X > 0$ for $X \neq 0$, that is, if $X^t A X > 0$ for $X \neq 0$.

Let (X, Y) and $X \cdot Y$ be as in (16). Let $\{X^1, X^2, \ldots, X^n\}$ be an orthonormal basis for V with respect to $X \cdot Y$. Suppose that $(X, Y) = PX \cdot Y$ and let A be the matrix of P with respect to $\{X^1, X^2, \ldots, X^n\}$. Because P is symmetric with respect to $X \cdot Y$, we know that $A = A^t$. Furthermore $A_{ij} = PX^j \cdot X^i$ for $i = 1, 2, \ldots, n$ and $j = 1, 2, \ldots, n$. [See (11) of Section 5, Chapter 2.] Since $PX^j \cdot X^i = (X^j, X^i)$, we have that $A_{ij} = (X^j, X^i)$ for $i = 1, 2, \ldots, n$ and $j = 1, 2, \ldots, n$. Because of this we usually call A the *matrix of (X, Y) with respect to $X \cdot Y$ and the orthonormal basis $\{X^1, X^2, \ldots, X^n\}$* (orthonormal with respect to $X \cdot Y$). Let $X = x_1 X^1 + x_2 X^2 + \cdots + x_n X^n$. Then $PX = x_1 PX^1 + x_2 PX^2 + \cdots + x_n PX^n$ so that

$$PX \cdot X = (x_1 \ x_2 \ \ldots \ x_n) A \begin{bmatrix} x_1 \\ x_2 \\ \vdots \\ x_n \end{bmatrix}.$$

Since $PX \cdot X > 0$, we see that A is a positive definite matrix. Conversely if A is a positive definite matrix and if P is a linear operator on V whose matrix with respect to the orthonormal basis $\{X^1, X^2, \ldots, X^n\}$ (orthonormal with respect to $X \cdot Y$) is A, then P is a positive operator on

V. If $(X, Y) = PX \cdot Y$, then A is the matrix of (X, Y) with respect to $X \cdot Y$ and $\{X^1, X^2, \ldots, X^n\}$. To see this let $X = x_1 X^1 + x_2 X^2 + \cdots + x_n X^n$ and note that

$$PX \cdot X = (x_1 \ x_2 \ \ldots \ x_n) A \begin{bmatrix} x_1 \\ x_2 \\ \vdots \\ x_n \end{bmatrix},$$

so that $PX \cdot X > 0$ if $X \neq 0$. Since A is symmetric, this tells us that P is a positive operator. The other results follow from

$$A_{ij} = PX^j \cdot X^i = (X^j, X^i), \qquad i = 1, 2, \ldots, n, \quad j = 1, 2, \ldots, n.$$

These results on positive operators and positive definite matrices can be extended to a slightly more general concept. We say that P is *positive semidefinite* or *nonnegative* if $P = P^*$ and $PX \cdot X \geq 0$ for all X. The results (15), (16), and (18) carry over without change in proof if we substitute "nonnegative" for "positive" throughout. An $n \times n$ matrix A is said to be positive semidefinite if $A = A^t$ and if $X^t A X \geq 0$ for all $n \times 1$ matrices X.

For matrices, the general forms of (15), (16), and (18) are given by the following.

(21)   Suppose that $A = A^t$. Then A is positive definite (semidefinite) if and only if the characteristic values of A are >0 (≥ 0). A is positive definite (semidefinite) if and only if there is a positive definite (semidefinite) matrix B such that $A = B^2$. The matrix B is uniquely determined by A.

These results can be established directly using the matrix forms of the results of Section 4, Chapter 3, or can be proved as matrix forms of the results in this section.

EXERCISES

1. Let $X \cdot Y$ denote the standard inner product on R^2. For each of the following functions (X, Y) show that (X, Y) is an inner product on R^2 and find a positive operator P such that $(X, Y) = PX \cdot Y$. We suppose that $X = (x_1, x_2)$ and $Y = (y_1, y_2)$.

  (a) $(X, Y) = x_1 y_1 + (x_1 + x_2)(y_1 + y_2)$
  (b) $(X, Y) = 3x_1 y_1 - x_2 y_1 - x_1 y_2 + 2x_2 y_2$
  (c) $(X, Y) = 100 x_1 y_1 + x_1 y_2 + x_2 y_1$

2. For each of the inner products of Exercise 1 find the matrix of (X, Y) with respect to $X \cdot Y$ and the basis $\{(1/\sqrt{2}, 1/\sqrt{2}), (1/\sqrt{2}, -1/\sqrt{2})\}$.

3. Let A be a symmetric 2×2 matrix. Show that A is positive definite if and only if $A_{11} > 0$ and det $(A) > 0$. Show that A is positive semi-definite if and only if $A_{11} \geq 0$ and det $(A) \geq 0$. [*Hint:* Show that $X^t A X$ can be <0 if $A_{11} < 0$ or det $(A) < 0$.]

4. (a) Let P be a linear operator on V such that P is positive semidefinite. Show that P is positive if and only if P is invertible. [*Hint:* Use (15).]
   (b) Let T be a linear operator on V. Show that both T^*T and TT^* are nonnegative operators.
   (c) Show that T^*T is a positive operator if and only if T is invertible.

5. Let P be a nonnegative operator on V. Let k be an integer ≥ 1. Show that there is a unique nonnegative operator Q such that $Q^k = P$. [*Hint:* If P is expressed as in (13), then $c_i \geq 0$ for $i = 1, 2, \ldots, r$. Let $Q = c_1^{1/k} E_1 + c_2^{1/k} E_2 + \cdots + c_r^{1/k} E_r$. The proof of the uniqueness of Q is similar to the proof of (18).]

6. For each of the following matrices A show that A is positive definite by finding the characteristic values of A.

   (a) $\begin{bmatrix} 10 & -9 \\ -9 & 9 \end{bmatrix}$ (b) $\begin{bmatrix} \frac{3}{2} & \frac{1}{2} & -1 \\ \frac{1}{2} & \frac{3}{2} & -1 \\ -1 & -1 & 3 \end{bmatrix}$

7. For each of the following matrices A find a positive semidefinite matrix B such that $B^2 = A$. [*Hint:* First find an orthogonal matrix P_0 such that $P^{-1} A P_0$ is diagonal.]

   (a) $\begin{bmatrix} 6 & \sqrt{3} \\ \sqrt{3} & 4 \end{bmatrix}$ (b) $\begin{bmatrix} 5 & -1 & -4 \\ -1 & 5 & -4 \\ -4 & -4 & 8 \end{bmatrix}$

8. Let

$$A = \begin{bmatrix} 1 & 0 \\ 0 & 1 \end{bmatrix} \quad \text{and} \quad B = \begin{bmatrix} 0 & 1 \\ 1 & 0 \end{bmatrix}.$$

Show that A is positive definite, that $B^2 = A$, and that B is *not* the positive square root of A. Can you find a matrix C such that $C \neq C^t$ and $C^2 = A$?

9. (a) Give an example of a 2×2 matrix A such that $X^t A X > 0$ for all 2×1 matrices $X \neq 0$, yet A is not a positive definite matrix.
   (b) Give an example of a 2×2 diagonalizable matrix A which is not positive definite, yet all of its characteristic values are >0.

10. (a) Show that if P and Q are nonnegative operators, then $aP + bQ$ is nonnegative for $a \geq 0$ and $b \geq 0$. [*Hint:* $aP + bQ$ is symmetric.]
    (b) Show that if P and Q are nonnegative and $PQ = QP$, then PQ is nonnegative. [*Hint:* Use Theorem 23, or show directly that PQ is symmetric and that the square roots of P and Q commute.]
    (c) Find two 2×2 matrices A and B such that both are positive and AB is not positive.

11. (a) Let T be a symmetric linear operator on V. Show that there are non-negative linear operators P and Q on V such that $T = P - Q$, T, P, and Q commute, and $PQ = 0$. [*Hint:* If $T = c_1E_1 + c_2E_2 + \cdots + c_rE_r$ as in Theorem 20, let P be the sum of those c_iE_i for which $c_i > 0$ and let $-Q$ be the sum of those c_iE_i for which $c_i < 0$.]

  (b) Show that if T, P, and Q are as in (a), and if $T = P_1 - Q_1$, where P_1 and Q_1 are nonnegative operators such that T, P_1, and Q_1 commute and $P_1Q_1 = 0$, then $P = P_1$ and $Q = Q_1$. [*Hint:* Show that if the $c_1, c_2, \ldots, c_r$ of (a) are distinct, then the conditions on P_1 and Q_1 imply that P_1 must be the sum of those c_iE_i such that $c_i > 0$. To do this, Theorem 20 might be helpful.]

The remaining exercises of this section are concerned with the concept of bilinear form, a slightly more general concept than inner product. We assume in these exercises that V is a finite dimensional vector space with an inner product, denoted by $X \cdot Y$.

A *bilinear form* on V is a real-valued function $h(X, Y)$ defined for X and Y in V and satisfying $h(aX^1 + bX^2, Y) = ah(X^1, Y) + bh(X^2, Y)$ and $h(X, aY^1 + bY^2) = ah(X, Y^1) + bh(X, Y^2)$.

12. Show that if $h(X, Y)$ is a bilinear form on V, then there is a unique operator T on V such that $h(X, Y) = TX \cdot Y$. [*Hint:* Use Theorem 16 as in the proof of (18). An alternative way is to let $\{X^1, X^2, \ldots, X^n\}$ be an orthonormal basis for V, let A be the $n \times n$ matrix defined by $A_{ij} = h(X^j, X^i)$ and let T be the operator on V whose matrix with respect to $\{X^1, X^2, \ldots, X^n\}$ is A. The matrix A is called the *matrix of h* with respect to $\{X^1, X^2, \ldots, X^n\}$.]

13. Show that $h(X, Y) = h(Y, X)$ for all X and Y in V if and only if $T = T^*$, where $h(X, Y) = TX \cdot Y$. [*Hint:* The matrix A in Exercise 12 is symmetric in this case.]

14. Suppose that $h(X, Y) = h(Y, X)$ for all X and Y in V. Show that there are real numbers $c_1, c_2, \ldots, c_n$ and an orthonormal basis $\{X^1, X^2, \ldots, X^n\}$ such that if $X = x_1X^1 + x_2X^2 + \cdots + x_nX^n$, then $h(X, X) = c_1x_1^2 + c_2x_2^2 + \cdots + c_nx_n^2$. [*Hint:* Use Exercise 13 and Theorem 22.]

15. (a) A *quadratic form* on R^n is a real-valued function $g(x_1, x_2, \ldots, x_n) = a_{11}x_1^2 + a_{22}x_2^2 + \cdots + a_{nn}x_n^2 + a_{12}x_1x_2 + a_{13}x_1x_3 + \cdots + a_{1n}x_1x_n + a_{23}x_2x_3 + a_{24}x_2x_4 + \cdots + a_{2n}x_2x_n + \cdots + a_{(n-1)n}x_{n-1}x_n$. Show that there is a bilinear form $h(X, Y)$ on R^n such that $h(X, Y) = h(Y, X)$ and $h(X, X) = g(X)$. [*Hint:* Let A be the $n \times n$ matrix defined by $A_{ii} = a_{ii}$ for $i = 1, 2, \ldots, n$ and $A_{ij} = A_{ji} = a_{ij}/2$ if $j > i$. Let T be the operator on R^n whose matrix is A and let $h(X, Y) = TX \cdot Y$, the dot product on R^n.]

  (b) Show that if k is bilinear, $k(X, Y) = k(Y, X)$ and $k(X, X) = g(X)$, then $k(X, Y) = h(X, Y)$ for all X and Y in V. [*Hint:* Show that $k(X, Y) = \frac{1}{4}g(X + Y) - \frac{1}{4}g(X - Y) = h(X, Y)$.]

16. (a) Show that $ax_1^2 + abx_1x_2 + cx^2 = 1$ is the equation of an ellipse if and only if $a > 0$ and $b^2 - ac < 0$. [*Hint:* Let $g(x_1, x_2) = ax_1^2 + 2bx_1x_2 + cx_2^2$; apply Exercises 14 and 15.]

(b) Show that $ax_1^2 + 2bx_1x_2 + cx_2^2 = 1$ is the equation of an hyperbola if and only if $a > 0$ and $b^2 - ac > 0$ or $a < 0$ and $b^2 - ac < 0$.

Section 3. ORTHOGONAL OPERATORS

In Section 4 of Chapter 3 we introduced the concept of orthogonal operator. In this section we shall investigate the properties of such operators. We will then apply these results to the two- and three-dimensional cases. The exercises will give a similar discussion of the four-dimensional case and will also apply our results to rigid motions.

Suppose that V is a vector space with the inner product (X, Y). Recall that a linear operator P on V is called an *orthogonal operator* if $P^* = P^{-1}$. An $n \times n$ matrix P_0 is called an *orthogonal matrix* if $P_0^t = P_0^{-1}$. [See (43) ff of Section 4, Chapter 3.]

Suppose that $P_0 = (P_{ij})$ is an orthogonal matrix. Then $P_0^t P_0 = I$. This tells us

$$(1) \quad P_{1j}P_{1j} + P_{2j}P_{2j} + \cdots + P_{nj}P_{nj} = 1, \qquad j = 1, 2, \ldots, n,$$

and

$$(2) \quad P_{1j}P_{1i} + P_{2j}P_{2i} + \cdots + P_{nj}P_{ni} = 0, \qquad i \neq j.$$

Using the notation $\delta_{ij} = 0$ if $i \neq j$ and $\delta_{ii} = 1$, we can rewrite this as:

The condition that $P_0^t P_0 = I$, where $P_0 = (P_{ij})$ is the same as
(3) $P_{1j}P_{1i} + P_{2j}P_{2i} + \cdots + P_{nj}P_{ni} = \delta_{ij}$ for $i = 1, 2, \ldots, n$ and $j = 1, 2, \ldots, n$.

Since $P_0^t P_0 = I$ if and only if $P_0 P_0^t = I$ (from Theorem 10), we have the following

The condition that $P_0^t P_0 = I$, where $P_0 = (P_{ij})$, is the same as
(4) $P_{i1}P_{j1} + P_{i2}P_{j2} + \cdots + P_{in}P_{jn} = \delta_{ij}$ for $i = 1, 2, \ldots, n$ and $j = 1, 2, \ldots, n$.

The condition given in (3) is that the columns of P_0 are orthonormal, while the condition given in (4) is that the rows of P_0 are orthonormal, in each case with respect to the standard inner product on R^n.

Suppose that P is an orthogonal linear transformation on V with respect to the inner product (X, Y). Let P_0 be the matrix of P with respect to the orthonormal basis $\{X^1, X^2, \ldots, X^n\}$ for V. Then P_0^t is the matrix of P^* with respect to this basis. Therefore the condition that $P^*P = I$ is the same as the condition that $P_0{}^t P_0 = I$. This establishes that

(5) P is orthogonal if and only if its matrix with respect to some orthonormal basis is orthogonal.

For example, suppose that dim $V = 2$ and that $\{X^1, X^2\}$ is an orthonormal basis for V with respect to the inner product (X, Y). Suppose that P is a linear operator on V whose matrix with respect to $\{X^1, X^2\}$ is

$$P_0 = \begin{bmatrix} 1/\sqrt{2} & 1/\sqrt{2} \\ -1/\sqrt{2} & 1/\sqrt{2} \end{bmatrix}.$$

Then from (3) or (4) we conclude that P_0 is an orthogonal matrix, so that from (5) P is an orthogonal transformation on V, with respect to the inner product (X, Y).

Suppose that $X = x_1 X^1 + x_2 X^2$ and $Y = y_1 X^1 + y_2 X^2$. Then

$$PX = \frac{x_1 + x_2}{\sqrt{2}} X^1 + \frac{-x_1 + x_2}{\sqrt{2}} X^2$$

and

$$PY = \frac{y_1 + y_2}{\sqrt{2}} X^1 + \frac{-y_1 + y_2}{\sqrt{2}} X^2.$$

We have

$$(PX, PY) = \frac{(x_1 + x_2)(y_1 + y_2)}{2} + \frac{(-x_1 + x_2)(-y_1 + y_2)}{2}$$

$$= x_1 y_1 + x_2 y_2 = (X, Y).$$

These identities hold because $\{X^1, X^2\}$ is orthonormal with respect to (X, Y). We have shown that

(6) $(PX, PY) = (X, Y)$ for all X and Y in V.

In particular this tells us that $(PX, PX) = (X, X)$, or taking square roots,

(7) $|PX| = |X|.$

This tells us that P preserves length. If $X \neq 0$ and $Y \neq 0$, then (6) and (7) combine to give

$$\frac{(X, Y)}{|X| \, |Y|} = \frac{(PX, PY)}{|PX| \, |PY|},$$

i.e.,

(8) P preserves the cosine of the angle between two vectors.

These results can be derived directly using only the condition that $P^* = P^{-1}$. Suppose that V is a finite dimensional vector space with the inner product (X, Y) and that P is a linear operator on V.

The following are equivalent.

(a) $P^* = P^{-1}$.
(b) $P^*P = I$.
(9) (c) $PP^* = I$.
(d) $(PX, PY) = (X, Y)$ for all X and Y in V.
(e) $|PX| = |X|$ for all X in V.

The equivalence of (9a, b, c) is given by Theorem 10. Suppose that $P^*P = I$. Then $(PX, PY) = (P^*PX, Y) = (X, Y)$ so that (9b) implies (9d). Suppose that $(PX, PY) = (X, Y)$ for all X and Y. Then $(P^*PX, Y) = (X, Y)$ so that $((P^*P - I)X, Y) = 0$ for all X and Y in V. In particular, letting $Y = (P^*P - I)X$ gives $(P^*P - I)X = 0$ for all X in V. Thus $P^*P = I$. This establishes the equivalence of (9b) and (9d).

If (9d) holds, then, in particular, $(PX, PX) = (X, X)$, so that $|PX| = |X|$ for all X in V. If $|PX| = |X|$ for all X, then $|PX|^2 = |X|^2$ for all X in V. We now use the polarization identity [see (13) of Section 2, Chapter 2]

$$\begin{aligned} (PX, PY) &= \tfrac{1}{4}|PX + PY|^2 - \tfrac{1}{4}|PX - PY|^2 \\ &= \tfrac{1}{4}|P(X + Y)|^2 - \tfrac{1}{4}|P(X - Y)|^2 \\ &= \tfrac{1}{4}|X + Y|^2 - \tfrac{1}{4}|X - Y|^2 \\ &= (X, Y). \end{aligned}$$

This shows that if (9e) is true, then (9d) is true and completes the proof of (9).

We have shown that an orthogonal transformation can be described in terms of any of the conditions of (9) as well as in terms of (5). Another useful condition is given by the following.

(10) P is an orthogonal operator if and only if P transforms orthonormal sets into orthonormal sets; i.e., $\{PX^1, PX^2, \ldots, PX^k\}$ is orthonormal whenever $\{X^1, X^2, \ldots, X^k\}$ is orthonormal.

Suppose that P is orthogonal and that $\{X^1, X^2, \ldots, X^k\}$ is orthonormal. Then (9d) gives $(PX^i, PX^j) = (X^i, X^j) = \delta_{ij}$ for $1 \leq i \leq k$ and $1 \leq j \leq k$. In other words, $\{PX^1, PX^2, \ldots, PX^k\}$ is orthonormal. Now suppose that P transforms orthonormal sets into orthonormal sets. Suppose that $\{X^1, X^2, \ldots, X^n\}$ is an orthonormal basis for V. Then $(P^*PX^i, X^j) = (PX^i, PX^j) = \delta_{ij} = (X^i, X^j) = (IX^i, X^j)$ for each i and j. Linearity gives $(P^*PX, Y) = (IX, Y)$ for all X and Y in V. From (10) of Section 5, Chapter 2, we have $P^*P = I$. From (9b) we know that P is orthogonal. This proves (10).

Remarks. The exercises will contain an example which shows that (9b) and (9c) are not the same in the infinite-dimensional case. This will also show that there are nonorthogonal operators on infinite-dimensional spaces satisfying (9d) and (9e).

In the above discussion we have limited ourselves to orthogonal operators. The concepts and most of the results extend to the case when the domain and range are different. Suppose that V has an inner product, say (X, Y), and W has an inner product, say $\langle X', Y' \rangle$. If P is an isomorphism of V onto W such that $\langle PX, PY \rangle = (X, Y)$ for all X and Y in V, then we say that P is an *orthogonal* transformation of V onto W. In the same manner as that used in the proof of (9), the condition $\langle PX, PY \rangle = (X, Y)$ is the same as the condition $|PX| = |X|$, where $|PX|^2 = \langle PX, PX \rangle$ and $|X|^2 = (X, X)$. For this reason an orthogonal transformation is often called an *isometric isomorphism* or *isometry*.

If dim $V =$ dim $W = n$, then we can construct an isometry of V onto W as follows. Suppose that $\{X^1, X^2, \ldots, X^n\}$ is an orthonormal basis for V and $\{Y^1, Y^2, \ldots, Y^n\}$ is an orthonormal basis for W. Let P be the linear transformation of V onto W defined by $PX^i = Y^i$ for $i = 1, 2, \ldots, n$. Then P is an isomorphism by Theorem 11. If $X = x_1 X^1 + x_2 X^2 + \cdots + x_n X^n$, then $PX = x_1 Y^1 + x_2 Y^2 + \cdots + x_n Y^n$. Thus $|PX|^2 = \langle PX, PX \rangle = x_1^2 + x_2^2 + \cdots + x_n^2 = (X, X) = |X|^2$ so that P is an isometry.

In order to describe the orthogonal operators on various spaces we need the following two results.

(11)   If P is an orthogonal operator on V and if c is a characteristic value of P, then $|c| = 1$.

(12)   If P is orthogonal, then det $(P) = \pm 1$.

Suppose that $PX = cX$ with $c \neq 0$. Then $(PX, PX) = c^2(X, X)$, so that $c^2 = 1$. This proves (11). Property (12) follows from the fact that det $(P) =$ det (P^*) and $1 =$ det $(I) =$ det $(P^*P) =$ det (P^*) det (P).

We shall now describe the orthogonal operators for dimensions 2 and 3. Suppose that dim $V = 2$ and that V has the inner product (X, Y). Let P be an orthogonal operator on V and let $\{X^1, X^2\}$ be an orthonormal basis for V. Let

$$P_0 = \begin{bmatrix} a & b \\ c & d \end{bmatrix}$$

be the matrix of P with respect to $\{X^1, X^2\}$. Then

$$P_0^{-1} = \frac{1}{ad - bc} \begin{bmatrix} d & -b \\ -c & a \end{bmatrix},$$

so that the conditions $P_0{}^t P_0 = I$, from (5) and (1), and det $(P) = ad - bc = \pm 1$, from (12), give

(13) $P_0 = \begin{bmatrix} a & b \\ -b & a \end{bmatrix}$ if det $(P_0) = 1$;

$P_0 = \begin{bmatrix} a & b \\ b & -a \end{bmatrix}$ if det $(P_0) = -1$.

Property (1) tells us that $a^2 + b^2 = 1$. Therefore there is a unique number θ such that $0 \le \theta < 2\pi$ and

(14) $P_0 = \begin{bmatrix} \cos\theta & -\sin\theta \\ \sin\theta & \cos\theta \end{bmatrix}$ if det $(P_0) = 1$,

(15) $P_0 = \begin{bmatrix} \cos\theta & \sin\theta \\ \sin\theta & -\cos\theta \end{bmatrix}$ if det $(P_0) = -1$.

These show that if det $(P_0) = 1$, then P is rotation through the angle θ, and if det $(P_0) = -1$, then P is reflection through the X^1 axis followed by rotation through θ.

If dim $V = 3$ and P is an orthogonal operator on V, then the characteristic polynomial of P is of degree 3. Thus the characteristic polynomial has a real root. (See Exercise 4, Section 2, Chapter 3.) This tells us that P has a characteristic value, say c. From (11) we must have $c = \pm 1$. Suppose that $PX = cX$, where $X \ne 0$. Then if $X^1 = X/|X|$, we have

$$PX^1 = cX^1, \quad \text{and} \quad (X^1, X^1) = 1.$$

Choose X^2 and X^3 so that $\{X^1, X^2, X^3\}$ is an orthonormal basis for V. Let P_0 be the matrix of P with respect to this basis. We have

(16) $$P_0 = \begin{bmatrix} c & P_{12} & P_{13} \\ 0 & P_{22} & P_{23} \\ 0 & P_{32} & P_{33} \end{bmatrix}.$$

From (1) we know that $c^2 + P_{12}^2 + P_{13}^2 = 1$. Since $c = \pm 1$, we must have $P_{12} = P_{13} = 0$. From (1) we also have:

$$P_{22}^2 + P_{23}^2 = P_{32}^2 + P_{33}^2 = 1 \quad \text{and} \quad P_{22}P_{23} + P_{32}P_{33} = 0.$$

Thus

$$\begin{bmatrix} P_{22} & P_{23} \\ P_{32} & P_{33} \end{bmatrix}$$

is an orthogonal matrix. As in the derivation of (14) and (15) we conclude that there is a unique number θ with $0 \leq \theta < 2\pi$ such that

$$\begin{bmatrix} P_{22} & P_{23} \\ P_{32} & P_{33} \end{bmatrix} = \begin{bmatrix} \cos \theta & -\sin \theta \\ \sin \theta & \cos \theta \end{bmatrix}$$

(17) or

$$\begin{bmatrix} P_{22} & P_{23} \\ P_{32} & P_{33} \end{bmatrix} = \begin{bmatrix} \cos \theta & \sin \theta \\ \sin \theta & -\cos \theta \end{bmatrix}.$$

We have shown that:

(18) If det $(P) = 1$ and $c = 1$, then

$$P_0 = \begin{bmatrix} 1 & 0 & 0 \\ 0 & \cos \theta & -\sin \theta \\ 0 & \sin \theta & \cos \theta \end{bmatrix}.$$

(19) If det $(P) = 1$ and $c = -1$, then

$$P_0 = \begin{bmatrix} -1 & 0 & 0 \\ 0 & \cos \theta & \sin \theta \\ 0 & \sin \theta & -\cos \theta \end{bmatrix}.$$

(20) If det $(P) = -1$ and $c = 1$, then

$$P_0 = \begin{bmatrix} 1 & 0 & 0 \\ 0 & \cos \theta & \sin \theta \\ 0 & \sin \theta & -\cos \theta \end{bmatrix}.$$

(21) If det $(P) = -1$ and $c = -1$, then

$$P_0 = \begin{bmatrix} -1 & 0 & 0 \\ 0 & \cos \theta & -\sin \theta \\ 0 & \sin \theta & \cos \theta \end{bmatrix}.$$

Each of these has a simple geometric description. If det $(P) = 1$, then (18) tells us that P leaves the X^1-axis, i.e., the line through 0 and X^1, fixed and is rotation through the angle θ about this axis. Statement (19) tells us that P reflects in the X^2-axis and then rotates through θ about the X^1-axis. When det $(P) = -1$, then (20) tells us that P reflects through the plane of the X^1- and X^2-axes, then rotates through θ about the X^1-axis, while (21) tells us that P reflects in the plane of the X^2- and X^3-axes, then rotates through θ about the X^1-axis.

Remarks. To assist in the study of higher dimensions we give the following two results.

(22) Suppose that P is an orthogonal operator on V. Suppose that M is an invariant subspace for P; i.e., PX is in M whenever X is in M. Then M is also an invariant subspace for P^*.

(23) Suppose that P, V, and M are as in (22). Let P_1 be the restriction of P to M; i.e., P_1 is the linear operator on M defined by $P_1 X = PX$ for X in M. Let Q_1 be the restriction of P^* to M. Then P_1 is an orthogonal operator on M and $P_1^* = Q_1$.

To establish (22) and (23) let $\{X^1, X^2, \ldots, X^k\}$ be an orthonormal basis for M. Since M is invariant for P, we have that PX^i is in M for $i = 1, 2, \ldots, k$. From (10) we conclude that $\{PX^1, PX^2, \ldots, PX^k\}$ is also an orthonormal basis for M. If X is in M, then $X = a_1 PX^1 + a_2 PX^2 + \cdots + a_k PX^k$ so that $P^*X = a_1 P^*PX^1 + a_2 P^*PX^2 + \cdots + a_k P^*PX^k = a_1 X^1 + a_2 X^2 + \cdots + a_k X^k$ which is in M. Here we used the fact that $P^* = P^{-1}$. This proves (22). If X and Y are in M, then $P_1 X = PX$ and $P_1 Y = PY$ are in M. Furthermore, (9d) gives $(P_1 X, P_1 Y) = (PX, PY) = (X, Y)$, so that (9) tells us that P_1 is an orthogonal operator on M. Since $Q_1 Y = P^*Y$ for Y in M, we have that $(P_1 X, Y) = (PX, Y) = (X, P^*Y) = (X, Q_1 Y)$ for all X and Y in M. This proves (23).

These results can be used to simplify the matrix of P. Let $\{X^1, X^2, \ldots, X^k, X^{k+1}, \ldots, X^n\}$ be an orthonormal basis for V such that $\{X^1, X^2, \ldots, X^k\}$ is an orthonormal basis for M. Then, as in the proof of Theorem 15, $\{X^{k+1}, X^{k+2}, \ldots, X^n\}$ is an orthonormal basis for $M^\perp$. Suppose that $P_0 = (P_{ij})$ is the matrix of P with respect to $\{X^1, X^2, \ldots, X^n\}$. Then $P_{ij} = (PX^j, X^i)$ for $i, j = 1, 2, \ldots, n$. Suppose that M is invariant under P. Then PX^j is in M for $1 \leq j \leq k$. Thus $P_{ij} = (PX^j, X^i) = 0$ if $j \leq k$ and $i > k$. Since $P_0{}^t$ is the matrix of P^* with respect to this basis, we have $P_{ji} = (P^*X^j, X^i) = (X^j, PX^i) = 0$ if $j > k$ and $i \leq k$. This shows that

$$(24) \quad P_0 = \begin{bmatrix} P_{11} & P_{12} \ldots P_{1k} & 0 & 0 & \ldots & 0 \\ P_{21} & P_{22} \ldots P_{2k} & 0 & 0 & \ldots & 0 \\ \vdots & & \vdots & \vdots & & \vdots \\ P_{k1} & P_{k2} \ldots P_{kk} & 0 & 0 & & 0 \\ 0 & 0 \ldots 0 & P_{k+1,k+1} & P_{k+1,k+2} \ldots P_{k+1,n} \\ 0 & 0 \ldots 0 & P_{k+2,k+1} & P_{k+2,k+2} \ldots P_{k+2,n} \\ \vdots & & \vdots & \\ 0 & 0 \ldots 0 & P_{n,k+1} & P_{n,k+2} & \ldots P_{n,n} \end{bmatrix}.$$

In other words,

$$P_0 = \begin{bmatrix} A & 0 \\ 0 & B \end{bmatrix},$$

where A is $k \times k$, B is $(n - k) \times (n - k)$, and 0 represents a zero matrix of appropriate size. A is clearly the matrix of the operator P_1 of (23) with respect to $\{X^1, X^2, \ldots, X^k\}$. Using (1), we see that both A and B are orthogonal matrices.

EXERCISES

1. Suppose that R^3 has the standard inner product. Which of the following operators on R^3 is an orthogonal operator?

(a) $P(x, y, z) = \left(\dfrac{x + y + z}{\sqrt{3}}, \dfrac{x + y - 2z}{\sqrt{6}}, x - y \right)$

(b) $P(x, y, z) = \left(\dfrac{x + y + 2z}{\sqrt{6}}, \dfrac{x + 3y - 2z}{\sqrt{14}}, \dfrac{-4x + 2y + z}{\sqrt{21}} \right)$

(c) $P(x, y, z) = \left(\dfrac{x + z}{\sqrt{2}}, \dfrac{x - 2y - z}{\sqrt{6}}, \dfrac{x + y - z}{\sqrt{3}} \right)$

2. On each of the vector spaces V with the indicated inner product, show that the given operator P is orthogonal.

(a) $V = R^4$; standard inner product, $P(x, y, z, w) = (-y, x, w, -z)$.

(b) V is the space of 2×2 matrices; $(A, B) = A_{11}B_{11} + A_{12}B_{12} + A_{21}B_{21} + A_{22}B_{22}$, $PA = C^t A C$, where

$$C = \begin{bmatrix} 0 & 1 \\ -1 & 0 \end{bmatrix}.$$

(c) $V = R^2$; $((x_1, x_2), (y_1, y_2)) = x_1 y_1 + (x_1 + x_2)(y_1 + y_2)$, $P(x_1, x_2) = (\sqrt{2}x_1 + (\sqrt{2}/2)x_2, -\sqrt{2}x_1)$.

3. Let V be the space of polynomials, with the inner product $(a_0 + a_1 t + a_2 t^2 + \cdots + a_n t^n, b_0 + b_1 t^2 + b_2 t^2 + \cdots + b_n t^n) = a_0 b_0 + a_1 b_1 + a_2 b_2 + \cdots + a_n b_n$; i.e., take the sum of the products of coefficients of like powers. We shall denote this inner product by (f, g). Let P be the operator on V defined by $Pf(t) = tf(t)$ and let Q be the operator on V defined by $Qf(t) = (1/t)(f(t) - f(0))$. Show that $P^* = Q$, that $PQ \neq I$, and $QP = I$. [This shows that the assumption of finite dimensionality in (9) is necessary. P is often called a *shift* operator since $Pt^k = t^{k+1}$.]

4. Show that if P and Q are orthogonal operators on V with respect to (X, Y), then PQ is an orthogonal operator on V with respect to (X, Y).

5. For each of the following pairs of vector spaces V and W with the indicated inner products, determine if the given transformation P from V into W is orthogonal.

(a) $V = R^2$; standard inner product,
$W = R^2$; $((x_1, x_2), (y_1, y_2)) = x_1y_1 + (x_1 + x_2)(y_1 + y_2)$,
$P(x_1, x_2) = (x_1, x_2 - x_1)$.

(b) $V = R^3$; standard inner product,
W is the space of polynomials of degree ≤ 2; $(f, g) = \int_0^1 f(t)g(t)\, dt$,
$P(x, y, z) = x + yt + zt^2$.

(c) V is the space of polynomials of degree ≤ 2; $(f, g) = \int_0^1 f(t)g(t)\, dt$,
$W = R^3$; standard inner product,

$$P(a_0 + a_1t + a_2t^2) = \left(a_0 + \frac{a_1}{2} + \frac{a_2}{3}, \frac{a_1 + a_2}{2\sqrt{3}}, \frac{a_2}{6\sqrt{5}}\right).$$

6. We suppose that V is finite dimensional and the (X, Y) is an inner product on V. A *rigid motion* on V is a transformation P (not necessarily linear) such that

$$|PX - PY| = |X - Y|.$$

(a) Show that if P is an orthogonal transformation then P is a rigid motion.

(b) Show that if $PX = X + Z$, where Z is a fixed vector, then P is *not* linear and P is a rigid motion.

(c) Suppose that P is a rigid motion such that $P0 = 0$. Show that $|PX| = |X|$.

(d) Suppose that P is a rigid motion such that $P0 = 0$. Show that $|PX + PY| = |X + Y|$. [*Hint:* Square both sides and use the parallelogram law to express $|PX + PY|^2$ in terms of $|PX - PY|^2$, $|PX|^2$, and $|PY|^2$.]

(e) Suppose that P is a rigid motion such that $P0 = 0$. Show that $(PX, PY) = (X, Y)$. [*Hint:* Use (d) and the polarization identity.]

(f) Suppose that P is a rigid motion such that $P0 = 0$. Show that $P(X + Y) = PX + PY$. [*Hint:* Express $|P(X + Y) - PX - PY|^2$ in terms of the inner product and use (e).]

(g) Suppose that P is a rigid motion such that $P0 = 0$. Show that $P(aX) = aPX$ for any real number a. [*Hint:* Express $|P(aX) - aPX|^2$ in terms of the inner product and use (e).]

(h) Suppose that P is a rigid motion. Let $QX = PX - P0$. Show that Q is an orthogonal linear transformation on V. This establishes that a rigid motion is the sum of two transformations, one of which is linear and orthogonal, the other being a translation.

7. Suppose that dim $V = 4$ and that P is an orthogonal operator on V with respect to (X, Y). From Exercise 32, Section 4, Chapter 3, there is an invariant subspace M for P such that dim $M = 1, 2,$ or 3.

(a) Using this and (22), (23), and (24) show that there is an orthonormal basis for V such that the matrix of P has the form

$$\begin{bmatrix} A & 0 \\ 0 & B \end{bmatrix},$$

where A is $k \times k$, B is $(4 - k) \times (4 - k)$ with $0 < k < 4$ and 0 represents a zero matrix of appropriate size.

(b) In part (8a) give a complete description of the possible nature of A and B. Use this to give a geometric description of the effect of P.

(c) Give a similar description in the case when dim $V = 5$.

8. Suppose that $P(x_1, x_2, \ldots, x_n) = (y_1, y_2, \ldots, y_n)$, where

$$y_1 = \frac{x_1 - x_2}{\sqrt{2}}, \qquad y_2 = \frac{x_1 + x_2 - 2x_3}{\sqrt{2 \cdot 3}},$$

$$y_3 = \frac{x_1 + x_2 + x_3 - 3x_4}{\sqrt{3 \cdot 4}}, \ldots,$$

$$y_{n-1} = \frac{x_1 + x_2 + \cdots + x_{n-1} - (n - 1)x_n}{\sqrt{(n - 1)n}},$$

$$y_n = \frac{x_1 + x_2 + \cdots + x_n}{\sqrt{n}}.$$

(a) Show that P is an orthogonal operator on R^n with respect to the standard inner product.

(b) Show that $x_1^2 + x_2^2 + \cdots + x_n^2 = y_1^2 + y_2^2 + \cdots + y_n^2$. [*Hint:* Use (9e).]

(c) Let $\bar{x} = (1/n)(x_1 + x_2 + \cdots + x_n)$ and

$$s^2 = \frac{(x_1 - \bar{x})^2 + (x_2 - \bar{x})^2 + \cdots + (x_n - \bar{x})^2}{n}.$$

Show that $ns^2 = y_1^2 + y_2^2 + \cdots + y_{n-1}^2$. This result is useful in statistics.

The remaining exercises of this section apply some of the methods of the section to the study of quadratic forms. (See Exercises 12 through 16 of Section 2 for definitions and results on quadratic forms.) All our results will be stated for R^n with the standard inner product, which we will denote by $X \cdot Y$. If $g(X)$ is a quadratic form on R^n and T is a linear operator, we say that T *preserves* g if $g(TX) = g(X)$ for all X in R^n.

9. Suppose that $g(x_1, x_2, \ldots, x_n) = x_1^2 + x_2^2 + \cdots + x_n^2$. Show that T preserves g if and only if T is orthogonal. [*Hint:* This is merely a restatement of (9e).]

10. Let $g(X)$ be a quadratic form on R^n and suppose that $g(X) \neq 0$ if $X \neq 0$. Show that if T preserves g, then T is invertible and T^{-1} also preserves g. Show that if S and T preserve g, then ST preserves g.

11. Let $g(x_1, x_2, x_3, x_4) = x_1^2 + x_2^2 + x_3^2 - x_4^2$. Show that if T preserves g, then $\det(T) = \pm 1$. [*Hint:* Using Exercises 12 through 16 of Section 2, write $g(X) = PX \cdot X$. Show that $\det(P) = -1$ and that T preserves g if and only if $T^*PT = I$. An operator preserving this form is called a *Lorentz* transformation.]

Section 4. THE COMPLEX CASE

In this and the next two sections we shall extend our results to the complex numbers. As we shall see, most of our results extend without change. We lose many of our geometric tools in this process, but we gain the use of the fact that all polynomials will factor into linear factors. Thus many of the results of Chapter 2 must be modified, while many of the results of Chapter 3 can be strengthened and the proofs shortened.

The complex numbers are those numbers of the form $a + ib$, where a and b are real and $i^2 = -1$. The sum and product of two complex numbers are defined by

$$(a + ib) + (c + id) = (a + c) + i(b + d)$$

and

$$(a + ib)(c + id) = (ac - bd) + i(ad + bc).$$

The same rules hold for these operations as hold for addition and multiplication of real numbers. If $a + ib \neq 0$, then we can write

$$\frac{1}{a + ib} = \frac{a - ib}{(a + ib)(a - ib)} = \frac{a}{a^2 + b^2} - i\frac{b}{a^2 + b^2},$$

so that we can also divide by nonzero complex numbers.

We shall usually denote a complex number by a single lower-case Greek letter, say α. If $\alpha = a + ib$, where a and b are real, then we call a *the real part of* α and b *the imaginary part of* α.

With these definitions, all our definitions and results of Chapter 1 carry over if we merely replace the word "real" by the word "complex." With this change, the results of Sections 1 and 2 on solving systems of equations carry over to systems of complex equations, i.e., systems in which the coefficients and constants are complex numbers. The definition of matrix is the same where "real number" is replaced by "complex number."

The definition of vector space is the same if we replace the concept of multiplication by a real number with that of multiplication by a complex number. The vector space of arrows has no useful complex analog, so we shall omit this. The space C^n of complex n-tuples is defined exactly as is R^n in Section 3, Chapter 1, by using complex instead of real numbers. The definitions of subspace, dimension, linear combination, dependence, independence, spanning, basis, row space, column space, and null space carry over in a similar fashion. Lemmas 1 and 2 and Theorems 5 and 6 carry over with the same proofs by substituting "complex numbers" for "real numbers." Clearly the space C^n has complex dimension n, with $\{(1, 0, \ldots, 0), (0, 1, 0, \ldots, 0), (0, 0, 1, 0, \ldots, 0), \ldots, (0, 0, \ldots, 0, 1)\}$ as a basis, again called the *standard (ordered) basis*. (Note that C^n can also be considered as a real vector space if we allow ourselves to multiply only by *real* numbers. In this case the real dimension of C^n is $2n$. We shall adopt the convention of using the symbol "$C^{n\prime\prime}$" for the complex space of n-tuples with multiplication by complex numbers.) The other results of Section 3, Chapter 1, extend immediately.

The definition of linear transformation is similar to that given for real spaces. Thus a transformation T of a complex vector space V into a complex space W is *linear* if $T(\alpha X + \beta Y) = \alpha TX + \beta YT$ for all X and Y in V and all *complex* numbers α and β. If $V = W$, we say that T is a linear operator. The results of Section 4, Chapter 1, carry over easily. The matrix of T is analogously defined, as are such special operators as 0 and I. Theorems 7, 8, and 9 extend to the complex case, again needing only the change from "real" to "complex" in their proofs. Transformation multiplication is defined analogously, as is matrix multiplication. Coordinates, isomorphism, invertible operator or matrix, automorphism, inverse, diagonal matrices, the diagonal of a matrix, change of coordinates, and upper triangular matrices have obvious complex analogs.

The definition and uniqueness of the determinant carry over to the complex case immediately, along with all the results of Section 6, Chapter 2. The results of Section 7, Chapter 2, however, have no complex analog of interest to us. The results of Sections 1 to 5, Chapter 2, can be extended with some modifications. This we shall now do.

Let $\alpha = a + ib$. Then we call the complex number $a - ib$, the *conjugate* of α and denote this by $\bar{\alpha}$ (often read "α-bar" or "α-conjugate"). The properties of conjugation are

    (a) $\bar{\bar{\alpha}} = \alpha$,

    (b) $(\alpha + \bar{\alpha})/2$ is the real part of α; $(\alpha - \bar{\alpha})/2i$ is the imaginary part of α,

(1)   (c) $\overline{(\alpha + \beta)} = \bar{\alpha} + \bar{\beta}$,

    (d) $\overline{(\alpha\beta)} = \bar{\alpha}\,\bar{\beta}$,

    (e) α is real if and only if $\alpha = \bar{\alpha}$,

    (f) $\alpha\bar{\alpha} = a^2 + b^2$ if $\alpha = a + ib$.

These are easily established. Property (1f) leads us to the following definition. The *absolute value* of α, denoted by $|\alpha|$, is defined by $|\alpha| = \sqrt{a^2 + b^2}$, if $\alpha = a + ib$. The properties of absolute value are

(2)
- (a) $|\alpha| > 0$ if $\alpha \neq 0$, $\quad |0| = 0$,
- (b) $|\alpha|^2 = \alpha\bar{\alpha}$,
- (c) $|\alpha\beta| = |\alpha|\,|\beta|$,
- (d) $|\alpha + \beta| \leq |\alpha| + |\beta|$.

These are also easily established, although (2d) is not completely trivial. We now define an *inner product* on a complex vector space V as a complex-valued function, which we will usually denote by (X, Y), of two vector variables, satisfying the following:

(3)
- (a) $(X, Y) = \overline{(Y, X)}$,
- (b) $(\alpha X + \beta Z, Y) = \alpha(X, Y) + \beta(Z, Y)$ for α and β complex,
- (c) $(X, \alpha Y + \beta Z) = \bar{\alpha}(X, Y) + \bar{\beta}(X, Z)$ for α and β complex,
- (d) $(X, X) > 0$ if $X \neq 0$.

Of course, (3c) is a consequence of (3a) and (3b). Note that (3a) already ensures that (X, X) is real, since $(X, X) = \overline{(X, X)}$. We denote $(X, X)^{1/2}$ by $|X|$ and call this nonnegative real number the *length* or *norm* of X. With this definition of inner product, the results of Sections 1 to 3, Chapter 1, immediately extend to complex vector spaces. We still use such phrases as *parallelogram law, projection of one vector on another, orthogonal, perpendicular, and the triangle inequality*, even though these have no immediate geometric analog in the complex case. For example, we have that X and Y are *perpendicular* or *orthogonal* if $(X, Y) = 0$. As before each of these concepts is given relative to a given inner product on the complex space V. The polarization identity [(13) of Section 2, Chapter 2] needs some modification. This will be given in the exercises.

The concepts of orthogonal and orthonormal basis, the Schwarz inequality, and the Gram-Schmidt process, carry over by substituting "complex" for "real" in the proofs and using the properties of conjugation.

The *standard inner product* in the space C^n is defined by

$$(4) \quad ((x_1, x_2, \ldots, x_n), (y_1, y_2, \ldots, y_n)) = x_1\bar{y}_1 + x_2\bar{y}_2 + \cdots + x_n\bar{y}_n.$$

Clearly this definition satisfies (3), so that this product is an inner product.

The results of Section 4, Chapter 2, extend immediately, in particular the very useful Theorem 16. The definition (and existence, in the finite-dimensional case) of the adjoint of an operator carries over immediately. The matrix description of the adjoint needs a small modification. Let (X, Y) be an inner product on the complex space V, let T be a linear operator on V, and let $\{X^1, X^2, \ldots, X^n\}$ be an orthonormal basis for V. Let A be the matrix of T and B the matrix of T^*. Then $A_{ij} = (TX^j, X^i)$ [see (11) of Section 5, Chapter 2], and $B_{ij} = (T^*X^j, X^i)$. But $(TX^j, X^i) = (X^j, T^*X^i) = \overline{(T^*X^i, X^j)}$, so that $B_{ij} = \overline{A_{ji}}$. For this reason we call B the *conjugate transpose* of A, and denote B by A^*. We shall continue to denote the transpose of A by A^t.

(5) If A is the matrix of T with respect to an orthonormal basis, then A^* is the matrix of T^* with respect to this basis.

With this modification, the results on the adjoint carry over immediately. An operator T is said to be *self-adjoint*, or *Hermitian*, if $T^* = T$, and *skew adjoint* or *skew Hermitian* if $T^* = -T$, with similar definitions for complex matrices. For example, we say that the complex $n \times n$ matrix A is *self-adjoint* or *Hermitian* if $A^* = A$. Note that if A is self-adjoint, then the diagonal entries of A must be real. This follows from the fact that $\overline{A_{ii}} = A_{ii}$ for $i = 1, 2, \ldots, n$.

The definitions and concepts of Sections 1 to 3, Chapter 3, carry over with the usual substitution of "complex" for "real." Theorems 20 and 21 of Section 4, Chapter 3, easily extend. The results on symmetric operators also carry over to Hermitian operators, although the proofs are much easier, as we shall see in the next section. The reason for this should be clear. The difficulties of the proof of Theorem 22 were caused chiefly by the necessity to treat the possible existence of quadratic factors without real roots in the minimum polynomial for T. These difficulties do not appear in the complex case, because any complex polynomial can be factored into complex linear factors.

The results of Section 1, Chapter 4, extend easily to the complex case. For example, we have the following.

(6) If S and T are diagonalizable operators on the complex finite dimensional space V such that $ST = TS$, then there is a basis $\{X^1, X^2, \ldots, X^n\}$ for V consisting of characteristic vectors for both S and T.

The proof of (6) is the same as the proof of Theorem 23 with the usual substitution of "complex number" for "real number."

The results of Sections 2 and 3, Chapter 4, will be extended to the complex case in Section 6.

EXERCISES

1. (a) Find the real and imaginary parts of $((3 + 7i) + (6 - 2i))(\sqrt{2} - i)$
    (b) Find the real and imaginary parts of $1/(2 + 3i)$.
    (c) Find the real and imaginary parts of $(2 - i)i(\overline{3 - 7i})((6 - 2i) + \overline{(1 + i)})$.
                                                                    (*cont.*)

(d) Show that if $|\alpha| = 1$, then $\bar{\alpha} = 1/\alpha$.

(e) Find $|\alpha|$, where $\alpha = (3 - 6i)/(2 - i)$.

(f) Prove that (2d) holds. [*Hint:* If $\alpha = a_1 + ia_2$ and $\beta = b_1 + ib_2$, compute $|\alpha + \beta|^2$ using (1f). Then apply the Schwarz inequality to obtain $2a_1b_1 + 2a_2b_2 \leq 2(a_1^2 + a_2^2)^{1/2}(b_1^2 + b_2^2)^{1/2}$.]

(g) Show that the polynomial $t^2 + \beta t + \gamma$ has two distinct complex roots if and only if $\beta^2 \neq 4\gamma$.

(h) Find the absolute value of

$$\det \begin{bmatrix} i + 1 & 3i \\ -1 & 2 + i \end{bmatrix}.$$

(i) We can find the square roots of α by writing α in polar form. If $\alpha = a + ib$, a and b real, then $a = r \cos \theta$, $b = r \sin \theta$, where $r^2 = a^2 + b^2$ and $\theta = \tan^{-1}(b/a)$. Show that if $\beta_1 = r^{1/2}[\cos (\theta/2) + i \sin (\theta/2)]$ and

$$\beta_2 = r^{1/2}\left[\cos \left(\frac{\theta + 2\pi}{2}\right) + i \sin \left(\frac{\theta + 2\pi}{2}\right)\right],$$

then $\alpha = \beta_1^2 = \beta_2^2$.

2. Find the rank, nullity, and inverse, if it exists, of each of the following complex matrices.

(a) $\begin{bmatrix} 1 & 1 & 1 & i \\ 1 & i & 1 & i \\ 0 & i+1 & 0 & 0 \\ 2 & 0 & 2 & 2i \end{bmatrix}$

(b) $\begin{bmatrix} 3 & i & 0 \\ 1 & -i & 1 \\ 2 & 1 & 1 \end{bmatrix}$

(c) $\begin{bmatrix} 0 & 1 & 1 \\ 0 & i & 1 \\ i & i & i \end{bmatrix}$

(d) $\begin{bmatrix} 4 - i & 1 + 3i & 1 - i & 6 \\ 1 & 3i & 0 & 1 \\ -i & 1 + i & 1 - i & -1 \\ 3 & -i & 0 & 6 \end{bmatrix}$

3. Find a basis for C^3 which includes a basis for the subspace M when:

(a) M is the subspace spanned by $\{(1, 1, 1), (1, i, 1), (0, i + 1, 0)\}$.

(b) M is the set of all (α, β, γ) such that $\alpha + \beta + \gamma = 0$.

(c) M is the set of all (α, β, γ) such that $\alpha = \beta$ and $\gamma = 0$.

4. Let T be the linear operator on C^3 defined by

$$T(\alpha, \beta, \gamma) = (i\alpha + \beta, \beta + i\gamma, i\gamma).$$

Find the matrix of T with respect to each of the following bases.

(a) $\{(1, i, 1), (i, 0, 0), (i, i, 0)\}$

(b) $\{(i + 1, i + 2, i + 3), (i + 4, i + 5, i + 6), (i, 2i, 3i)\}$

5. Let A be the matrix constructed in Exercise 4(a) and let B be the matrix constructed in Exercise 4(b). Find a matrix P_0 such that $P_0^{-1} A P_0 = B$.

6. Show that $\{(1, i, 1), (-i, 1, 0), (2i + 1, 0, 3)\}$ is a basis for C^3. Apply the Gram-Schmidt process to this basis to find an orthonormal basis for C^3 with respect to the inner product $((\alpha_1, \beta_1, \gamma_1), (\alpha_2, \beta_2, \gamma_2)) = \alpha_1\bar{\alpha}_2 + (\alpha_1 + \beta_1)\overline{(\alpha_2 + \beta_2)} + (\beta_1 + \gamma_1)\overline{(\beta_2 + \gamma_2)}$.

7. Let V be the space of *complex* polynomials of degree ≤ 2 with the inner product $(f, g) = \int_0^1 f(t)\overline{g(t)}\, dt$.

    (a) Find the orthogonal complement of the subspace spanned by $\{1, t\}$.

    (b) Let K be the complex-valued function defined on V by $Kf = f(0)$. Find a polynomial g in V such that $Kf = (f, g)$. [*Hint:* See the proof of Theorem 16.]

    (c) Let D be the linear operator on V defined by $Df = df/dt$. Find an expression for D^*.

8. Let (X, Y) be a complex-valued function defined for pairs of vectors X and Y in the complex space V. Suppose that (X, Y) satisfies (3b) and the two conditions $(X, Y) = (Y, X)$ and $(X, X) \geq 0$ for all X and Y in V. Show that $(X, Y) = 0$ for all X and Y. [*Hint:* Show first that $(X, X) = 0$ by computing (iX, iX). Then show that $(X, Y) = \frac{1}{4}(X + Y, X + Y) - \frac{1}{4}(X - Y, X - Y)$.]

9. Let (X, Y) be an inner product on the complex space V. Establish the polarization identity $(X, Y) = \frac{1}{4}(X + Y, X + Y) - \frac{1}{4}(X - Y, X - Y) + (i/4)(X + iY, X + iY) - (i/4)(X - iY, X - iY)$.

10. Let T be the transformation defined on C^2 by $T(\alpha, \beta) = (\bar{\alpha}, \bar{\beta})$. Show that $T(aX + bY) = aTX + bTY$ for all X and Y in C^2 and all *real* numbers a and b. Show that T is *not* complex linear.

11. Show that

$$\begin{bmatrix} 1 & 2 \\ -1 & -1 \end{bmatrix}$$

is complex diagonalizable but *not* real diagonalizable.

12. For each of the following matrices A find a matrix P_0 such that $P_0^{-1}AP_0$ is a diagonal matrix.

    (a) $A = \begin{bmatrix} i & 1 \\ 1 & i \end{bmatrix}$
        (b) $A = \begin{bmatrix} 2 & 1+i & 0 \\ 0 & i & 0 \\ 0 & 0 & 1-i \end{bmatrix}$

13. Show that

$$\begin{bmatrix} 1 & 1 \\ 0 & 1 \end{bmatrix}$$

is not complex diagonalizable.

14. Let

$$A = \begin{bmatrix} 3 - i & 2 + 2i \\ \dfrac{1}{1-i} & 3i \end{bmatrix}.$$

Find two Hermitian matrices B and C such that $A = B + iC$. [*Hint:* Suppose that $A = B + iC$. What is A^*?]

15. Let V be the collection of $n \times n$ Hermitian matrices. Show that we can make V into a real vector space by defining $A + B$ by our usual matrix addition and aA by our usual scalar multiplication for real numbers a. What is the dimension of V?

16. Let A be an $n \times n$ complex matrix. Show that

$$\det (A^*) = \overline{\det (A)}.$$

[*Hint:* See the proof of (18) of Section 6, Chapter 2.]

17. Let

$$A = \begin{bmatrix} \dfrac{1+i}{2} & \dfrac{-1+i}{2} \\ \dfrac{-1+i}{2} & \dfrac{1+i}{2} \end{bmatrix}, \qquad B = \begin{bmatrix} 0 & -i \\ -i & 0 \end{bmatrix}.$$

Show that there is an invertible matrix P_0 such that $P_0^{-1}AP_0$ and $P_0^{-1}BP_0$ are diagonal.

18. Let

$$A = \begin{bmatrix} 1 + 2i & 1 + i \\ -i & 0 \end{bmatrix}.$$

Find A^{10}.

Section 5. NORMAL OPERATORS AND THE SPECTRAL THEOREM

Theorem 21 gives a characterization of diagonalizable operators. This theorem extends immediately to the complex case with the simple substitution of "complex" for "real" in its proof. In this section we shall give the complex analog of Theorem 22.

For convenience we shall restate the results of Theorems 20 and 21 for the complex case. Let V be a finite dimensional complex vector space and let T be a linear operator on V. Denote the minimum polynomial of T by p. We have

T is diagonalizable if and only if $p = (t - \alpha_1)(t - \alpha_2) \ldots (t - \alpha_r)$, where $\alpha_1, \alpha_2, \ldots, \alpha_r$ are distinct complex numbers. If T is diagonalizable, then α is a characteristic value of T if and only if $\alpha = \alpha_i$ for some i, $1 \leq i \leq r$. Furthermore, there are unique projections

(1) $E_1, E_2, \ldots, E_r$ such that

(a) $T = \alpha_1 E_1 + \alpha_2 E_2 + \cdots + \alpha_r E_r$,
(b) $I = E_1 + E_2 + \cdots + E_r$,
(c) $E_i E_j = 0, \qquad i \neq j$.

If $P_1, P_2, \ldots, P_r$ are the Lagrange interpolation polynomials for $\alpha_1, \alpha_2, \ldots, \alpha_r$, then $E_i = P_i(T)$ for $i = 1, 2, \ldots, r$.

Relaxing the conditions on $\alpha_1, \alpha_1, \ldots, \alpha_r$ we also have

(2) T is diagonalizable if and only if there are complex numbers α_1, α_2, $\ldots, \alpha_r$ (not necessarily distinct) and projections $E_1, E_2, \ldots, E_r$ such that conditions (1a, b, c) hold.

We now suppose that V has an inner product which we shall denote by (X, Y). We shall attempt to give an answer to the following question.

(3) For which operators T on V can we find an orthonormal basis consisting of characteristic vectors for T?

Let us look at some examples on C^2 with (X, Y) denoting the standard inner product. Suppose that T is Hermitian. Let

$$A = \begin{bmatrix} \alpha & \beta \\ \gamma & \delta \end{bmatrix}$$

be the matrix of T with respect to $\{(1, 0), (0, 1)\}$. Then $A = A^*$. Since

$$A^* = \begin{bmatrix} \bar{\alpha} & \bar{\gamma} \\ \bar{\beta} & \bar{\delta} \end{bmatrix},$$

we have that $\bar{\alpha} = \alpha$, $\bar{\delta} = \delta$, and $\gamma = \bar{\beta}$. Thus α and δ are real so that

$$A = \begin{bmatrix} a & b + ic \\ b - ic & d \end{bmatrix},$$

where a, b, c, and d are real numbers. We have

(4) $\qquad \det (tI - A) = t^2 - (a + d)t + ad - (b^2 + c^2).$

The roots of (4) are given by

$$t = \frac{a + d \pm \sqrt{(a + d)^2 - 4(ad - b^2 - c^2)}}{2}$$

$$= \frac{a + d \pm \sqrt{(a - d)^2 + 4(b^2 + c^2)}}{2}.$$

This shows that (4) has real roots which are unequal if $a \neq d$ or $b \neq 0$ or $c \neq 0$. If $a = d$ and $b = c = 0$, then $A = aI$. Otherwise let c_1 and c_2 be the distinct roots of (4). Let $TX^1 = c_1X^1$ and $TX^2 = c_2X^2$, where $|X^1| = |X^2| = 1$. The following general result tells us that $\{X^1, X^2\}$ is an orthonormal basis for C^2 consisting of characteristic vectors for T.

(5) Suppose that V is a finite dimensional complex space with the inner product (X, Y). Suppose that T is a linear operator on V and that $TX^1 = \alpha_1X^1$, $T^*X^2 = \alpha_2X^2$ with $\alpha_1 \neq \bar{\alpha}_2$. Then $(X^1, X^2) = 0$.

We have $(\alpha_1 - \bar{\alpha}_2)(X^1, X^2) = (\alpha_1 X^1, X^2) - (X^1, \alpha_2 X^2) = (TX^1, X^2) - (X^1, T^*X^2) = 0$. Since $\alpha_1 \neq \bar{\alpha}_2$, we must have $(X^1, X^2) = 0$.

Now suppose that T is a linear operator on R^2 such that $T^*T = I$. Let

$$A = \begin{bmatrix} \alpha & \beta \\ \gamma & \delta \end{bmatrix}$$

be the matrix of T with respect to $\{(1, 0), (0, 1)\}$. Then $A^*A = I$ which gives

(6) $|\alpha|^2 + |\beta|^2 = |\gamma|^2 + |\delta|^2 = 1, \qquad \alpha\bar{\gamma} + \beta\bar{\delta} = 0.$

We also have

(7) $|\det(A)| = 1, \qquad$ so that $\qquad |\alpha\delta - \beta\gamma| = 1.$

The properties (6) and (7) do not make it easy to determine the roots of $\det(tI - A)$. We do know from (15) of Section 2, Chapter 3, that this polynomial does have a root. We have

(8) $\det(tI - A) = (t - \lambda)(t - \mu).$

Thus λ and μ are the characteristic values of T. Let $X \neq 0$ be such that $TX = \lambda X$. Then $(X, X) = (T^*TX, X) = (TX, TX) = (\lambda X, \lambda X) = |\lambda|^2(X, X)$, so that $|\lambda|^2 = 1$. Similarly $|\mu|^2 = 1$. We know that $T^*T = I$ so that $TT^* = I$ from Theorem 10. Thus $0 = |TX - \lambda X|^2 = (TX, TX) - (TX, \lambda X) - (\lambda X, TX) + (\lambda X, \lambda X) = (T^*TX, X) - \bar{\lambda}(TX, X) - \lambda(X, TX) + (\lambda X, \lambda X) = (TT^*X, X) - \bar{\lambda}(X, T^*X) - \lambda(T^*X, X) + |\lambda|^2(X, X) = (T^*X, T^*X) - (\bar{\lambda}X, T^*X) - (T^*X, \bar{\lambda}X) + (\bar{\lambda}X, \bar{\lambda}X) = |T^*X - \bar{\lambda}X|^2$.

Thus $T^*X = \bar{\lambda}X$. This collection of identities only used the properties of the inner product and the fact that $T^*T = TT^*$ so that we actually proved the following.

(9)   Suppose that V is a complex vector space with the inner product (X, Y) and suppose that T is a linear operator on V such that $T^*T = TT^*$. Then $TX = \lambda X$ if and only if $T^*X = \bar{\lambda}X$.

Let us return to our example. If $\lambda \neq \mu$, choose X^1 and X^2 such that $|X^1| = |X^2| = 1$ and $TX^1 = \lambda X^1$, $TX^2 = \mu X^2$. Then $T^*X^2 = \bar{\mu}X^2$. Since $\bar{\bar{\mu}} = \mu$, (5) tells us that $(X^1, X^2) = 0$. Thus $\{X^1, X^2\}$ is an orthonormal basis for C^2 consisting of characteristic vectors for T. We shall leave the case where $\lambda = \mu$ for an exercise. Note that our proof that $(X^1, X^2) = 0$ generalizes without change to establish the following.

(10)   Suppose that V and T are as in (9) so that $T^*T = TT^*$. If $\lambda \neq \mu$ and $TX^1 = \lambda X^1$, $TX^2 = \mu X^2$, then $(X^1, X^2) = 0$.

We have shown that if T is a linear operator on C^2 such that $T = T^*$ or $T^*T = I$, then the answer to (3) is affirmative. As we saw in the case $T^*T = I$, computation using the entries of the matrix of T is quite difficult. The results (9) and (10) were obtained by elementary computations with the inner product and suggest that the condition $T^*T = TT^*$ may be critical in obtaining an answer to (3). The condition $T^*T = TT^*$ is certainly necessary for T to satisfy (3). For suppose that T is a linear operator for which the answer to (3) is affirmative. Let $\{X^1, X^2, \ldots, X^n\}$ be an orthonormal basis for V consisting of characteristic vectors for T. Suppose that $TX^i = \alpha_i X^i$ for $i = 1, 2, \ldots, n$. Let A be the matrix of T with respect to $\{X^1, X^2, \ldots, X^n\}$. Then

(11)
$$A = \begin{bmatrix} \alpha_1 & 0 & \ldots & 0 \\ 0 & \alpha_2 & \ldots & 0 \\ \vdots & & & \\ 0 & 0 & \ldots & \alpha_n \end{bmatrix}.$$

Since A^* is the matrix of T^* with respect to this basis and

(12)
$$A^* = \begin{bmatrix} \bar{\alpha}_1 & 0 & \ldots & 0 \\ 0 & \bar{\alpha}_2 & \ldots & 0 \\ \vdots & & & \\ 0 & 0 & \ldots & \bar{\alpha}_n \end{bmatrix},$$

we see immediately that $A^*A = AA^*$. Therefore $T^*T = TT^*$.

A linear operator on V is said to be *normal* if $T^*T = TT^*$. The answer to (3) is given in the next theorem.

Theorem 24 (The Spectral Theorem). Suppose that V is a finite dimensional complex vector space with the inner product (X, Y) and that T is a linear operator on V. Then V has an orthonormal basis consisting of characteristic vectors for T if and only if T is normal.

Proof. In (11) and (12) we showed that if V has such a basis, then T is normal, so we need only prove the converse.

Suppose that T is normal and that p is the minimum polynomial for T. Then from (15) of Section 2, Chapter 3, p does factor into linear factors. We shall show that p has no repeated factors. Suppose that $p = (t - \alpha)^2 q$. Since p does not divide $(t - \alpha)q$, we know that $(T - \alpha I)q(T) \neq 0$. Let X be in V such that $(T - \alpha I)q(T)X \neq 0$ and let $Y = (T - \alpha I)q(T)X$. Then $(T - \alpha I)Y = (T - \alpha I)^2 q(T)X = p(T)X = 0$. From (9) we see that $(T^* - \bar{\alpha}I)Y = 0$. Since $Y \neq 0$, we have $0 < (Y, Y) = (Y, (T - \alpha I)q(T)X) = ((T^* - \bar{\alpha}I)Y, q(T)X) = 0$. This is a contradiction. We conclude that p has no repeated factors, so that Theorem 21 tells us that T is diagonalizable.

We now duplicate the proof of Theorem 21. Let $\alpha_1, \alpha_2, \ldots, \alpha_r$ be the distinct characteristic values of T and let $P_1, P_2, \ldots, P_r$ be the Lagrange interpolation polynomials for $\alpha_1, \alpha_2, \ldots, \alpha_r$. Denote $P_i(T)$ by E_i. Then $E_i^2 = E_i$, $i = 1, 2, \ldots, r$ and the conditions (1a, b, c) hold. Let $\{X_i^1, X_i^2, \ldots, X_i^{k_i}\}$ be an orthonormal basis for the range of E_i for $1 \leq i \leq r$ and let $D = \{X_1^1, X_1^2, \ldots, X_1^{k_1}, X_2^1, X_2^2, \ldots, X_2^{k_2}, \ldots, X_r^1, X_r^2, \ldots, X_r^{k_r}\}$. Then, as in the proof of Theorem 20, each vector in D is a characteristic vector for T and D is a basis for V. From the construction of D, we have $(X_i^l, X_i^s) = 0$ if $l \neq s$ and $|X_i^l| = 1$ for $l = 1, 2, \ldots, k_i$ and $i = 1, 2, \ldots, r$. We now apply (10). We have $TX_i^l = \alpha_i X_i^l$ and $TX_j^s = \alpha_j X_j^s$ for $l = 1, 2, \ldots, k_i$ and $s = 1, 2, \ldots, k_j$, and $i = 1, 2, \ldots, r$ and $j = 1, 2, \ldots, r$. If $i \neq j$, then (10) gives $(X_i^l, X_j^s) = 0$ because $\alpha_i \neq \alpha_j$. This shows that D is an orthonormal basis for V. Q.E.D.

As before, the projections E_i are uniquely determined by T and are called the *spectral projections* for T, $1 \leq i \leq r$. Although it is not obvious from our results thus far, we have

$$(13) \qquad\qquad E_i^* = E_i, \qquad i = 1, 2, \ldots, r.$$

There are several ways to prove this. We shall give a proof of (13) which introduces new tools for the study of operators in the following two results.

(14)   If T is normal and g is a complex polynomial, then $g(T)$ is normal.

(15)   If $S^*S = 0$,   then $S = 0$.

To establish (14) we write $g = \beta_0 + \beta_1 t + \beta_2 t^2 + \cdots + \beta_n t^n$. Then $g(T) = \beta_0 I + \beta_1 T + \beta_2 T^2 + \cdots + \beta_n T^n$, so that $(g(T))^* = \bar{\beta}_0 I + \bar{\beta}_1 T^* + \bar{\beta}_2 (T^*)^2 + \cdots + \bar{\beta}_n (T^*)^n$. If $f = \bar{\beta}_0 + \bar{\beta}_1 t + \bar{\beta}_2 t^2 + \cdots + \bar{\beta}_n t^n$, then this shows that $f(T^*) = (g(T))^*$. If $TT^* = T^*T$, then $T^2 T^* = T(TT^*) = T(T^*T) = (TT^*)T = (T^*T)T = T^*T^2$. Similarly $T^k T^* = T^* T^k$ for any integer $k \geq 1$. We conclude that $g(T)f(T^*) = f(T^*)g(T)$. Since $f(T^*) = (g(T))^*$, this tells us that $g(T)$ is normal and establishes (14).

To prove (15) we suppose that $S^*SX = 0$. Then $(S^*SX, X) = 0$. Since $(S^*SX, X) = (SX, SX)$, we conclude that $SX = 0$. The condition that $S^*S = 0$ is the same as $S^*SX = 0$ for all X. We have shown that this implies that $SX = 0$ for all X, so that (15) is established.

Returning to the proof of (13), we note that each E_i is a polynomial in T, since $E_i = P_i(T)$. Thus E_i is normal. The general form of (13) is as follows.

(16)   If E is a normal projection, then E is self-adjoint.

Suppose that E is a normal projection and let $S = E - EE^*$. Then $S^* = E^* - (EE^*)^* = E^* - E^{**}E^* = E^* - EE^* = E^* - E^*E$. Thus $S = E(I - E^*)$ and $S^* = E^*(I - E)$. Since $E = E^2$, we have $(I - E)E = 0$. Therefore $S^*S = E^*(I - E)E(I - E^*) = 0$. From (15) we conclude that $S = 0$, that is, $E = EE^*$. Therefore $E^* = (EE^*)^* = E^{**}E^* = EE^* = E$. This proves (16). Statement (13) now follows from (14) and (16).

Remarks. Several classes of operators are easily seen to be normal. For example, if T is self-adjoint, then $T = T^*$, so that $TT^* = T^2 = T^*T$. If $U^*U = I$, then from Theorem 10, $UU^* = I$, so that $U^*U = UU^*$. This is the general form of our results (6), (7), and (8). A linear operator U such that $U^* = U^{-1}$ is called a *unitary operator* on V. In the next section we shall give an analysis of the various types of normal operators using Theorem 24.

The results of this section can, of course, be given for matrices. If A is an $n \times n$ complex matrix, then we say that A is *normal* if $A^*A = AA^*$. Suppose that C^n is given the standard inner product and let T be the linear operator on C^n whose matrix with respect to the standard basis is A. Then the matrix of T^* is A^*. Thus A is normal if and only if T is normal.

Suppose that A is normal. Then Theorem 24 tells us that C^n has an orthonormal basis $\{X^1, X^2, \ldots, X^n\}$ consisting of characteristic vectors for T. Suppose that $TX^j = \alpha_j X^j$ for $j = 1, 2, \ldots, n$ and that $X^j = (\beta_{1j}, \beta_{2j}, \ldots, \beta_{nj})$. The condition that $\{X^1, X^2, \ldots, X^n\}$ be orthonormal is

$$(17) \qquad \beta_{1j}\bar{\beta}_{1k} + \beta_{2j}\bar{\beta}_{2k} + \cdots + \beta_{nj}\bar{\beta}_{nk} = \delta_{jk},$$
$$1 \le j \le n \quad \text{and} \quad 1 \le k \le n.$$

Let U be the matrix whose jth column is X^j for $j = 1, 2, \ldots, n$; that is, $U_{ij} = \beta_{ij}$ for $1 \le i \le n$ and $1 \le j \le n$. If $U^* = (\alpha_{ij})$, then $\alpha_{ij} = \bar{\beta}_{ji}$, for $1 \le i \le n$ and $1 \le j \le n$. Thus (17) is the same as

$$(18) \qquad\qquad U^*U = I.$$

The jth column of AU is $TX^j = \alpha_j X^j$. [See (19) of Section 6, Chapter 1.] Thus

$$U^*AU = \begin{bmatrix} \alpha_1 & 0 & \ldots & 0 \\ 0 & \alpha_2 & \ldots & 0 \\ \vdots & & & \\ 0 & 0 & \ldots & \alpha_n \end{bmatrix}.$$

A matrix U satisfying (18) is called a *unitary matrix*. The matrix form of Theorem 24 is as follows.

(19)   If A is a normal $n \times n$ matrix, then there is a unitary $n \times n$ matrix U such that U^*AU is a diagonal matrix.

EXERCISES

1. Let

$$A = \begin{bmatrix} \alpha & b \\ \gamma & \delta \end{bmatrix}$$

and suppose that $A^*A = I$. Show by direct computation that if λ is a complex number such that $(\lambda I - A)^2 = 0$, then $A = \lambda I$. This shows that if $\lambda = \mu$ in (8), then there is an orthonormal basis for C^2 consisting of characteristic vectors for T.

2. Which of the following operators T on C^3 are normal with respect to the standard inner product?
   (a) $T(\alpha, \beta, \gamma) = (3\alpha + i\beta + (2 - i)\gamma, -i\alpha + i\gamma, (2 + i)\alpha - i\beta + 6\gamma)$
   (b) $T(\alpha, \beta, \gamma) = (\alpha, i\alpha + \beta, i\alpha - i\beta + \gamma)$
   (c) $T(\alpha, \beta, \gamma) = (\beta, \gamma, i\alpha + i\beta + i\gamma)$
   (d) $T(\alpha, \beta, \gamma) = ((2 + i)\alpha - (1 + 2i)\beta, (1 + 2i)\alpha + (2 + i)\beta, \gamma)$

3. Let V be the space of 2×2 complex matrices with the inner product $(A, B) = \text{tr}(B^*A)$, where $\text{tr}(A) = A_{11} + A_{22}$. Which of the following operators T on V are self-adjoint? Skew adjoint? Unitary? Self-adjoint projections? Normal? [*Hint:* First compute T^*. The fact that $\text{tr}(ABD) = \text{tr}(DAB)$ is helpful.]

   (a) $TA = AC$, where $C = \begin{bmatrix} i & 7 \\ 1 & 0 \end{bmatrix}$

   (b) $TA = AC$, where $C = \begin{bmatrix} 1 & i \\ -i & 2 \end{bmatrix}$

   (c) $TA = AC$, where $C = \begin{bmatrix} i/\sqrt{2} & 1/\sqrt{2} \\ 1/\sqrt{2} & i/\sqrt{2} \end{bmatrix}$

   (d) $TA = CA$, where $C = \begin{bmatrix} 1 & i \\ 0 & 0 \end{bmatrix}$

   (e) $TA = AC - CA$, where $C = \begin{bmatrix} i & 2 - i \\ -2 - i & 2i \end{bmatrix}$

   (f) $TA = C^*AC$, where $C = \begin{bmatrix} 1 & 0 \\ i & 0 \end{bmatrix}$

   (g) $TA = C^*AC$, where $C = \begin{bmatrix} i & 2 + i \\ 0 & 1 \end{bmatrix}$

(h) $TA = AC + CA$, where $C = \begin{bmatrix} \dfrac{2+i}{2} & \dfrac{1+2i}{2} \\ \dfrac{-1-2i}{2} & \dfrac{2+i}{2} \end{bmatrix}$

4. (a) Let

$$A = \begin{bmatrix} 1 & i \\ -i & 1 \end{bmatrix} \quad \text{and} \quad B = \begin{bmatrix} 0 & i \\ i & 0 \end{bmatrix}.$$

Show that A and B are normal while $A + B$ and AB are not normal.
(b) Find 2×2 Hermitian matrices A and B such that AB is not normal.
(c) Show that the product of unitary operators is unitary.

5. Show that each of the following operators T on C^2 or C^3 is diagonalizable. Find the spectral projections of each and verify that these are self-adjoint if and only if T is normal. (See Exercise 11.)

(a) $T(\alpha, \beta) = (2\alpha - i\beta, i\alpha + \beta)$
(b) $T(\alpha, \beta) = (i\alpha + (1 + i)\beta, -i\alpha + \beta)$
(c) $T(\alpha, \beta) = (i\alpha + \beta, -\alpha + 2i\beta)$
(d) $T(\alpha, \beta, \gamma) = ((2 + i)\alpha - (1 + 2i)\beta, (1 + 2i)\alpha + (2 + i)\beta, \gamma)$

6. For each of the following 2×2 matrices A, find a unitary matrix U such that U^*AU is diagonal.

(a) $A = \begin{bmatrix} 2 & 1+i \\ 1-i & 1 \end{bmatrix}$ **(b)** $A = \begin{bmatrix} 2i & -1+i \\ 1+i & i \end{bmatrix}$

(c) $A = \begin{bmatrix} i/\sqrt{2} & 1/\sqrt{2} \\ 1/\sqrt{2} & i/\sqrt{2} \end{bmatrix}$

7. We showed in (4) ff that if T is a self-adjoint operator on C^2, then the characteristic values of T are real. This exercise generalizes that result.

(a) Show that if A is a self-adjoint $n \times n$ matrix, then the entries on the diagonal of A are real.
(b) Suppose that T is a linear operator on the complex space V with the inner product (X, Y). Show that if $T = T^*$, then the characteristic values of T are real. [*Hint:* This can be proved using part (a) and (19) or directly. If $TX = \alpha X$, $X \neq 0$, then compute using $(X, T^*X) = (TX, X) = \overline{(X, TX)}$.]

8. Show that if S and T are normal and $ST = TS$, then ST is normal. [*Hint:* It is necessary to show that $ST^* = T^*S$ and $S^*T = TS^*$. Write $T = \alpha_1 E_1 + \alpha_2 E_2 + \cdots + \alpha_r E_r$ as in (1). Then each E_i is a polynomial in T and $E_i^* = E_i$ from (13). Thus $SE_i = E_iS$ for $1 \leq i \leq r$. Since $T^* = \bar{\alpha}_1 E_1 + \bar{\alpha}_2 E_2 + \cdots + \bar{\alpha}_r E_r$, it follows that $ST^* = T^*S$.]

9. Show that T is normal if and only if $|TX| = |T^*X|$ for each X in V. [*Hint:* Show that $((T^*T - TT^*)X, X) = 0$ for all X and use the polarization identity. See Exercise 9, Section 4.]

10. Show that T is normal if and only if T^* is a polynomial in T. [*Hint:* If $T = \alpha_1 E_1 + \alpha_2 E_2 + \cdots + \alpha_r E_r$ as in (1), then $T^* = \bar{\alpha}_1 E_1 + \bar{\alpha}_2 E_2 + \cdots + \bar{\alpha}_r E_r$ from (13). Each E_i is a polynomial in T.]

11. Let T be diagonalizable. Show that if the spectral projections of T are normal, then T is normal. [*Hint:* Use (16) and compute T^* from (1).]

12. This exercise outlines an alternative proof of Theorem 24.

   (a) Show that if M is an invariant subspace for T, then $M^\perp$ is an invariant subspace for T^*. [*Hint:* If X is in M and Y is in $M^\perp$, then $(T^*Y, X) = (Y, TX) = 0$.]

   (b) Suppose that T is normal. Let α be a characteristic value of T (at least one such characteristic value exists, from (15) of Section 2, Chapter 3.) Let $TX^1 = \alpha X^1$ with $|X^1| = 1$. Let M_1 be the subspace spanned by $\{X^1\}$. Show that M_1 and $M_1^\perp$ are invariant for both T and T^*. [*Hint:* Use part (a) and (9).]

   (c) Let M_1 be as in (b). Let T_1 be the operator on $M_1^\perp$ defined by $T_1 X = TX$ for X in $M_1^\perp$. Show that T_1 is normal. [*Hint:* Using (b), show that $T_1^* Y = T^* Y$ for all Y in $M_1^\perp$.]

   (d) Prove Theorem 24 by repeated application of parts (b) and (c). [*Hint:* The construction of $M_1^\perp$ shows that if X^2 is a characteristic vector for T_1 of length one, then $(X^1, X^2) = 0$.]

Section 6. SOME CONSEQUENCES OF THE SPECTRAL THEOREM

In this section we shall study various classes of normal operators. Each of the classes can be given a simple description in terms of characteristic values. This can be done in two ways, which are essentially the same. We could show that the properties hold for any matrix representation of T with respect to an orthonormal basis, and thus can be described in terms of a diagonal matrix; or we can use the expression for T in terms of its spectral projections. We shall use the latter tool. As we shall see, normal operators behave much like complex numbers.

Throughout this section we shall suppose that V is a finite dimensional complex vector space, with an inner product (X, Y). All mention of length, angle, and adjoint will refer to this inner product. For convenience of reference we shall state the results of Section 5 in the form in which they will be used.

T is a normal operator on V if and only if there are complex numbers $\alpha_1, \alpha_2, \ldots, \alpha_r$ and projections $E_1, E_2, \ldots, E_r$ such that

(1)
   (a) $T = \alpha_1 E_1 + \alpha_2 E_2 + \cdots + \alpha_r E_r$,
   (b) $I = E_1 + E_2 + \cdots + E_r$,
   (c) $E_i E_j = 0, \quad i \neq j$,
   (d) $E_i^* = E_i^2 = E_i \neq 0, \quad i = 1, 2, \ldots, r$.

Furthermore if $\alpha_1, \alpha_2, \ldots, \alpha_r$ are distinct, then the projections E_i are uniquely determined by conditions (a, b, c, d).

This is a restatement of Theorem 24 and (1) and (13) of Section 5. When we use (1) in this section we shall assume that the numbers α_1, $\alpha_2, \ldots, \alpha_r$ are distinct.

The following result is not true for symmetric operators on real vector spaces. It is a consequence of the properties of complex conjugation and the polarization identity (see Exercise 9, Section 4).

(2) T is self-adjoint if and only if (TX, X) is real for each X in V.

Suppose that $T = T^*$. Then $(TX, X) = \overline{(X, TX)} = \overline{(T^*X, X)} = \overline{(TX, X)}$, so that (TX, X) is real. Conversely, suppose that (TX, X) is real for each X in V. Then $\overline{(TX, X)} = (TX, X)$, so that $(TX, X) = \overline{(X, TX)} = (X, TX)$. Also $(TX, X) = (X, T^*X)$, so that $(TX, X) = (X, T^*X) = \overline{(T^*X, X)} = (T^*X, X)$. We have

$$
\begin{aligned}
(TX, Y) &= \tfrac{1}{4}(T(X + Y), X + Y) \\
&\quad - \tfrac{1}{4}(T(X - Y), X - Y) \\
&\quad + (i/4)(T(X + iY), X + iY) \\
&\quad - (i/4)(T(X - iY), X - iY) \\
&= \tfrac{1}{4}(T^*(X + Y), X + Y) \\
&\quad - \tfrac{1}{4}(T^*(X - Y), X - Y) \\
&\quad + (i/4)(T^*(X + iY), X + iY) \\
&\quad - (i/4)(T^*(X - iY), X - iY) \\
&= (T^*X, Y).
\end{aligned}
$$

Thus $((T - T^*)X, Y) = 0$ for all X and Y, so that $T = T^*$.

We shall say that an operator P is *nonnegative* if $(PX, X) \geq 0$ for all X and *positive* if $(PX, X) > 0$ for $X \neq 0$. We shall use the notation $S \geq T$ if $S - T$ is nonnegative and $S > T$ if $S - T$ is positive. From (2) we see that if $P \geq 0$ or $P > 0$, then $P = P^*$. Theorem 24 gives us the tools to establish the following theorem.

Theorem 25. If T is normal, then:

(3) $T = T^*$ if and only if the characteristic values of T are real.

(4) $T \geq 0$ if and only if the characteristic values of T are ≥ 0.

(5) $T > 0$ if and only if the characteristic values of T are > 0.

(6) $T = -T^*$ if and only if the characteristic values of T are pure imaginary (a complex number $\alpha = a + ib$, where a and b are real is *pure imaginary* if $a = 0$).

(7) T is unitary if and only if the characteristic values of T are of absolute value 1.

(8) T is a projection if and only if the characteristic values of T are either 0 or 1 or both.

(9) T is invertible if and only if the characteristic values of T are all nonzero.

Proof. Let T be expressed as in (1).

If $\alpha_1, \alpha_2, \ldots, \alpha_r$ are real, then $T^* = \alpha_1 E_1 + \alpha_2 E_2 + \cdots + \alpha_r E_r = T$. Suppose that $T = T^*$ and that α is a characteristic value of T. Let $TX = \alpha X$, $X \neq 0$. Then $\alpha(X, X) = (\alpha X, X) = (TX, X)$. From (2), (TX, X) is real. Since

$$\alpha = \frac{(TX, X)}{(X, X)},$$

α must be real. This proves (3). If $T \geq 0$ and $TX = \alpha X$, $X \neq 0$, then

$$\alpha = \frac{(TX, X)}{(X, X)} \geq 0,$$

since $(TX, X) \geq 0$. If $(TX, X) > 0$ for $X \neq 0$, then

$$\alpha = \frac{(TX, X)}{(X, X)} > 0.$$

This shows that the characteristic values of a nonnegative (positive) operator are nonnegative (positive).

Suppose that each $\alpha_i \geq 0$ in (1). Let X be in V. Then $X = E_1 X + E_2 X + \cdots + E_r X$ from (1b). Also $TX = \alpha_1 E_1 X + \alpha_2 E_2 X + \cdots + \alpha_r E_r X$ from (1a). Thus, using (1c) and (1d), we have $(TX, X) = \alpha_1 |E_1 X|^2 + \alpha_2 |E_2 X|^2 + \cdots + \alpha_r |E_r X|^2 \geq 0$. If each $\alpha_i > 0$ and $X \neq 0$, then $|E_i X| > 0$ for some i since $X = E_1 X + E_2 X + \cdots + E_r X$. Thus $(TX, X) > 0$. This completes the proof of (4) and (5).

To prove (6) let $S = iT$. Thus $S = S^*$ if and only if $T^* = -T$. Since α is a characteristic value of T if and only if $i\alpha$ is a characteristic value of S, (6) follows from (3).

We have $T^* = \bar{\alpha}_1 E_1 + \bar{\alpha}_2 E_2 + \cdots + \bar{\alpha}_r E_r$, so that (1b, c, d) gives $T^* T = |\alpha_1|^2 E_1 + |\alpha_2|^2 E_2 + \cdots + |\alpha_r|^2 E_r$. Thus if $|\alpha_1| = |\alpha_2| = \cdots = |\alpha_r| = 1$, then (1b) gives $T^* T = I$. Conversely if $T^* T = I$ and $TX = \alpha X$, $X \neq 0$, then $(X, X) = (T^* TX, X) = (TX, TX) = (\alpha X, \alpha X) = |\alpha|^2 (X, X)$. Thus $|\alpha|^2 = 1$. This completes the proof of (7).

If $T = \alpha_1 E_1 + \alpha_2 E_2 + \cdots + \alpha_r E_r$ as in (1) and each $\alpha_i = 0$ or 1, then $T^2 = \alpha_1^2 E_1 + \alpha_2^2 E_2 + \cdots + \alpha_r^2 E_r = T$. Conversely if $T^2 = T$, then the minimum polynomial for T must divide $t^2 - t$. This proves (8).

Statement (9) does not use normality. T is invertible if and only if $TX = 0$ has no solutions other than $X = 0$, i.e., if and only if 0 is not a characteristic value of T. Q.E.D.

The assumption that T is normal is necessary for all parts of Theorem 25, except (9). The exercises will give examples to show this. The results of Theorem 25 are the operator analogs of the following results about complex numbers. Let α be a complex number, $\alpha = a + ib$, a and b real. Then $\alpha = \bar{\alpha}$ if and only if $b = 0$; $\alpha \geq 0$ if and only if $b = 0$ and $a \geq 0$; $\alpha = -\bar{\alpha}$ if and only if $a = 0$; $\alpha\bar{\alpha} = 1$ if and only if $|\alpha| = 1$; $\alpha = \alpha^2$ if and only if $\alpha = 0$ or 1; α is invertible if and only if $\alpha \neq 0$. Several other properties of complex numbers have operator analogs. For example, if $\alpha = a + ib$, a and b real, then

$$a = \frac{\alpha + \bar{\alpha}}{2} \quad \text{and} \quad b = \frac{\alpha - \bar{\alpha}}{2i}.$$

We have

$$T = \frac{T + T^*}{2} + i\frac{T - T^*}{2i},$$

where

$$\frac{T + T^*}{2} \quad \text{and} \quad \frac{T - T^*}{2i}$$

are both self-adjoint, so that $T = H + iK$, where $H = H^*$ and $K = K^*$. We sometimes call $H = (T + T^*)/2$ the *real part* of T, and $K = (T - T^*)/2i$ the *imaginary part* of T. These give another characterization of normal operators.

(10) T is normal if and only if $HK = KH$.

For if $T^*T = TT^*$, then certainly $HK = KH$. Conversely if $HK = KH$, then $T = H + iK$ and $T^* = H - iK$ so that $TT^* = T^*T$.

Now suppose that $\alpha \geq 0$. Then α has a positive square root. For operators we have the following.

(11) $P \geq 0$ if and only if there is a $Q \geq 0$ such that $Q^2 = P$. Furthermore if $P \geq 0$, then Q is uniquely determined by the conditions, $Q \geq 0$ and $Q^2 = P$.

We call Q the *nonnegative square root* of P. To prove (11) note that if $P = T^*T$, then $(PX, X) = (T^*TX, X) = (TX, TX) \geq 0$. Thus if $P = Q^2$, where $Q \geq 0$, then $P \geq 0$. To prove the converse write $P = \alpha_1 E_1 + \alpha_2 E_2 + \cdots + \alpha_r E_r$ as in (1). If $P \geq 0$, then each $\alpha_i \geq 0$. Let $Q = \sqrt{\alpha_1}E_1 + \sqrt{\alpha_2}E_2 + \cdots + \sqrt{\alpha_r}E_r$. Then (1c) and (1d) give $Q = Q^*$ and $Q^2 = P$. From (1) of Section 5, α is a characteristic value of Q if and only if $\alpha = \sqrt{\alpha_i}$ for some i, $1 \leq i \leq r$. Thus (4) tells us that $Q \geq 0$.

Suppose that $Q_1 \geq 0$ and $Q_1^2 = P$. Then apply (1) to Q_1 yielding: $Q_1 = \beta_1 F_1 + \beta_2 F_2 + \cdots + \beta_k F_k$, where $\beta_1, \beta_2, \ldots, \beta_k$ are distinct complex numbers, $I = F_1 + F_2 + \cdots + F_k$, $F_i F_j = 0$ if $i \neq j$, $F_i^2 = F_i = F_i^* \neq 0$, for $i = 1, 2, \ldots, k$. From (4) we know that $\beta_i \geq 0$ for $1 \leq i \leq k$. Thus $P = Q^2 = \beta_1^2 F_1 + \beta_2^2 F_2 + \cdots + \beta_k^2 F_k$. Since $\beta_1, \beta_2, \ldots, \beta_k$ are distinct and ≥ 0, we must have $\beta_1^2, \beta_2^2, \ldots, \beta_k^2$ distinct. Thus the uniqueness of the spectral projections tells us that $k = r$ and reordering, if necessary, that $E_i = F_i$, $\beta_i = \alpha_i$ for $1 \leq i \leq r$. Therefore $Q_1 = Q$. This establishes (11).

If $\alpha = a + ib$, where a and b are real, then $\alpha = 0$ or

$$\alpha = |\alpha| \, \frac{\alpha}{|\alpha|}.$$

If $\alpha \neq 0$, then

$$\left| \frac{\alpha}{|\alpha|} \right| = 1.$$

In either case $\alpha = ru$, where $|u| = 1$ and $r \geq 0$. This also has an operator analog. We shall give this only for normal operators although a similar result also holds for nonnormal operators.

> (12) If T is normal, then $T = UP$, where $P \geq 0$, $P^2 = T^*T$, and U is unitary. If T is invertible, then U is unique. Furthermore $UP = PU$, $TU = UT$, and $TP = PT$.

Let $T = \alpha_1 E_1 + \alpha_2 E_2 + \cdots + \alpha_r E_r$ as in (1). Then $T^* = \bar{\alpha}_1 E_1 + \bar{\alpha}_2 E_2 + \cdots + \bar{\alpha}_r E_r$, since $E_i^* = E_i$ for $i = 1, 2, \ldots, r$. Thus, using (1c) and (1d), we have $T^*T = |\alpha_1|^2 E_1 + |\alpha_2|^2 E_2 + \cdots + |\alpha_r|^2 E_r$. Let $P = |\alpha_1| E_1 + |\alpha_2| E_2 + \cdots + |\alpha_r| E_r$. From Theorem 25, $P \geq 0$. Also $P^2 = T^*T$. If $\alpha_i \neq 0$ for each i let

$$U = \frac{\alpha_1}{|\alpha_1|} E_1 + \frac{\alpha_2}{|\alpha_2|} E_2 + \cdots + \frac{\alpha_r}{|\alpha_r|} E_r.$$

Then $T = UP$. If $\alpha_i = 0$ for some i, we can suppose that $\alpha_1 = 0$. Then $\alpha_i \neq 0$ for $i > 1$. Let

$$U = E_1 + \frac{\alpha_2}{|\alpha_2|} E_2 + \cdots + \frac{\alpha_r}{|\alpha_r|} E_r.$$

Again $T = UP$. In either case Theorem 25 tells us that U is unitary. From Theorem 25, T is invertible if and only if $\alpha_i \neq 0$, for $i = 1, 2, \ldots, r$. Thus if T is invertible, Theorem 25 tells us that P is invertible. Therefore $U = TP^{-1}$, so that U is unique. The construction of U and P shows that $UP = PU$, $UT = TU$, and $PT = TP$.

If T is normal, then the computation of $f(T)$, where f is a polynomial, is easy. If $T = \alpha_1 E_1 + \alpha_2 E_2 + \cdots + \alpha_r E_r$ as in (1), then $T^2 = \alpha_1^2 E_1 + \alpha_2^2 E_2 + \cdots + \alpha_r^2 E_r$, using (1c) and (1d). In general, $T^k =$

$\alpha_1^k E_1 + \alpha_2^k E_2 + \cdots + \alpha_r^k E_r$ for any integer $k \geq 1$. From these results it follows that

(13) $$f(T) = f(\alpha_1)E_1 + f(\alpha_2)E_2 + \cdots + f(\alpha_r)E_r.$$

If f is *any* complex-valued function such that $f(\alpha_1), f(\alpha_2), \ldots, f(\alpha_r)$ are defined, then we define $f(T)$ by the formula (13). Thus in order to compute $f(T)$ we need to compute the characteristic values of T and the spectral projections of T. The definition of $f(T)$ is really nothing new. It is merely a device for symbolizing various operators related to T. The computational use of this definition resides in the following rules.

(14)
(a) $(f + g)(T) = f(T) + g(T)$,
(b) $(\alpha f)(T) = \alpha f(T)$,
(c) $(fg)(T) = f(T)g(T)$.

For example if $f(\alpha) = e^\alpha$ and $g(\alpha) = e^{-\alpha}$, then $f(T) = e^{\alpha_1}E_1 + e^{\alpha_2}E_2 + \cdots + e^{\alpha_r}E_r$, $g(T) = e^{-\alpha_1}E_1 + e^{-\alpha_2}E_2 + \cdots + e^{-\alpha_r}E_r$; and $f(T)g(T) = E_1 + E_2 + \cdots + E_r = I$. Since $fg(\alpha) = 1$, this result also follows from (14c).

Our results easily extend to matrices. The proofs can be given directly for matrices or can be established by considering the matrix as the matrix of an operator on C^n.

EXERCISES

1. Show that each of the following operators on C^2 is normal with respect to the standard inner product. Find the characteristic values of each operator. Which are self-adjoint? Positive? Nonnegative? Skew adjoint? Unitary? Projections?

(a) $T(\alpha, \beta) = (\alpha + i\beta, -i\alpha + \beta)$
(b) $T(\alpha, \beta) = ((2i + 2)\alpha + (-1 + 2i)\beta, (1 - 2i)\alpha + i\beta)$
(c) $T(\alpha, \beta) = (\alpha + i\beta, -i\alpha)$
(d) $T(\alpha, \beta) = (2i\alpha - \beta, (1 + i)\alpha + (2 - 2i)\beta)$
(e) $T(\alpha, \beta) = (i\alpha + (i + 1)\beta, -i\alpha + (i + 1)\beta)$
(f) $T(\alpha, \beta) = (\alpha + (1 + i)\beta, (1 - i)\alpha + \beta)$

(g) $T(\alpha, \beta) = \left(\dfrac{i\alpha + \beta}{\sqrt{2}}, \dfrac{\alpha + i\beta}{\sqrt{2}} \right)$

(h) $T(\alpha, \beta) = \left(\dfrac{\alpha + i\beta}{2}, \dfrac{-i\alpha + \beta}{2} \right)$

2. Show that $T = T^*$ if and only if $T = (T + T^*)/2$. [*Hint:* Show that $(T - T^*)/2i = 0$.]

3. Show that if S and T are linear, then $(SX, X) = (TX, X)$ for all X in V if and only if $S = T$. [*Hint:* See the proof of (2).]

4. Let V be the space of 2×2 complex matrices with the inner product $(A, B) = \text{tr}(B^*A)$. (See Exercise 3, Section 5.) Show that each of the following operators on V is normal. Which are unitary? Positive? Skew adjoint?

(a) $TA = AC - CA$, where $C = \begin{bmatrix} 0 & i \\ i & 0 \end{bmatrix}$.

(b) $TA = AC - CA$, where $C = \begin{bmatrix} i/\sqrt{2} & 1/\sqrt{2} \\ 1/\sqrt{2} & i/\sqrt{2} \end{bmatrix}$.

(c) $TA = C^*AC$, where $C = \begin{bmatrix} 1 & i \\ -i & 0 \end{bmatrix}$.

(d) $TA = AC$, where $C = \begin{bmatrix} 2i+1 & i-1 \\ 1-i & i \end{bmatrix}$.

5. Let $T(\alpha, \beta) = ((3i+6)\alpha + (2-7i)\beta, 6i\alpha - \beta)$. Assuming that C^2 has the standard inner product find the real and imaginary parts of T.

6. (a) Suppose that $P_1 \geq 0$ and $P_2 \geq 0$. Show that $P_1 + P_2 \geq 0$. [*Hint:* Use the definition rather than Theorem 25.]

(b) Suppose that $P_1 \geq 0$, $P_2 \geq 0$, and $P_1P_2 = P_2P_1$. Show that $P_1P_2 \geq 0$. [*Hint:* Use the results of (11) and (13) of Section 1 in order to express P_1P_2. Then use Theorem 25.]

7. Let

$$P = \begin{bmatrix} 1 & i \\ -i & 1 \end{bmatrix}.$$

Show that $P \geq 0$; find the spectral projections for P and find the square root of P.

8. (a) Show that $T^*T \geq 0$.

(b) Show that if P is normal and if $0 \leq \alpha \leq 1$ for all the characteristic values α of P, then $P \geq 0$ and $I \geq P$.

9. Let C^2 have the standard inner product and let

$$T(\alpha, \beta) = (2i\alpha - \beta, \alpha + i\beta).$$

Find the square root of T^*T. Find operators P and U such that (12) holds. Verify that $PU = UP$.

10. Find the characteristic values of each of the following operators T. Show that each serves to show that the assumption of normality is necessary in (5), (6), (7), and (8), respectively.

(a) $T(\alpha, \beta) = (\alpha + i\beta, 2\beta)$
(b) $T(\alpha, \beta) = (i\alpha, i\alpha + 2i\beta)$
(c) $T(\alpha, \beta) = (i\alpha + \beta, i\beta)$
(d) $T(\alpha, \beta) = (\alpha + \beta, \beta)$

11. Show that if T is normal, $T = \alpha_1 E_1 + \alpha_2 E_2 + \cdots + \alpha_r E_r$ as in (1) with $\alpha_1, \alpha_2, \ldots, \alpha_r$ distinct and $\alpha_1 = 0$, then there are many operators U such that U and P satisfy (12). [*Hint:*

$$U = iE_1 + \frac{\alpha_2}{|\alpha_2|} E_2 + \cdots + \frac{\alpha_r}{|\alpha_r|} E_r$$

satisfies the same conditions as the operator given in the proof of (12).]

12. **(a)** If a is a real number, then $a \geq 0$ or $a < 0$. Show that the analogy between operators and numbers is not complete by finding a self-adjoint operator T such that $T \not\geq 0$ and $-T \not\geq 0$. [*Hint:* Use (4).]

   (b) Let T be a self-adjoint operator on V (V finite dimensional). Show that there are operators P_1 and P_2 on V such that $P_1 \geq 0$, $P_2 \geq 0$, and $T = P_1 - P_2$. [*Hint:* If $T = \alpha_1 E_1 + \alpha_2 E_2 + \cdots + \alpha_r E_r$ as in (1), let P_1 be the sum of those $\alpha_i E_i$ such that $\alpha_i \geq 0$.]

13. Let V be a finite dimensional complex vector space with an inner product, which for convenience we will denote by $X \cdot Y$.

   (a) Suppose that P is an operator on V such that $P \geq 0$. Let $h(X, Y) = PX \cdot Y$. Show that $h(X, Y) = \overline{h(Y, X)}$, $h(\alpha X^1 + \beta X^2, Y) = \alpha h(X^1, Y) + \beta h(X^2, Y)$, and $h(X, X) \geq 0$.

   (b) Suppose that $h(X, Y)$ is a complex-valued function of the two vector variables X and Y which satisfies $h(X, Y) = \overline{h(Y, X)}$, $h(\alpha X^1 + \beta X^2, Y) = \alpha h(X^1, Y) + \beta h(X^2, Y)$, and $h(X, X) \geq 0$. Show that there is a unique operator P such that $h(X, Y) = PX \cdot Y$. Show also that $P \geq 0$. [*Hint:* Fix X and let $f(Y) = \overline{h(X, Y)}$. Apply Theorem 16, to show that there is a unique vector X' such that $\overline{f(Y)} = X' \cdot Y$. Denote X' by PX.]

14. Let

$$A = \begin{bmatrix} i/2 & -\frac{1}{2} \\ \frac{1}{2} & i/2 \end{bmatrix}, \qquad f(t) = \frac{1}{1 - t}, \qquad g(t) = \frac{1}{1 + t^2},$$

$$h(t) = 3i(1 - t^2), \qquad k(t) = t^4 + 2t + 1, \qquad m(t) = t^{10}.$$

Determine if the following are defined. If so, compute them. [*Hint:* Find the spectral projections of A.]

   (a) $g(A)$ **(b)** $f(A)h(A)$
   (c) $(kg)(A)$ **(d)** $m(A)$
   (e) $h(A)k(A)m(A)\big(f(A)\big)^2$

15. Let

$$A = \begin{bmatrix} 3 & i \\ -i & 1 \end{bmatrix}.$$

   (a) Find all self-adjoint matrices B such that $AB = BA$.
   (b) Find all normal matrices C such that A is the real part of C. [*Hint:* Use part (a) and (10).]

16. Let

$$A = \begin{bmatrix} \alpha & \beta \\ 0 & \gamma \end{bmatrix}.$$

Show that A is normal if and only if $\beta = 0$. State and prove a generalization of this to $n \times n$ matrices.

17. Let V be a finite dimensional complex vector space with the inner product (X, Y). Let T be the linear operator on V. Then there is an orthonormal basis for V such that the matrix of T is lower triangular. The parts of this exercise will lead to a proof of this.

(a) Let α_1 be a characteristic value of T^*. Let X^1 be in V such that $|X^1| = 1$ and $T^*X^1 = \alpha_1 X^1$. Denote the subspace spanned by X^1 by M_1. Show that $M_1^\perp$ is an invariant subspace for T. [*Hint:* See Exercise 12, Section 5.]

(b) Denote the restriction of T to $M_1^\perp$ by T_1, that is, $T_1X = TX$ for X in $M_1^\perp$. Let α_2 be a characteristic value of T_1^*. Choose X^2 in $M_1^\perp$ such that $|X^2| = 1$ and $T_1^*X^2 = \alpha_2 X^2$. Denote the subspace spanned by X^2 by M_2. Let $(M_2^\perp)_1^\perp$ denote the orthogonal complement of M_2 in $M_1^\perp$; that is, $(M_2^\perp)_1^\perp$ is the collection of all X in $M_1^\perp$ such that $(X, X^2) = 0$. Show that $(M_2^\perp)_1^\perp$ is an invariant subspace for T_1 and that dim $(M_2^\perp)_1^\perp = $ dim $V - 2$. [*Hint:* dim $(M_2^\perp)_1^\perp = $ dim $M_1^\perp - 1$.]

(c) Denote the restriction of T_1 to $(M_2^\perp)_1^\perp$ by T_2 and repeat part (b) for T_2 and $(M_2^\perp)_1^\perp$. Repetition of this process leads to an orthonormal basis $\{X^1, X^2, \ldots, X^n\}$ for V such that TX^i is a linear combination of $\{X^i, X^{i+1}, \ldots, X^n\}$ for $i = 1, 2, \ldots, n$. Note that if T is normal, then this process is the same as that given in Exercise 12, Section 5.

NOTES

The results of Sections 1 and 2 are used in many places in Courant and Hilbert [5]. This book shows that many questions in physics can be reduced to questions about quadratic and bilinear forms. Other applications and further results can be found in Smirnov [24, Chapter 4]. Part III of Smirnov's book contains a study of representations of orthogonal and Lorentz transformations. A very complete algebraic study of bilinear and quadratic forms over arbitrary fields can be found in Jacobson [15, Chapters 5 and 6]. An application of Exercise 9 of Section 3 in statistics can be found in Cramér [6, p. 184 ff].

An extension of Theorems 25 and 26 to the infinite dimensional case can be found in Berberian [2]. The polar decomposition [(12) of Section 5] can be obtained without using normality although without the given commuting relation. For a proof of this see Hoffman and Kunze [14, p. 279 ff].

Power series methods can be used to extend the concept of $f(T)$ to more general functions than polynomials and more general operators than normal operators. Alternative approaches to this are given in the introduction to Courant and Hilbert [5] and in Jacobson [15, Chapter 6].

REFERENCES

1. AITKEN, A. C., *Determinants and Matrices.* 3rd ed., New York: Interscience, 1944.

2. BERBERIAN, S., *Introduction to Hilbert Space.* New York: Oxford University Press, 1961.

3. CHURCHILL, R. V., *Operational Mathematics.* 2nd ed., New York: McGraw-Hill, 1958.

4. CHURCHILL, R. V., *Introduction to Complex Variables and Applications.* New York: McGraw-Hill, 1948.

5. COURANT, R. and D. HILBERT, *Methods of Mathematical Physics.* Vol. 1, New York: Interscience, 1953.

6. CRAMÉR, H., *The Elements of Probability Theory.* New York: Wiley, 1955.

7. ERDÉLYI, A., *Operational Calculus and Generalized Functions.* New York: Holt, Rinehart, and Winston, 1962.

8. FADDEEVA, V. N., *Computational Methods of Linear Algebra.* C. D. Benster, translator, New York: Dover, 1959.

9. FICKEN, F. A., *The Simplex Method of Linear Programming.* New York: Holt, Rinehart, and Winston, 1961.

10. FRIEDMAN, B., *Principles and Techniques of Applied Mathematics.* New York: Wiley, 1956.

11. GANTMACHER, F. R., *Applications of the Theory of Matrices.* Translated and revised by J. L. Brenner with the assistance of D. W. Bushaw and S. Evanusa. New York: Interscience, 1959.

12. GUILLEMIN, E. A., *Introductory Circuit Theory.* New York: Wiley, 1953.

13. HALMOS, P., *Finite-Dimensional Vector Spaces.* 2nd ed., Princeton, N. J.: Van Nostrand, 1958.

14. HOFFMAN, K. and R. KUNZE, *Linear Algebra.* Englewood Cliffs, N. J.: Prentice-Hall, 1961.

15. JACOBSON, N., *Lectures in Abstract Algebra.* Vol. 2, New York: Van Nostrand, 1953.

16. KAPLAN, W., *Ordinary Differential Equations.* Reading, Mass.: Addison-Wesley, 1958.

17. KAPLAN, W., *Advanced Calculus.* Reading, Mass.: Addison-Wesley, 1953.

18. KLEIN, F., *Elementary Mathematics from an Advanced Standpoint, Geometry.* E. R. Hedrick and C. A. Noble, translators, New York: Dover, 1939.

19. LANCZOS, C., *Applied Analysis.* Englewood Cliffs, N. J.: Prentice-Hall, 1956.

20. LOVITT, W. V., *Linear Integral Equations.* New York: Dover, 1950.

21. NICKERSON, H. K., D. C. SPENCER, and N. E. STEENROD, *Advanced Calculus.* Princeton, N. J.: Van Nostrand, 1959.

22. ROBINSON, G., *Vector Geometry.* Boston: Allyn and Bacon, 1962.

23. RUDIN, W., *Principles of Mathematical Analysis.* New York: McGraw-Hill, 1953.

24. SMIRNOV, V. I., *Linear Algebra and Group Theory.* Revised, edited, and adapted by R. A. Silverman. New York: McGraw-Hill, 1961.

25. TOLSTOV, G. P., *Fourier Series.* R. A. Silverman, translator, Englewood Cliffs, N. J.: Prentice-Hall, 1961.

ANSWERS TO SELECTED EXERCISES

Section 1.

1. (a) $[2 \quad 1]$

(c) $\begin{bmatrix} 1 & 2 \\ 3 & 4 \end{bmatrix}$

(e) $\begin{bmatrix} 0 & 6 & 1 \\ 9 & 12 & -8 \\ 12 & 62 & -3 \\ -3 & 8 & -2 \end{bmatrix}$

(g) $\begin{bmatrix} 0 & 1 & 2 & -1 \\ 1 & -3 & 0 & 0 \\ -1 & 1 & 0 & 0 \end{bmatrix}$

(i) $\begin{bmatrix} 1 & 1 & 1 \\ a & a & a \\ a^2 & a^2 & a^2 \end{bmatrix}$

2. Echelon forms.

(a) $[1 \quad \frac{1}{2}]$

(c) $\begin{bmatrix} 1 & 0 \\ 0 & 1 \end{bmatrix}$

(e) $\begin{bmatrix} 1 & 0 & 0 \\ 0 & 1 & 0 \\ 0 & 0 & 1 \\ 0 & 0 & 0 \end{bmatrix}$

(g) $\begin{bmatrix} 1 & 0 & 0 & 0 \\ 0 & 1 & 0 & 0 \\ 0 & 0 & 1 & -\frac{1}{2} \end{bmatrix}$

(i) $\begin{bmatrix} 1 & 1 & 1 \\ 0 & 0 & 0 \\ 0 & 0 & 0 \end{bmatrix}$

3. (a) $x_1 = -\frac{1}{2}x_3$
$x_2 = -\frac{3}{2}x_3$

(c) $x_1 = x_3 + 2x_4$
$x_2 = -2x_3 - 3x_4$

4. (a) Has nontrivial solutions. (c) Has nontrivial solutions.
(e) Has no nontrivial solutions. (g) Has nontrivial solutions.

6. (a) $x_1 = -\dfrac{3-i}{2}x_3, \qquad x_2 = -\dfrac{1-3i}{2}x_3$

13. The maximum number for a 3×3 system is eighteen.

Section 2.

1. (a) No solutions.
(c) $x = \frac{3}{4}, \qquad y = \frac{5}{4}, \qquad z = \frac{3}{4}$
(e) $x = \frac{2}{3}w + \frac{1}{3}, \qquad y = -\frac{4}{3}w + \frac{1}{3}, \qquad z = -3w$
(g) $x = 2, \qquad y = 1, \qquad z = 0, \qquad w = -1$
(i) $x = y + 2$

2. (a) Unique solutions.   (c) No solutions.

3. (a) $y_1 - y_2 - y_3 + 3y_4 = 0$
   (c) $y_1 + y_3 = 0$

4. (a) $x = (7 - 2i)/3,$ $y = (-2 - i)/3$
   (c) No solution.

Section 3.

6. (a) No.   (c) 0, 1, 2, 3

7. (a) Independent.   (c) Dependent.   (e) Independent.

8. (a) Dependent.   (c) Independent.   (e) Independent.

9. (a) Independent.   (c) Dependent.

10. (a) Not a linear combination.
    (c) $(4, 2, 1, 0) = 2(6, -1, 2, 1) + (1, 7, -3, -2)$
    $- 3(3, 1, 0, 0) + 0(3, 3, -2, -1)$

11. (a) Basis for $M = \{(1, 0, 1), (0, 1, 0)\}$.
    Basis for $V = \{(1, 0, 1), (0, 1, 0), (1, 0, 0)\}$.
    (c) $M = V$.
    (e) Basis for $M = \{t - 1, t^2 + 1\}$.
    Basis for $V = \{t - 1, t^2 + 1, 1\}$.
    (Of course there are many other possibilities.)

12. (a) $[1 \quad 0 \quad -1]$ (c) $\begin{bmatrix} 0 & 0 & 0 & 0 \\ 0 & 0 & 0 & 0 \\ 0 & 0 & 0 & 0 \\ 0 & 0 & 0 & 0 \end{bmatrix}$

13. (a) Rank $= 2$.
    Basis for row space $= \{(2, 1), (1, 2)\}$.
    Null space is the zero subspace
    (c) Rank $= 3$.
    Basis for row space $= \{(1, 0, 0, \frac{22}{15}), (0, 1, 0, \frac{1}{15}), (0, 0, 1, -\frac{42}{15})\}$.
    Basis for null space $= \{(-\frac{22}{15}, -\frac{1}{15}, \frac{42}{15}, 1)\}$.

14. Many choices are possible. The following are some simple examples.
    (a) $\{1, t, t^2, \ldots, t^n\}$ (c) $\{x, y, z\}$
    (e) $\{l_1, l_2\}$, where l_1 and l_2 do not pass through 0 and the perpendicular
    from l_1 to l_0 is *not* parallel to the perpendicular from l_2 to l_0.

Section 4.

1. (a) Linear.   (c) Not linear.   (e) Not linear.   (g) Linear.

4. (2a) $\begin{bmatrix} 1 & 0 & 0 \\ 0 & \frac{1}{2} & \sqrt{3}/2 \\ 0 & -\sqrt{3}/2 & \frac{1}{2} \end{bmatrix}$ or $\begin{bmatrix} 1 & 0 & 0 \\ 0 & \frac{1}{2} & -\sqrt{3}/2 \\ 0 & \sqrt{3}/2 & \frac{1}{2} \end{bmatrix}$

depending upon the orientation.

(2c) $\begin{bmatrix} 1 & 0 & 0 \\ 0 & 0 & 0 \\ 0 & 0 & 1 \end{bmatrix}$

(3a) $\begin{bmatrix} 1 & -1 & 0 \\ 0 & 1 & 1 \\ 1 & 0 & 0 \end{bmatrix}$ (3c) $\begin{bmatrix} 1 & 1 & 0 \\ -1 & -1 & 0 \\ 0 & 0 & 1 \end{bmatrix}$

5. (a) $n = m = 3$; $T(x, y, z) = (3x + y + 2z, y + z, -x + y + z)$
   (c) $n = 3$, $m = 2$; $T(x, y, z) = (2x + y + z, x + y + z)$

7. (a) Range is R^3; null space is the zero subspace.
   (c) Range is the plane $x + y = 0$; null space is the line $x = t$, $y = -t$, $z = 0$.

8. (a) Rank $= 2$, nullity $= 1$.   **(c)** Rank $= 2$, nullity $= 1$.

9. (a) Basis for range $= \{(2, 1), (-1, 1)\}$.
   Basis for null space $= \{(-1, -2, 1)\}$.
   (c) Basis for range $= \{(3, -1, 0), (2, 1, 5)\}$.
   Basis for null space $= \{(1, 1, -5)\}$.

10. (a) $T(x, y) = (-x + 4y, -x + 5y)$
   $T(1, 0) = (-1, -1)$

12. (a) $ST(x, y, z) = (3x - 4y - z, 0, x)$
         $TS(x, y, z) = (3x - y, z, 3x - y)$
         $(S + T)(x, y, z) = (4x - 2y, y + z, x + z)$
         $(3S^2 - 2T^3)(x, y, z) = (27x - 3y + 4z, -4x - 2z,$
                                                   $-2x + 4y + 5z)$

   (c) $ST(x, y, z) = (4x + 4y, 0, z)$
         $TS(x, y, z) = (3x - y, -3x + y, z)$
         $(S + T)(x, y, z) = (4x, -x - y, 2z)$
         $(3S^2 - 2T^3)(x, y, z) = (27x - 9y, 0, z)$

13. (a) $\begin{bmatrix} -1 & 3 \\ 0 & 2 \end{bmatrix}$ **(c)** $\begin{bmatrix} 6 & -1 \\ 0 & 1 \end{bmatrix}$ **(e)** $\begin{bmatrix} 1 & 2 \\ -5 & -1 \end{bmatrix}$

14. There are many examples. Here are some simple ones.
   (a) $T(x, y, z) = (y, z, 0)$ **(c)** $T = I$
   (e) $T = I$, $S(x, y, z) = (x, y, -z)$
   (g) $S(x, y, z) = (x + y + z, y + z, z)$, $T(x, y, z) = (x, y, -z)$

Section 5.

2. (a) $T^{-1}(x, y, z) = (x - y, y - z, z)$
   (c) Not invertible.

3. (a) Not invertible.
   (c) T^{-1} is rotation through $-\pi/2$ about the line through $(0, 0, 0)$ and $(1, 1, 1)$ leaving $(0, 0, 0)$ fixed.

4. (a) Not invertible.

5. (a) The matrix of T^{-1} is $\begin{bmatrix} 0 & 1 \\ \frac{1}{2} & -\frac{3}{2} \end{bmatrix}$.

(c) Not invertible.

(e) The matrix of T^{-1} is $\begin{bmatrix} 0 & 1 \\ 1 & 0 \end{bmatrix}\begin{bmatrix} 1 & 0 \\ 0 & \frac{1}{3} \end{bmatrix}\begin{bmatrix} 1 & -2 \\ 0 & 1 \end{bmatrix}$.

(g) Invertible if $a^2 \neq 3$. The matrix of T^{-1} is

$$\begin{bmatrix} \dfrac{a+1}{a^2-3} & \dfrac{-2}{a^2-3} \\[2mm] \dfrac{-1}{a^2-3} & \dfrac{a-1}{a^2-3} \end{bmatrix}.$$

12. (a) Not an isomorphism.

(c) Not an isomorphism.

13. (a) For example, $T(a_0 + a_1 t + a_2 t^2) = (a_0, a_1, a_2)$.

Section 6.

1. (a) $[6 \quad 9]$

(c) $\begin{bmatrix} 12 - \pi + 3\sqrt{2} & 2 + 2\pi + \sqrt{2} & 2 + \pi & 2 + \sqrt{2} & 3 + \pi & 3 + \pi \\ 3 + \sqrt{2} & 1 - 2\sqrt{2} & -\sqrt{2} & 1 & 3 - \sqrt{2} & 3 - \sqrt{2} \\ 2 & 3 & 1 & 1 & 2 & 2 \end{bmatrix}$

(e) $\begin{bmatrix} 1 & 1 & 0 \\ 3 & 2 & 0 \\ 3 & 5 & 0 \end{bmatrix}$

(g) $\begin{bmatrix} 1 & 0 & 0 & 0 \\ 2 & 0 & 0 & 0 \\ 4 & 1 & 4 & 10 \\ 1 & 0 & 1 & 2 \end{bmatrix}$

(i) $\begin{bmatrix} -\frac{3}{40} & -\frac{1}{84} \\ \frac{103}{630} & \frac{317}{3528} \end{bmatrix}$

(k) $\begin{bmatrix} 9 & 6 \\ 1 & 1 \\ -2 & 0 \end{bmatrix}$

(m) $\begin{bmatrix} -3 & 4 & 3 \\ 0 & 2 & 0 \\ 0 & 0 & 0 \end{bmatrix}$

(o) $\begin{bmatrix} 10 & 1 & 0 \\ 1 & 5 & 2 \\ 0 & 2 & 1 \end{bmatrix}$

5. (a) $\begin{bmatrix} 1 & 0 & 0 \\ 0 & 3^{10} & 0 \\ 0 & 0 & 2^{10} \end{bmatrix}$

(c) $\begin{bmatrix} 0 & 0 & 0 & 0 \\ 0 & 0 & 0 & 0 \\ 0 & 0 & 0 & 0 \\ 0 & 0 & 0 & 0 \end{bmatrix}$

7. (a) Not invertible.

(c)
$$\frac{1}{24}\begin{bmatrix} 5 & -12 & -6 \\ -2 & 0 & 12 \\ -1 & 12 & 6 \end{bmatrix}$$

(e)
$$\frac{1}{23}\begin{bmatrix} -2 & -7 & 7 & 7 & 9 \\ 10 & 12 & -35 & -12 & 1 \\ -15 & -18 & 18 & 41 & 10 \\ 3 & -1 & 1 & 1 & -2 \\ -1 & 8 & 15 & -8 & -7 \end{bmatrix}$$

8. (a)
$$\begin{bmatrix} -1 & 0 & \frac{2}{3} \\ 0 & 1 & -\frac{1}{3} \\ 0 & 0 & \frac{1}{3} \end{bmatrix}\begin{bmatrix} 1 & 0 & 0 \\ 0 & \frac{1}{2} & 0 \\ 0 & 0 & \frac{1}{3} \end{bmatrix}\begin{bmatrix} 1 & -1 & 2 \\ -2 & 3 & -6 \\ 1 & -1 & 3 \end{bmatrix}$$

(c) Not invertible.

10. (a) Invertible if $a \neq 1$ and $a \neq -3$.
(c) Invertible for all real λ.

16. (a) $(3, 7, -6)$ **(c)** $(1, 1, 1, 0, 1, 2)$

17. (a) Independent.   **(c)** Dependent.

18. (a) Dependent.

20.
$$\begin{bmatrix} 2 & 0 & 0 & 2 & 0 & 0 \\ 0 & 4 & 0 & 2 & 0 & 0 \\ 0 & 0 & 6 & 0 & 0 & 0 \\ 1 & 1 & 0 & 3 & 0 & 0 \\ 0 & 0 & 0 & 0 & 4 & 1 \\ 0 & 0 & 0 & 0 & 1 & 5 \end{bmatrix}$$

21. (a) $(1, 1, 0)$

22. (b) $(1, 4, 15, 40)$

23. (a) $(1, 3, -1)$ **(c)** $(6, 1, -1)$

24. (a)
$$\begin{bmatrix} 1 & 0 & -1 \\ 0 & 0 & 1 \\ 0 & 0 & 0 \end{bmatrix}$$
(c)
$$\begin{bmatrix} 2 & 0 & 0 \\ 0 & 3 & 0 \\ 0 & 0 & 0 \end{bmatrix}$$

25. (a)
$$\begin{bmatrix} 0 & 0 & 0 \\ 1 & 0 & 0 \\ 0 & 1 & 0 \\ 0 & 0 & 1 \end{bmatrix}$$

27. (a)

$$\begin{bmatrix} 1 & 0 \\ 2 & 6 \end{bmatrix}\begin{bmatrix} 0 & 1 \\ 1 & 0 \end{bmatrix}\begin{bmatrix} 2 & 1 \\ 1 & 1 \end{bmatrix}\begin{bmatrix} 1 & 0 \\ 0 & 1 \end{bmatrix}$$
$$\begin{bmatrix} 1 & 0 \\ 0 & 1 \end{bmatrix}\begin{bmatrix} 3 & 1 \\ 0 & 2 \end{bmatrix}\begin{bmatrix} 0 & 0 \\ 0 & 0 \end{bmatrix}\begin{bmatrix} 1 & 0 \\ 0 & 1 \end{bmatrix} = \begin{bmatrix} 2 & 1 & 1 & 1 \\ 10 & 8 & 3 & 6 \\ 2 & 1 & 4 & 1 \\ 1 & 1 & 0 & 3 \end{bmatrix}$$

(c)

$$\begin{bmatrix} 0 & 1 \\ 0 & 0 \end{bmatrix}\begin{bmatrix} 1 & 1 \\ 1 & 1 \end{bmatrix}\begin{bmatrix} 1 & 1 \\ 1 & 1 \end{bmatrix}^2$$
$$\begin{bmatrix} 0 & 0 \\ 0 & 0 \end{bmatrix}\begin{bmatrix} 0 & 1 \\ 0 & 0 \end{bmatrix}\begin{bmatrix} 1 & 1 \\ 1 & 1 \end{bmatrix} = \begin{bmatrix} 0 & 0 & 1 & 2 & 3 & 4 \\ 0 & 0 & 0 & 1 & 2 & 3 \\ 0 & 0 & 0 & 0 & 1 & 2 \\ 0 & 0 & 0 & 0 & 0 & 1 \\ 0 & 0 & 0 & 0 & 0 & 0 \\ 0 & 0 & 0 & 0 & 0 & 0 \end{bmatrix}$$
$$\begin{bmatrix} 0 & 0 \\ 0 & 0 \end{bmatrix}\begin{bmatrix} 0 & 0 \\ 0 & 0 \end{bmatrix}\begin{bmatrix} 0 & 1 \\ 0 & 0 \end{bmatrix}$$

CHAPTER 2

Section 1.

2. (a) $4\mathbf{i} + \mathbf{k}$ **(c)** -8
(e) $-18/5\sqrt{14}$ **(g)** $2|\mathbf{v}_1|^2 + 2|\mathbf{v}_2|^2 = 26$
(i) $\frac{1}{5}\mathbf{v}_1$

4. (b) $ax + by + cz = \dfrac{d}{\sqrt{a^2 + b^2 + c^2}}$

or

$ax + by + cz = -\dfrac{d}{\sqrt{a^2 + b^2 + c^2}}$

(e) $\dfrac{x - x_0}{A} = \dfrac{y - y_0}{B} = \dfrac{z - z_0}{C}$

6. $(\mathbf{v} \cdot \mathbf{v}_1)\mathbf{v}_1/|\mathbf{v}_1|^2$ if $\{\mathbf{v}_1, \mathbf{v}_2\}$ is dependent and $\mathbf{v}_1 \neq 0$. Otherwise this projection is $(\mathbf{v} \cdot \mathbf{v}_1)\mathbf{v}_1/|\mathbf{v}_1|^2 + (\mathbf{v} \cdot \mathbf{v}_3)\mathbf{v}_3/|\mathbf{v}_3|^2$, where $\mathbf{v}_3 = \mathbf{v}_2 - (\mathbf{v}_2 \cdot \mathbf{v}_1)\mathbf{v}_1/|\mathbf{v}_1|^2$, so that $\mathbf{v}_1 \cdot \mathbf{v}_3 = 0$.

Section 2.

6. (a) -16 **(c)** $\sqrt{7}$ **(e)** $-\frac{2}{7}Y$ **(g)** $5/\sqrt{42}$
7. (a) -79 **(c)** $\sqrt{29}$ **(e)** $-\frac{23}{3}Y$ **(g)** $27/\sqrt{28 \cdot 29}$
8. (a) $\frac{397}{924}$ **(c)** $1/\sqrt{11}$ **(e)** $\frac{55}{408}Y$ **(g)** $\sqrt{33}/42$
11. (b) Parallel, $(-1/\pi) \sin 2\pi t$.
     Perpendicular, $t + (1/\pi) \sin 2\pi t$.

Section 3.

1. (a) Not orthogonal.   **(c)** Orthonormal.
2. (b) Orthonormal.   **(d)** Not orthogonal.
3. (a) The standard basis.
     (c) $\{1, \sqrt{12}\,(t - \frac{1}{2}), \sqrt{180}\,(t^2 - t + \frac{1}{6}), 20\sqrt{7}\,(t^3 - \frac{3}{2}t^2 + \frac{3}{5}t - \frac{1}{20})\}$

4. (a) Coordinates of $(2, 1, 0)$ with respect to first basis: $(1/\sqrt{2}, 3/\sqrt{2}, 0)$.
Coordinates of $(3, -1, 2)$ with respect to second basis: $(3, \frac{3}{2}, -\frac{5}{2})$.

(c) Coordinates of $\begin{bmatrix} 2 & 1 \\ 0 & 1 \end{bmatrix}$: $(1, -1/\sqrt{3}, 4/\sqrt{6}, -\sqrt{2})$.

Coordinates of $\begin{bmatrix} 1 & -1 \\ -1 & 1 \end{bmatrix}$: $(1, \sqrt{3}, 0, 0)$.

6. $U = \begin{bmatrix} 2/\sqrt{5} & 3/\sqrt{70} & -1/\sqrt{14} \\ 1/\sqrt{5} & -6/\sqrt{70} & 2/\sqrt{14} \\ 0 & 5/\sqrt{70} & 3/\sqrt{14} \end{bmatrix}$ $\Delta = \begin{bmatrix} \sqrt{5} & 1/\sqrt{5} & 1/\sqrt{5} \\ 0 & \sqrt{70}/5 & 2\sqrt{70}/35 \\ 0 & 0 & 4\sqrt{14}/7 \end{bmatrix}$

Section 4.

1. (a) The subspace spanned by $(1, 1, -1)$.
 (c) The subspace spanned by $(1, 1, 1, \ldots, 1)$.
 (e) The subspace spanned by $\{(3, 0, 1, 2), (1, 0, 1, 1)\}$.

2. (a) For M: $\{(-1/\sqrt{35}, 5/\sqrt{35}, 3/\sqrt{35})\}$.
   For $M^{\perp}$: $\{(1/\sqrt{6}, -1/\sqrt{6}, 2/\sqrt{6}), (2/\sqrt{6}, 1/\sqrt{6}, -1/\sqrt{6})\}$.
 (c) For M: $\{(-2/\sqrt{5}, 1/\sqrt{5}, 0), (-3/\sqrt{70}, -6/\sqrt{70}, 5/\sqrt{70})\}$.
   For $M^{\perp}$: $\{(1/\sqrt{14}, 2/\sqrt{14}, 3/\sqrt{14})\}$.

3. (a) $(\frac{6}{35}, -\frac{30}{35}, -\frac{18}{35})$ **(c)** $(\frac{15}{14}, -\frac{6}{7}, \frac{3}{14})$

4. (a) $\{a(7, 0, -10), b(61, -107, 81)\}$, where $a^2 = \frac{1}{107}, 1/b^2 = 61^2 + 46^2 + 35^2$.
 (c) $\{1/\sqrt{11}\,(-1, 0, 4)\}$

5. (a) $-\frac{1}{66}(-1, 5, 3)$ **(c)** $(\frac{10}{11}, -1, \frac{4}{11})$

6. (a) $Y = (3, -1, 0)$

7. (a) $\{a(18t^2 - 7), b(420t^2 - 447t + 85)\}$, where $1/a^2 = \frac{149}{5}$ and $1/b^2 = \int_0^1 (420t^2 - 447t + 85)^2 \, dt$.
 (c) $g = 390t^2 - 372t + 57$

10. (a) (x, y) is extreme if and only if $x^2 + y^2 = 1$.
 (d) g has its maximum for $y = 3, -1 \le x \le 1$.

Section 5.

1. (a) $T^*(x, y, z) = (x + y + z, y + z, z)$
 (c) $T^* = T$
 (e) $T^*(x, y, z) = (-y - 2z, x - 3z, 2x + 3y)$

2. (a) $T^*(x, y) = (3x + y, -4x - y)$

3. (a) $T_1^* f = -T_1 f + f(1)(30t^2 - 24t + 3) - f(0)(30t^2 - 36t + 9)$
 (c) $T_3^* f = -T_2 f + f(1)(30t^2 - 24t + 3)$
 (e) $T_5^* = T_5$

4. (a) Basis: $\{(1/\sqrt{2},\, 0),\, (1/\sqrt{2},\, -2/\sqrt{2})\}$.

Matrix of T: $\begin{bmatrix} 1 & 2 \\ 0 & 1 \end{bmatrix}$.   Matrix of T^*: $\begin{bmatrix} 1 & 0 \\ 2 & 1 \end{bmatrix}$.

5. (a) $T_1^* T_2(f) = -t\dfrac{d^2 f(t)}{dt^2} - \dfrac{df(t)}{dt} + \dfrac{df(1)}{dt}(30t^2 - 24t + 3)$

(c) $(T_2^* T_1^*)(1) = 180t^2 - 168t + 24$; $T_2^* T_1^*(t) = 150t^2 - 144t + 22$;
$(T_2^* T_1^*)(t^2) = 120t^2 - 116t + 18$

(e) $2T_5$

6. (a) $T^* A = C^t A$ **(c)** $T^* A = AC^t + C^t A$

9. (a) Parts 1(b) and 1(c) are orthogonal; 1(c) and 1(d) are symmetric and
1(e) is skew symmetric. If T is the operator of part 1(b), then $T = T_1 + T_2$, where $T_1(x,\, y,\, z) = ((\sqrt{2}/2)x,\, y,\, (\sqrt{2}/2)z)$, $T_2 = ((-\sqrt{2}/2)z,\, 0,\, (\sqrt{2}/2)z)$.

(b) If T is the operator of 2(a), then $T = T_1 + T_2$, where $T_1(x,\, y) = (2x,\, -2x)$ and $T_2(x,\, y) = (-x - y,\, 2x + y)$.

Section 6.

2. (a) -6 **(c)** -13 **(e)** 4

6. (a) 0

7. (a) Not invertible.

(c) $\begin{bmatrix} -\frac{1}{2} & -\frac{1}{6} & \frac{5}{6} & \frac{1}{6} \\ -\frac{1}{2} & \frac{1}{2} & -\frac{1}{2} & \frac{1}{2} \\ -\frac{1}{2} & \frac{1}{6} & \frac{7}{6} & -\frac{1}{6} \\ 1 & 0 & -1 & 0 \end{bmatrix}$

11. (a) $x = \frac{7}{5}$, $y = \frac{8}{5}$ **(c)** $x = \frac{2}{5}$, $y = \frac{3}{5}$, $z = -\frac{2}{5}$

Section 7.

3. (a) Empty if $(Z,\, Y) \neq 0$. If $(Z,\, Y) = 0$ and $Y \neq 0$, then this is the line through $Y \times Z/|Y|^2$ parallel to Y.

(c) If $(Z,\, Y) = 0$, this is the two planes given by $(X,\, Z) = 0$ or $(X,\, Y) = 0$.

4. (a) -1 **(c)** $(-1,\, -4,\, 4)$ **(e)** $(30,\, -24,\, 6)$ **(g)** $\frac{1}{6}$ **(i)** $\frac{1}{3}$

CHAPTER 3

Section 1.

1. (a) Any vector in the plane $x = z$ is a characteristic vector belonging to 1 and any vector perpendicular to this plane is a characteristic vector belonging to -1.

(c) For example, $T(1,\, 1,\, 0) = (1,\, 1,\, 0)$.

(e) For example, $T(0,\, 1,\, -1) = (0,\, 1,\, -1)$.

3. (a) Not diagonalizable.   **(c)** Diagonalizable.

4. (a) (2a) $T^k(x, y, z) =$
$\left(x, 2(2^k - 1)x + 2^k y, \frac{3}{2}(1 - 2^{k+2} + 3^{k+1})x + 3(3^k - 2^k)y + 3^k z\right)$
  (2c) $T^k = 3^{k-1}T$

  (2e) $T^k A = B^k A$, where $B^k = \begin{bmatrix} 1 & 0 \\ 0 & (-3)^k \end{bmatrix}$

  (b) (2a) Yes.   **(2c)** Yes.   **(2e)** No.
  (c) (2a) $\lambda \neq 1$, $\lambda \neq 2$,   and $\lambda \neq 3$
  (2c) $\lambda \neq 0$ and $\lambda \neq 3$
  (2e) $\lambda \neq 1$ and $\lambda \neq -3$

9. (a) Yes.   **(c)** No.   **(e)** No.

11. $A^{23} = A$

14. $y_1 = 2e^{2t} - e^{4t}$, $y_2 = 2e^{2t} + e^{4t}$

Section 2.

1. (a) $q = t^2 + t + 1$, $r = 0$
  (c) $q = 0$, $r = f$ **(e)** $q = 0$, $r = f$

6. (a) $P_1 = \dfrac{(t - 2)(t - 3)(t - 4)(t - 5)}{24}$,

  $P_2 = \dfrac{(t - 1)(t - 3)(t - 4)(t - 5)}{-6}$,   etc.

  (c) $(1 - t)(t - 5)(\frac{13}{12}t^2 - \frac{20}{3}t + 10)$

8. (a) $f(T)(x, y, z) = (34x - 27y - 2z, 56x + 142y + 23z, 15x - 2y + 8z)$
  (c) $(-386x - 4748y - 705z, 10201x + 18606y + 3338z,$
  $518x - 705y - 12z)$
  (e) $(396x - 2118y - 97z, 1617x + 3240y + 566z, 181x - 91y + 38z)$

9. (a) $f(A) = \begin{bmatrix} 14 & 33 \\ 0 & 14 \end{bmatrix}$, $g(A) = \begin{bmatrix} 4 & 6 \\ 0 & 4 \end{bmatrix}$

  $q(A) = \begin{bmatrix} \frac{5}{3} & \frac{13}{3} \\ 0 & \frac{5}{3} \end{bmatrix}$, $r(A) = \begin{bmatrix} \frac{22}{3} & \frac{17}{3} \\ 0 & \frac{22}{3} \end{bmatrix}$

  $(gq + r)(A) = f(A) = \begin{bmatrix} 14 & 33 \\ 0 & 14 \end{bmatrix}$

  (c) $f(A) = \begin{bmatrix} 1 & 6 \\ 0 & 1 \end{bmatrix}$, $g(A) = \begin{bmatrix} 1 & 0 \\ 0 & 1 \end{bmatrix}$

  $q(A) = \begin{bmatrix} -\frac{2}{3} & \frac{1}{3} \\ 0 & -\frac{2}{3} \end{bmatrix}$, $r(A) = \begin{bmatrix} \frac{5}{3} & \frac{17}{3} \\ 0 & \frac{5}{3} \end{bmatrix}$

  $(gq + r)(A) = f(A) = \begin{bmatrix} 1 & 6 \\ 0 & 1 \end{bmatrix}$

10. $f(A) = \begin{bmatrix} 64 + 3^{16} & 25 + 3^{16} - 2^{16} & 0 \\ 0 & 29 + 2^{16} & 0 \\ 0 & 0 & 9 \end{bmatrix}$

Section 3.

1. **(a)** $t^3 - 5t^2 + 7t - 12$ **(c)** $t(t-1)^2$
   (e) $t(t-1)(t-2)$

2. **(a)** t^3 **(c)** $(t^2 - 5t + 3)(t^2 - 2t - 1)$

3. $T^{-1} = (-1/a_0)(a_1 I + a_2 T + \cdots + a_n T^{n-1})$

4. **(a)** **(1a)** $p = \Delta$ **(1c)** $p = t(t-1)$
        (1e) $p = \Delta$
   (b) **(2a)** t^3 **(2c)** $p = \Delta$

8. **(a)** $p = (t-1)^4$ **(c)** $p = (t^2 - 2t + 3)^2$

Section 4.

1. **(a)** No.   **(c)** Yes.   **(e)** No.   **(g)** Yes.   **(i)** No.

2. **(a)** Range is the line $y = x$; null space is the line $x = 0$.
   (c) Range is the plane $x + y = 0$; null space is the line $x + z = y = 0$.
   (e) Range is the symmetric matrices; null space is the skew symmetric matrices.
   (g) Range is the set of functions f such that $f'(t) = 0$ for $\frac{1}{2} < t \le 1$; null space is the set of f such that $f(t) = 0, 0 \le t \le \frac{1}{2}$.

3. **(a)** One example, $E(x, y) = (y/2, y)$.

   (d) One example, $E\begin{bmatrix} a & b \\ c & d \end{bmatrix} = \begin{bmatrix} 0 & \dfrac{b-c}{2} \\ \dfrac{c-b}{2} & 0 \end{bmatrix}$.

4. **(a)** $E(x, y) = (-x/3 + 2y/3, -2x/3 + 4y/3)$

11. **(a)** $\begin{bmatrix} 1 & 1 & 0 \\ 0 & 0 & 0 \\ 0 & 0 & 0 \end{bmatrix}$, $\begin{bmatrix} 0 & 1 & -1 \\ 0 & 1 & -1 \\ 0 & 0 & 0 \end{bmatrix}$, $\begin{bmatrix} 0 & 0 & 1 \\ 0 & 0 & 1 \\ 0 & 0 & 1 \end{bmatrix}$

   (c) $\begin{bmatrix} 2 & -1 & 0 & 0 \\ 2 & -1 & 0 & 0 \\ 0 & 0 & \frac{3}{2} & -\frac{1}{2} \\ 0 & 0 & \frac{3}{2} & -\frac{1}{2} \end{bmatrix}$, $\begin{bmatrix} -1 & 1 & 0 & 0 \\ -2 & 2 & 0 & 0 \\ 0 & 0 & 0 & 0 \\ 0 & 0 & 0 & 0 \end{bmatrix}$,

   $\begin{bmatrix} 0 & 0 & 0 & 0 \\ 0 & 0 & 0 & 0 \\ 0 & 0 & -\frac{1}{2} & \frac{1}{2} \\ 0 & 0 & -\frac{3}{2} & \frac{3}{2} \end{bmatrix}$

(e) $\begin{bmatrix} 1 & -1 & 0 & 0 \\ 0 & 0 & 0 & 0 \\ 0 & 0 & 1 & -1 \\ 0 & 0 & 0 & 0 \end{bmatrix}$, $\begin{bmatrix} 0 & 1 & 0 & 0 \\ 0 & 1 & 0 & 0 \\ 0 & 0 & 0 & 1 \\ 0 & 0 & 0 & 1 \end{bmatrix}$

(g) $\dfrac{-1}{2\sqrt{2}} \begin{bmatrix} -1-\sqrt{2} & 1 & 0 & 0 \\ 1 & 1-\sqrt{2} & 0 & 0 \\ 0 & 0 & 0 & 0 \\ 0 & 0 & 0 & 0 \end{bmatrix}$,

$\dfrac{1}{2\sqrt{2}} \begin{bmatrix} -1+\sqrt{2} & 1 & 0 & 0 \\ 1 & 1+\sqrt{2} & 0 & 0 \\ 0 & 0 & 0 & 0 \\ 0 & 0 & 0 & 0 \end{bmatrix}$,

$\begin{bmatrix} 0 & 0 & 0 & 0 \\ 0 & 0 & 0 & 0 \\ 0 & 0 & \frac{1}{2} & \frac{1}{2} \\ 0 & 0 & \frac{1}{2} & \frac{1}{2} \end{bmatrix}$, $\begin{bmatrix} 0 & 0 & 0 & 0 \\ 0 & 0 & 0 & 0 \\ 0 & 0 & \frac{1}{2} & -\frac{1}{2} \\ 0 & 0 & -\frac{1}{2} & \frac{1}{2} \end{bmatrix}$

13. **(a)** This projection is orthogonal with respect to the standard inner product, but not with respect to the other inner product.

   (c) This projection is orthogonal with respect to the second inner product.

14. **(a)** $P_0 = \begin{bmatrix} \dfrac{5+\sqrt{29}}{2a} & \dfrac{5-\sqrt{29}}{2b} \\ \dfrac{1}{a} & \dfrac{1}{b} \end{bmatrix}$,

   $a^2 = (29+5\sqrt{29})/2, \qquad b^2 = (29-5\sqrt{29})/2$

   (c) $P_0 = \begin{bmatrix} \dfrac{1+\sqrt{17}}{4a} & \dfrac{1-\sqrt{17}}{4b} & 0 & 0 \\ 1/a & 1/b & 0 & 0 \\ 0 & 0 & \dfrac{1+\sqrt{5}}{2c} & \dfrac{1-\sqrt{5}}{2d} \\ 0 & 0 & -1/c & -1/d \end{bmatrix}$,

   $a^2 = \dfrac{17+\sqrt{17}}{8}, \qquad b^2 = \dfrac{17-\sqrt{17}}{8}, \qquad c^2 = \dfrac{5+\sqrt{5}}{2},$

   $d^2 = \dfrac{5-\sqrt{5}}{2}$

15. $\begin{bmatrix} 1 & 0 & 0 \\ -1 & 0 & 0 \\ 0 & 0 & 0 \end{bmatrix}$, $\begin{bmatrix} 0 & 0 & 0 \\ 1 & 1 & 0 \\ -1 & -1 & 0 \end{bmatrix}$, $\begin{bmatrix} 0 & 0 & 0 \\ 0 & 0 & 0 \\ 1 & 1 & 1 \end{bmatrix}$

24. $f(A) = \begin{bmatrix} 0 & \log 2 & \log \frac{3}{2} \\ 0 & \log 2 & \log \frac{3}{2} \\ 0 & 0 & \log 3 \end{bmatrix}$

26. (b) $\begin{bmatrix} 1 & 0 \\ 0 & 2 \end{bmatrix}$

27. (c) R^2, $\{(0, 0)\}$ and the x-axis.

CHAPTER 4

Section 1.

1. (a) No.   **(c)** No.   **(e)** Yes.   **(g)** No.   **(i)** No.

2. (a) $\{(1, 1, 1), (1, 2, 1), (1, 1, 2)\}$

4. $(A + B)^{10} = \begin{bmatrix} 4^{10} & 0 \\ 0 & 6^{10} \end{bmatrix}$, $f(A + B) = \begin{bmatrix} e^4 & 0 \\ 0 & e^6 \end{bmatrix}$

Section 2.

1. (a) $P(x, y) = (2x + y, x + y)$ **(c)** $P(x, y) = (100x + y, x)$

2. (a) $\begin{bmatrix} \frac{5}{2} & \frac{1}{2} \\ \frac{1}{2} & \frac{1}{2} \end{bmatrix}$ **(c)** $\begin{bmatrix} 51 & 50 \\ 50 & 49 \end{bmatrix}$

6. (a) $\dfrac{19 \pm 5\sqrt{13}}{2}$ and $19 > 5\sqrt{13}$

7. (a) $B = \begin{bmatrix} \dfrac{3\sqrt{7} + \sqrt{3}}{4} & \dfrac{-3 + \sqrt{21}}{4} \\ \dfrac{-3 + \sqrt{21}}{4} & \dfrac{\sqrt{7} + 3\sqrt{3}}{4} \end{bmatrix}$

Section 3.

1. (a) No.   **(c)** Yes.

5. (a) Yes.   **(c)** Yes.

Section 4.

1. (a) Real part: $9\sqrt{2} - 5$; Imaginary part: $-5\sqrt{2} - 9$.
(c) Real part: -38; Imaginary part: 124.
(e) 9

2. **(a)** Rank = nullity = 2.

(c) The inverse is
$$\begin{bmatrix} -1 & 0 & -i \\ \dfrac{1+i}{2} & \dfrac{-(1+i)}{2} & 0 \\ \dfrac{1-i}{2} & \dfrac{1+i}{2} & 0 \end{bmatrix}.$$

3. **(a)** For example, $\{(1, 0, 1), (0\ 1, 0)\}$ is a basis for M and $\{(1, 0, 1),$ $(0, 1, 0), (0, 0, 1)\}$ for C^3.

   (b) For example, $\{(1, 1, 0)\}$ is a basis for M and $\{(1, 0, 0), (1, 1, 0),$ $(1, 1, 1)\}$ for C^3.

4. **(a)** $\begin{bmatrix} i & 0 & 0 \\ -1+i & i & i \\ 2-i & 0 & 1 \end{bmatrix}$

5. $\begin{bmatrix} i+3 & i+5 & 3i \\ 2+5i & 5+6i & -4+3i \\ -2-3i & -5-6i & 2-3i \end{bmatrix}$, for example.

6. $\Big\{1/\sqrt{5}\,(1, i, 1),\ 1/\sqrt{15}\,(-1-i,\ 1-i,\ -1+4i),$

$$\frac{1}{\sqrt{15}}\left(3i-1,\quad \frac{3-4i}{3},\quad \frac{-3+4i}{3}\right)\Big\}$$

7. **(a)** The subspace spanned by $\sqrt{180}\,(t^2 - t + \tfrac{1}{6})$.

   (c) $D^*1 = 12t - 6,\ D^*t = 30t^2 - 24t + 2,\ D^*t^2 = 30t^2 - 26t + 3$

12. **(a)** $P_0 = \begin{bmatrix} 1 & 1 \\ 1 & -1 \end{bmatrix}$, for example.

14. $B = \begin{bmatrix} 3 & \dfrac{5+3i}{4} \\ \dfrac{5-3i}{4} & 0 \end{bmatrix}$, $\quad C = \begin{bmatrix} -1 & \dfrac{5-3i}{4} \\ \dfrac{5+3i}{4} & 3 \end{bmatrix}$

15. n^2

17. $P_0 = \begin{bmatrix} 1/\sqrt{2} & 1/\sqrt{2} \\ -1/\sqrt{2} & 1/\sqrt{2} \end{bmatrix}$, for example.

18. $\begin{bmatrix} 33i-32 & 33i-31 \\ 32-i & 31-i \end{bmatrix}$

Section 5.

2. **(a)** Normal.   **(c)** Not normal.

3. (a) Not normal.   **(c)** Unitary.
(e) Skew adjoint.   **(g)** Not normal.

5. (a) Spectral projections:

$$\frac{1}{\sqrt{5}}\begin{bmatrix} \dfrac{1+\sqrt{5}}{2} & -i \\[2mm] i & \dfrac{-1+\sqrt{5}}{2} \end{bmatrix},\qquad -\frac{1}{\sqrt{5}}\begin{bmatrix} \dfrac{1-\sqrt{5}}{2} & -i \\[2mm] i & \dfrac{-1-\sqrt{5}}{2} \end{bmatrix}.$$

(c) Spectral projections:

$$\frac{-i}{\sqrt{5}}\begin{bmatrix} i\dfrac{-1-\sqrt{5}}{2} & 1 \\[2mm] -1 & i\dfrac{1-\sqrt{5}}{2} \end{bmatrix},\qquad \frac{i}{\sqrt{5}}\begin{bmatrix} i\dfrac{-1+\sqrt{5}}{2} & 1 \\[2mm] -1 & i\dfrac{1+\sqrt{5}}{2} \end{bmatrix}.$$

6. (a) $U = \begin{bmatrix} \dfrac{\sqrt{2}\,(1+i)}{2\sqrt{3}} & \dfrac{1+i}{\sqrt{3}} \\[3mm] -\sqrt{2/3} & 1/\sqrt{3} \end{bmatrix}$

(c) $U = \begin{bmatrix} 1/\sqrt{2} & 1/\sqrt{2} \\ 1/\sqrt{2} & -1/\sqrt{2} \end{bmatrix}$

Section 6.

1. (a) $2, 0$; Nonnegative.
(c) $(1+\sqrt{5})/2,\ (1-\sqrt{5})/2$; Self-adjoint.

(e) $\dfrac{1}{2}\left[2i+1 \pm (41)^{1/4}\left(\dfrac{-4}{82-10\sqrt{41}} + \dfrac{\sqrt{41}-5}{82-10\sqrt{41}}\,i\right)\right]$

(g) $\dfrac{i\pm 1}{\sqrt{2}}$; Unitary.

4. (a) Skew adjoint.
(c) Not unitary, positive, nor skew adjoint.

5. Real part:

$$H(\alpha,\beta) = \left[6\alpha + \left(\frac{2-13i}{2}\right)\beta,\ \left(\frac{2+13i}{2}\right)\alpha - \beta\right].$$

Imaginary part:

$$K(\alpha,\beta) = \left[3\alpha - \left(\frac{1+2i}{2}\right)\beta,\ \left(\frac{-1+2i}{2}\right)\alpha\right].$$

7. $P^{1/2} = 0\begin{bmatrix} \frac{1}{2} & -i/2 \\ i/2 & \frac{1}{2} \end{bmatrix} + \sqrt{2}\begin{bmatrix} \frac{1}{2} & i/2 \\ -i/2 & \frac{1}{2} \end{bmatrix}$

9. $P = \begin{bmatrix} 2 & i \\ -i & 1 \end{bmatrix},\qquad U = \begin{bmatrix} i & 0 \\ 0 & i \end{bmatrix}$

10. (a) 1, 2,   **(c)** i

14. (a) $g(A)$ is not defined.

   (c) $(kg)(A) = (t^2 + 1)(A) = \begin{bmatrix} \frac{1}{2} & -i/2 \\ i/2 & \frac{1}{2} \end{bmatrix}$

   (e) $h(A)k(A)m(A) \left(f(A)\right)^2 = 0$

15. (a) $AB = BA$ if and only if B is of the form $\begin{bmatrix} \alpha & \beta \\ -\beta & \alpha + 2i\beta \end{bmatrix}$.

Index

INDEX

Adjoint, classical, 154
 of a linear operator, 141, 144
 matrix of (with respect to an
  orthonormal basis), 142
Affine subspace, 48
Affine transformation, 57
Algebras, 71
Angle between two vectors, 110, 118
Augmented matrix, 17

Basis, 39, 40
 orthogonal, 123
 orthonormal, 123
 standard (of C^n), 243
 standard (of R^n), 99
Bessel's inequality, 130 (Ex. 7a)
Bilinear form, 231
 matrix of, 231 (Ex. 12)

C^n, 243
Cayley-Hamilton Theorem, 191
Characteristic equation, 174
Characteristic polynomial, 190
Characteristic subspace, 173
Characteristic value, 173
Characteristic vector, 173
Commuting operators, 218
Complex number, 13, 242
 absolute value of, 244
 conjugate of, 243
 imaginary part of, 242
 pure imaginary, 257
 real part of, 242
Components of a vector, 113, 114, 118
Convex polyhedron, 138 (Ex. 11)
Convex set, 52 (Ex. 20)
Coordinates of a vector, relative to an
  ordered basis, 92
Cosine law, 111, 120
Cramer's rule, 158 (Ex. 10)
Cross product, 160

Determinant, Laplace expansion of,
  154
 of a linear operator, 147, 155
 of a matrix, 148, 149
 permutation form, 159 (Ex. 13b)
 uniqueness of, 150
Determinant function, 149
Determinant rank, 158 (Ex. 12)
Diagonalizable, simultaneously, 217
Diagonalizable matrix, 179
Diagonalizable operator, 171
 characteristic polynomial of, 195
 minimum polynomial of, 195
 spectral projections of, 202
Dimension, 39
Division algorithm, 183
Dot product, 110, 113, 117
Dual space, 136

Echelon (row reduced) matrix, 10
Extremal subset, 138 (Ex. 10)
 extreme point, 138 (Ex. 10)

Factor-root theorem, 184
Field, 13
Finite dimensional vector space, 39
Function, 54
 of matrix, 187, 261
 of operator, 186, 203, 261
Fundamental theorem of algebra, 185

Geometric representation of R^3, 27–30
Gram-Schmidt process, 125
 (Theorem 14)

Hermitian (*see* Self-adjoint)
Homogeneous system of linear
  equations, 3
 method for solving, 10 (Theorem 1)
 nontrivial solution, 3, 12
 trivial solution, 3